STALKING THE WILD VERB PHRASE

A SELF-PACED SELF-CORRECTING ADVENTURE INTO THE GRAMMAR OF ENGLISH FOR ENGLISH-SPEAKING LEARNERS OF OTHER LANGUAGES

ROBERT FRADKIN

Old Dominion University

Lanham • New York • London

University Press of America®, Inc.
4720 Boston Way
Lanham, Maryland 20706

3 Henrietta Street
London WC2E 8LU England

Printed in the United States of America
British Cataloging in Publication Information Available

Library of Congress Cataloging-in-Publication Data

Fradkin, Robert A., 1951-
Stalking the wild verb phrase : a self-paced, self-correcting adventure into the grammar of English for English-speaking learners of other languages / Robert Fradkin.
p. cm.
Includes bibliographical references and indexes.
1. English language—Grammar—Self-instruction.
2. Grammar, Comparative and general—Self-instruction.
I. Title.
PE1112.3.F7 1991
428.2'4—dc20 90–22539 CIP

ISBN 0–8191–8102–1 (cloth)
ISBN 0–8191–8103–X (paper)

To

Mom and Pop,

who taught me always to love life and
be dedicated to my work--
even if it's ***grammar!***

ACKNOWLEDGEMENTS

Thanks, first of all, to the students I have had the privilege of knowing and introducing to Russian, Hebrew, and general linguistics at Indiana University (Bloomington), University of Washington (Seattle), Brown University (Providence), and to those I am about to meet at Old Dominion University (Norfolk). They have made my language teaching career a joy so far, as well as inspired, encouraged--even violently protested--the writing of this book and both loved and loathed working through the earlier xeroxed versions.

My friends and colleagues in the fields of both theoretical linguistics and foreign language teaching at these same four universities, as well as University of California (Berkeley), Moscow State University, Hebrew University in Jerusalem, and Ben Gurion University in the Negev have knowingly and unknowingly contributed to my education and development as a linguist, polyglot, and teacher of other languages to English-speaking students.

Special thanks to the Judaic Studies Program at Brown University--Annette Boulay, Vicki Caron, Ernie Frerichs, Cal Goldscheider--for their friendship and support during my years on the faculty there, not to mention their abundant Macintosh resources, without which I could not have prepared this camera-ready copy.

To my wonderful wife and eagle-eyed proofreader, Goedele Gulikers, thanks for enduring my endless ruminations on English grammar and linguistic structure and for catching the myriad typos and inconsistencies in the previous versions of the manuscript. Naturally, I alone take responsibility for the final copy.

TABLE OF CONTENTS 1:
CHAPTER HEADINGS AT A GLANCE

SECTION 1: THE FOREST

SECTION 2: THE TREES

SECTION 3: THE LEAVES

TABLE OF CONTENTS 2: CHAPTERS HEADINGS AND MAJOR SUB-DIVISIONS

SECTION 2: THE TREES
(CLOSER LOOKS AT THE BUILDING BLOCKS)

SECTION 3: THE LEAVES (SPECIAL ISSUES OF IMPORTANCE TO THE LANGUAGE LEARNER)

LIST OF EXERCISES AND ANSWER KEYS

BOTH "ON LOCATION" AND IN THE APPENDIX

LIST OF CHARTS AND TABLES

PREFACE

TO THE USER, BE YOU STUDENT OR TEACHER

The purpose of this book is to provide you with three opportunities:

⇒ to review--or meet for the first time--the terms and concepts of language study, in general, with an eye toward foreign language study, in particular.

⇒ to listen to yourself speak normal 20th century American English and give yourself a framework for getting sensitive to and appreciating the complex and elegant **patterns** of sound and meaning you execute every thinking-seeing-speaking-hearing minute of the day.

⇒ to suggest in traditional terms, as unstuffy and non-technical as possible, how you can apply this material to your advantage in learning another language.

WHO SHOULD USE THIS BOOK?

This book will be especially useful to you if you are learning--or teaching--a language *other than* English in any high school, college, or community education program. (Of course, it will open your eyes to English even if you are not studying another language and are just plain interested in your own thought and behavior.)

⇒ **If you are a student**, you will do yourself a great favor by getting familiar with the processes of your own language, and you will give yourself survival training for dealing with the terms of your target language textbook. If creatures like "subordinate clause" or "transitive verb" gave you the willies in earlier school days--if, indeed, you were ever taught them to begin with--now is the time to meet them head-on in a way that will make them meaningful and may smooth your path through the wonderful world of learning another language. (In this regard, you will get a kick out of Chapter 9 of Herman Wouk's novel, *The City Boy*, listed in the Further Reading appendix.)

⇒ **If you are a teacher**, you and your students can have a reference tool and common vocabulary for how English deals with concepts like "direct object" or "definite article." And because the whole thing is self-correcting, the student can use it outside of class ***without costing you a moment of precious class time***. You can work it into your syllabus and hold them responsible for basic terms so that you do not have to explain in class. Even if your method is to teach strictly communicative language and avoid formal grammar, you can find useful material on the "culture of speaking."

It does not matter what your purpose is for studying a language, whether for travel, research, business, community work, or just fun. Some people have the idea that "learning the grammar" of your target language is somehow different from--or even a barrier to--effective communication in it. Not so. The discipline of "thinking grammar" is an important accompaniment to learning daily conversation. True enough, reciting grammar rules and their exceptions, memorizing long lists of words out of context, or translating from or into English will not make you a fluent speaker of another language, if your goal is to be one, but it is still useful to equip yourself with the tools to help you see the more or less systematic ways your language groups items together. Language is patterns. At the very least, if you know that English puts its articles *before* its nouns and its verbs in the *middle* of its clauses in regular ways, you will not be intimidated when you open the textbook of your new language and read that it puts its articles *after* its nouns or puts its verbs at the *end* of its clauses. You do not need a degree in linguistics to do this, but as long as you are making the effort to learn another language, you might as well take the opportunity to get an adult-level idea of what the pieces of language are and how they operate and interact.

The many "grammar/reference/self-help" books on the market today are not meant to meet the needs of the adult other-language learner. (Some of these are listed in the Further Reading appendix, and they are worth glancing at, too.) The assumption in most of them seems to be that your language is "deficient" and that you need to "improve" or "polish up" your language in order to be successful in business or to snatch society from the jaws of degradation and doom. Such books stress "correct grammar," "word power," good composition, spelling, or punctuation. These are important, to be sure, but they are individual facts and not overall processes. Even some of the better grammar books feel they have to sugar-coat or water-down their presentation, and as a result, you do not get any more enlightened than when you started out.

⇒ By not concentrating on showing you the interconnections among parts of language these books miss the forest for the trees. You come away thinking that "grammar" is only what is "good and correct" based on somebody else's judgment, but they have not given you the tools for judging for yourself whether something is "correct" or not. Fact is, grammar is what you *do* do with your marvelous language capacity, not just what you *should* do.

Instead of worrying about whether your grammar is "right" or "wrong" ask yourself if it follows a consistent pattern. Then you can ask later whether that pattern is considered appropriate verbal behavior for the speaking or writing situation you are in. There are lots of varieties of English: some are appropriate to writing and some, to speaking, with hundreds of gradations in between. They all *are* grammar, and they all *have* grammar. (Some people would say you use several co-existing and overlapping "grammars" at the same time all day long.) When somebody tells you your grammar is wrong, they probably mean, as you will see just below, that you have either chosen a possible but inappropriate pattern or put into an existing pattern elements that do not usually fit into it. You rarely do totally "wrong" things.

WHAT THIS BOOK IS FOR

The aim of this book is to focus not on the little things someone considers wrong and the mistakes you should fix, but rather, on the thousands of intricate operations you do *right* just by being a member of the one species on this planet that uses language as a means of communication. (We're not sure about dolphins yet.) This is not a "how-to" book that will make you speak "better." The hope is that it will help you be more aware of English and gain easier access to other languages. This is not an exhaustive grammar of English, and it is not a rigorous linguistic analysis, though the author draws heavily on linguistic theory and method.* It is meant both to "raise your consciousness" and increase your sensitivity by hinting at some of the hundreds of issues you could discuss in the context of learning any human language. (Students of foreign languages do not necessarily seek out courses in general linguistics, so for most people, foreign language class is the only place they are likely to be exposed to such matters. Formal linguistics is its own subject, and not all of its concerns are useful for practical language learning. Not all language teachers have a background or interest in it, either, but it certainly doesn't hurt to be familiar with it.)

As for learning another language, this book *does* try to separate the forest from the trees, as you see from the three sections in the table of contents. The point is that you *have* "grammar," whether you like it or not, and you already *had* it in remarkably sophisticated form by the age of four! If you were a normal human, you could not escape. You could not *not* learn your own native language! You never sat down and *learned* grammar, but you somehow knew that "Old MacDonald had a farm" was a pattern of English sound and meaning and that "MacDonald Old farm a had" was not an English pattern. That means you *know* your own grammar, and all the rest is commentary. You just do not have the terms to talk *about* your grammar. The truth is, you almost never *need* to talk about it, either, until you start taking another language. Only then do you start getting concerned with "phrases," "clauses," and "verb conjugations." The practical upshot of this is that your new language may do things similarly to or quite differently from you, but you may not recognize it because of the technical terms your textbook does or does not use.

THE STRUCTURE OF THE BOOK AND HINTS ON USING IT

This is a self-paced, self-correcting book of twenty chapters. Some are short and sweet; others, more involved and demanding. Work through each of the twenty chapters at the rate of about one a day to avoid "grammar burn-out." The index is quite detailed for your convenience, and there are a lot of internal references to other parts of the book to stress the patterns and the interconnectedness of things. The

* The reader familiar with the field of linguistics will recognize in the body of the text nods at some of the great linguists of this century: Roman Jakobson, Jerzy Kurylowicz, Cornelis van Schooneveld, Michael Silverstein, Robert van Valin, even Noam Chomsky. Some of the formulations are based on their theories of language, and some are the author's own.

outline format used throughout is designed to help you zero in on the most important items and then get additional information, depending on your energy level. You can just go down the Roman numeral headings in a chapter to get a perspective one day and then go back and do the deeper levels the next. Most chapters have exercises, which you should always try to "hear yourself saying." (Remember, language is mostly an oral-aural experience. Writing sometimes masks the more exciting aspects of language.) The answer key is either right below the exercise or in the appendix at the back.

Each of the three sections-- "The Forest" (Chapters 1-7), "The Trees" (Chapters 8-11), and "The Leaves" (Chapters 12-20)--goes deeper into aspects of language structure. Section 1 covers "the big basics" of sentence structure. Section 2 deals with the properties of verbs, nouns, and pronous in ways your high school English teacher never dreamed of (no offense!). Section 3 tries to bring out in the open several issues that traditional grammar terms do not handle very well but that are very important in many of the languages you are likely to study.

As for time, once you start your language course, you will be very busy practicing vocabulary and how to ask for the bus stop in Madrid, so get a head start a month or two *before* you begin and keep right on using it outside of class. In a college setting you can use the summer before first semester you are signed up for or the long winter vacation. Give yourself time to assimilate this material and get into the mindset of thinking in terms of these structures. If you are not in the habit, it will not come overnight and you may wonder what all the commotion is about.

The examples are drawn from the whole range of spoken and written English: new and old, good and bad, polite and vulgar, including the language of fine literature, cheap novels, political speeches, sermons, commerials, sports, pizza-delivery, poetry, nursery rhymes, popular songs. Anything goes, because it is all English and all part of your daily linguistic experience. Operate on these sentences as required, concentrating not on "learning the rule," but on becoming aware of the process that you or someone you hear uses in producing language. Then you have a chance of sensing whether your new language is similar or dissimilar, or whether English is "exotic." (Please do not think that you have to measure all languages in terms of English!) Do the exercises and check the key. If you do not understand--or do not agree with the key--ask your teacher or a fellow-user.

⇒ *Above all,* ENJOY IT! *This is a discovery process. Bringing the material to a slow, conscious level might seem counter-intuitive--your brain does these things in billionths of a second, after all--and it may never have occurred to you to put your language under a microscope or analyze it as an elegant symbiosis of the tangible world and the intangible sounds you utter all the time. But it is wonderfully enlightening!*

SECTION 1

THE FOREST

BIG CHUNKS OF SENTENCES

CHAPTER 1

SUBJECT AND PREDICATE

I. THE SENTENCE AND ITS TWO BIG HALVES

Elementary school English books usually tell you that, "A sentence is a group of words that expresses a complete thought." You immediately think of examples like "my pet dog" or "What a beautiful day!" Aren't these thoughts complete? Yes, but they are not expressed in sentences. It is enough for school children to hang on to, but you need a more precise definition, something like, "A sentence is a group of words **containing a subject and a predicate** and expressing a complete thought." The terms **subject** and **prédicate** (rhymes with *etiquette*) refer to the two major parts of a sentence.

A. Read the following very ordinary sentences out loud:

1. Harry studies in the library.

2. The rain in Spain stays mainly in the plain.

3. Your mother dresses you funny.

4. The honored guest was greeted with great fanfare.

B. You pronounce all of them so that you feel a natural division between

1. someone or something who is doing something or is somehow being acted upon and. . .

2. what he/she/it is doing or having done to it. The "someone or something" is termed the **subject**. It is the starting point, the item on which you are going to comment, namely **Harry, the rain, your mother, the guest.** What you say about the subject is termed the **predicate**, namely **studies** (in the library), **stays** (in the plain), **dresses** (you funny),**was greeted** (with fanfare). So the minimal

sentences you can get away with--the smallest units that make sense by themselves, even though these are not "complete" sentences--are: **Harry studies. Rain stays. Mother dresses. Guest was honored.**

II. WHAT BELONGS WHERE?

For now, we can say that any word or phrase in a sentence is part of either the subject or the predicate. The parentheses just give additional information.

A. Some traditional grammar books want to make it easy for you by lulling you into the common misconception that the subject is "what comes first" in the sentence. They are not doing you any favor. Notice what happens in questions and poetic style:

1. What does Mathilda want?
2. How much sugar do you take in your coffee?
3. What kind of bird is that?
4. Why wasn't she promoted?
5. Whose woods these are I think I know. . . (R. Frost)

B. Here the subjects--the "doers" or "get-done-to-ers"--are in the middle of the sentence: **you, she, that, she, I,** and **what**, respectively. Everything else comprises the predicate. You should still feel the division between the two parts of the sentence and may even find it helpful to re-arrange them into their "natural" order, e.g., if you answer the questions you can't help but come out with sentences:

1. Mathilda wants a sundae.
2. He takes a teaspoon of sugar in his coffee.
3. That is a strange kind of bird.
4. She wasn't promoted because she didn't publish enough.
5. I think I know whose woods these are. . .

EXERCISE 1
SUBJECTS AND PREDICATES
Key: page 337

Examine the following run-of-the-mill sentences from proverbs, nursery rhymes, and advertizing and analyze them into subject and predicate, that is, underline the subject once and the predicate twice. Don't be alarmed if one of those lines has to be disconnected: it often happens that one part occurs in the middle of the other. Most important is that you "feel" where the natural division between the "actor or acted-upon" and the "act" lies. Then consult the answer key.

Examples:

a. Harry studies in the library.
b. The rain in Spain stays mainly in the plain.
c. Many happy years did these little creatures romp and play.
d. Who squeezed the Charmin'?
e. Who are you boys trying to kid? (See why?)

1. April showers bring May flowers.

2. My bonnie lies over the ocean.

3. I pledge allegiance to the flag.

4. Peter Piper picked a peck of pickled peppers.

5. She sells sea shells by the sea shore.

6. Mary had a little lamb; its fleece was white as snow.

7. Coke adds life!

8. Over the river and through the woods to Grandmother's house we go.

9. My name is McNamara. I'm the leader of the band.

10. The square of the hypotenuse is equal to the sum of the squares of the other two sides.

11. George Washington threw a silver dollar across the Potomac.

12. The amazing Veg-O-Matic slices, dices, and peels!

13. The rockets' red glare, the bombs' bursting in air gave proof through the night that our flag was still there.

14. Four score and seven years ago our foreparents brought forth a great nation. . .

15. By the shores of Gitche Gumee by the shining Big-Sea-Waters stood the wigwam of Nokomis. . . (H. Longfellow, *Hiawatha*, Chp. 3)

CHAPTER 2

CLAUSES AND PHRASES

I. CLAUSES

A **clause** is defined traditionally as "a group of words containing a subject and a predicate."

A. Given what you just did in Chapter 1, logic will not have failed you if you conclude that a sentence is just one type of clause. Since a sentence can stand alone and make sense by itself, it goes under the alias of **independent clause** or **main clause**.

B. A clause can also be **dependent**, also termed **subordinate**. A dependent clause also has a subject and predicate, by definition, but it does not "make sense" by itself. It usually serves to amplify a part of the main clause. It has to be part of a sentence, hence its "dependency." There is a small group of words part of whose mission in life is to "introduce" dependent clauses. Here are the most frequent among them.

1. **that**:

   a. This is the house **that Jack built**. or
   b. We agreed **that he should lose a few pounds.**

2. **which**:

   a. Marriage is an institution **which society values highly**.
   b. Marriage is an institution, **which is OK** if you like institutions.

3. **who**: People **who live in glass houses** shouldn't throw stones.

4. **when**: Driver, please let me know **when we get to Altoona.**

5. **if:** We'll be lucky **if we get there in time for cocktails.**

6. **while:** Keep on eye on my luggage **while I look for a taxi.**

7. **after:** I'll leave **after the rush hour traffic dies down.**

8. **before:** The quality goes in **before the name goes on!**

9. **until:** Don't fire **until you see the whites of their eyes!**

10. **because:** He cried **because he was so happy.**

There are others, but these will do for now. Be careful not to think that every time you see or hear these words they will be followed by a clause. Do you feel that the clauses in 1-3 serve different kinds of functions in the sentence from those in 4-10? They do. More later.

II. WHAT ABOUT PHRASES?

It is almost trivial at this point to make an issue of phrases. They are, as implied earlier, any group of words that fits together in some sort of natural way: my life, world opinion, the presidential campaign, get around, back up, making a cheesecake, fill in for somebody at work, on the beach, within a year, because of the weather. They all have their own characteristics and terms for referring to them, and the next few sections will provide you the tools for differentiating these various groups and learning what information you expect them to relate to you in a given sentence.

EXERCISE 2a.
CLAUSES GALORE!
Key: p. 338

In the sentences below, one part of the independent clause is elaborated on by a dependent clause. As you did in Exercise 1, underline the minimal subject of the whole sentence once and the minimal predicate twice. In addition, set off the dependent clause with curly brackets and within it follow the same procedure as before: subject underlined once; predicate, twice. (Don't be surprised if you find yourself feeling compelled to underline the very word that "introduces" the clause--usually **that**.) Use your intuition. Then check the answer key. Examples:

I want a girl just like the girl {that married dear old Dad}.

Little Bo Beep doesn't know {where she lost her sheep}.

1. I write the songs that make the whole world sing. (B. Manilow)

2. People who live in glass houses should get dressed in the basement.

3. He who is without sin may cast the first stone.

4. This is a day that will long live in infamy. (F. Roosevelt)

5. He who laughs last laughs best.

6. The evil that men do lives after them. (M. Antony)

7. God bless America, land that I love. . . (I. Berlin)

8. Beware the Jabberwock, my son, the jaws that bite, the claws that catch (L. Carroll)

9. This, Mr. Corlione, is a deal that you cannot refuse. . .

10. *Ten Days That Shook the World* is a book by John Reed about the 1917 Russian revolution.

EXERCISE 2b.
MORE CLAUSES
Key: p. 339

The following sentences also contain dependent clauses. Do they feel a bit different in character? Follow the same identification procedure as above, separating the dependent clauses with curly brackets.

1. When it rains it pours.

2. Do you know where she lives?

3. I won't go unless you do.

4. Children should do as they're told!

5. I wouldn't do that if I were you.

6. You can't always get what you want.

7. I'll understand this grammar stuff when hell freezes over!

8. (Take me out to the ball game . . . .) I don't care if I ever come back. . .

9. (Rockabye baby in the tree tops). . .When the wind blows the cradle will rock.

10. If I had a hammer I'd hammer in the morning. . .

CHAPTER 3

PARTS OF SPEECH

We have not yet finished labelling the parts of sentences, but in order to do that efficiently you have to arm yourself with a certain set of grammar vocabulary of what age-old tradition recognizes as the eight parts of speech. This little section isn't really adequate to cover all the possibilities, and there will be more specialized discussions of these items later on. Identifying parts of speech is a major occupation of traditional schoolbook grammars. The definitions given below are largely the traditional ones, even though they don't always work, that is, they don't always help you understand what role any particular word plays in building up the meaning of a sentence. Later on, you will see why you need to deal with these concepts if the subject, predicate, and clause introducer you just worked with are going to make any sense whatsoever:

I. NOUN A noun names a person, place, thing, or idea.

Examples:
noun, person, place, thing, idea, example, part, speech, classroom, beauty, idiocy, president, anarchy, aardvark.

You can refine this classification with several subdivisions:

A. **Common nouns** (all of the above), which you can further specify as

1. **Concrete nouns** like **person, place, tablecloth** (yes, this includes things that aren't so concrete like **air, unicorn, microbe**).

2. **Abstract nouns** like **beauty, laziness, speed, democracy, charisma, empathy.**

B. **Proper nouns,** which give people's names, geographical places, titles of books, basically those that would be spelled in English with a capital letter: **Tom, Betty, Susan, Miss Piggy, Dollface, Hunk** (as in "Hey, there, Hunk." but not "He's such a hunk!"), **Sugarlump, Shorty, Mama, Spokane, East Overshoe, Watergate**

C. Another useful way to class nouns by meaning is **count nouns** vs. **mass nouns.**

1. Count nouns are the names of things you can think of as individual items and groups of items: **table(s), chair(s), contest(s), digital watch(es), boom box(es), democracy-ies** (in the sense of "a country with that form of government"), and zillions more. These usually go with either "a" or "the".

2. Mass nouns refer to substances and indivisible things that you cannot count, only measure: **air, fire, water, milk, work, money**. These can go with "the" but not usually with "a". (As soon as you say "a fire" you mean "a place where the substance **fire** is visible in great quantities", so you already get the idea that mass and count are types of **meaning** and not just words. More on this in Chapter 10.)

D. A **noun phrase** is a noun with its accompaniments of one or more words: **the apple, a glorious extravaganza, our next door neighbor**

E. Along with the concept of noun comes the grammatical category of **number**, that is, English shows by the form of the word itself whether it represents **more than one item**--called **plural**--or whether it is a question of either one or more than one item. The term for this form is **singular**, but beware: it does not always mean "just one."

1. In generic meanings like **The pen is mightier than the sword**, you really mean **pens** in general and **swords** in general. More in Chapter 10.

2. The most normal way to form the plural from the singular in English is to add **-(e)s** to the singular.

   a. There are many rules for spelling this, but don't confuse spelling rules with grammar rules. You may recognize handy hints like "Change **y** to **i** and add **-es**" for, e.g., **city-cities**, but of course, you don't hear that extra **e**-letter. You <u>do</u> hear it in **wish-wishes, tax-taxes.** We will not be concerned with these here.

b. There are a few plural formations we call "irregular" because they do not conform to this **-(e)s** principle.

(1). A few nouns change the vowel in the middle: **man-men, goose-geese, tooth-teeth, foot-feet, mouse-mice, louse-lice.**

(2). Only three nouns have an **-n** instead of **-s**, and two of those have other changes or additions: **ox, oxen; child, children**; **brother, brethren** alongside the "regular" plural **brothers**, but they have different meanings, namely, "related by spirit or community" vs. "related by blood."

(3). One noun uses entirely different words: **person-people**, but people like regularity, so you often hear **persons**, as well, but usually only in counting or in official contexts where, perhaps **persons** sounds more "precise."

(4). A few add nothing to the singular: **moose, sheep, fish.**

There are several others, like **index-indices** (also **indexes**), **vertebra-vertebrae, bacterium-bacteria** and some others we need not bother with just now.

II. A **PRONOUN** "stands for a noun," in the traditional definition.

A. Normally these refer to things that have already been mentioned or assumed in the context. That thing is called the **antecedent** of the pronoun.

B. A sentence like

"**My** brother's not home. **He**'ll be back soon. **That**'s **what he** told **me**."

illustrates several different kinds of pronouns: "**My**" assumes that some "**I**" is speaking and has a brother. "**He**" refers, of course, to brother. "**That**" refers to the whole message about absence and assumed return, and "**me** " still refers to the speaker but in a different role, namely, direct object (cf. Chapter 4, below) instead of "possessor".

1. Personal pronouns come in different varieties for different kinds of reference.

    a. Used as subject of a sentence:
    I, you, he, she, it, we, they, who

    b. Used as anything else:
    me, you, him, her, it, us, them, whom
    (Wonder why **you** and **it** are in both sets? Check out Chapters 4, 11.)

    c. "Indefinite" pronouns: **everybody, anybody, somebody**

    d. Strictly speaking, this definition of "standing for a noun" works only for **he-she-it-they**. The others--**I, you, we, everybody**--refer not to nouns but directly to people in the real world. More in Chapter 11.

    e. The interesting property of pronouns in English, and most other languages, is that they have different forms that have to do with the different **roles** their referents play in the sentence. This is a phenomenon called **case** in many languages. You could say that English pronouns have two cases: **subject vs. non-subject,** because you can tell by looking what they do and what they do not do. For English nouns, you have to understand the whole sentence before you can look back and decide who played what role, more on which in Chapters 4, 5, 11, and 18.

2. Personal pronouns can also indicate **possession**.

    a. Possessive **pronouns** occur by themselves:
    mine, yours, his, hers, its, ours, theirs, as in

    "What's mine is mine. What's yours is negotiable."

    b. Use them with a noun and they are **possessive adjectives**:
    my, your, his, her, its, our, their, as in

    "My dog's better than your dog." More on this in IV.E., below.

C. The **Pointers**, also called **demónstratives,** are **this-that** and the plurals, **these-those**.

a. You choose **this-these** for things you consider to be in **proximity** to you, dwithin your immediate sphere, close by.

b. You choose **that-those** for a thing that is either

(1). **distant** from you or within your immediate vicinity, but not in your immediate concern.

(2). outside your sight or grasp.

c. Another way to look at this contrast is to think of **this-these** as "the thing near me," and **that-those** as "the thing near you" or "near him/her/them." This also suggests that when you are contrasting two or more things, **this-these** is the "first one pointed out" and **that-those** is the "second one pointed out."

d. The problem is that nearness or farness is not always the crucial factor in tagging something **this** or **that**. You can look at something right up close and ask, "Hey, what's **that**?" Of course you mean, "I assume **you** know more about this than **I** do." Some languages do not make that distinction and are satisfied to mean "the thing pointed out." Some languages have a finer gradation, something like "this one close by, that one over there but still within sight or reach," and "the one out of range."

e. When there is no question of choosing between first thing or second thing, **this** and **that** have another interesting difference, especially in telling a story about something you experienced:

(1). **This** in a story introduces an item that you are familiar with but are mentioning for the first time and do not assume your audience knows, as in:

"So we're standing on the corner, and **this car** pulls up. **This guy** gets out and asks for directions to . . ."

(2). **That** in a story says, "I have already mentioned the thing and assume you know what I'm referring to," as in:

"Officer McDougal made a daring rescue today. **That woman** will go down in history!"

It is an entirely separate issue that the above uses are not recommended in formal writing. They are still part of the English language.

D. As long as the subject comes up, we might as well get used to the idea of **relative pronouns**. These are the ones that introduce a kind of dependent clause called a **relative clause**, as you saw in Chapter 2 (I.B.1-3), more about which later. The relative pronouns are **who**, (also **whom**, if you're inclined to say it), **which**, and **that**. (What? Wasn't **that** called a demonstrative just above? Yes. The word **that** does lots of different things in this language. So do lots of words.)

E. Pronouns usually stand for something **already mentioned** or identified in the text or speech, but it is also possible for pronouns to **anticipate** the reference to a person or thing you have not yet mentioned. Take the utterance:

"When **he** comes home, tell **my brother** somebody called."

"**My**" refers to the speaker, **who** already knows **who he/she** is, and so do **you,** the listener; "**somebody**" obviously refers to **whoever** called. As for "**he,**" well, **you** the listener don't know **who that** is until later in the sentence. This is **anticipatory** instead of **retrospective reference**. (Could **you** help but notice how chock full of pronouns **this** sentence was?)

III. A **VERB** relates:

A. an action, like **walk, write, scream, tear, eat**

B. a process, like **become, grow, think**

C. a state, such as **sit, stand, live, exist**

D. A **verb phrase** is just that: several "verb words" acting together as a unit: **is sitting, does stand, will write, has been dancing, would go, would have sent, to do**

E. There are several terms associated with verbs in grammar. Briefly we can say that:

1. **Tense** shows--at the risk of grossly oversimplifying--the time relation of the action to the speaker. There are also **aspect, mood, and voice**, more on which in Chapters 8, 9, and 18 below.

2. Verbs in English also mark number, similarly to nouns. There are two forms for the present tense: the kind with an **-s** and the kind without. The kind with **-s** are strictly for the **3rd person singular**--more on which in Chapter 8, and the kind without are for anything else. The past tense uses one form for everything with no distinction between singular and plural. The single exception is the verb **be: was/were**.

IV. An **ADJECTIVE** describes or "modifies" a noun.

A. These may be inherent **qualities** of objects:

big car, **little** cat, **interesting** discussion, **smooth** sailing

B. They may also be **relationships** to other areas of life without any inherent or natural association:

rented house, **French** government, **stolen** goods

C. In English adjectives **come before** the nouns they modify 99.9% of the time. The only time they do not is in special phrases like Mother **Dear**, all things **great** and **small**, the secretary **general**.

D. The **articles** are also a kind of adjective, more about which in Chapter 10.

1. The **definite** article **THE** marks items or entire classes of items whose identity is already known or assumed, as in either

a. The hot dog is the all-American food. (generic) or

b. The hot dog you just snarfed down is full of nitrites and nitrates!!

2. The **indefinite** article A marks an item as a member of a class of similar items but does not identify which member of the class you mean:

   a. You may not have picked one out yet, as in **Gimme a hot dog with mustard and relish.**

   b. You may, indeed, have picked one out but are mentioning it for the first time, as in **She walked in and saw him snarfing down a hot dog with mustard and relish.**

3. A lot of languages have only a definite article and no indefinite one (Hebrew, Bulgarian, Turkish), but never the other way around, that is, they have the equivalent of **the book** but just plain **book** covers **a book** and, say, **(what kind of) book**. A lot of languages have no articles at all (Russian, Latin). Speakers of these languages have other means to express what our articles express, and they have a hell of a time learning what English speakers consider "definite" and "indefinite."

E. **Possessive** adjectives are related to the personal pronouns (II.B.2 above):

1. **my, your, his, her, its, our, their** come before nouns.

2. **mine, yours, his, hers, its, ours, theirs** stand for the whole noun phrase, e.g., **my dog**,, so they are pronouns.

3. The pronouns are either the same as the adjectives (**his, its**) or are longer than the adjectives by one sound: mostly **-s (your-her-our-their+s)** and also one case of **-n (my+n**, spelled **mine.**)

4. Otherwise, you express possession either of two ways:

   a. The **-s** type **"X's Y"**. Add the sound "s", spelled "apostrophe **'s**" on a singular possessor-noun and "**s'**-apostrophe" on a plural possessor-noun. This is fine for your eye, but the two types usually *sound* identical in speech: **the student's book(s)** and **the students' book(s).**

b. The **of** type **"the Y of X,"** as in **the book(s) of the student(s)**.

c. Here are the possibilities in terms of each other. You always know how many possessors you are dealing with, but the number of possessed items is not always immediately clear. Let "2" mean "more than one":

the student's book:	the book of the student	(1s., 1b.)
the student's books:	the books of the student	(1s., 2 b.)
the students' book:	the book of the students	(2 s., 1b., co-owned)
the students' books:	the books of the students = 2 s. and either 1b. each or 2 b. each	

d. The two types, furthermore, usually have different meanings or can be used with some types of nous but not others. As for the **of** type, possession is only one of its possible meanings. Sometimes the two types mean almost the same thing, and other times they are quite different.You say only "the House of the Senate" and not *"the Senate's house." "John's book" is hardly the same as "the Book of John." But you can say "the airplane's wing" even if school books tell you to say "the wing of the airplane." At any rate, some languages have only one pattern or the other. Some have both.

5. Languages that have **cases**--more on which at the end of Chapter 4--often express possession by a form called **genitive case**--at least the common ones like German, Latin, Russian, and Turkish. English grammar books refer to the **possessive case form** with **-'s**.

6. The rule of spelling possessives with "apostrophe **-'s**" works for every noun in English. There are spelling rules about writing **-'s, -s'**, or just **'** depending on whether the word already ends in an **-s**: "the **Morse's** house" alongside "**Moses'** staff". But that is a visual nicety, not part of language structure.)

7. The one exception is the pronoun **it**. First of all, while the other pronuns use separate words for their possessive form (**I-my, he-his, she-her, we-our**) or have similar-looking forms **(you-your,**

they-their), only **it** forms its possessive like a "regular" noun by adding **-s**.

a. Grammar books warn you that **its** (no apostrophe) is a possessive and **it's** (with apostrophe) is the contraction of **it is**. First of all, this is a rule of spelling and not of language. The "correct" spellings turn up in the following sentences:

(1). Have you seen John**'s** new skateboard? **It's** a beauty!

(2). The cat licked **its** paws.

b. Second of all, you frequently see these two forms mixed up in writing, and some language purists tear their hair out over the downfall of the English language. Relax. If you write "the cat licked **it's** paws", it just means that you are applying the otherwise regular rule and forgot to stop when you got to the word **it**. (Funny it does not seem to bother anybody that possessive **John's** is identical to the contraction of **John is**. . . There is no form ***Johns**, but there is both **its** and **it's**.) So, unlike the pairs **John-John's** or **the judge-the judge's**, the trio **it-its-it's** is one of a kind. No wonder people don't want to bother with it. You could even say that the rule itself is partly to blame for the frequent confusion.

F. Adjectives form three **degrees**:

1. **Plain**: My house is **big**.

2. **Comparative**: Add **-er** My house is **bigger than** your house.

3. **Supérlative**: Add **-est** My house is **the biggest** in town.

4. These mean:

a. The plain is just that. You can also, of course, form a "comparison of equality," that is, "My house is **as big as** your house. It would be fair to call this a "comparative," too, but that term is generally reserved for the **-er** form.

b. The comparative is, strictly speaking, between **two unequal** things, whether two individuals, as in in 2., above, or when one thing is compared to a whole group of things, as in **My house is bigger than all the other houses on the block**.

c. The superlative compares one things to at least two others.

5. As for forms:

a. You get **"X-er than"** and **"the X-est (of, in)"** only with adjectives of one syllable (**big-bigger-biggest, tall-taller-tallest**) and the two-syllable ones that have the strέss on the first syllable (**nóisy-noisier-noisiest, úgly-uglier-ugliest**), but not all of them (***sénile-seniler-senilest, *cívil-civiller-civillest**).

b. The two-syllable ones with stress on the second syllable and anything longer than two syllables use **"more X than"** (yes, spelled with an <u>**a**</u>.) and **"the most X."** There is no ***seréne-serener-serenest, *beautiful-beautifuller-beautifullest,** or ***intelligent-intelligenter-intelligentest**.

c. Two adjectives use a different stem to add the comparative and superlative endings to: **good** but **better-best** and **bad** but **worse-worst.**

6. It is worth mentioning, alongside the superlative **the most X**, the phrase **a most X**. This is not a superlative, just an **intensifier** of the adjective, cf. Chapter 10, V.H. There is no real comparison involved.

V. An **ADVERB** describes the action of a verb or embellishes an adjective.

A. Adverbs usually answer the question "How? In what way" These are very often formed from adjectives by adding **-ly**: hungri**ly**, smooth**ly**, sensuous**ly**. The most obvious case of an adverb not derived from its corresponding adjective is the pair **good-well.** The word **fast** can be either adjective or adverb, although grammar books may tell you to use **quickly** for the adverb.

B. Some independent words not formed from adjectives are also considered adverbs, though they have nothing to do with qualities, but rather, with intensity or "setting the scene" in time and place: **now, then, often, seldom, very.**

C. Adverbs also have three degrees, like adjectives, and you form them the same two ways:

1. **Plain** and **Equal Comparison**:

   a. Her dog runs **fast** and jumps **beautifully**.

   b. Her dog runs **as fast as** yours and jumps **as beautifully**.

2. **Unequal comparison**: Our dog runs **faster than** hers and jumps **more beautifully**.

3. **Superlative**: Your dog runs **the fastest of** any in the county and jumps **the most beautifully.**

4. Two adverbs use a different stem to add the comparative and superlative endings to: **well** but **better-best** and **badly** but **worse-worst.** (That's right: **better-best** and **worse-worst** stop distinguishing between adjective and adverb, but their corresponding **plain** forms do distinguish: **good-well, bad-badly**.)

VI. A **PREPOSITION** is a big name for a little word.

A. It shows a relationship between two things, usually two nouns or two general situations.

1. The relationship usually involves the position of one item relative to the other, like **in, on, at, around** or time relative to each other, like **before, after, since.**

2. The relationship can be more abstract, like subject content (**about**), physical composition (**of**), comparison (**like, as**), contradiction (**despite**), and many others that space does not permit us to delve into.

B. Prepositions--really "pre"+"pose" meaning "placed in front of"--is followed by a noun or pronoun, which is then called the **object of the preposition**, and the whole phrase is called, naturally enough, a **prepositional phrase**. Here are some typical prepositional phrases with their objects as they occur in well-known titles and other common expressions. Ask yourself what kind of relationship they designate:

1. **in:** The Cat **In The Hat**, The Wind **In The Willows**

2. **on:** Cat **On A Hot Tin Roof**, Little House **On The Prairie**

3. **over:** Bridge **Over The River Kwai**

4. **of:** Tale **Of Two Cities, Of Mice and Men**, Patch **Of Blue**

5. **without:** Parents **Without Partners**

VII. A **CONJUNCTION** simply join things together (con+join). They come in two varieties:

A. **Coordinating conjunctions** connect similar parts of sentences: nouns with nouns, verbs with verbs, adjectives with adjectives, sentences with sentences, etc. **and, but, yet,** also **for** in more formal usage.

B. **Subordinating conjunctions** introduce subordinate clauses, as you saw in Chapter 2 above: **although, when, if, while, because, as, since,** and several others. They have meanings like "giving a reason, cause, condition, or other "accompanying circumstance" to the main clause.

VIII. There are also **INTERJECTIONS**, the emotional words you can't do without but that, strictly speaking, are not part of the structure of a sentence. **Oh!, Gawldarnit!, Wow! Fiddlesticks! Well, now!** They will not concern us here, but they do add a certain something.

EXERCISE 3
PARSE YOUR SPEECH
Key: p. 339

With this mini-glossary under your control, go through the following sentences and operate on them as follows (the text is deliberately spaced wide):

a. Underline all nouns and noun phrases.
b. Double underline all verbs and verb phrases.
c. Indicate adjectives by drawing an arrow between them and the noun they modify.
d. Do the same with adverbs modifying verbs.
e. Bracket all prepositional phrases and show by an arrow what the phrase modifies.

Example: The quick brown fox jumped [over the lazy dog].

1. The Cat in the Hat came back.

2. The rain in Spain falls mainly on the plain.

3. Put that in your pipe and smoke it!

4. Somewhere over the rainbow bluebirds fly.

5. The square of the hypotenuse is equal to the sum of the squares of the other two sides.

6. Peter Piper picked a peck of pickled peppers.

7. Go to the polls in November and vote for the candidate of your choice.

8. Some enchanted evening you may meet a stranger across a crowded room.

9. I pledge allegiance to the flag of the United States of America.

10. In a cabin in the woods a little old man by the window stood.

∞∞

IX. POST-SCRIPT: MOVING IN AND OUT OF PARTS OF SPEECH

This is just a quick look at the fact that you can determine the part of speech of a word in English not so much by the way it looks as by the way it acts in the sentence. In many languages the form also tells you the part of speech: once a verb always a verb; once a noun always a noun, and if you want to use a noun as a verb you have to change its form. Not necessarily so in English.

A. Take these nouns and use them as verbs without changing them at all. Just stick them in the "verb slot" in the sentence:

1. Nouns signifying "superficial covering or natural coating" become verbs meaning "take off the natural covering" or "put on the non-natural covering."

a. natural:
peel a banana, **skin** an animal, **shell** an egg, **dust** the furniture

b. additional, asociated, or non-natural covering:
paint a house, **varnish** a table, **wax** a car, **carpet** the living room, and even **dust** the crops (compare with 'furniture'!)

2. Nouns signifying "anatomical parts" become verbs meaning "use that part in some functionally appropriate way."

   a. obvious connection:
   hand me the cup, **shoulder** responsibility, **face** a crisis, **elbow** your way through a crowd, **eye** a situation, **knee** an attacker (ouch!)

   b. marginal or not so obvious:
   stomach a person, **back** a cause, **head** a committee, and the barely recognizable **foot** the bill. (Is there any connection at all?)

3. Nouns for some containers can become verbs:
bottle the water, **can** the peas, but note that **cup** your hands does not mean "put your hands in a cup," but "make youre hands into the *shape* of a cup so that they can hold liquid."

B. **Derivation**

1. This is the process by which you change one kind of word into another. There are also many ways of changing words by adding things to them. What you just did in A. above--use a noun as a verb (or is it vice-versa?)--is a kind of derivation. Since you did not actually change the word itself, you can call it **zero derivation**.

2. Adjectives or nouns, for example, can become verbs in several ways and have different, though related meanings. These include:

   a. Start with **en-: enrich, enlarge; entomb, entangle,** and with minor spelling change to represent actual sound: **embitter**

   b. End with **-en: widen, broaden, loosen, flatten, shorten.** Also: **lengthen, strengthen** (cf. **long-length, strong-strength**). Compare the past (participle) suffix **-(e)n**, Chapter 8, chart, p. 110, 2e.-h.

   c. Both: **enliven, embolden** (note spelling of **-em** before **b**)

   d. End with **-ify,** chopping off some of the original end, if need be: **terror-terrify, electricity-electrify, humid-humidify, quantity-quantify, liquid-liquefy** (spelling!).

e. End with **-ize**: **maximum-maximize, human-ize, brutal-ize, normal-ize, national-ize.**

3. There are lots of such processes, but there is not space to go into them here. What is important for language learning is that derivational processes like the ones just mentioned--and the ones elaborated on in Chapter 12, below--applies only to some words, and you have to learn which ones. The adjective **large** becomes a verb by starting with **en-**. But to make **short** into a verb you *end* with **-en**, and from **liquid** you cannot form either ***liquiden** or ***enliquid**. So there is only **enlarge** and **shorten** but no ***largen** or ***enshort**. The similar adjectives **big** and **small** are "derivational dead ends": you cannot form any other words from them, except the questionable nouns **bigness** and **smallness**.

⇒ This does not mean that English is "crazy," "illogical," or impossible to learn. It just illustrates that derivation is not an automatic process and that not all words are created equal.

C. Inflection

1. This is the **automatic** (or nearly so!) type of formation, like the plural formation of nouns (adding some kind of **-s**) or the formation of past tense from present (adding some kind of **-d**, more on which in Chapter 8). By inflection you mean that, in principle, any noun forms a plural. By derivation you mean that not every noun can become a verb by form or by use.

2. Languages can deal with inflection and derivation very differently--that is, with different kinds of endings or other kinds of changes within the word itself. It is not always easy to tell which grammatical categories are inflectional and which are derivational, but it helps to have an idea that the notion exists. More in Chapter 12.

CHAPTER 4

SENTENCE FUNCTIONS: PREDICATES AND OBJECTS

By now you can look at a sentence and identify the nouns and verbs. But if you think your job ends there, you are in for a surprise. That was just the beginning. Now you have to see what that knowledge will do for you in terms of how these parts interact to build up a sentence that means something.

I. SUBJECTS AND OBJECTS

A. It is now clear not only that nouns and pronouns exist as classes of words, but also that they perform a crucial function in a sentence. Nouns and pronouns serve as **subjects of verbs** and **objects of verbs and prepositions**.

1. Every sentence in English is composed minimally of a one-word subject and a one-word predicate. (Many languages have "predicate sentences," which have no subject.) The minimal subject in English is a noun or pronoun. The minimal predicate is a verb. In these examples the one-word noun/pronoun-subject is underlined once, and the one-word verb-predicate, twice:

   This stinks! Who coughed? Dogs bark. Heat rises. What happened?

2. Careful, though: not every 2-word group is a noun-verb sentence. What do you say about these:

   Why bother? Since when? What for? Pure chewing satisfaction!

B. You can expand--potentially to infinity--either part of such sentences by modifying it with adjectives, adverbs, dependent clauses, or prepositional phrases. You should still see the minimal frame intact:

1. Big dogs (with cold noses) bark.

2. Dogs bark loudly (at all hours) (of the day).

3. And you can, of course, combine the two and continue expanding, but the basic core remains:

⇒ **Too many big, husky-voiced dogs with cold noses bark loudly and threateningly at all hours of the day at any moving thing that passes for no apparent reason.**

C. A verb like **bark** can, then, form a whole predicate by itself. It needs no other information to complete it, though it can take a lot. Other verbs do not form a predicate all by themselves. Say these almost-sentences to yourself:

1. I am. She appears. Kid feels. Car looks. Weather became. Hair turns.

2. If you wanted to complete them, you might try:

   a. I am **fine** or I am **the baby sitter.**

   b. She appears **tired**.

   c. The kids feel **crummy**.

   d. Your car looks **brand new**.

   e. The weather became **lovely**.

   f. My hair is turning **grey**.

3. The verb in each of these sentences is followed by a noun or adjective that basically **equals** or **identifies** the subject, namely:

a.-d. are 1-stage:	I = fine; I = sitter; she = tired; kids = ±crummy; car = new.
e.-f. are 2-stage:	weather ≠ lovely → weather = lovely;
	hair ≠ grey → hair = grey.

Since this noun or pronoun is in the predicate part of the sentence and serves to complete the verb, it is called the **predicate adjective** or **predicate noun**. The verbs in this case--**is, appear, feel, look**--are not actions, but rather, mere connectors. They are, therefore, called **linking verbs or helping verbs** or, in fancier terminology, the **cópula**.

II. MORE OBJECTS AND VERB CLASSIFICATIONS

A. Now look what you need to complete these verbs, and see if you don't feel that they are different animals:

1. Dogs love [Alpo]. (Commercial)
2. Kids watch [T.V.]
3. You're bothering [us].
4. I like [her] and she likes [me].
5. The Giants win [the pennant]!! The Giants win [the pennant]!!
   (Shrieked over and over by sportscaster in 1951 World Series)

Verbs that are not copula but nonetheless require a third element to complete them--that is, to rescue a sentence from sounding like it is hanging in mid-air--are called **transitive**. The term refers to the fact that the action of the verb "goes over" (transits!) onto an object, called a **direct object**. In the above examples, in addition to the usual subject-predicate underlining, the direct object is enclosed in [square brackets]. Do you feel an intimate connection between the action and the object?

B. The direct object, like the subject, is a noun, noun phrase, or pronoun. In theory, it is the item that gets the direct effect of the verbal action the subject performs. Of course, in the real world this can take several shapes:

1. This effect can be creative, as in: Jack built [his house].

2. It can be destructive, as in: Jack destroyed [his house].

3. It can be steady-state, as in: Jack loves [his house].

Given your knowledge of the real world, you know that if you apply a **build** action to **house** then you can guess there first was no house, then there was one. The reverse is true if you apply **destroy** to the house: first you have one, then you don't! The grammatical structure of English considers the two situations equally: "some verb" applies to "some noun". The grammar of some other languages distinguishes these dynamic vs. stative meanings by different forms of the verb or the noun!

4. As you guessed from sentence II.A.4 just above, pronouns have different forms depending on whether they function as subject or object. Many languages are equally concerned that their nouns, too, show by their form whether they are subjects or objects. This is part of the **case** phenomenon mentioned in Chapter 3 II.B.1.d., above. More on this later.

C. Unlike transitive verbs, verbs that either do not require a third element to complete their meaning or do require one and insist that it be connected by a preposition are **intransitive**. A lot of intransitive verbs, for example, refer to motions or noises characteristic of the subject. In these examples there are no square brackets, but rather:

1. These verbs are complete, and the prepositional phrases in parentheses provide optional information:

   Dogs bark (at people). Birds fly (south in winter). You coughed.

2. These verbs are also intransitive but do require some prepositional phrase, which appears in bold type. (Even if you spoke these sentences in telegraphic form with no preposition, you would still hear one in your "mind's ear."):

We listen **to the news** every day.

Mr. Bush lives **in Washington.**

Joey stepped **on a shell** at the beach.

Her lawyer talked **to my lawyer.**

Do you agree it would sound funnier to say just, e.g., "Joey stepped," than, e.g., "Dogs bark"?

D. **Be Warned!**

Just in case you come to the mechanical conclusion that a verb followed by a prepositional phrase is intransitive, here are some normal transitive verbs that, in addition to a direct object, also require, or frequently occur with, prepositional phrases. The proof is not in the linear order of words but in the **meaning of the resulting phrase**:

1. The researcher put [the brew] **in the test tube**.

2. Did you sweep [that dust] **under the bed**?

3. We couldn't retrieve [the important file] **from the ruined disk.**

That is, even though **put** and **sweep** are transitive verbs, you cannot say just **put the brew** and **sweep the dust**. You need some additional information about the destination of that direct object. (After all, **put** and **sweep** are verbs that depict a kind of motion, so it stands to reason you need to know where that motion goes.

4. Now, if you wonder why you can say **sweep the floor** without adding another phrase, think of the different relationship between your **sweep** action and the dust vs. the floor. When you apply motion to the dust it ends up somewhere else. The floor, however, does not move. This is not just a quirk or a logical game. You are incredibly careful and clever about the way you use your grammar to package information. The sentence structure looks the same, but the kinds of words that can fill in the subject-verb-[object] slots interact with each other in ways you are totally unaware of. In other words, a verb like **sweep** can mean either:

a. change the nature of an object but not its location, as in **floor** or

b. change the location of an object but not its nature, as in **dust**.

English grammar considers both things the direct object of **sweep**, which makes the notion of "direct object" kind of wishy-washy.

⇒ The upshot of this exercise in apparent nit-pickiness is that when you learn verbs in your new language, part of learning them is learning what other kinds of words they combine with to make normal-sounding sentences in that language. Not every language may allow you to express such different relationships as **sweep the dust** and **sweep the floor** with the same sentence type.

The unfortunate thing is that neither textbooks for beginners nor "English-Whatever" dictionaries give you that information very reliably. (In fact, this is not even always clear from the American Heritage or Webster's dictionaries.)

5. Here are two more verbs like **sweep** that are often discussed by people who recognize that traditional grammar terms are not precise enough to show you what you really express with your language:

a. **load**: (1). Penelope loaded onions on the truck.
(2). Penelope loaded the truck with onions.

b. **plant**: (1). Hortense planted flowers in the garden.
(2). Hortense planted the garden with flowers.

The situations you describe with such verbs involve the same elements in each case (person-onions-truck; person-flowers-garden), and each sentence has a transitive verb with a direct object. Traditional grammar is content if you get that far. But the relationships among the elements are different.

c. In (1) the onions and flowers literally "change location", while the truck and the garden do not. In (2) the truck and the garden go from empty to occupied. In each case, whichever is the direct object is "directly affected" by the prepositional phrase, while the object of the preposition is seen as "less affected." The difference in meaning--rather, in focus of attention--may not be particularly important 99 out of 100 times you use such sentences, but their grammatical structure is, nonetheless, differnent.

d. Other such "two-way transitive verbs" in English are **splash**, as in "splash the wall with paint" vs. "splash paint on the wall," and **strip**, as in "strip the dissident of his citizenship" vs. "strip the citizenship from the dissident." (Note that this does not work with, say, **spill**: "spill the milk on the floor" is fine, but *"spill the floor with milk" is nonsense. Seems like hair-splitting, but some languages use different verb forms to show that relationship.

E. English can often express the same--or apparently the same--idea with either a transitive or intransitive verb. There is usually some slight difference in meaning.

1. Compare the transitive a. and intransitive b.:

   a. Mosquitos inhabit [the swamp].

   b. Mosquitos live **in the swamp.**

   The two sentences are nearly the same, but do you feel that in the first there is a tighter bond between subject and object than in the second? With **inhabit** it sounds as if they have really put down roots and are quite comfortable and numerous. **Live in** is much more neutral, both physically and emotionally.

2. The relevance for your target language is that it may express by a transitive verb what English expresses by an intransitive verb and vice-versa. Here are some more examples of English pairs of transitive verb + [direct object] vs. intransitive verb + **prepositional phrase** (in bold). Do they mean exactly the same? Maybe one feels more concrete, more formal, more forceful? Would you be more likely to use one in speech and the other in writing? (That is also an important difference.) The point is, for our immediate concerns, that the two structures are different, even if the meaning appears to be the same.

a. The beast entered [the room]. The beast came **into the room.**

b. The student attends [class]. The student goes **to class.**

III. THINGS THAT LOOK SIMILAR MAY NOT BE!

A. Not every noun that follows a verb directly is a direct object, either. The verb must "feel" transitive. Transitivity is above all a question of sense, not of position in the sentence. All these sentences have the form

noun + verb + noun

but what's the difference?

1. a. He sees a student. b. He is a student.

2. a. She met a teacher. b. She became a teacher.

3. a. You bored them. b. They looked bored.

The a. sentences all have transitive verbs and direct objects. The b. sentences all have copular verbs with either a predicate noun, as in 1 and 2, or predicate adjective, as in 3. It is more of an "equivalent" of the subject and therefore not a direct object of the verb. In short, we can say that a direct object is a noun or noun phrase that represents an entity separate from the subject. A predicate noun or adjective more or less describes or gives new information about the subject. This is a real meaning difference, so you cannot be ruled by the mere position of the noun that comes after the verb.

B. Now, what about pronouns? English is more or less careful about using a different set of pronouns for subject--**I, you, he, she, it, we, they**--from those for object--**me, you, him, her, it, us, them**. What about predicate pronouns?

1. Strictly speaking, according to a certain logic, you can say that since the predicate noun more or less equals the subject you should use the same form for predicate pronouns as you do for subject pronouns. Formal English and high school grammar books want you to observe this logic and say:

a. "Who is at the door?" "It is **I**."

b. Was it **he** with whom we saw you?

c. "May I please speak with Ms. Bildgebottom?" "This is **she**."

d. "Is that the guests arriving?" "Why, yes, it appears to be **they**."

2. Now, it is not the purpose of this book to be renegade or preach anti-establishmentism and grammatical anarchy, but the fact is that normal 20th century American English, for whatever reason, has reassigned the **me-us-him-her-them** group to be used as **anything except subject**. So most people say,

   "Did you see that handsome guy on the 6:00 news? That was **me**."

   You do not have to go around thinking that spoken language is somehow inferior to written language. In speaking, anything else but "That was **me**" sounds pretty stilted. However, the norm for writing term papers and business letters is still, e.g., "That was **I**."

3. In the same spirit, the distinction between **who** and **whom** is not part of most people's active repertoire, and **whom** is slowly losing ground, that is, becoming less acceptable, even in writing.

   a. Traditional grammar books want you to say "**Who** are you?" and "**Whom** do you see?" because the answers are, respectively, "I am /your congress person/" (with a predicate noun) and "I see [them]" (with a direct object).

   b. Most people no longer feel that **whom** is an object form, but they still have an idea that **whom** is somehow formal and supposedly "correct," so they use it anytime they want to sound formal--maybe to appear authoritative--or deliberately imitate or mock fancy speech, as in, "**Whom** are you?" It's really a very interesting phenomenon, one of several where the textbooks are lagging way behind the reality of the speech community. You do not have to assume that textbooks are right. They are, after all, written by people who have particular ideas and agendas.

C. **Transitivity** or **intransitivity**, then, is a property of meaning inherent in the verb itself. Traditional definitions of a **transitive** verb as "a verb that takes a direct object" and of **intransitive** as "a verb that does not take a direct object" are circular and misleading. Dictionaries class verbs as *v.t.* and *v.i.,* respectively. More on this in Chapter 18 below, but here are some things to think about in the meantime:

1. In **He's cooking supper** you immediately say **cook** is transitive. You could operate on it as follows: He's cooking [supper].

2. But in **Supper is cooking** you see no direct object, so many grammars would call **cook** intransitive: Supper is cooking.

3. On the one hand, **supper** can not "do" anything transitively in the same sense that **he** can: you don't *expect* the **supper** to cook anything transitively, and you don't expect **he** to cook intransitively in the way **supper** does. Many languages have different verb forms or entirely different sentence patterns for expressing this relationship. The point here is that the verb **cook is inherently transitive**: there will always be a "cook-**er**" and "cook-**ee**", but the cook**er** may or may not always be expressed. More on this in Chapter 18.

4. Along similar lines, in **He's eating supper** it is obvious that **eat** is transitive and **supper** is the direct object, that is, **he** is the "eat**er**", and **supper** is the "eat**ee**": He's eating [supper].

   a. In a sentence like plain **He's eating** there is no object expressed, but you cannot claim that **eat is** any less transitive. There is still an "eat-**er**" and an "eat-**ee**", though the "eat-**ee**" is not expressed by a word.

   b. So traditional grammar often says **eat** in such cases is a "transitive verb used intransitively." This definition, based on the number of words, misrepresents both concepts. There is a fundamental difference between "intransitive with no object" and "transitive with object assumed but not expressed." Many verbs like **eat, drink, cook, read, write** in English have the option of specifying their object or not. Verbs like **put, build, lock, like** do not have the option. They have to have an object. You can not say:

(1). "Leave me alone. I'm locking," without getting strange looks. (Forget for now that you can say "I'm locking up.")

(2). In a third-rate spy movie you might hear the foreign female villain kiss the unwitting hero seductively and ask, "**You like?**" for "Do/Did you like **it**?" It sounds pretty comical not to supply a direct object there. Rather than assume from this that the spy has just learned English poorly, you might guess instead that her language has a structure which does *not* require you to supply a direct object the way English often--but not always!--does. (Russian happens to be such a language, by the way.)

⇒ The point is that in language and in learning the grammar of a language, what you **don't say** is often as important as what you **do say!** The trickiest part of learning a new language is not memorizing vocabulary and verb conjugations. It is learning what words go together with what other words and in what ways!

IV. TO '-ly' OR NOT TO '-ly' ? *THAT* IS THE QUESTION! (A NOTE ON "FEELING GOOD" AND "FEELING WELL")

A. You are now quite expert in identifying subjects and predicates and, further, separating those predicates into verbs and direct objects or verbs and predicate nouns and adjectives.

B. Now let's look at how **adjectives** and **adverbs** function within predicates. This is one of those points of normative grammar that send many teachers tearing their hair out because people mess it up all the time. They do what the "rule" says, but the rule is not formulated finely enough in most school grammar books of English, and this makes all kinds of problems for the foreign language learner armed with misconceptions.

1. Take the adjective/adverb pair **good-well**. In these two sentences the adjective modifies the noun **writer**, and the adverb modifies the verb **write**:

a. She is a **good writer**.

b. She **writes well.**

2. Most adjective-adverb pairs are characterized by the ending **-ly** on the adverb. Take the above sentences and replace **good** with **bad** or **delightful**:

   a. He is a **bad-delightful writer.**

   b. He **writes badly-delightfully**.

3. The rules of standard English say that modifiers that follow verbs are adverbs. In fact, there are several verbs in English for which this is not true, and a lot of confusion arises over whether you should add **-ly** or not. These are mostly the copula verbs discussed above:

   a. She **is good** in math.

   b. We **are awful** when it comes to doing our tax returns on time.

4. The verbs that relate to the five senses--**taste, smell, sound, look, feel**--are also kind of copular in their behavior. They mean, essentially, "My sense of taste tells me that the subject **is good, bad,** or **indifferent**."

   a. The verbs **taste, smell, feel** can also be transitive, if a potential "doer" is doing them. (The transitive **hear** and **see** correspond to the copular **sound** and **look**.) If the subject has none of these senses, you have to assume that someone who does have them is using them. This is why you say:

      (1). They tasted the coffee, and the coffee **tasted bitter** (and not **bitterly**). Specifically, "They deduced through their sense of taste that the coffee **was bitter**."

      (2). I smelled the cottage cheese, and it didn't **smell fresh** (not **freshly**).

      (3). We heard you on the radio, and you **sounded nervous** (not **nervously**).

      (4). She saw him on T.V., and he **looked terrific** (not **terrifically**).

(5). The child's mother felt his forehead, and he **felt feverish** (not **feverishly**).

b. This last one is the one you were probably most corrected for in school. Teachers probably said, "Don't say 'I don't feel good.' Say 'I don't feel **well**.'" They were over-applying the rule that says, "Use adverbs after verbs" as in B.2. above. The more natural-feeling rule is:

Use predicate adjectives after verbs of sensing and not adverbs.

c. The truth is that **well** here is the adjective "healthy", and it has no adverb pair ***welly**. No one would correct you for saying, "I **feel good** about my work," because you mean **good** and not **well**.

d. Similarly for **bad**, you can certainly **feel bad** about something, although you often hear people over-applying the adverb rule and saying **feel badly**. You can, of course, encounter genuine adverbs after these sensing verbs, but only if you refer to the manner in which you perform the action, as in the somewhat far-fetched:

(1). He wanted to be a professional wine taster, but he **tasted badly** (= did a bad job of tasting).

(2). The bell **sounded loud** because they **sounded the bell loudly**. (two different uses of **sound**.)

V. "DOUBLE OBJECTS?" Just a short note on examples like these:

A. What is the direct object in sentences like these:

1. We consider them experts in the field.

2. They elected her president.
(Both **hér** and **président** receive strong stress, and not as the single phrase [her président].)

B. At first glance you seem to have two objects: **them** and **experts, her** and **president.** The best we can say at this point is that the second noun in the predicate of each sentence is not itself the direct object. Instead, it does tell you about **a particular facet of the direct object**.

C. You could paraphrase these to show the relationship between the subject, verb and direct object, something like:

1. "She became /the president/ as a result of our action." or
   "They elected [a president], and it was /her/ (/she/).

2. "They are /experts/ in our opinion."

3. That is, while the first noun after the verb is really its direct object, you could consider the second noun, that describes the direct object, a kind of hidden predicate noun. If you parse them, then, you can use both square brackets and also diagonal slashes:

   a. We consider [them] /experts/ in the field.

   b. They elected [her] /president/.

4. Not many verbs permit this construction. Some verbs prefer some preposition or even an intervening verb:

   a. Bush chose Quayle **as** his running mate. . .

   b. They believe him **to be** an honest candidate.

VI. REFLEXIVE AND RECIPROCAL OBJECTS

A. Reflexive Objects.

This is actually a big topic and will receive more attention in Chapter 18, but for now we can just say that in the real world a subject can be its own direct object, whether intentionally or unintentionally. You indicate this in English by the pronouns with **-self**. This is called the **reflexive pronoun**.

1. Lush Liquid gets dishes so clean, you can see [yourself] in them. (You are both the "see-or"--intentionally--and the "see-ee.")

2. We fell down and hurt [ourselves]. (We are both the "hurt-or"--unintentionally--and the "hurt-ee."

B. Notice that a lot people use the **-self** form even when they do not mean it. This usually happens in conjoined phrases, more on which in Chapter 11, IV. Some people think it sounds "nicer" or more "precise." Do you see why sentences like:

1. My wife and myself thank you.

2. You can get a ride with my wife and myself.

are considered "incorrect" in grammar books? The **-self** form here does not "reflect" back on to any "me" in the sentence. Strictly speaking, no **-self** form can occur in the subject for the same reason. The same people who say the above sentence would never say, "Myself thank(s?) you," or, "You can get a ride with myself."

C. **Reciprocal objects.**

When you have a **plural subject**, and one element of the subject is the direct object of the other element of the subject and vice-versa, you use **each other**.

1. I don't know you and you don't know me, so we should get to know **each other**.

2. These politicians can't keep **themselves** out of trouble. Maybe if they get together they can help keep **each other** out of trouble.

VII. NOMINATIVE AND ACCUSATIVE CASE

A. Recall the notion of **case** mentioned briefly in Chapter 3, II. B. In many languages, nouns have different forms to show at a glance (and whatever the audio equivalent of a glance is) what role the noun is playing in the given sentence. Usually this appears as an **ending** on the noun. Even if your target language does not do this, it is a good idea to be familiar with the term and concept in any case.

B. The centuries-old tradition of teaching Latin grammar has emblazoned on the pages of language textbooks everywhere the terms **nominative case** for the form the noun has when it is **subject** and **accusative case** for the form the word has when it is **direct object**. In many languages this applies to adjectives modifying nouns, too.

1. Imagine that, as in Latin, the nominative ending of a noun--and for argument's sake, the adjective, too--is **-us**. That means whenever you use the noun as subject it will end in **-us**, and every time you see or hear an **-us**, you will know that the noun in question is the subject. Let's also say that the accusative case ending for the same noun is **-um**.

2. Take the sentence: **The Swedish movie delighted the viewers, but the critics panned the Swedish movie.**

   a. In this book you indicate subject and object by underlining and bracketing. Imagine that English is like Latin and adds audible endings instead. Try to say this, allowing for occasional "squishes" of the ending with the body of the word (and if you know Latin, try to contain your revulsion at this perversion of it):

      Th**us** Swedish-**us** movi**us** delighted the viewers-**um**, but the critics-**us** panned th**um** Swedish-**um** movi**um**.

   b. English used to do this quite naturally until the Norman Conquest of 1066 got in the way. One typical phenomenon that goes hand-in-hand with this case business is this: since you can tell by the form of the word what function it has, you can put it in different positions in the sentence and not confuse your listener. And in fact, a lot of languages with a **case system** also have free, or relatively free, **word order**. English and Chinese, which do not have cases of nouns, have fairly strict word order. (See Chapter 7, IV.)

3. What this means for English sentence structure, in terms of the way we are operating on it with brackets and underlines, is that there is no *audible* way to distinguish, say, <u>John</u> from [John], but there *is* an

important kind of case system in English, namely, for pronouns, more on which in Chapter 11. For now, just think about the fact that you *must* distinguish--and you do, quite automatically--between I and [me], he and [him], she and [her], we and [us], they and [them]. In some grammar books of English you see the terms **nominative case** for the underlined items and **objective case** for the bracketed ones. (To the extent that you can talk about **case** at all in English, there is also the so-called **possessive case**, mentioned in Chapter 3, IV.E.)

C. DISCLAIMER!!

This does not mean that every language that has a case form called **nominative** and a case form called **accusative** uses those forms only for subject and object, respectively.

1. The forms that grammarians call by the same name in different languages can have different uses in different languages. By the same token, if a language has a lot of case forms, it might use several of them for what we consider a direct object. Keep an open mind and let your language do what it needs to, not what you, the English-speaking learner, think it ought to. . .

2. The names for the five Latin cases get applied to many languages, whether they actually fit or not. Here are the names of those five forms and at least one of the functions they typically serve. This is far from the whole story. English grammars of several generations back used to present English nouns according to this Latin model, too. It looked a bit like this:

Nominative	for subject	**The boy** ate cake.
Accusative	for direct object	We love **the boy**.
Genitive	for possession	**The boy's** book or the book **of the boy,**
	for composition	a group **of boys**
Dative	for indirect object	I gave **the boy** a treat.
Ablative	for origin	I took the book **from the boy.**
	for source	I'm afraid **of the boy.**

EXERCISE 4a.

RECOGNIZING DIRECT OBJECTS

Key: p. 340

Given: All the clauses in the following sentences have transitive verbs with explicit direct objects. Identify them by underlining the subject once, the verb, twice, and bracket the D.O. When there is a dependent clause, set it off by curly brackets and apply the same procedure within it. Don't bother with prepositions for now.

Example:

Our product guarantees relief from the aches and pains that ruin your day. →

Our product guarantees [relief] from the aches and pains {that ruin your [day]}.

1. Real men eat quiche.
2. Beef gives strength.
3. If you touch me I'll call the police!
4. Grammar will not baffle you any more.
5. What are you writing, your memoirs? (Careful)
6. Drink Coca Cola.
7. Support your local union. (What's the problem with 6 and 7?)
8. May I take your order, please?
9. I'd like a Big Mac and fries, please.
10. The phone company cancelled my service because I didn't pay my bill.

EXERCISE 4b.

DISTINGUISHING DIRECT OBJECTS AND PREDICATE NOUNS

Key: p. 341

Which clauses contain direct objects and which do not? Underline all subjects once, all verbs (not the whole predicate) twice. If there is a direct object, bracket it. If there is a predicate noun or adjective put diagonal slashes around it. (In sentences with more than one clause, curly-bracket the dependent clause and apply the same procedure within it.) Examples:

Trans. Verb + Dir. Obj.: Coke adds [life].

Intrans. Verb + Pred. Noun or Adj.: The tree grew /tall/ and /straight/.

Object in dep. clause only: We lounge around {whenever we have [time]}.

1. Try it: you'll like it!

2. These are the times that try men's souls.

3. You have ring around the collar!

4. Maybelline makes beautiful eyes.

5. Ms. Smith defeated the incumbent mayor and became the new mayor.

6. You can take Salem out of the country but you can't take the country out of Salem. (TV cigarette jingle, ca. 1960's.)

7. How much wood would a woodchuck chuck if a woodchuck could chuck wood?

8. If Peter Piper picked a peck of pickled peppers, how many pecks of pickled peppers did Peter Piper pick?

9. “All the world’s a stage.” (Hamlet)

10. Do you take this person to be your lawfully wedded spouse. . .and will you be a faithful spouse and parent?

CHAPTER 5

INDIRECT OBJECTS

I. A FOURTH PART OF THE SENTENCE

According to Chapter 4, a direct object is the third major component of a sentence, along with the subject and transitive verb. So is a predicate noun or adjective, along with the subject and copula verb. The direct object, though, is the thing which receives the effect of the transitive verb. Take it one step further and the **indirect object** is the fourth major component of many sentence structures. It is the thing--most often a person--which receives the **benefit from** or **effect of** the direct object.

A. The indirect object almost always precedes the direct object in the sentence. In these examples, subjects are underlined once; verbs, twice.

The [direct object] is square-bracketed, as usual. The ⟨**indirect object**⟩ is in boldface and angle brackets with an arrow to it from the direct object to drive home the tight connection between the direct and indirect object.

1. He gave ⟨**her** ⟩ [some candy].

2. The crooked car dealer sold ⟨**the millionairess**⟩ [a lovely Edsel].

3. Mommy bought ⟨**me**⟩ a [book].

4. Will the baby sitter tell ⟨**us**⟩ a [story]?

B. Some verbs in English require indirect objects in addition to their direct objects:

1. **give** Grammar really gives ⟨**me**⟩ [a headache].

2. **bring** I'll bring ⟨**you**⟩ [your fries] right away, Mr. McDonald.

3. **send** The bank sends ⟨**us**⟩ [statements] every month.

4. **buy** Now you can buy ⟨**your whole family**⟩ [a big dinner] at Shmo's Snack Shack for mere pennies!

5. **promise** I never promised ⟨**you**⟩ [a rose garden].

6. **tell** Daddy told ⟨**me**⟩ [a scary story].

7. Verbs like **promise** and **tell** are a little trickier than meets the eye: their direct objects are very often whole noun clauses or infinitive phrases like **to go, to analyze** (more on which in Chapters 6, 8, 9), but the indirect object is still indirect. Look at the intricate bracketing of these:

   a. You promised ⟨**me**⟩ {[that you 'd be home on time tonight]}.

   b. The reporter told ⟨**the editor**⟩ {[that this was /the story/ of the week]}.

   c. The editor told ⟨**the reporter**⟩ [to go ahead with the story].

   (Note that in the case of **tell**, if you do not state the indirect object and have only the infinitive clause "to go ahead. . ." you have to replace **tell** with **say**: "The editor said [to go ahead with the story].")

8. Even if the direct object is unexpressed, as in a. below, the indirect object is still indirect **by sense**, that is, you could supply a direct object. The space is provided in your head. Likewise, if the indirect object is unexpressed, as in b. below, it is still "there." Either the sentence sounds a little unfulfilled, or you understand it to mean "to anybody and everybody."

a. {If I've told ⟨**you**⟩ [?] once} I've told ⟨**you**⟩ a thousand times [to sit still]!

b. This supermarket gives ⟨**??**⟩ [Green Stamps]!

C. Beware the usual dangers of relying on mechanical rules of position instead of on your sense of meaning. Take, for example,

1. They send [**their child**] to summer camp. versus

2. They send ⟨**their child**⟩ [a meager allowance].

Do you feel that **child** is serving a different function in the two sentences? In the first, it is the one affected by the action **send,** namely, the direct object. (The child is changing location!) In the second, **child** is the recipient of the direct object: the **allowance** is doing the relocating. So, **child** is the indirect object. Other languages might use different forms for these functions.

⇒ **It is not just that the "noun that follows the verb" is the direct object. You have to ask yourself who the principle players are in the scene, what they're doing, and who the supporting cast is. Then see how your own or your new language expresses those realities.**

3. One more note on verbs like **tell** and **pay**. They take both a direct and an indirect object, but either one may be unexpressed. Which is which in these?

a. **tell** (1). The scout leader told a scary story.

(2). The scout leader told the campers a scary story.

(3). The scout leader told the campers about his canoe trip.

b. **pay** (1). Peter paid the bus fare.

(2). Peter paid the driver the bus fare.

(3). Peter paid the driver and sat down.

In the (1) examples the direct objects **story** and **fare** have to have recipients in the real world, even if you do not express them. Do **campers** and **driver** play the same role in the (2) and (3) examples? Yes, they do. They are indirect objects regardless of the fact that in (3) there is no expressed direct object. The **story** changed hands in (2) and the **campers** got it, and there was a story in (3) though no word "story." Similarly in b. there is a **fare** in (3) whether you say so or not, so the **driver** is the recipient of it no matter what you do. This is the crucial difference between pure grammatical rules based on layout and grammatical processes based on knowledge of who does what to whom.

4. As you can guess, the reason it is important to be aware of this is that many languages use different forms to express these functions: one form for subject; one for direct object; possibly another, for indirect object. You have to feel, or be able to determine, the function in order to use the right form and produce target language that speakers of that language do not have to "retranslate" in order to understand and respond to.

II. ANOTHER KIND OF INDIRECT OBJECT

A. English allows another way of expressing this indirect object relation, namely, with the prepositions **to** and **for**, which usually come later in the sentence.

1. a. She **bought me** a present.
   → She **bought** a present **for me.**

   b. The butler **packed us** a lunch.
   → The butler **packed** a lunch **for us.**

2. a. The voters **gave the president** their mandate.
   → The voters **gave** their mandate **to the president.**

   b. Honey, I've **brought you** a surprise. . .
   → Honey, I've **brought** a surprise **for you**. . .

B. Some grammar books call both the a. and b. constructions **indirect object**. Both constructions are normal English, and sometimes you may prefer one over the other. Do you detect any subtle difference in their meaning? Are they really the same? Does one sound better than the other? Think about when you use which one and ask yourself why you chose it. You might, for example, want to draw more attention to the indirect object by placing it "later" in the sentence. Some languages allow only one or the other construction.

III. YET ANOTHER KIND

One more kind of indirect object is the one where the subject is the recipient of his or her own direct object.

A. One kind is the **reflexive -self**, similar to reflexive direct objects. Compare these pairs:

1. a. He gave ⟨**himself**⟩ [a talking to].

   b. He gave [himself] up.

2. a. She threw ⟨**herself**⟩ [a birthday party].

   b. She threw [herself] off the bridge.

3. a. Go get ⟨**yourself**⟩ [a haircut].

   b. Go get [yourself] checked out!

4. a. "Have ⟨**yourself**⟩ [a merry little Christmas]. . ." (Bing Crosby)

   b. Have [yourself] stuffed and mounted!

B. You often have straight object pronouns without **-self**. To northern city folk this usually sounds--as Hollywood has taught us the stereotype--"folksy" or "back-woodsy". In fact, the object-looking pronoun is not necessarily an object at all. It is not so much a "beneficiary" of an action as "the person most relevant for the given story" and usually the same person as the subject. This is a very important use of pronouns in some languages, including those areas of the United States where it is normal to say things like:

1. I got **me** a right perty little filly.

2. Ol' Zeke's got **him** a new bride.

3. We had **us** a grand ol' time.

4. I do believe I'll have **me** a chiliburger.

C. You also have the **reciprocal** indirect object with **each other**:

1. They send ⟨**each other**⟩ [birthday cards], but they never get ⟨**themselves**⟩ [anything].

2. Those feuding neighbors don't give ⟨**each other**⟩ [a moment's peace].

IV. DATIVE CASE

A. As we mentioned in Chapter 4, VII. above, Latin, Russian, German and many other languages express this indirect object function by tacking on the ending of the **dative case** (from Latin for "give"). Imagine, as in Russian, that the dative ending is **-ye**, that the accusative ending is **-u**, and that the nominative ending is **-a**. You could "translate" this English sentence into "Renglish" or "Russglish":

1. My mother gave my sister a book.

2. My-**a** mother-**a** gave my-**ye** sister-**ye** a-**u** book-**u**.

B. This means, to continue the pattern suggested in Chapter 4, VII.B.3, above, that English has one noun form for the three functions <u>John</u>, [John] and ⟨John⟩ or <u>book</u>, [book] and ⟨book⟩, and two pronoun forms, one for <u>I</u>, and one for both [me] and ⟨me⟩.

EXERCISE 5
INDIRECT OBJECTS
Key: p. 342

Follow the identification procedure outlined in I.A., above:

subject verb ⟨indirect object⟩ [direct object]. (without the **bold**, of course)

What is the point of the sentences with an (a) and a (b) part?

1. I gave my love a cherry without no stone. (folk song)

2. Promise her anything, but give her Arpège. (T.V. commercial)

3. Will you buy me something nice?

4. Sing us a song; Tell us a tale.

5. a. The parents sent their daughter a nice surprise.

   b. The parents sent their daughter on an important errand.

6. a. People who buy their poodles wholesale are cheap.

   b. People who buy their poodles presents must be rich.

7. a. Friends, Romans, Countrymen, lend me your ears! (M. Antony)

   b. In some cultures, men lend their wives money, and in some other cultures they lend their wives to their friends.

8. Ask me no questions and I'll tell you no lies.

9. I'll leave you my fortune if you leave me alone!

(If you really insist, you could squeeze a grammatical pun out of this by saying, "I'll leave you a loan if you leave me alone," but it sounds rather unnatural. At any rate, is it clear that **you** and **me** are playing different roles in the two clauses?)

10. a. I cut myself shaving.

b. I cut myself a piece of cake.

11. a. You've had your supper. Now you have to pay the bill.

b. You've done your dance. Now you have to pay the piper.

WHOA!

REGROUP AND DIGEST CHAPTERS 1-5:

NOTES ON PARSING VS. DIAGRAMMING

You deserve a break before going on to grander things! Just stop a minute and reflect on what you are really doing here and what generations of students before you have done.

The identification exercises you have been doing so far are examples of **parsing** a sentence. That is the general procedure you will use throughout this book. It used to be the major activity of elementary and secondary school English classes and is still the main thrust of many a Latin and Greek class.

Another formerly popular teaching tool is **diagramming** sentences. (The procedure goes back at least to Reed and Kellogg, 1886--see the Further Reading section at the end of this book.) While parsing involves the highly intellectual process of labelling parts of sentences by form and function, diagramming has the advantage of forcing you to manipulate the components of the sentence and arrange them on a sort of graph so as to highlight their relationship to each other visually. Given that the two major parts of any English sentence are subject and predicate, most often occurring in that order, in diagramming you put them on a divided horizontal line.

I. Take as an example a minimal 1-clause, 2-part sentence like **Birds fly.**

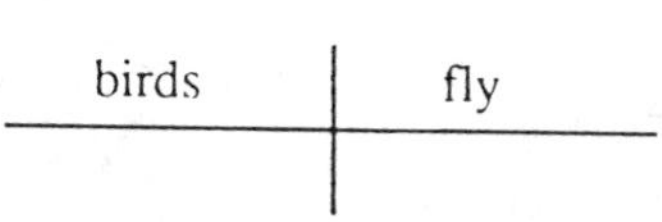

```
   birds   |   fly
-----------+-----------
           |
```

A. Now take the more elaborate **Big birds fly fast**. Modifiers will go on diagonal lines under the part of the sentence they modify. The diagonals in the subject half are adjectives, and those in the predicate half are most likely adverbs.

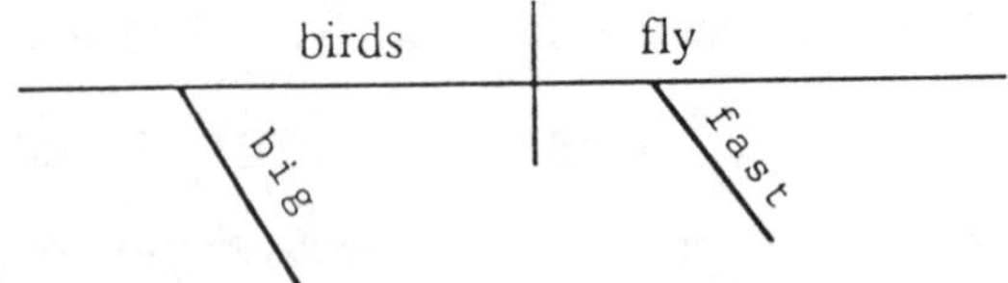

B. Expand the sentence a little more:

The big birds of the Great Lakes fly fast in beautiful formation.

Prepositions are also modifiers, of course. Their objects go on lower-level lines, and their modifiers in turn go on lower-level diagonals:

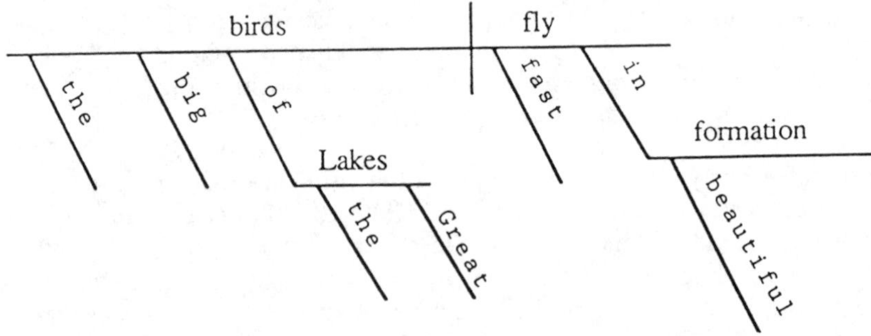

C. The same logic dictates how you deal with adverbs, that is, modifiers of modifiers. They also get diagonal lines. Take: **The beautifully colored birds in our back yard flew off with a wonderfully inspiring clatter.** This kind of procedure shows you very clearly how a simple basic core can build itself into an impressive structure.

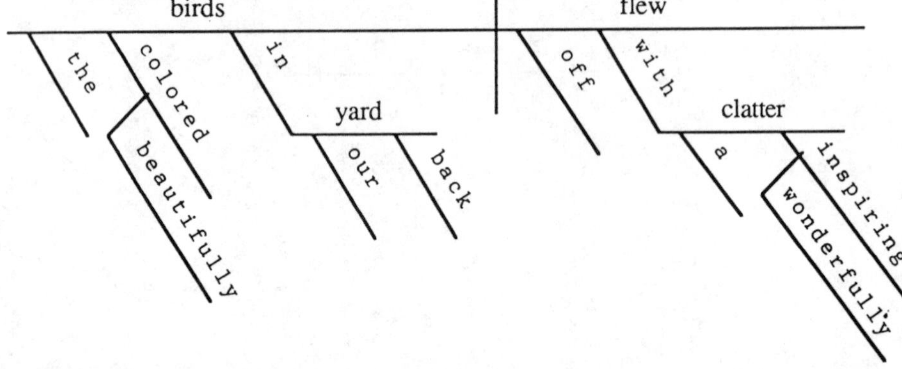

II. 3-part sentences put that crucial third element--direct object, if the verb is transitive or predicate nominal if the verb is a copula--on the main line.

A. Direct objects are separated by a vertical line that meets but does not cut the main line, since they are, after all, part of the predicate:

Good pilots fly new planes willingly.

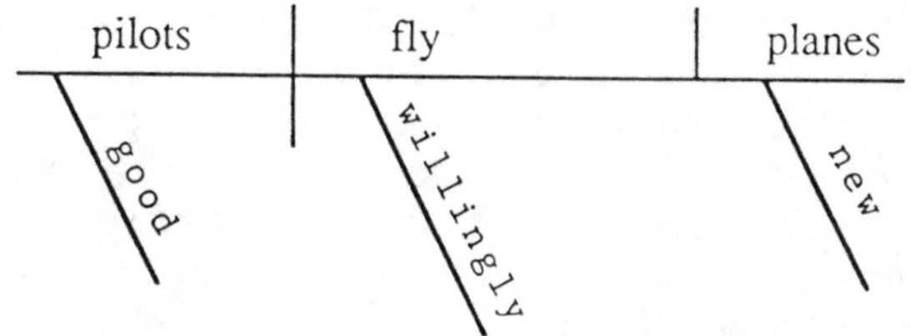

B. Predicate Nominals are indicated by a slant line that does not cross the main line: **My mother is an experienced pilot.**

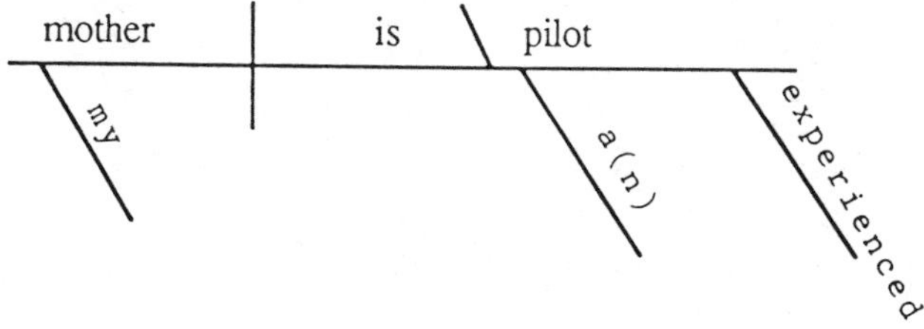

This is sufficient to give you an idea of the procedure and the possibilities. Diagramming sentences with subordinate clauses can be very daunting if your artistic prowess lags behind your analytical skills. You really have to study the finished product to understand what the sentence really means. (In my day, fourth and fifth grade English consisted of a lot of diagramming. My fifth grade teacher even admonished us,"When you diagram for me it will be a work of art!" I think I was the last generation to get this training, back in the early 1960's. My students a mere fifteen years later had never heard of it and were amazed when I diagrammed an English sentence on the board one day.)

In this book you will continue to parse. Parsing in its gourmet variety makes you go the extra step of giving more grammatical information about the parts you identify. In **Birds fly** you would say, "Birds: noun, plural, acting as subject. Fly: verb, present tense," and so on. Neither exercise can capture everything there is to say about the components of a sentence and their interrelations. For example, as you will discover in Chapter 10 below, you can not diagram the difference between, say, **experienced pilots** (Adj.+N) and **airline pilots** (N+N). They seem to have the same structure and will be diagrammed identically, even though **airline** is a noun, not an adjective. In many languages that difference is crucial because the forms of the words change. Going back to the example of **sweep** in Chapter 4, II.D.4-5, above, both **dust** and **floor** can be objects of **sweep** and will be diagrammed identically, but the different kind of relationship we uncovered there is too subtle for either parsing or diagramming. At any rate, both procedures are respectible and have their purpose in elementary schools. If your too-progressive English teacher deprived you of the experience of getting inside your language process, it's not too late to make up for it!

CHAPTER 6

PULLING IT ALL TOGETHER: PHRASES AND CLAUSES

Now that phrases and clauses are no problem to identify, you can take a closer look and see how you use them in normal speech. In fact, if you have a good idea of nouns, adjectives, and adverbs, you can see in this chapter just how phrases and clauses do the same things that nouns, adjectives, and adverbs do.

I. PHRASES

Any group of words that makes sense together can be called a phrase. You know from Chapter 2 that any phrase beginning with a preposition can be called a **prepositional phrase**.

A. A prepositional phrase that modifies a noun the way an adjective does is called an **adjective phrase**. Compare the same noun with an adjective and an adjective phrase:

1. a. the book **in the library** vs. the **fascinating** book

   b. "The Cat **In The Hat**" vs. the **mischievous** cat

   c. the fool **on the hill** vs. the **silly** fool

   ⇒ Both the adjective and the adjective phrase modify the **book** and **cat**. They answer the question, **"Which one?"** or **"What kind?"**

2. The difference is that the plain adjective goes **before** the noun, while the adjective phrase usually **follows** the noun.

a. Many languages treat single-word and phrase-length modifiers the same: either both before their noun, as in Chinese, or both may follow, as in French.

b. Some prepositional phrases are treated like single whole adjectives, in which case they precede the noun and are usually spelled hyphenated: an **in-depth** report, **on-the-spot** coverage, that **down-home** feeling.

B. Similarly, a prepositional phrase that modifies a verb the way an adverb does is called an **adverb phrase** or **adverbial phrase**. Note these questions and their answers:

1. **Where**? adverb: We live **there**.

   adverbial phrase: We live **on Elm St.**

> ⇒ Both the adverb and the adverbial phrase modify the verb **live** and answer the question, "**Where**?"

2. **Where to**? adverb: Let's go **home**.

   adverbial phrase: Let's go **to the movies**.

> Both the adverb and the adverbial phrase modify the verb **go** and answer the question, "**Where to**?"

(See Chapter 17 below on this "location-destination" distinction.)

C. Obviously the only way to tell whether your prepositional phrase is adjectival or adverbial is in a live context. Perhaps it is more precise, then, to say that a given prepositional phrase is "used adjectivally" or "used adverbially." Only context will tell you:

1. We live **on Elm St.**, modifies **live** by answering "**Where**?"
   (adv.)

2. The house **on Elm St.**, modifies **house**, answering "**Which one**?"
   (adj.) (and also "where", indirectly)

EXERCISE 6a.
PREPOSITIONAL PHRASE FROLIC
Key: p. 343

Underline all the prepositions and bracket the prepositional phrases they introduce. Indicate what the phrase modifies using an arrow, and label it as **Adj. Phr.** or **Adv. Phr.** Ask yourself what question it answers.

Example: The rain [in Spain] stays mainly [in the plain].
Adj. Phr. *Adv. Phr.*
= *which rain?* = *Where does it stay?*

1. Hurry to K-Mart for the sale of a lifetime!!

2. We were sailin' along on Moonlight Bay....

3. a. "What light through yonder window breaks?. . .

   b. . . .she hangs upon the cheeks of night like a rich jewel in an Ethiop's ear." (R. Montague)

4. a. 'Twas the night before Christmas and all through the house not a creature was stirring. . .

   b. The stockings were hung by the chimney with care in hopes that St. Nicholas soon would be there..."

5. a. "I'm getting married in the morning. . .

   b. . . . so get me to the church on time." (H.Higgins/L.Lowe)

6. a. "I pledge allegiance to the flag of the United States of America. . .

   b. . . .one nation under God with liberty and justice for all."

7. "The quality of mercy is not strained. It droppeth as the gentle rain of heaven upon the place beneath. . ." (Portia of Venice)

8. I am the very model of a modern major general. (Gilbert and Sullivan)

∞∞

II. CLAUSES, ESPECIALLY ADJECTIVE CLAUSES

You already know that a phrase with a subject and a predicate is called a clause. Now you can fine-tune that definition.

A. A clause that can make sense standing alone is called an **independent clause**. Normal folks call it a sentence. The term **main clause** is also applicable.

B. Any other clause is, therefore, **dependent** because it has to be part of a larger sentence unit. The other term for dependent clause is **subordinate clause**.

C. A subordinate clause that modifies a noun is called an **adjective clause**. This also goes under the alias of **relative clause**. They usually begin with **that**, **which**, or **who(m)**. When these pronouns are used this way they are called **relative pronouns** or simply **relativizer**. In these examples, all clauses are set off in curly brackets, with the other usual underlinings and brackets for the subject, verb, and direct object:

1. adjective: the **interesting** book, the **friendly** people

2. adjective phrase: the book **on the table**, the kid **up the block**

3. adjective clause: a. the book {that caught [her eye]}

   b. the people {who moved in next door}

   c. the book {[that] she bought }

   d. the people {[who(m)] we met }

4. The relativizers **that** and **who** refer to the nouns just before them. Regardless of what role **book** and **people** play in their own clause, you can see clearly that the relativizers in 3a. and 3b. act as **subject of the subordinate clause**, on the one hand, and in 3c. and 3d. they act as **direct object of the subordinate clause**. The one unusual fact is that the direct objects come **before** the verb.

D. Omittable THAT and stylistic gradations.

1. Notice that when the relativizers **that** or **who(m)** functions as object of the clause, normal English has the option of leaving it out altogether without disturbing the meaning or structure of the sentence. Observe these:

   a. the book {[that] she bought} → the book {she bought }

   b. the people {[who] we met → the people {we met}

2. This is not possible if the relativizer is the subject of its clause. In these two you cannot drop **who** or **that** without changing the structure of the sentence drastically. Both are "correct," but one is a sentence and one is a noun phrase modified by a relative clause:

   a. the mouse {that roared} → The mouse roared.

   b. the people {who live here} → The people live here.

3. The important thing is that the **THAT**-less versions of 1a., b. are still subordinate clauses, as the curly bracket parsing indicates to you. Many languages just do not permit such relativizer omission, so if you are translating such a clause from English into your target language, you have to keep the **THAT** in there or supply one. Otherwise, you'll come out with unacceptable target language.

4. A note on **who-whom** and **which**.

   a. Recall from Chapter 4, Section III.B.3, that formal English distinguishes the subject pronoun **who** from the object pronoun **whom.** This applies to subordinate clauses, too, so you could rephrase D.2 above as **the people whom we met** in contrast with D.3. **the people who live here**.

   b. The other interesting property of these relativizers is that you can almost always substitute **that** for **who(m)**.

      (1). That is, **who** refers only to people, but **that** can refer to **either** non-people **or** people. This is why **the people that we met** is a perfectly normal sentence for spoken English.

      (2). You can go one step further and omit the **THAT** → the people we met.

   c. As for **which**, it, quite the opposite of **who**, can not refer to people. You would not say ***the people which we met**.. You can replace **which** by **that**. So **that** is the most versatile relativizer, more on which in III. below.

5. As object of the preposition in the relative clause you get **which** and **who(m)**, but never **that**:

   a. in formal written English:

      (1). the book {**about which** we spoke}

      (2). the teacher {**against who(m)** we conspired}

   b. In less formal English--which is what most of us use most of the time--the prepositional phrase splits up and "frames" the clause.

The **which** or **who(m)** introduces the clause and the preposition shifts to the end of the clause. The preposition becomes "distanced" from its object, but the boldfaced items below still constitute a prepositional phrase.

(1). the book {**which** we spoke **about**}

(2). the teacher {**who(m)** we conspired **against**}

If (1) sounds a little funny to you as is, the reason is that **which** as a relativizer tends to belong to more formal language.

c. In this case you can replace both **who** and **which** with **that**. **THAT**, then, appears to be the distant object of the dislocated preposition, but you would never "prepose" the preposition.

(1). the book {**that** we spoke **about**}

(2). the teacher {**that** we conspired **against**}

but never *"the book **about that** we spoke" or "the teacher **against that** we conspired"

d. One further step is that no matter which relativizer you might have, it becomes optionally omittable:

(1). the book { we spoke **about**}

(2). the teacher { we conspired **against**}

6. Perhaps your high school grammar textbook warned you that the 5a. types were "correct" and the 5d. types, "incorrect", typical of "sloppy" or "casual" speech. The fact is that there is nothing sloppy about omitting **that**. You do not do so randomly, and you know exactly when you can and cannot. (You will not usually find rules like b.-c.-d. in textbooks because textbooks teach **written** language, and they do not consider spoken language as having rules. It does, of course, but they are the kind you learn intuitively and not in classrooms.)

a. The truth is that the formal "about which" type structure sounds rather artificial to most American speakers and sometimes is even wrong. This does not mean that American English is deteriorating or inferior to British English. Recall how Winston Churchill demonstrated how odd the so-called "correct" formal construction can sound by quipping, "That is a lot of nonsense **up with which** I will not put." (Actually, the example is not a great one: the verb **put up with** acts like a single complex word and does not want to be broken up. More on this in Chapter 7, III. below.)

b. So, in English, saying "the pen **with which** I write" or "the pen I write **with**" can be a marker of formal vs. not-necessarily-formal style. Other languages may not leave you such options, in which case this kind of construction cannot serve as a style marker.

III. RESTRICTIVE VS. NON-RESTRICTIVE RELATIVE CLAUSES

You know that pronouns refer back to nouns, so in relative clauses the relativizer refers back to a noun in the preceding clause, as in **the book which she read**, where **which** refers back to **book**. (If you want to understand this as a compressed paraphrase of the larger process, "There is a book, and she read **it**, so this is the book **which** she read," go ahead.) But is that all they can refer to?

A. The reason **which** is a special relativizer is that it can refer not only to single nouns, but also to whole ideas, phrases, or propositions. Traditional grammar books do not like this because it stretches the definition of "pronoun", but it is a fact. In these sentences, note the clauses in curly brackets and ask yourself which **which** refers to nouns and which to propositions:

1. The assignment {which is due next week} will determine your grade in this course.

2. This assignment, {which you should have handed in by now}, will determine your grade.

3. This assignment will determine your grade, {which should worry many of you. . .}

B. Do these **which**-clauses feel different? In 1 you merely select one assignment from the set of other assignments. This kind of adjective clause is called a **restrictive relative** clause because it identifies a particular item and gives essential information about it. You would literally not know "which" assignment was so crucial without that clause in the sentence. In 2, you assume everyone knows which assignment you mean, but you add a side remark about it, that is, non-essential information. Do you hear that you sort of slip it in under your breath? This is called a **non-restrictive relative** clause, because its purpose is to comment and not to identify. In both of these, the antecedent of **which** is the single noun **assignment**.

C. In 3 you get something English grammar hardly has a name for. It is a kind of non-restrictive relative clause, except that the **which** here refers to the whole fact of the importance of the assignment and not to any one word. It is clearly a clause, but is it an adjective clause? Hard to tell. It is more like an **editorial**. The other way you know that is that it comes at the end of the sentence. This allows it to refer to the whole proposition. In spoken language this is by far the most significant use of **which**. Do you feel you have a big pause in your speech between the two clauses? Here are some other examples of the **restrictive/non-restrictive/editorial** contrast:

1. **Restrictive**: "This is a day which will long live in infamy."
   (The only day referred to and the only information about it.)

2. **Non-restrictive:** This is a special day, for which we have ourselves to thank.
   (Already idenitifed day with extra information added.)

3. **Editorial**: This has been a wonderful day, which it's a good thing it was 'cuz if it hadn't been somebody would have been in trouble!
   (General comment apart from singling out the day.)

D. Note that your eye and ear can catch these right away: the non-restrictives are the ones set off by a big space in your voice, as represented by the commas in writing. Grammar books usually make an issue of this because of the correctnes or incorrectness of writing those commas, but far more important is the kind of information they are meant to convey and the way you use your voice to convey it.

E. You also have restrictive and non-restrictive relative clauses with **who.** With **that** you get only restrictive clauses. You never pause before a **THAT**-clause in speaking and never set it off with commas in writing, for example. So **who** and **which** have something else in common that distinguishes them as a group from **THAT**, cf. II.D.4, above.

1. **Restrictive**: The neighbors who moved in next door seem like decent folks.
(You need the clause to identify them.)

2. **Non-restrictive:** The new neighbors, who we helped move in, seem like decent folks.
(You know which neighbors, but maybe you didn't know that we helped them move in.)

3. **Editorial**: The new neighbors don't play their stereo too loud, which saves us the trouble of complaining to the police.
(More a comment about us than about them.)

IV. NOUN CLAUSES

A subordinate clause can function, the way a noun does, as a subject of a verb or object of a verb or preposition. It is then called a **noun clause**.

A. Most often they, too, are introduced with **that**, or **who(m)**, and also **what**. You can also include the so-called **question words**, cf. Chapter 14, below: **when, where, how, why**. (Notice that **which** does not work for noun clauses.)

1. You can add their related "indefinite pronouns" with **-ever**: **whoever, whatever, whichever**, as wel as **whenever, wherever, however** (and maybe even **whyever?**)

2. A lot of these can break down into some kind of **which** or **who**, at least in theory if not in practice.

   a. **What** can usually be paraphrased by "**that which**," namely, a pronoun **that** modified by an adjective-clause introduced by **which**. You probably do not say it very often, but other languages do exactly this.

   b. By the same token, **why** is "**for what**" or even "**that for which**." (But note that there is a slight difference in the meaning of questions with "Why?" and "What for?")

   c. The relative **whose** is dissectable into "**of whom.**"

   d. Also, the question words **when** (**=at which time**) and **where** (= **at which place**) can serve to introduce noun clauses, with or without **-ever**.

B. **Noun clause as subject or predicate noun** after **to be**. Note the bracketing.

1. Subject

   a. That you are right is quite evident. →

   {That you are /right/} is quite /evident/.

   b. What you say contradicts current theory.→

   {[What] you say} contradicts [current theory].

   c. Whatever you touch seems to turn to gold, Mr. Midas. →

   {[Whatever] you touch } seems to turn **to gold.**

2. Predicate "Noun"

   a. This is what they asked for." →

      This is /{**what** they asked **for**}/. or more "literally":

      This is /that/ {**for which** they asked}.
      (**Which**-clause modifies predicate pronoun **that**.)

   b. Shirley is who you need to talk to about that. →

      Shirley is /{**who** you need to talk **to** (about that)}/. OR →

      Shirley is /the one/ {**to whom** you need to talk {about that)}.
      (**Who-**clause modifies predicate pronoun **the one**.)

C. Noun clause as direct object

Compare a plain noun object with different kinds of noun clauses as object. The clauses are set off in curly brackets and have the usual subject and verb underlining, and the function of the noun clause introducer, itself, is given within its own clause. (To go the whole nine yards and put the curly-bracketed noun clause into its own set of square brackets just to show that it is serving as driect object would be a bit of overkill. Just imagine it!)

1. She knows [your name]. (noun phrase as dir.obj.)
   [everything.] (pronoun as dir. obj.)

   {/what/ your name is}. (noun clause as dir. obj.)

   {[whatever] you know. }

   {[what] they bought}.

   {/who/ you are}.

   {who planned [the party]}.

{[who] you surprised at the party}.

{[which sonata] she's performing tonight}.

{why you're here}.

{where we hid}.

{(*that*) you're leaving}. (More on this just below.)

2. Tell ⟨us⟩ [your address]. (noun phrase as dir.obj.)

{who ate [the leftovers]} . (noun clause as dir. obj.)

{/what time/ it is}.

{why you 're /mad/}.

{where you live}

{when things settle down}.

{(*that*) everything is /O.K./}.

3. Mommy bought [an ice cream cone]. (noun phrase as dir.obj.)

{[what] we wanted}. (noun clause as dir. obj.)

4. Naturally, such noun clauses can also serve as **indirect object,** but those are harder to represent on the page without a mega-computer program. You would put the curly bracket, with all its internal underlinings inside angle brackets. Go ahead and try one. It looks pretty awful, but it shows you all the right relationships:

Mommy bought whoever wanted one an ice cream cone. →

Mommy bought ⟨{whoever wanted [one]}⟩ [an ice cream cone].

D. More on Omittable THAT

In the last clauses of the above sentences, you will certainly agree (that) that **THAT** is droppable. This is true not only after **know** and **tell** in the above examples, but also after a whole group of verbs that are related to **say, know, think** or **understand**. These include **promise, decide, answer, retort, conclude, suspect, suppose, swear, declare, affirm, assert, deny, hope** and on and on. There are also a few others like **seem, appear, be sure**. Note that the following noun clauses introduced by droppable **THAT** function as direct object of a transitive verb or predicate noun of a copula. Compare them with noun direct objects or predicate adjectives.

1. You promised us [a visit].

   [{(*that*) you'd visit}].

2. Did you think [good thoughts]?

   [{(*that*) you'd pass [the exam]}]?

3. He suspects [them].

   [{(*that*) they have [a plan]}].

4. I suppose [{(*that*) the weather will change}].

   (This one doesn't work so well with a plain noun object.)

5. It seems /better/ now.

   /{(*that*) things will get /better/}/.

Many other languages are quite particular and insist that this **that** be present in all such sentences.

E. Beware the look-alikes!

This is another of many proofs that language works in **patterns** and **structures**, not individual words. Expanding the sentences you examined in C., above, you can see how attuned your *ear* is to language structure, even if your *eye* is not. Some **THAT**'s are present; others "omitted."

1. She knows **your name.** → She knows [your name].

2. She knows **your name is Ringo.**
   → She knows {(*that*) your name is /Ringo/}.

3. She knows **that hit tune.** → She knows [that hit tune].

4. She knows **that hit tune is #1 this week.**
   → She knows {(*that*) that hit tune is /#1 this week/}.

5. She knows **that hit tunes don't stay popular long.**
   → She knows [{**that** hit tunes don't stay popular long}].

5. Tell us **your address.** → Tell ⟨us⟩ [your address].

6. Tell us **your address hasn't changed.**
   → Tell ⟨us⟩ [{(*that*) your address hasn't changed}].

7. Tell us **that scary story.** → Tell ⟨us⟩ [that scary story].

8. Tell us **that scary stories are only make-believe!**
   → Tell ⟨us⟩ [{**that** scary stories are /only make-believe/}]!

F. **Noun clause as object of preposition**:

1. We're calling **about your son's behavior.** (phrase)

   {[what] your son did in school today}. (clause)

   {what happened in school}.

2. We thank you **for your help.**

   {[what] you did **for us**}.

V. ADVERBIAL CLAUSES

A subordinate clause that modifies a verb is an **adverbial clause**. As you saw in Chapter 2, they typically begin with **when, if, as, while, until, after, before, although, whether, because**. These little words go under the fifty-cent title of **subordinating conjunction**, cf. Chapter 3, VII.B., above. They join the subordinate clause to the main clause and answer the usual adverb questions "When? Why? How? Where?" Compare these plain adverbs, adverb phrases, and adverb clauses:

A. **When**?	1. adverb:	We're going	**now.**
	2. adverbial phrase:		**in a minute.**
	3. adverbial clause:		**{when the movie's over}.**
B. **How**?	1. adverb:	She speaks	**confidently.**
	2. adverbial phrase:		**in a confident manner.**
	3. adverbial clause:		**{as if she is at her best}.**
C. **Why**?	1. adverb:	He smiled	**shyly.**
	2. adverbial phrase:		**out of shyness.**
	3. adverbial clause:		**{because he was shy}.**
D. **Where**?	1. adverb:	Put this	**away.**
	2. adverbial phrase:		**in the drawer.**
	3. adverbial clause:		**{where they can't get [it]}.**

E. Look back at Chapter 2, Exercises 2a., 2b. You will now see that the "difference" you felt between the types of clauses in the two sets was that 2a. had only adjective clauses, and 2b. had only adverbial clauses, each with its own structure and type of information it conveys.

VI. SENTENCE TYPES

This is as good a time as any to go through some traditional labels that help you classify a sentence's make-up in terms of main and subordinate clauses and the way they package their information.

A. Sentence Structures.

Most grammar books spend a lot of time on this topic, but we will spend very little. Here are the usual terms for the types.

1. A **simple sentence** contains only one main clause and no subordinate clauses, as in a. Of course, they can be very long with lots of prepositional phrases, as in b.

   a. April showers bring [May flowers].

   b. I pledge [allegiance] **to** the flag **of** the United States **of** America.

2. A **complex sentence** is composed of a main clause and a subordinate clause, be it adjective, noun, or adverb.

   a. adjective: This is the house {that Jack built}.

   b. noun: Who knows {where the time goes}?

   c. adverbial: Make hay {while the sun shines}.

3. A **compound sentence** is composed of two main clauses connected by **and, but**, or the other **coordinating conjunctions** mentioned in Chapter 3, VII.A., above. In these sentences the lower-case conjunction connects similar parts of a phrase, and the upper-case "coordinates" the two main clauses:

   a. I ordered pepperoni and mushroom, AND you brought me anchovy!

b. My friends and I went out and voted Republican, BUT the Democratic candidate won anyway.

4. A **compound-complex** sentence is composed of two main clauses--in this case connected by **but**--and either one or both of the main clauses also has a subordinate clause:

   We wish {(that) you had called {before you came over}, BUT {since you 're here}, you might as well relax.

5. A word about **run-on sentences**. Traditional grammar detests the **run-on** and warns you to shun it at all cost. A run-on is essentially a visual problem, rather than one of speech: two main clauses connected by a mere comma. Norms of writing want you either to make it two separate sentences with a period or insert a coordinating conjunction after the comma. Know that this concept exists and do what you will with it. Recast, for example, **You pay the check, I'll get the car** as:

   a. → 2 simple sentences: You pay the check. I'll get the car. (Replace comma by period.)

   b. → compound sentence: You pay the check, and I'll get the car. (Insert **and**).

   c. The same goes for the familiar, "Roses are red, violets are blue."

B. Sentence Meanings

Here are some other terms you usually encounter in grammar books. Although it seems like fancy names for simple things, you should be aware that not all languages treat these types the same way:

1. **Declarative** sentences are those that make a statement (like this one, if you're in to self-referentiality). This is the "basic" sentence type, and the others below are ways of operating on it.

2. **Negative** sentences do **not** assert that their information is true, **do** assert that it is **untrue**, or say you'd better make another choice.

Some languages, for example, have different kinds of verb forms for positive vs. negative statements. Others use a different form of a noun depending on whether it is, say, the object of a positive verb or a negative verb. More on English negation in Chapter 15.

3. **Interrogative** sentences ask a question. English accomplishes this by changing the order of the words or using a **question word**, depending on the kind of answer you expect to get. Some languages do this by merely changing voice inflection without changing the words or their order. More on questions in Chapter 14.

4. **Negative-interrogative** sentences are the kind you already think you know the answer to, such as, "Aren't you having a good time?" These are important not so much for the forms of nouns or verbs they use, but rather, for the way you use them to convey information and opinion in conversation. It is more a subtle way of saying, "You should be having a good time, though I see you are not." It can serve as a way of asking a favor in a non-invasive way, as in, "Won't you go and pick up the dry cleaning?" instead of the direct request, "Please pick up the dry cleaning." Different languages exploit these possibilities differently.

EXERCISE 6b.

SCHIZOPHRENIC PARTS OF SPEECH:
RECOGNIZING AMBIGUITIES

Key: p. 344

A. **Adverb or Preposition?**

Items these items as Adverbs or Prepositions by simply bracketing the whole unit that goes together: if an adverb, just the adverb; if a preposition, the whole phrase. Let context be your guide.

1. up ________ a. Come up and see me sometime.

________ b. Come up the stairs.

2. down ________ a. Don't put that down!

________ b. Don't put that down the laundry chute!

3. around ________ a. Let's go to the schoolyard and hang around.

________ b. They live around the corner.

B. **Triple Jeopardy**

Identify these as Adverbs, Prepositions, or Subordinating Conjunctions. Square-bracket the plain adverb and the preposition+object. Curly-bracket the subordinating conjunction and underline the subject of the clause once and the verb of the clause twice.

1. after ________ a. I don't want to do it now. I'll do it after.

________ b. I'll do it after the movie.

________ c. I'll do it after the movie ends.

2. before ________ a. He'd never seen anything like it before.

________ b. Don't eat that before supper!

________ c. Don't eat that before you go running!

3. since ________ a. We haven't done that since childhood.

________ b. We haven't done that since we were kids.

________ c. We haven't done anything like that before or since!

EXERCISE 6c.

GREAT BIG I.D. REVIEW
Key: p. 345

1. Underline the subject of the main clause once and the main verb, twice.

2. Set off all prepositional phrases with square brackets--no, they're not direct objects here!--and all subordinate clauses with curly brackets.

3. Label each adjective phrase **AjP,** each adverbial phrase **AvP**, each adjective, adverbial or noun clause as **AjC, AvC, NC**, and there is nothing to prevent one from being "inside" the other.

4. Within each clause underline the subject once and the predicate twice. If you come upon a subordinate clause with a "dropped **that**" (Cf. II.D, above), put it "back" in, even if you wouldn't normally say it yourself. If there are two sentences do both.

GOOD LUCK!!

Example: My friends agree with me when I tell them that this is the most absurd assignment we've ever done in our lives! →

My friends agree [with me] {when I tell them} {that this is the
AvP *AvC* *NC*

most absurd assignment} {(that!) we've ever done [in our lives]}.
AjC *AvP*

1. What you think of them is no business of mine.

2. I wouldn't go in that old house if I were you....

3. Whoever thought this stuff up is off his/her rocker!

4. If you miss the train I'm on you will know that I am gone. . . (folk song)

5. I'm leavin' on a jet plane; I don't know when I'll be back again. ("folk" song)

6. Everything we've achieved until now will go for naught unless you accept the task I'm putting before you....

7. We were doing fine without help until they showed up!

8. They met before class and had made arrangements before the teacher walked into the classroom.

9. Anyone who finds the answer to the magic riddle can have anything he desires!!!

10. Do you know that guy who's campaigning for governor?

11. Do you know that guy's campaigning for governor?

The pièces de résistance:
How would you express these two in the King's English?
Spell out all the relationships in "normal order."
It might help to re-write this one separately:

12. Whose woods these are I think I know. His house is in the village, though.

Bonus:

This one is a now-famous sentence a child is reported to have said while arguing with his parents. Isn't it perfectly comprehensible? You often pile up little preposition-looking things at the ends of sentences and you have no trouble sorting them out.)

"What did you bring the book I don't like to be read to out of up for?!"

(Actually this also involves a sticky topic we will take up later. Do you notice the problem?)

CHAPTER 7

TROUBLESHOOTING:

THINGS THAT CAN CATCH YOU UNAWARES

I. WHO DOES WHAT TO WHOM?

A. As we saw in Chapter 6 above, it is perfectly possible and normal in language for items that go together by sense or structure not to occur right next to each other, as in **the book <u>that</u> we spoke <u>about</u>.** In such cases the *pre*position is separated from its object and, in fact comes *after* the object!

B. This section provides an opportunity for you to consolidate everything you have done so far and focus on ways in which English usually separates things, thus masking their relationship to each other. Just because a sentence starts with the pronouns **who** or **what** does not mean that that's the subject. You have to hear the whole sentence and decide who or what is doing what to whom or what. One way to tell is to answer the question and see what role the replacement for **what** or **who** plays. For example:

1. Q:**Who** said that? A: **<u>My neighbor</u>** said that.

2. Q:**Who** is that? A: That is **/my neighbor/.**

3. Q: **Who** do you trust? A: I trust [**my neighbor**].

4. Q: **Who** are you subbing **for**? A: I'm subbing **for my neighbor.**

The underlining and bracketing in the answers help make it clear that **who** in 1. is a subject; in 2., a predicate (pro)noun; in 3., a direct object, and in 4., the object of the preposition. **Who** and **what** have only one form to serve all these function. Your target language may well have **case** forms for these question words to distinguish these functions right up front.

a. In 3. you do have the option of, "**Whom** do you trust?" but you would risk sounding unnatural in 20th century America. More on this later.

b. Is something missing? Yes, you cannot have **who** as an **indirect object** without supplying **to** or **for**: **Who** are you giving that Picasso **to**? or **Who** did you buy this cheap thing **for**? (In a language with a genuine **dative case** (cf. Chapter 5, IV.) this would not be a problem.

EXERCISE 7a.
WHO'S WHO(M)?

Identify the function of **who** or **what** in the following sentences without bothering to underline and bracket. (If you want to see underlining, it is on page 347.) Pick from **S** for subject, **P** for predicate noun, **D** for direct object, or **O** for object of preposition. Draw an arrow to the preposition it is the object of (sic!).

1. _____ Who are you?
2. _____ Who do you trust?
3. _____ What are you driving nowadays, Mario?
4. _____ What are you driving at, anyway?
5. _____ What makes you so sure?
6. _____ What is the moon made of?
7. _____ Who was that lady I saw you with?
8. _____ Who are those new kids on the block?
9. _____ Who are those new kids on the block bothering?
10. _____ Who are those new kids on the block talking to?

KEY TO 7a.	1-P, 2-D, 3-D, 4-O, 5-S, 6-O, 7-P, 8-P, 9-D, 10-O

∞∞

II. WHEN *WHAT* MEANS *WHICH ONE, WHAT KIND OF*

A. English **what** modifying a noun can be paraphrased by **which, which (one),** or **what kind of.** That is, the English word **what** can function as both a pronoun *and* an adjective. Most other languages you study probably will differentiate between the two functions with separate words, so you'd better get sensitive to that difference now.

B. Besides that, English **what** can also be a modifier in exclamations like **What a beautiful day! What a mess! What happiness**! It's hard to put a name on this one. Is it an identifier like **which one**? Better to just recognize that the same word does all three things and not try to name the exclamation function.

C. As for the adjective **whose**, it is usually paraphrasable into **of whom,** although you wouldn't say it that way. (It's its own built-in prepositional phrase, if you will.)

∞∞

EXERCISE 7b. WHICHWHAT?

In the sentences below, determine whether **what** is an **A**djective or an independent **PR**onoun. then, designate the function of the **what** phrase as **S**ubject, **P**redicate noun, **D**irect object, **O**bject of preposition, or just **E**xclamation.

Example: "Gee, Grandma, **what big eyes** you have. . ." A-D(E)

***What Ever Happened** To Baby Jane?* PR-S

1._____ What day is it today?

2. _____ What is the date today?

3. _____ What school do you go to?

4. _____ What do you study in school?

5. _____ "Are you ready for the exam today!?" "AUGH! What exam???!!!"

6. _____ What fun it is to ride in a one-horse open sleigh!

7. _____ What light through yonder window breaks?

KEY TO 7b. | 1. A-P, 2. PR-P, 3. A-O, 4. PR-D, 5. A-E, 6. A-E, 7. A-S

III. PREPOSITIONS, PARTICLES, GOVERNMENT

A. Verbs in a sentence are said to "take" or "govern" certain kinds of constructions, that is, the verb combines in some regular way with other words in the sentence. Transitive verbs, for example, "take" a direct object, and as suggested above in Chapter 4, this literally means there is no other word between the verb word and the direct-object-noun word. Other verbs choose a particular preposition to connect it with and suggest some definable relationship to the following noun.

1. Different languages choose different prepositions, so that there is almost never a one-to-one correspondence across languages, and you cannot tell by the individual meaning of the words which one the given language chooses to go with which verb.

2. In English you **listen to music,** but in French, Russian, or Hebrew you **listen music.** In English you **help somebody,** while in the same three languages and also German you **help to somebody.** In

English you can either **believe somebody** or **believe in somebody**, and the meaning is not the same, while in the four just-mentioned languages you can either **believe to somebody** or **in somebody.** In English you can either **marry somebody** or **get married to somebody,** while in Hebrew you **get married with somebody.** English speakers **depend on** something, but French and Russians **depend from,** and Hebrew speakers **depend in.**

a. Perhaps some combinations make more intuitive "sense" than others, but that is not for you, the language learner, to decide. You take it as a given, and maybe once you get deeper into the language you can ask what language-internal logic seems to determine the verb-preposition partnership.

b. At any rate, you have to be aware that the government concept is a normal and essential part of language learning. You cannot translate word for word from English into your target language because you will produce as funny a target language as a Frenchman who says, "I want to help to you."

3. The ideal dictionary should tell you as part of the word what preposition it governs, so that you can be assured of producing acceptable language. But you should know that not all dictionaries have the space for this. Sometimes you simply have to glean it from the example sentences the dictionary gives of the usage of the verb.

4. The government notion is not just for verbs, either. Some adjectives have their own required completers. In English, a country can be **rich in minerals,** and a speaker of Russian or Arabic will say **rich minerals-wise.** In English one place can be **close to** or **far from** another place. In Arabic they can be both **close from** and **far from,** and in Russian they can be either **close to** or **close from** but only **far from.** In English you can be **pleased with something,** while in Hebrew you are **pleased from** it and in Russian you are **pleased "something-wise".** The examples and contrasts are endless, and the purpose here is neither to belabor the obvious nor to emphasize the apparent arbitrariness or scare you away from learning French, German, Russian, Hebrew, or Arabic. As far as you and your target language are concerned, keep your mind flexible and learn the government of the word as part of your

vocabulary. Get the sound of the phrase in your ear, so that you can rely on it and not try to translate word for word.

B. Verb-Particle Combinations

What's a **particle**?! This is the next logical step after Exercise 6b. you did just above. That set was meant to alert you to the fact that you cannot just identify parts of speech by their linear order of occurrence. The same word was a preposition or adverb or conjunction depending on the sentence structure it participated in. Now we see situations where traditional labels like **adverb** and **preposition** are just not adequate for those little **up**'s and **down**'s, not to mention the **on**'s, **around**'s, or **about**'s. Very often the verb cannot get along without that word and still mean what you want it to. Better to say, the combination of a certain verb and a preposition-looking thing often creates a meaning not derivable from the meanings of the two words separately. Compare these sentences in terms of the units in square brackets:

1. a. He looked **up** and saw her coming.

   b. He looked **up the street** and saw her coming.

   c. He **looked up** the word in the dictionary.

2. In all of them you have the verb **look**, meaning "set your gaze" followed by **up**. Break them up as follows:

   a. In 1a. you usually call **up** an adverb because it gives the direction of the gaze.

   b. In 1b. you **look [up the street]**, with the phrase giving the direction of the looking in relation to the street, so you have to call **up** a preposition.

   c.. In c., however, you **[look up]** the word and do not **look [up the word]**, with **up** tacked on to **look**. The meaning of the entire resulting phrase is only loosely related to the meaning of **look** alone and not at all related to what we think of as the "normal" meaning of **up**. That is, **up** here is neither an adverb nor a prepositon-plus-object. In such cases, you have little choice but to refer to **up** by the catch-all title **particle.**

3. You can consider the whole phrase [**look up**] as a fusion of [**verb+particle**] **+object** making a transitive two-part verb and the direct object **word**.

   a. It is important to note that these particles always **follow** the verb and are written separately.

   b. In a few cases you get a different meaning if the particle comes before or after. First, if it comes before, it is usually called a **prefix** and is always written as part of the word. **Up** and **over** seem to provide this contrast most readily:

      (1). You **hold up** the bank, and the court **upholds** its decisions.

      (2). You **turn over** a new leaf, and the court **overturns** a ruling.

   c. This is not just a parlor trick or an example of how illogical or capricious English is. The dictionary lists these separately, and sometimes you would not even notice that the verb root is the same because the meaning is so different.

4. Some verb-particle fusions are "tighter" than others. Usually the particle can go either between the verb and the object or right after the object, but some *must* come together:

   a. You can **hold up** the meeting or **hold** the meeting **up**, but you can only **hold up** the bank and not ***hold** the bank **up**.

   b. You can **turn over** the record ont he stereo or you can **turn** the record **over**, but you can only **turn over** a new leaf and not ***turn** a new leaf **over**. In terms of your target language, this is a question of learning vocabulary as whole units, and the units do not have to be single words.

   c. In the type that can split up, a pronoun object *must* come between the verb and the particle, and this can even split up the "unsplittables":

(1). "We want to finish the meeting, so don't **hold** it **up**." You might even say, "Hey, there's a bank. I think I'll **hold** it **up.**" (*"I'll **hold up** it" is not English.)

(2). The record's done. **Turn** it **over**, will you? But you definitely cannot say, "Yup, that's my new leaf. *I **turned** it **over** yesterday" because you would then mean an actual leaf, and that is not the meaning of that expression. Of course, the option, *"I **turned over** it" is no option at all. (Here you probably have to admit that the whole unit is **turn over a new leaf** and not **turn over** + a new leaf.)

5. There are not too many particles in English, and all of them double as prepositions. The most common particles are the three pairs of opposites: **up-down, out-in, off-on**. The others include **after, across, around**. Try to think of sentences with these and you'll see. Traditional school book grammar has difficulty labelling them a separate part of speech. A lot of dictionaries and grammars simply avoid the issue by calling such combinations "idioms." The entry **look up** with its special application to "seeking information" is normally buried in the dictionary under **look**. There you will find "~ up", even though the meaning of **look up** has little to do with **look.** Just listen to yourself and see how small you can make the units of your sentences and still have them mean what you want. As with all this sensitivity-training, be ready for the possibility that your new language might express these English compounds as whole words.

C. The verb **look** is a handy example because it is right on the border of being a verb-plus-regular-preposition, where you can still see the meaning of the preposition, and a verb-particle cooperation. You can **look** aghast, and you can **look at** the children playing. You can do the latter and not [**look after**] those children (look [**after the children**]?). If they lose something they will [**look for**] it (look **for it?**). You can look **out the window (look out** the window?) and **look out for** falling rocks. The question is, are these all separate verbs: **look, look at, look for, look out, look out for?** True they all involve some kind of "**looking**" but the other additions give all kinds of directions, purposes, and responsibilities that have little to do with the **looking** itself. It is crucial to emphasize that if you use, for example, an English-Tibetan dictionary and you want to know how to say "look at", you should not assume that you can look up **look** and then **at** and just put them together. Tibetan **look** might be an entirely different word from **look at**. Other such contrasts include:

1. **Stick** the stamp on the envelope by **sticking out** your tongue. (direction?) Furthermore, once you form the "expanded word" **stick out,** it, in turn, has its own government, since you **stick out** your tongue **at somebody.**

2. You can **put** the book **up on the shelf** and **put up with** the noise. Again, it is questionable whether:

   a. the verb is **put up** plus the phrase **with the noise** or the verb **put up with** plus the direct object **noise** or. . .

   b. the verb is **put** plus the adverb **up**, although it is not a question of physical direction, plus the phrase **with the noise.**

3. Again, that the position of the particle or adverb or whatever you choose to call it is variable. You can **stick** your tongue **out** and **stick out** your tongue. However, you can only **put up with** the noise and not ***put up** the noise **with.** That is, a noun object can go on either side of the particle. A pronoun object, however, will always come right next to the verb and push the particle to the "right" if it is movable. Going back to **tongue**, you can only **stick** it **out** and not ***stick out** it. If it is not movable, it looks more preposition-like: **put up with** it.

D. There is a note of consistency about the use and meaning of some of these additions to the verb.

   1. Take the particle **up**. Very often it adds to the meaning of the verb the nuance of **do the given action to completion or attainment of a goal** or **operating to a natural conclusion on a given object.** If the conclusion is really obvious, this **up** feels like a mere filler that does not add or change meaning. This produces, e.g.,

      a. **eat the pizza** vs. **eat up the pizza** (= there's none left)

      b. **clean the house** vs. **clean up the house** (= it's all clean)

c. **lock the door** vs. **lock up the house** seem the same.

d. In **finish the assignment** vs. **finish up the assignment** the latter one suggests "be near the end anyway and just put the finishing touches on it."

e. Other nuances: **sign** the document vs. **sign up** for a course (=do something that puts your name on the roster), and also **put the guests up with the neighbors** vs. **put up with the guests.**

f. Some verbs exist only as particle verbs with **up**. These usually involve some change of state with a "before-and-after" feeling: **smarten up, wise up, limber up, liven up, fatten up.**

2. Similarly, **down** also suggests totality of action, as in **fall** vs.**fall down,** where the latter removes all doubt that you hit the ground. In **sit** vs. **sit down** you can get the idea of steady-state sitting vs. transition into a sitting position. (You say, "Sit!" to your dog but, "Please sit down," to your guest.) As for transitives, you can **break the door** as well as **break down the door.** (Of course, you can also **break in** the door and **break into** a house.) As for change of state, similar to **up**, you have **cool down, wind down, get down to business.**

3. Another of these is **out**. It also implies that the action is done "till it can't be done anymore," as in **print a document** vs. **print out a document** (What's the difference between this and the very similar **print up a document**?), **clean the house** vs. **clean out the house** (very different from **clean up the house,** where **out** focuses on the container properties of **house**).

4. In parallel fashion, **in** frequently gives the sense of completion with some leftover feeling of "ending up in an **in**-type situation": **settle in, write in** a candidate's name--hardly the same as write (a letter) *in the candidate's name*--**sign in** at work, and on and on.

5. Another word family that shows you how particles work is **dry**. You simply **dry the dishes** or **the clothes** you washed normally. But think of the different effects drying has on different things. Depending

on your expectations of the thing's use or knowledge of its "essential nature" you get:

a. **dry off** become dry on the surface but not otherwise change its essential nature, as when you come out of the pool.

b. **dry out** something that normally either should not be wet and gets wet or should be wet and becomes dry. In either case, it becomes temporarily unsuitable for its expected purpose. Becoming dry allows it to regain its usability, like the clothes you were wearing when you got caught in a downpour. Something that *should* be wet or moist becomes unusable by becoming dry, as in yesterday's bread or the roast in the oven. So **out** here means "do the action completely in such a way that the item becomes either usable or unusable without changing its essential nature." It is still recognizable.

c. **dry up** become unrecognizable by changing its essential nature, as in a puddle or a resource: it is no longer what it was.

Threre are many hundreds of these in English, and to discuss themin detail would make this book very large, indeed. How many such families can you come up with? Is there any sense to which particles occur with which verbs?

6. Sometimes you see this property of "doing the action of a verb to some expected or natural conclusion" or "doing in a certain way" referred to as **verbal aspect**. This topic comes back in Chapter 9, X.

E. Grammar Rules vs. Reality: Ending a sentence with a preposition!

The structure of Latin absolutely prohibits a preposition from occurring without its object after it, so a Latin sentence or subordinate clause cannot possibly end with a preposition. That rule has ruled English grammar for centuries, but you now see why that rule is totally unnatural for English speakers: some of the items the rule is supposed to apply to are just not prepositions. They look like them, but they don't act like them. Some verbs have to have their completers after them and cannot have them shunted to the beginning of a relative clause. This is part of the definition of a particle! Here are some more examples of what you saw in B., C., and D., above.

1. A preposition can "front" in so-called formal style. The sentence, "**We live on the corner**" can become just part of a sentence in either of two ways:

   a. **The corner we live on. . .** neutral (formal or not)

   b. **The corner on which we live. . .** formal only

   A particle cannot do this, as in **we turned on the television** → **the television we turned on,** and there's no other way--like ***the television on which we turned**--because **turn on** is a unit.

2. Recall the important property of particles that establishes them as something separate from prepositions: they can come on either side of the direct object, while a pronoun direct object *has* to come between the verb and its particle.

   a. Imagine the question, "Who's sitting **on my antique chair**?" and the answer, "Joannie's sitting **on it**." Perfectly normally, the object pronoun **it** follows its preposition **on**.

   b. Now ask, "Who **turned** the television **on**?" or "Who **turned on** the television?" The answer *must* be only, "Sam turned **it on,**" where **it** has to be considered the direct object of the verb-unit **turn on**.

3. There is an anecdote about a "hick"--by which educated city folk mean country folk--who is walking around Harvard Yard. He approaches a student and queries, "'Skyooz me, sir, can you tell me where the lie-berry's at?" The student looks down his nose at the fellow and says, "The *library* is over there, and young man, at Hahvahd we do not end sentences with prepositions." "Oh, I see," replies the hick. "Well, can you tell me where the lie-berry's at, jerk?"

EXERCISE 7c.
PREP YOUR PARTICLE!
Key: p. 347

Just sensitive yourself to units that make sense together. Merely bracket the prepositional phrase or the **verb+particle**, as we did in B.2., above.

1. He finished his cigarette and flipped the butt out the window.
2. He looked at his mail and flipped out the minute he saw her handwriting.
3. Help me out here. I need some advice.
4. Help me out of this monkey suit, will you please?
5. She's been looking for you all day.
6. She's been looking for a present for Clara's birthday all day.
7. The shuttle blasted off from Cape Canaveral just after dawn.
8. Take your blasted fishing gear off my white shag carpet, if you don't mind!
9. When we raise sufficient funds this program will take off all over the world.
10. That new nuclear plant gives off more radiation in an hour than you can scrub off the whole white-coated staff in a day!

IV. WORDS AND WORD ORDER

A. It is worth taking a few minutes to reflect on the normal sequence of words in normal language usage. Above we made some references to putting "out of order" sentences back into their "natural order." The majority of the sentences you've operated on start with the subject, and that is followed by the predicate. If there is an object in the predicate, it usually follows the verb. You can symbolize this **subject-then-verb-then object** state of affairs by saying that **English is an S-V-O language.**

1. A regular corollary to this is that you can switch the S and the V in, for example, questions: "**You are** doing a fine job" → "**Are you** doing a fine job" but the O still follows the V.

2. Some kinds of constructions regularly flip the S and the V, especially ones that point to a direction (a, b) or a contrast (c-d):

    a. Here comes the judge!

    b. There goes Grossman!

    c. You are no politician and neither is your mother!

    d. You're a wonderful cook and so is your brother!

3. You can, of course, reverse the normal order for effect and special contrast. Not everybody does this, and it is more prevalent in certain areas of the country:

    a. I don't like tacos. Now, **pízza** I like!

    b. Your sister's OK. **Your kid bróther** I could do without!

    c. **Right** you are, sonny!

4. The reason for mentioning this is that many languages follow different patterns. German, for example, is S-V-O in main clauses but S-O-V in subordinate clauses. (Whew! Aren't you glad you know what those are by now!) Others, like Turkish, are always verb-final. A sentence

like "We to the store before it closes go" sounds very poetic or archaic in English, as in nursery rhymes, but may be the norm elsewhere. Now go rent the video of *Return of the Jedi* and characterize the speech of Yoda.

B. **Word order within a phrase.**

1. It seems obvious, but adjectives and articles that modify nouns **precede** the noun. You can say only **the ball, a good neighbor, my close friend,** etc. Lots of languages put adjectives *after* the nouns they modify, like French and Spanish. Nonetheless, they leave the articles in front. Some languages have the *article* after the noun, too. This is called **post-posed article**, as in Bulgarian, Norwegian, or Turkish.

2. Adverbs are sneakier. In English they precede adjectives--**very good, so bad, deliciously evil**. As for verbs, they can either precede or follow them:

   a. Only before the verb: He **barely withstood** the strain.
   We **almost lost** the race.

   b. Only after (almost): You **play beautifully.**
   They **approached** the house **quietly.**
   (They **quietly** approached the house.)

   c. Either before the verb or at the end of the whole sentence:

   You **completely missed** the point.
   You **missed** the point **completely** .

   d. Only at the beginning of the sentence followed by a pause:

   Fortunately, the traffic has died down.
   "Your reindeer are in violation of the leash law, Mr. Kringle. **Consequently**, we are impounding them."

3. Prepositions are called that because they come *before* nouns, but in some languages they come at the *end* of their phrase, so you call them

post-positions. A normal English sentence translated into, say, Turkish--which has postpositions, post-posed articles, and is verb final--might look like this:

Eng.: The boy who lives next door goes to school with my son.

Trk.: Next-door living boy-the son-my-with school-the-to goes.

Sounds like spinning a record backwards on the turntable, doesn't it?

C. Phrases and Clauses as Modifiers.

1. Noun phrases usually begin with the article and end with the noun, forming a kind of frame for all the other adjectival modifiers:

   [**the window**] (+ dirty) → [**the** dirty **window**] (+big) → [**the** big dirty **window**].

2. Prepositional phrases and adjective clauses normally **follow** the noun they modify, so you dilute that "framing" effect.
   a. [**the window**] + big, in the corner →
      [**the** big **window**] *in the corner*

   b. [**the window**] + big, that I broke →
      [**the** big **window**] *that I broke*

3. This is important to be aware of because many languages, including Turkish, Korean, Chinese, extend the "modifiers before nouns" rule to include **all** modifiers, whether adjective, phrase, or clause, so you get in literal translation phrases like: **the that-roared mouse, the that-Jack-built house, the who-is-walking person, the on-the-corner house.** Of course, you get the same thing in English when a prepositional phrase becomes a single-word adjective. You usually spell it with a hyphen, as in **in-depth analysis, on-the-scene coverage, out-of-sight music**. (Notice, though, that you can do this only with adjective **phrases** and never with **clauses**.)

SECTION 2

THE TREES

CLOSER LOOKS AT THE BUILDING BLOCKS

CHAPTER 8

TIPTOE THROUGH THE TENSES

PART 1: VERB FORMS

I. VERBS IN TIME

Philosophers since the beginning of time have been discussing and pondering the notion of **time**. Whether or not time really exists in some metaphysical sense, grammarians have for centuries divided events into three time frames along an assumed "time line" from **past** to **present**, and on through to **future.** Every language has ways of referring to the time an action or event takes place, and the most common means is by using different forms of **verbs**. As soon as you take a closer look, though, you see that most languages do not have only three verb forms, or if they do, they do not fit neatly into these assumed time designations. Furthermore, they break up that time line at different points to communicate different kinds of relationships. There are no absolutes.

A. These notions of "time reference" usually mean "time relative to the perception or point of view of some language-possessing creature having an exchange of language with another language-possessing creature at some space-time coordinates." The one who sends speech into the air is the **speaker**. The one that the speaker addresses is the **addressee**, cf. Chapter 11, below. Consequently:

   1. **Present Tense** means "present from somebody's vantage point in time and space," that is, within the speaker's direct or potential perception.

   2. **Past Tense** means "previous to or earlier than the speaker's perception."

   3. **Future Tense** means "later than the speaker's perception."

B. In English and other languages you cannot always rely on the verb form alone to tell you *when* the action took place relative to the speaker and addressee. The more accurate indicator of time is often "time words" like **today, yesterday, tomorrow**, or **now, a minute ago, in a minute**, or **this week, last week, next week**.

1. Obviously, these terms are provisional and imprecise. No one stands around with a stopwatch to tell you when the **present** is over and becomes **past**, but learning that division in your target language is very important.

2. By the same token, no one can say exactly when the **future**· "collides" with the present and slides on into the past. It is all a continuum, and no language is really successful at having one word or grammatical form that always and only reflects the abstract notion of **time**.

3. For now let us simplify things and imagine that most languages use different forms of their **verbs** to suggest that an action is located in a certain time frame with respect to the speaker of the message. Verb forms that express some kind of time relation are called **tenses**. That is, **tense** is the prototypical verbal category, but the physical past **time**, present **time**, and future **time** do not always coincide with the verb forms that grammar books for a language label past **tense**, present **tense**, and future **tense**! You will see in Part 2 of this chapter how *in*frequently the name fits the time, even in English. (The range of relations among events in time is too great to fit into just these three categories. It is like assuming that Democrat and Republican always coicide with liberal and conservative. The range of political views is just too broad to be lumped into only two baskets. The two sets of terms are not equivalent and even criss-cross: you have liberal Republicans and conservative Democrats.)

C. English verb forms also express other considerations besides just "when" the action happens. English is also concerned with "what else is in the scene described", namely, whether the action in question is isolated or in progress relative to some other action.

1. An action seen as general or generic is termed **plain**, as in, "The sun **rises** in the east." It is just the one-word verb form you find in the dictionary (here: **rise** is in the dictionary, not **rises**).

2. An action seen as being "in progress" at a certain moment is termed **progressive**, as in, "Oh, look: the sun **is rising**. How beautiful!"

3. English can also express "relevance or lasting effect of a past action for a later time," as in, "Now that the sun **has risen** we can do our morning yoga exercises." This is termed **perfect**.

4. It is also possible to combine **do** or **did** with the plain form to express **emphatic**, as in, "We **do want** you to have a good time at our resort!"

II. THE NOTION OF "VERB SYSTEM"

A. Tenses

The following chart shows that English has a very neat system wherein each "time frame" can be expressed with all four of the above-mentioned nuances (with the exception of an "emphatic future"), yielding eleven tenses for English. (Here it becomes clear that the term **tense** is used very broadly in most grammar books to mean just about any kind of verb phrase, regardless of whether "time reference" is its main business.) Other English grammars may give other numbers of tenses, depending on their criteria. Some languages have many fewer "tenses." Other have many more, expressing even more nuances and finer time frames. In some languages the forms themselves are complicated with lots of endings or other things added to the basic verb word. The English ones are pretty simple and transparent, as verb systems in the world go. As an example we can use the very regular verb **LOOK**.

tense → **↓nuance**	**PRESENT**	**PAST**	**FUTURE**
PLAIN	*look(s)*	*looked*	*will look*
EMPHATIC	*do look*	*did look*	* * * *
PROGRESSIVE	*is looking*	*was looking*	*will be looking*
PERFECT	*has looked*	*had looked*	*will have looked*

B. Other Verb Forms

The following are hard to label as "tenses," but they are nonetheless verb phrases with reasonably consistent meanings, and you have to recognize them as whole units and not individual words. (Some books do include them in the tense inventory of English.) We will deal with them below. Many other languages, after all, have distinct forms for them instead of these multi-parted compounds:

INFINITIVE	*to look*
PERFECT INFINITIVE	*to have looked*
PAST HABITUAL	*used to look*
PAST FREQUENTATIVE	*would look* (also. . .)
CONDITIONAL	*would look* (yep, same form!)
CONDITIONAL PERFECT	*would have looked*
PERFECT PROGRESSIVES	*had-(will)have-been looking*
IMPERATIVE	*Look!*
PASSIVE VOICE	*be looked (at)*

So you see there are not many actual verb forms--just **look(s)-looking-looked**--but they are very agile and make a lot of regular combinations with the verbs called **auxiliaries**: **be, have, do, will,** and **would**. Some languages do not use auxiliaries at all. Instead they use a lot more endings on the verb itself or other means to express these or other verb categories.

III. THE NOTION OF "VERB CONJUGATION"

English does very little to change the "plain" form of the verb. In a few cases it adds **endings** to the plain base. There are three such endings. Spell them **-s**, or **-es**, **-d** or **-ed**--schematically **-(e)s, -(e)d** (including the occasional **-t** and **-(e)n)--and -ing**. The inflectional process (cf. Chapter 3, IX.) of tacking endings onto verb stems is called **conjugation**. In other words, **conjugation** is the process of inflecting verbs for **tense** and usually **person**, as well. (More in Chapter 11.)

A. To **conjugate a verb** in English the tradition is to state the infinitive and recite the list of subject pronouns--I, you, he, she, it, we, you, they--with their appropriate verb forms, as in the jingle, "I scream, you scream, we all scream for ice cream."

1. In most language textbooks a typical present-tense or past tense verb conjugation is listed like this (of course, for English it is kind of silly since the forms hardly change at all, but it is still a useful organizational habit):

to scream: Present Tense

I	**scream**	we	**scream**
you	**scream**	you	**scream**
he, she, it	**screams**	they	**scream**

to scream: Past Tense (one form fits all!)

I	**screamed**	we	**screamed**
you	**screamed**	you	**screamed**
he, she, it	**screamed**	they	**screamed**

2. This sort of list is called a **paradigm** (sounds like the old depression-era song "Brother, can you (s)páre a dime"). Only the form for **he-she-it** gets the ending **-(e)s**. Aside from trivial spelling adjustments of the **try-tries** variety, two verbs in English experience a change in **sound**, which you do not represent in writing: I **say**-he **says,** you **do**-she **does** (compare **pay-pays, go-goes**). One verb loses a consonant sound: we **have**-it **has** (compare **halve-halves**).

3. Of course, the verb **be** is one of a kind, with distinct forms for several of pronoun subjects:

I	**am**	we	**are**
you	**are**	you	**are**
he, she, it	**is**	they	**are**

You get a hint that all used to do this in general when you read Shakespeare or the King James Bible:

you say, do = **thou sayest, dost** (pl.: **ye say; do**)
he says, does = **he sayeth, doth** .

B. Verb Phrases

There are three verbs that, besides their regular meanings, are used together with other verbs to form compounds. These are the **auxiliary** verbs **be, have,** and **do.**

1. The combinations they form in conjunction with the verb forms themselves are called, not unexpectedly, **verb phrases.** The phrases count as whole forms, even though the two or more parts may not always occur right next to each other.

2. Each compound tense form has its own meaning and contributes its own special flavor to the larger context.

   a. The **plain** form **+ing** is called the **present participle** in most books. It combines with the auxiliary **be** to give the form called **progressive**: I **am playing**, she **is filibustering**, we **were psychoanalyzing.**

   b. The **plain past** form in **-(e)d**, when it comes with the auxiliary **have**, goes under the alternate name of **past participle**.

   c. The auxiliary **do** plus the plain form gives the so-called **emphatic**. (This is a little strange. After all, if you want to say something emphatically, you *just* **say** ***it*** ***EMPHATICALLY!***, no? But it is a real part of English grammar. Sometimes you can do without it. Other times you have to use it.)

C. "Irregular Verbs" and the Notion of Principle Parts

1. For a verb to be "regular" verb in English means that you can automatically make several forms by regular processes of sound using the plain form as a base. These are:

   a. the past tense by adding **-ed**, spelling peculiarities aside: **look-looked, bake-baked, refrigerate-refrigerated**, and this form automatically combines with the auxiliary **have** to express the **perfect**. (See Part 2, IV below.)

   b. the present participle by adding **-ing**.

c. the infinitive by prefacing the plain form with "**to**".

d. the **he-she-it** form of the present tense by adding **-(e)s**

e. the future with the auxiliary **will**.

2. As far as b.-e. are concerned, all verbs in English are regular, that is, "conjugate regularly" except, of course, **be** and the **modals**, on which see Chapter 9, VII.

3. For several dozen English verbs, though, the past form is not automatically predictable from the plain. You have to learn it as a separate form. This is called "irregular." In addition, the past participle may be the same as the past or even a separate, third, form.

4. Traditional grammar has developed a handy trick for keeping track of how much information you can extract from a verb form. This is the notion of **principle parts of the verb**. These are the essential forms that help you predict everything you need to know to make the correct forms of verbs. As we hinted just above, for most verbs this is hardly necessary, but for the verbs like **sing, teach, buy, catch, see, freeze**, and the entire list that any full-sized grammar book will give you, you have to learn the past form separately, and often the past participle, too.

   a. Sometimes you see the term **strong verbs** for these, and what we call "regular" are sometimes called **weak verbs**. It just means that the weak ones need help from the outside--the ending **-(e)d**--while the strong ones can "take care of themselves from the inside," so to speak.

   b. Of course, "irregular" does not mean "having no pattern," just a different one form the "norm" and one that is aplicable o only a small number of items. They are not just random. Here is an idea of how you can systematize some of them. Don't let spelling fool you: use your ears.

	PLAIN (=pl.)	PAST (=ps.)	PAST PARTICIPLE (=pp.with *have*)
3-PRINCIPLE PARTS			
a. change vowel, no endings	*ring* *swim*	*rang* *swam*	*rung* *swum*
b. change vowel, and add **-n** to pp.	*drive* *write* *fly*	*drove* *wrote* *flew*	*driven* (sound !) *written* *flown*
2-PRINCIPLE PARTS			
a. change vowel, (several patterns) no ending	*hold* *meet* *read* *cling* *hang* *fight*	*held* *met* *read* (sound!!) *clung* *hung* (e.g., 'picture') *fought* ? (or d.-type?)	
b. "regular": no vowel change, ps. end in **-ed**	*tuck* *tug* *strut*	*tucked* (sound: **-t**) *tugged* (sound: **-d**) *strutted* (sound: **-id**)	
c. both: change vowel and add **-t**	*keep* *dream*	*kept* *dreamt* (sound!!)	
d. change stem, ps. with **-t**	*catch* *teach* *seek* *buy*	*caught* *taught* *sought* *bought*	
e. pp. same as pl.**+n**	*throw* *take*	*threw* *took*	*thrown* *taken*
f. pp.same as ps.**+n**	*steal* *lie* *bite*	*stole* *lay* *bit*	*stolen* *lain* *bitten*
g. pl., ps. are "reg.", **pp**. has vowel change and **-n**	*swell*	*swelled*	*swollen*
h. pl. same as ps., pp. has **-n**	*beat*		*beaten*
1-PRINCIPLE PART (one form fits all):	*hit, cut, put*		

This is not all. How many more patterns can you see in the rest of the so-called "irregular" verbs?

D. Contractions

These are the shortened forms of some of the auxiliary verbs that teachers probably warned you against using in writing. They may even have condemned them as "sloppy", "careless", or--God forbid!--"colloquial" forms. Face it: they are a normal and necessary part of English **speaking**. Even when you read something aloud that spells out "is not" or "she would say" your natural tendency is to read "isn't" and "she'd say." These variant forms have their own place in English grammar. That is, it makes a difference to the meaning of your message--or your listener's reaction to it--whether or not you "contract." You can consider the apostrophe as a visual boundary marker between the subject and predicate. Here is how you usually make contractions:

1. Take the auxiliaries **be, have/had, will, would**. Attach them to the word that comes immediately before them, usually the subject.

   a. **be** (present tense only, though)

      (1). Pronouns: I'm going, you're whistling, it's raining, they're joshing

      (2). Pronouns or nouns: he's deliberating, John's working she's calculating, Mary's deciding

      (3). Note that this also applies to "whole verb" **be**, even without a following **-ing** participle: I'm late, you're a goon, she's a senator, they're just kids.

      (4). In old-fashioned writing you see the contraction with **it** from the other side in both present and past tense: 'Tis I! 'Twas the night before Chrsitmas. You can also contract main-verb **have** in the same style and former time period: "I've little concern for the downtrodden." "You've nothing to worry about."

   b. **have/had**: I've/I'd been, you've/you'd arrived, we've/we'd appealed, they've/they'd signed, she's/she'd won, he's/he'd conceded, it's taken so long (Compare: she's winning, he's conceding. See how you tell the contraction of **she has** from **she is**? What do you do with **it**? It'd happened so fast. . ."?

c. **will/would:** I'll/I'd recant, you'll/you'd squander, they'll/they'd disembark, he'll/he'd reconsider, she'll/she'd reconnoiter. Note, too, that the contraction for **I would** is the same as for **I had**, but there is hardly any chance of confusing them because **I'd go** has to be **I would go** and **I'd gone** has to be **I had gone**.

2. This contraction business is a product of the fact that you do not put the stréss on these auxíliaries únder nórmal condítions. Naturally, if you méan to stréss the auxíliary, you do nót contract it: ". ..but I **am** doing the best I can. . .", "Oh, I see: you already **have** hired six new errand runners." We will take these up again in Chapters 14 and 15 on questions and negations.

EXERCISE 8a:

WHOLE VERBS OR AUXILIARIES?
Key p. 348

Simply underline the entire verb phrase in each clause of the following sentences and identify its tense by traditional name.

Examples: a. "Baa, Baa, Black Sheep, have you any wool?"
present

b. "Baa, Baa, Black Sheep, have you bought any wool lately?"
present perfect

1. You have a lot of guts to do that!

2. You have earned everybody's admiration!

3. A 4-leaf clover! I do believe I'll have good luck today.

4. While my wife is busy in corporate dealings I do the dishes and the laundry.

5. "Who did that?" "What? I didn't do anything!"

6. It was such a nostalgic trip. We hadn't been back there in years!

7. Mr. Gorbachev has taken bold steps toward *glastnost*.

8. Mr. Gorbachev has less support in the government now than he used to.

9. Who are you and who do you think you're kidding?

10. We were so happy when we were carrying a mortgage and car payments. . .

CHAPTER 8, PART 2:

MEANINGS AND USES OF THE TENSES

Observe the various ways English uses each of its forms. You will notice that information about the physical time of the action is not always the most important factor. Expect that forms called **present, past,** and **future** might have uses not limited to those time designations and, most important, that other languages with forms of the same names may use them in very different ways.

I. "PLAIN" FORM

A. Plain Present Form

1. Statements of generality, regularity, or habit, even if they are not happening "right now" in the so-called "present":

    a. The sun **rises** in the East.

    b. The English **drive** on the left side of the street.

    c. The workers **control** the means of production.

    d. We **walk** to school, but they **take** the bus.

    e. We **elect** the president in November.

    f. Sequoia trees **live** for thousands of years.

    g. Olympic athletes **train** rigorously.

2. Other terms used for these meanings of the English plain form that some languages have separate forms for include:

    a. **áorist** (sounds like (p)áy your wrist), literally, "timeless, always valid," as in 1a., 1b.

    b. **durative present** for actions that go and on, as in 1a., f., g.

3. In legal, official, or poetic usage, the plain form might also refer to an action taking place at the moment. Most of these are actions that you name as you do them. Some people refer to them as **performatives** because the very act of saying the word constitutes doing the action. (They feel sort of progressive because they are literally happening as you utter them, but you stick with the plain form, anyway)

   a. I **refer** you to page 27 of the textbook.

   b. I now **pronounce** you spouse and spouse.

   c. The prosecution **calls** John Doe to the stand.

   d. The bench **recognizes** the Honorable Ms. Smith.

   e. I **object**!

   f. "The sun **shines** bright on my old Kentucky home. . ." (You can read this as either "in general" or "is shining at the moment")

   g. Here I **come**, ready or not!

   h. Now, there you **go** making those wild claims again!

B. **Plain Past Form**

1. General statements about the past, such as states that last over a long period or separate events that recur again and again.

   a. When he **was** a kid he often **had** bad dreams.

   b. The Romans **built** aqueducts.
   (occupation, way of life, emphasis on fact of building in the past without stressing the completion of one particular aqueduct)

   c. He **got** A's all through school.

   d. The Republicans **won** 7 out of the 11 presidential elections in the post-World War II era.

2. The context of a sentence may point to a single instance of the action in the past. (This seems like a fine distinction, and English does not use a special verb form to tip you off to which of the meanings of the past is meant, but some languages are very fussy about this and do use a different form to express this "one-timeness" vs. regularity of an action.)

   a. Columbus "**discovered**" America in 1492.

   b. The Romans **built** these aqueducts.
      (legacy, emphasis on accomplishment and observable result. Compare B.1.b., above)

   c. He **got** your letter yesterday.

   d. Ronald Reagan **won** by a landslide in 1980.

3. Here, too, you can encounter the term **durative past** for situations like B.1.b., though English has no special form for it. The term **aorist** also has a tendency to be applied to past tenses, at least in the grammatical traditions for Classical Greek and the Slavic languages.

C. **Future Form (will + plain)**

1. The usual "later than now":

   a. **We'll be** there at 8:30.

   b. The delegation **will arrive** in an hour.

2. "Supposition", "Prediction" or "Potential" action (another kind of regularity), and not so much "future time":

   a. Oh, there's the door bell. That **will be** the mailman.

   b. O.K., Buddy, that **will cost** you 2 bucks. (The price is fixed anyway. This is not a statement of actual "future.")

   c. Boys **will be** boys.

d. Oil **will float** on water. (Compare with "Oil **floats** on water.")

e. (As you put down your cards in a poker game you say) "I'**ll see** your five and **(will) raise** you ten. (usually spoken as a reaction and already in process. No time designation or even prediction. It feels more like a **performative**, cf. I.A.2, above.)

D. **Uses of Plain Tense Forms for Other Purposes**

1. Plain present as "Near, Imminent, or Scheduled Future"

a. We **leave** tomorrow: first we **go** to England, then we **head** for France, and finally **arrive** in Vienna next Tuesday.

b. The show **starts** in 5 minutes.

c. Hmm, lemme check my date book. Ah, yes: I **give** a lecture at 2:00, then **hold** a press conference, then **meet** my buddies for happy hour.

2. "Implied Future", especially in subordinate clauses with **if, when, after, before, until, by the time that** when main clause has real future (note curly brackets):

a. {If you **eat** that} you **'ll get** sick. (The "eating" is in the future as well as the "getting sick". You haven't eaten it yet.)

b. {If you **study** well for the exam} you **'ll pass**. (So get to it!)

c. {When she **gets** out of school} she **'ll run** for mayor.

She hasn't finished school yet. But compare this with, "When he **gets** out of school, he rushes home to see *General Hospital.*" This **get** is a habitual and not a future, but you can only tell from the following context.

d. **I'll tell** you about it {when we **have** more time}. (so I'm not telling you now because we do not, in fact, have the time.)

e. I **'ll tell** you about it {after the guests **leave**}. (same deal)

f. We **will sell** no wine {before it **is** ready}.

g. By the time I **get** to Phoenix, she **'ll be rising**. (popular song)

3. Present as "Narrative Past", typical of casual speech, journalism, sports casting, and lots of other styles (applies to both plain and progressive present):

   a. Casual:

      "So **I'm walking** down the street the other day, and I **see** this guy changing clothes in a phone. So I ask him what he thinks he**'s doing**, and he **tells** me he's Superman!"

   b. News or history:

      (1). Today's headlines: Switzerland **invades** Germany. The Japanese **revalue** the yen.

      (2). "Now let's review, class: In 1776 the American colonists **revolt** against King George. In 1789 the French peasants **eat** cake and **storm** the Bastille. Any questions?"

   c. Sports: And there**'s** the wind up and the pitch: he **swings** and **misses**. (Obviously narrated after the fact, even if immediately after; still physically "past.")

4. The end result is that one verb form--with the ending **-(e)d**--*always* indicates past tense, while the form without the ending can signal just about anything *except* "specifically past tense." So you can call the plain form simply the **non-past**. The English tense system, then, centers around the opposition **definitely past** vs. **not-definitely-past**. The form called "past" gives definite information. The form called "non-past" can refer, in principle to the past, present, or future.

II. EMPHATIC: DO/DOES-DID + PLAIN FORM

A. Emphatic in Statements

1. **Present**: Yessiree, I **do believe** it looks like rain.

2. **Past**: I tawt I taw a pooty tat. I did, I **did see** a pooty tat!!
(Tweety Bird re: Sylvester)

3. **Future**: English cannot express this by a special form. At best, you can stress the auxiliary **will** with your voice:

"Are you sure you don't want any ice cream?"
"If you insist, I guess I **wíll** have some after all."

B. The most important use of this **do**-form, though, is not to emphasize, but rather, to make questions and negations of the Plain form, more on which in Chapters 14, 15. This is the so-called **do-insertion**. The resulting split verb phrase does not have to mean "emphatic" anymore and is considered a single unit.

1. Questions

a. Does the sun rise in the west? No, it rises in the east.

b. Did the Romans build aqueducts? Yes, they built hundreds of them.

c. Do you see {what I see}? (That is, do see vs. plain see.)

d. Did you see {what I saw}?

2. Negation. (The negative marker **not** does not count as part of the verb phrase, just as a modifier of it.)

a. The sun does not rise in the West.

b. The buses do not run on Sunday.

c. You didn't pay your taxes last year, did you, Mr. Mud?

III. PROGRESSIVE: IS/AM/ARE-WAS/WERE + PLAIN WITH -ING

A. Action in progress at a given observed moment:

1. It's **raining**; it's **pouring**; the old man **is snoring**.

2. Where **are** you **going**? I'**m going** home.

3. Quiet, please, I'**m working** on a big project!

B. An action in progress which serves as the backdrop for another plain form. Such sentences often suggest this "foreground" and "background" with a subordinate clause with **when, while,** or **as**:

1. You know I **can't hear** you {when the water's **running**}.

2. Where **were** you **going** {when I **saw** you downtown}?

3. She **walked** in {while he **was working**}.

4. "As I **was a-walkin'** to town one day, I **spied** a fair lady a-comin'' my way. . ." (folk song-like)

5. You'**ll recognize** her: she'**ll be wearing** the tuxedo.

C. An action considered as extending over a fairly long and steady time but taking place in short bursts, like a habit or occasional physical condition:

1. So, you'**re playing** a lot of tennis these days, eh?

2. Look, Doc, I'**m getting** these headaches a lot lately.

3. My car's **burning** gas like crazy. (even if it's in the driveway at the moment you say that.)

4. Sorry, gotta go. I'**m working** on a big project. (Compare A3.)

D. As for terminology, you often see **continous** for **progressive**, and the tenses are named with both parts, e.g., **present progressive** (= present continuous), **past progressive** (past continuous), etc. Languages often use the same form to express both **progressives** and **duratives**.

IV. PERFECT: HAVE/HAS-HAD + -ED

A. In general, an action preceding some other action in time. What is important is not the "pastness" of the action so much as its **consequences or relevance for a later action**. These perfect forms are a bridge between two situations. As you go through these examples, try to replace the perfect with the plain past and see if the sentence means something different or is possible at all.

1. **Present Perfect**, e.g., "**has tweezed**"

This form signals a past action relevant for the present, often with the sense of an accomplishment of one thing that allows another one to proceed. English signals this by using the present-tense auxiliary **have/has**. Try replacing the compound **have**-forms with the plain past. Does the meaning of the sentence change?

a. Now that we **have moved** to town we can look for work.

b. Yes, Mother, I'**ve practiced** piano. Now can I go out?

c. Don't change the channel: the hero **has**n't **arrived** yet!

d. The Republicans **have won** 7 out of the last 11 presidential elections. (Compare I.B.1.d, above.)

2. **Past Perfect**, e.g., "**had defrosted**", also called **Pluperfect**

This compound past form gives one past action **relevant for a later past** signalled by the past-tense auxiliary **had**. You usually find it in subordinate clauses in sentences with a main clause in the plain past.

a. We **had**n't **been** there 5 minutes when the phone rang.

b. They **had met** a hundred times, but each time was more intriguing than the last.

c. No one was home because they **had** all **gone** to the beach.

d. We **had** barely **been introduced** but we knew this would be no ordinary friendship.

In these sentences, does the "layering" effect of the past tenses come through? Try substituting the plain past tense for the compound. Does it feel different? Can you do it in all of them? Would you use these forms yourself or would you rather expect to find them in a Nancy Drew novel or Harlequin romance?

3. **Future Perfect**, e.g., "**will have re-established**"

Here is a form that shows a layering of futures, one before the other, signalled by future **will have** plus perfect **-ed**.

a. By New Year's Day we **will have lived** here 6 weeks.

You could be saying this on November 15 and have just moved in, or on December 28, in which case a lot of the living you refer to has already gone by, or in October before you even move in. The important thing is that New Year's Day be later than when you speak and the living precedes it. the order of events in the real world can be "speak-live-total" or "live-speak-total." English grammar does not distinguish the two.

b. Don't bother rushing: the train **will have left** by the time you **get** there. (Note also plain present **get** as implied future.)

c. Oh, but we can't leave town on Tuesday: I **won't have seen** the new play.

You can see that the circumstances requiring this kind of form are quite specific, one of the reasons you do not encounter it very frequently.

B. Action completed either once, several times, or in accordance with some prior expectation or arrangement

1. If **I've told** you once I'**ve told** you a million times....

2. Friends, Romans, Countrymen...I'**ve come** to bury Caesar...
(M. Antony)

3. "The time **has come**," the Walrus said, "to talk of many things. . ."

C. What's the difference between the present perfect **has tweezed** and the plain past **tweezed**?

1. The trick with the present perfect form is that even though it refers to an action in the past--or that started in the past--you cannot localize any point in the past when it happened. The consequence is that you cannot use a present perfect with any adverb that specifies a time. Say these sentences to yourself and see if you accept them as English sentences. (Remember the asterisk means unacceptable or non-existent, so obviously the author has a definite opinion):

a. *I have done the dishes two hours ago.

b. *We have gone to Paris last year.

c. *They have finished the job yesterday.

2. It just doesn't work. The best you can do is broad time expressions like **ever, yet, recently, in the past 3 days**, or **since last Christmas**. These include past time but stress the connection between the past and the present.

a. **Have** you ever **seen** such a sight in your life as 3 blind mice?

b. This town **has witnessed** a lot of change in recent years.

3. The present perfect does **not** combine with specific time words, and the plain past does. But it is important to recognize that most speakers of American English have no problem replacing the present perfect with the plain past, even with these vague, "connector" time words.

a. Many people say both:

(1). "**Have** you **eaten** yet?" and "**Did** you **eat** yet?"

(2). "**Have** you ever **seen** such a sight?" and "**Did** you ever **see** such a sight in your life (. . .as three blind mice. . .)?"

(3). "That's the hottest chili I**'ve** ever **tasted**!" and "That's the hottest chili I ever **tasted**!"

b. Grammar books tell you, with a certain logic, that the "did-ever-see" type is wrong. The reasoning behind the rule is that you **can** localize a plain past form in the past, while **yet** and **ever** mean "no specific past but, rather, relevance for the present." You get a clash of time references. Observe your own usage.

c. Does it ever really make a difference which of these you choose? It certainly does. Think about George Washington or any other politician and see if this doesn't drive the point home. If you say,

(1). "George Washington never **told** a lie," you are making a statement for history books. In order to claim this you need to know the whole of G.W.'s past. (The practical implications of such a use of the plain past could be either that ol' George has retired from politics or, indeed, has gone off to that great Mount Vernon in the sky.)

(2). If you say, "George Washington **has** never **told** a lie!" you are probably at the podium making a campaign speech on G.W.'s behalf in 1775. The extreme formulation here is that in order for you to make this statement, George has to be **alive**!

d. Your target language may or may not make such a difference, or it may make even finer distinctions. There are lots of intricate tense systems among the languages of the world.

V. OTHER VERB PHRASES: "PRESENT" "PAST" AND "FUTURE" IN OTHER GUISES

A. Imperative

There is no distinct form for this in English. "Imperative" is, more precisely, a special kind of sentence featuring the plain form.

1. You easily recognize this one by its lack of subject. You assume that **you** is the so-called "understood subject" and often write it with an exclamation point!

2. The other major property of imperatives is that, unlike regular tense forms, you cannot make an imperative sentence into a question. Compare these:

   a. The statement, "I'm going home" makes the question, "Am I going home?", but the imperative, "Go home!" can at best be paraphrased into a future form, "Will you please go home?!"

   b. You can "tag" a tensed statement (cf. Chapter 15, V.B., below): I'm going home, *aren't I*?, She went home, *didn't she*? But an imperative can have, at best, "Go home, *will you/won't you*!" and then it is not really a question, just a reinforcement.

2. Grammar books often call the imperative "the command form," but they are giving an unnecessarily restricted idea. You also use the imperative--in English and many other languages--to express a whole range of requests, appeals, suggestions, advertisements, or warnings. What motivates these "orders":

   a. **Call** me Ishmael. (= Go ahead!) (M. Dick)

   b. **Stand up** and **be counted**... (= You should, either because it is my personal opinion or the general society's notion of the right thing to do.)

   c. "**Ask** not what your country can do for you: **ask** what you can do for your country." (J.F. Kennedy, 1960)

   d. **Drink** Coca-cola. (commercial)

e. Friends, Romans, Countrymen, **lend** me your ears! (M. Antony, cf. IV.B.2, above)

f. **Read** my lips. (=I invite you to. . .) (G. Bush, 1988)

g. **Don't fire** 'til you see the whites in their eyes! (Bunker Hill)

h. **See** the U.S.A. in your Chevrolet. . . (T.V. commercial, ca. late 1950's.)

4. You can, of course, express commands, demands, or strong requests, namely, impose your "will" on someone, by using the future tense form. This usually sounds impatient, even angry, and you do not normally use such a form unless society gives you the authority, as in parents to children or teachers to students. These are not statements of "future time" but of expected fact. So the imperative really has a "future-like" meaning.

   a. Children, you will stop that racket --now!

   b. You will hand in your term papers next week.

B. "Near Imperatives", Wishes, and Appeals

The same kind of appeal to some "**you**" can apply to **me-us** or **him-her-them.** In this case you get the so-called:

1. **1st person imperative**, the **Let's go**-type form.

   a. Strictly speaking, this construction is formed with the imperative of **let** plus direct object **us** plus **plain** verb, but nobody thinks of it as literally asking permission: **Let's get** the show on the road. **Let's blow** this pop stand.

   b. In the singular this comes out as **let me,** as in "Now, let me just see what we're going to do about that," where, again, no permission is implied. In English this is just a polite "figure of speech" or "manner of speaking," but your target language may express these as separate forms.

2. **3rd person imperative**, the **let him go** type. (in principal the same kind of formation as "let+us+go" where both **him** and **us** are direct objects of **let**)

    a. The **let him-her-it-them go** type sometimes asks permission, as in, "He's a good boy, Sheriff. **Let him have** another chance.

    b. **Let him rot** in prison for all I care! (sounds like any number of grade C westerns: no permission sought here, more like, "I hope he rots.")

    c. It can also sound very high-flown in modern English, as in "**Let** there **be** light!" or "**Let** freedom **ring**!" where there is hardly a question of permission.

3. **Wish forms** are the **may I-you (ye)-he-she-it-they go** type. This expresses a wish--whether positive or negative, nice or nasty:

    a. **May it be** Thy will. . .

    b. **May ye** never **know** sorrow.

    c. **May** the Bird of Paradise **take** target practice from 50 feet above your bald head!

    Unlike **let**, it can really go with any person, including **you**.

4. Very much like the **may** form are the special usages of the plain form in some fixed expressions for possibility, probability, or something you have no control over. It is hard to tell whether it is the present or imperative. It's just plain. The trick is that with **he-she-it** subjects, where you normally have an **-s** you suddenly don't have one. This kind of usage is often termed **subjunctive**, on which, see Chapter 9, VIII.D.4.

    a. Some are typical of religious usage, especially the kind you tack on to the end of a sentence:

(1). He's a fine boy, Lord **love** him.
(More like "May the Lord love him" or "I hope the Lord will love him", not present tense "The Lord loves him).

(2). Thy will **be** done.
(This is the noun **will**, not the verb **will be**. How many thousands of times have you recited this line, asking yourself, "Thy ***what*** will be done?!")

(3). God **save** the queen! or God **damn** you!

(4). The devil **take** him!

b. The other kind of expression is where the plain form and the subject switch places. They sound flowery or high-brow and are also the kind you stick on the end of a sentence. Here are some of them with suggested paraphrases into more normal-sounding word order, even though you wouldn't say it like that. Note the relation of subject (single-underline) and verb (double-underline).

(1). come {what may}	→	whatever may come
(2). be that {as it may}	→	let that be {as it may}
(3). come hell or high water	→	{whether/even if hell or high water should come}
(4). Long live the king.	→	May the king live long.

5. **Implied Conditions**

These are two-part statements connected by **and** that have the sense of a condition. The form is either "Imperative **and** future", meaning, **If you (present), then I will (future)** or "Imperative **and** imperative." (More on "if" in E., below.)

a. "**Marry** me, **and I will pay** the mor-r-r-rtgage!" (old-time melodrama) → "If you marry me, I will pay. . ."

b. **Take** one step closer, **and you'll wish** you hadn't! → "If you take. . .you will wish. . ."

c. "**Say** de secret woid and **win** a thousand dollars." (Groucho Marx television quiz show, *You Bet Your Life*, circa 1955) → "You may say. . .and try to win. . ." or "If you do say. . you will win. . ."

C. Habitual Forms: used to fly, would smile

1. **used to do**: statement of former regularity, habit, or frequency, whether of actions or general abilities--hence the alternate title **frequéntative**--but no commitment to whether the habit still is one.

   "In those carefree years we used to go camping, but we haven't gone in years."

   a. Strictly speaking, **used to** is made up of the old-fashioned verb **use** 'to do frequently' (cf. the adverb **usually**) with a following infinitive. Of course now you can use it only in the past to mean you **were** in the habit and not you **are** in the habit.

   b. Notice that the **used to** part is pronounced **yóosta** in normal speech, almost as if the phrase were re-interpreted as a new auxiliary. (This is not "sloppy speech". If you try to pronounce it too carefully you sound ridiculous.)

   c. There are really two phrases **used to** with different structures. One is a verb phrase for past habits, namely, **used to do**. The other is a predicate adjective for "being accustomed," namely, **used to doing**. They form different kinds of sentences and behave differently in repetitions and answers to questions.

   (1). Uncle Jake used to live there, and Aunt Bessy used to, too.

   (2). Jake is /used to living there/, but Bessy isn't /used to it/.

2. **would do**: also indicates former regularity of events, as in

   a. "Ah, such fun we would have at parties: you would speak French and I would pretend to understand. . ."

b. "Those were the days: we would go camping on fine summer nights; you would pitch the tent... " (It sounds story-book-like, suitable for warm, relaxing summer evenings. . . of course, it can also sound affected and snobbish, can't it?)

3. The two habitual forms are different. Notice that you can say both:

a. (1). I used to speak French and I would speak French.

(2). They used to go camping and they would go camping.

b. **Used to** means either repeated events or general ability in the past, while **would do** seems limited to repeated events. (You can actually call both of them **frequéntative**.) It depends whether the verb you use tends to imply steady states or discreet events. Note that it would be normal to say, for example,

(1). We used to live in Hackensack, but somewhat odd to say

(2). Before we settled in Hoboken we would live in Hackensack.

c. So, **would do** means part of what **used to** means, and **used to** means everything **would do** means and more. This may be why the **used to** construction is used more often and **would** feels so stylized.

D. **Perfect Progressives**, e.g., **have been snoring, had been drawing, will have been sipping**

This two-part form--literally the combination of both the form and the meaning of the perfect **have been /had been/will have been** plus the progressive in **-ing**--signals that an action began previously and is/was/will be still in progress at a later moment, whichever tense you start in:

1. **Past into present:**

a. We've been waiting for him over an hour! (started over an hour ago and are still waiting.)

b. How long have you been studying physics?

c. So, what has little Joey been doing lately?
(=Catch me up to date, and I assume he's still doing whatever you tell me, even if not at the very moment.)

2. **Earlier past into later past.**

a. The party had been going on for hours when the neighbors finally complained of the noise.

b. How long had you been living there when the house was condemned?

3. **Past , present, or future into future**

a. He has been working at the bean cannery for 20 years. By the time he retires he will have been working there 30 years.

b. We'll leave for Antwerp next week and wait for you to rendezvous with us. When you get there we will already have been sightseeing for several days.

E. Conditionals

We will deal with these in more detail in Chapter 9, but for now we can just outline the basic types and note what verb forms they use.

1. **Real Conditions** are those which are potentially realizable or fulfillable. Note that the tense forms in the dependent if clause are **plain present**, while the independent clause is usually **future**.

a. If you drink this, you'll feel better.

b. If you vote for me, I'll lower taxes!

2. **Unreal** or **Hypothetical Conditions** might be realizable but involve doubt or lack of control to bring them about. They are formed with past-tense verb forms.

a. If you drank this, you would feel better (but it appears you do not want to drink it, and I can't make you.)

b. If you voted for me, I would lower your taxes. (I have no control over your vote, but I plant the seeds of a guilt trip.)

3. **Contrary to Fact Conditions** are already invalid. The condition was not met, so there was no result.

a. If you had drunk this, you would have felt better (but you didn't. What's a parent to do?!)

b. If you had voted for me, I would have lowered taxes (but you didn't give me the chance...)

F. **Infinitive = to+ plain**

This form is so designated because it is not "finite" or limited to any particular tense or person. It names the verbal action as an abstract that may or may not be observable at the moment. It is usually considered to be a kind of cross between a noun and a verb. That is, it can come in noun-like places in the sentence--subject, predicate noun after copula, direct object--and also have verb-like properties--like take a direct object or a predicate noun or adjective:

1. As direct object of transitive verbs like **want, wish, like, decide**

a. He wants **to eat** [cake].
(**to eat** is dir.obj. of want and cake, in turn, is direct object of eat, so you would have to double-bracket, as in He wants [to eat [cake]], but it gets so messy.)

b. We do not want **to be** /unemployed/!
(Here **to be** is direct object of want, but since it is itself a copula, it takes its own predicate adjective **unemployed**, so you would label it We do not want [to be /unemployed/].)

2. The infinitive can also occur as either subject or predicate noun-like thing:

a. **To err** is human. **To forgive** is divine.

b. It is nice **to stroll** in the woods.

c. **To be** or not **to be**: that is the question!

d. Your mission, should you decide to accept it, is **to find** the villain and **(to) stop** him!

3. Note that in the above sentences the person who wants is the same as the person who eats (or in this case, will eat). Both verbs have the same doer, so the one subject applies to both actions, in principle.

4. English, unlike many other languages, also has the following construction:

   a. He wants **me** to eat.

   b. They asked **her** to hurry up.

   In these, the two actions in the sentence--**want, eat; ask, hurry**--have different actors, hence the additional **me** or **her**. That is, **he** does the wanting but **I** do the eating. They do the asking but she does the hurrying. This is called **subject of the infinitive**. See why? More in Chapter 9.

G. **Changes in Tense in Direct vs. Indirect Speech.**
This is a quick introduction. There's more in Chapter 9, Sections II, III.

Imagine situations like these:

1. Johnny said, "I'**m going** home." This is **direct speech**. Then you report: "I saw Johnny. He said he **was going** home." This is **indirect speech.**

2. "You'**ll hear** from us later," and you relay: They said we **would hear** from them later.

3. "Where **do** you **live**?" In relating the scene, you say: He asked us where **we lived**.

4. Backwards: take an indirect speech and imagine what direct speech it came from. Notice the tense forms:

   a. Indirect: He told us where he **was going** but didn't say when he **would be** back.

   b. Direct: He said, "**I'm going** somewhere, but I don't know when **I'll be** back."

5. Note how slippery this can be:

   a. She said, "I **love** him!" (= and still does.)
   → Ah, she said she **loved** him! (= and still does.)

   b. She said, "I **loved** him." (= It's history.)
   → Oh, woe! She said she **had loved/used to love** him. (=Forget it!)

   c. "I **am** a doctor." → He said he **was** a doctor. (and still is!)

   d. "I **was** a doctor in Tacoma but decided to go into painting."
   → He said he **had been/ used to be** a doctor, but decided to paint instead.

VI. RECAP ON ENGLISH AUXILIARIES

A. The verbs **be, do, have**, and **will** (some would include **would** as well), when they combine with the verb forms, e.g. **look/looked**, to form phrases, are called **auxiliaries**.

1. **do-did** is the **emphatic auxiliary**. (Of course it is also indispensable in forming questions and negations.)

2. The group **be-is-am-are-was-were** is the **progressive auxiliary**. They combine with the **-ing** form--often called the **present participle**. You will see in Chapter 9 that **be** also combines with the

past participle to form the **passive voice**, which we have otherwise not discussed in this chapter.

3. **will** (no other forms) is, of course, the **future auxiliary.** (In Chapter 9 you will see it discussed as a **modal.**)

4. **have-has-had** are the **perfect auxiliaries,** not because they are so flawless, but because with the so-called **past participle** in **-ed** they form **perfect** tenses, signifying the **later relevance** of one action for a later situation.

B. Obviously, the term auxiliary refers to these verbs only in their combinatory capacity. If they are the main verb in the clause, they are not auxiliaries. These sentences do not contain auxiliaries: She **is** fine. You **have** a dog. Who **did** that?

C. **What About Tenses?**

1. If you have a single verb like **look,** you can distinguish past **looked** from non-past **look,** usually interpreted as **present.** (Of course in the present you also need to distinguish 3rd person singular from everything else by adding **-s.**) In a verb phrase with an auxiliary, you usually need to mark tense in the auxiliary only. This is why "**you do** look", "**he does** look", and "you or he **did** look" differ only by auxiliary. More on this in Chapter 11 on pronouns.

2. The verb **be** is basically the "verb of simultaneity" and combines with **-ing**, which we can now rename the **participle of simultaneity**, to form progressives, since its action happens at the same time as another.

3. **Have** is itself present tense but combines with the so-called "past participle" in **-ed**. Make sense? What does ***present*** **perfect** mean, after all, anyway?

4. **Will** combines, not surprisingly, with the non-past verb form. (Historically speaking, **will** is a present tense and its past form is **woul-d**, though this latter now has other meanings and uses. Also **shall**, hardly used in 20th-century American English, has a past form **shoul-d,** which has become specialized in its own way.)

D. You might well ask the question, "How many tenses does English have, anyway?" Different textbooks of English grammar give you different answers.

1. The chart in Part 1, II of this chapter suggests a nearly symmetrical system of eleven tenses (with one hole in the system for emphatic future) and several stragglers, listed in Part 1, III C., above. In terms of forms with an associated meaning, though, there are only two real verb forms: **past** in **-(e)d**, exemplified by forms like **looked**, and a vague thing called **non-past**, exemplified by what we have been calling the **plain** form **look**. In a sense, the meaning of **look** *includes* the meaning of **looked**, but not vice versa. (This is why you can use the plain, so-called present, form to refer to the past, cf. Part 2, I.D.3 above.)

2. All the rest are combinations of these with auxiliaries or special types of sentences, like the **if**-type. The **-ing** form is as much an adjective and noun as verb, more on which in Chapter 9 below.

3. A lot of languages have very elaborate tense systems with many distinct forms for many meanings. Some languages have simpler systems than English.

EXERCISE 8

VERB TENSES VS. TIME REFERENCE
Key: p. 349

Determine the whole verb in each clause, underline it and label what tense it is. If the tense form is being used differently from what its name implies, indicate this by give the actual time reference or specific use. Abbreviations: **pst., prs., fut., pf.** (perfect), **prg** (progressive), **cond**itional, **contr**ary to fact pst., **hyp**othetical condition, **imp**erative, **frq** (frequentative), **hab**itual, **inf**initive, **ind**irect speech, that is, past used as pres., etc), **emph**atic.

Examples: She <u>had</u> a better idea than she <u>had</u> ever <u>had</u> before.
pst. pst.pf.

I'<u>ll see</u> you when I <u>get</u> home.
fut. pres.= fut. (form called **present** refers to **future**)

1. If I had known you were coming I would have baked a cake.

2. If I had my way, I would tear this building down.

3. Why are you asking so many questions?

4. Why are you so mad?

5. Do you want anything?

6. Do me a favor.

7. We've been looking for you all day long!

8. I looked over Jordan, and what did I see: a band of angels was coming after me...

9. Friends, Romans, Countrymen, lend me your ears often.

10. Friends, Romans, and countrymen lend me their ears often.

11. Michael rows the boat ashore.

12. Michael, row the boat ashore.

13. Deep in my heart I do believe that we shall overcome someday.

14. Who was that lady I saw you with?

15. Who was that lady helping across the street?

CHAPTER 9

SPECIAL USES OF VERB FORMS AND PARTICULAR SENTENCE TYPES:

CONDITIONS, INDIRECT SPEECH, MODALS, MOODS, PARTICIPLES, GERUNDS, VOICE, ASPECT

AND OTHER DENIZENS OF GRAMMARDOM

PACE ALERT:
THIS IS A HEFTY CHAPTER AND IT COVERS LOTS OF SUBTLE TOPICS. YOU MAY WANT TO BREAK IT UP INTO TWO OR THREE SITTINGS.

I. MORE ON CONDITIONAL SENTENCES

A. You often see the term **conditional** used in grammar books as if it were a tense. It is not, at least in English. Conditional is, rather, a type of sentence. In English, conditionals are characterized by special uses of verb forms that we otherwise think of as **tenses**, but their time designation in the usual sense takes a back seat.

B. Conditional sentences usually contain an subordinate clause introduced by **if** and a main clause with particular patterns of tense forms in each. The main clause describes a situation which is contingent upon the situation described in the **if** clause. Many languages have specialized verb forms that are used only in such sentences. English just gets extra mileage out of its regular tense forms.

C. As you saw in Chapter 8, Part 2, V.E above, there are basically 3 kinds of **if**-type sentences. In this chapter we can see more clearly that there are really only two main types, each with its own characteristic patterns of verb tenses and associated meaning: **real** and **unreal**. The unreal type has two sub-types: **hypothetical future** and **contrary to fact past**.

Tense Patterns in English IF-Sentences

		Subordinate Clause	Main Clause
REAL		If you **go** *present*	I 'll **go** *future*
UNREAL	Hypothetical:	If you **went** *past*	I 'd **go** *would + plain*
	Contrary to Fact:	If you **had gone**, *past perf.*	I 'd **have gone** *would+present perf.*

D. The two types are signalled by the tense forms: the **unreal** type uses past or past-like forms, and the **real** type uses anything but past forms. Note that the verb forms do not refer primarily to the time of the action. The names **present, past, future** become nothing but nicknames for the forms and not necessarily for their total meaning. Their meaning in complex sentences may seem not to be the same as in simple sentences. (Whether there is, indeed, a connection between the time-usage and the special usage is a big theoretical can of worms. For now you can marvel at the power of names. All your life you thought **went** was a past tense, and now you suddenly realize it can refer to a **hypothetical future**!)

1. Listen to when you say these and you will find that the **real** type is a sort of **50-50 condition.** It expresses that "you have as good a chance of going as not going, but my going is guaranteed based on your going."

2. The **unreal** type injects doubt into the fulfillment of the condition. In the **hypothetical** type, e.g., "If you **went**, **I'd go**, too," you use a form called **past** to express any of the following nuances:

   a. I doubt that you will go. I may not go myself.

   b. I don't want to impose my opinion on you but I think it's a good idea.

   c. A gentle nudge: I know you want to go, so I'm dangling my going as a carrot in front of your nose.

d. A mild guilt trip: *I'm* the one who wants to go but I'm depending on you to push me, and it'll be your fault if I don't go. . .

3. In the **contrary to fact** type, "If I **had gone**, you **would have gone**," you already know you did **not** go, but you hypothesize about the past anyway.

4. A lot of languages use their past forms for hypothesis in the future. They often have only one type of unreal condition sentence, as if, "Once it's unreal, pal, I don't care whether it is possibly fulfillable or unfulfillable." When translating into English, the English speaker has to make the distinction between "hypothetical future" vs. "already invalid past" depending on the circumstances, the way English does.

5. You can paraphrase these conditions with **unless** to show the reverse perspective on the relationship between the two parts, and the verb tenses will be the same as in the **if** type:

Tense Patterns in English "Unless"-Sentences
(Compare I.C., above)

		Main Clause	Subordinate Clause
REAL		I **won't go** *future*	unless you **go** *present*
UNREAL	Hypothetical:	I **wouldn't go** *would + plain*	unless you **went** *past*
	Contrary to Fact:	I **wouldn't have gone** *would+present perf.*	unless you **had gone** *past perf.*

(Many people say "unless you **went**" for the last type and regularly replace the past perfect by the plain past.)

E. Some possible variations on these constructions are:

1. Real conditions are usually given by a **present** tense in the **if**-clause and **future** in the main clause. But you also frequently find **should**

in the **if**-clause, as well as the plain present. In this case you can do without the **if** altogether and start off with **should**, making a split verb phrase, and you still have future in the main clause:

a. If the weather should turn bad
} we won't go out.
b. Should the weather turn bad

This type tends to sound formal or stilted, or else it suggests that you really don't want the weather to change or if it does it might do so suddenly or unexpectedly. At any rate, it occurs and you have to recognize it as part of English grammar.

c. There is also the variation with **suppose**, usually in two "half-sentences":

Suppose the weather turns bad. Will we still go out?

2. Hypothetical conditions use the past form in the **if**-clause and the **would+plain** form in the main clause. A variation that makes the condition sound just a bit more arbitrary has the past tense of **were + infinitive**, where the past-form **were** is also a hypothetical future. You get inversion here, and the "suppose" option, too:

a. If she left,

b. If she were to leave, } we would cry.

c. Were she to leave,

d. **Suppose** she were to leave. We would cry.

e. Note, too, that the normally plural **were** goes for all subjects. Many people have a different strategy, more on which in VIII.D., below.

3. **Contrary to Fact Conditions** use compound forms in both clauses: the past perfect (**had done**) in the **if**-clause and the so-called conditional perfect (**would have done**, that is, would+present perfect) in the main clause. You do not normally compound the form

further by adding **were**, but you do get inversion and the "suppose" option:

a. If you had left,
} we would have cried.
b. Had you left,

c. **Suppose** you had left. We would have cried.

Each of these has its own stylistic flavor, but you should at least see the consistency in tense usage. (As a logical parallel to the b-variant for Hypotheticals, you can get a third variant of Contrary to Fact "if you were to have left" or "were you to have left," though this tends to sound a little too "stuffed.")

C. There is, however, nothing to prevent the present tense after **if** from meaning what present tense usually means: **general validity of action**, cf. Chapter 8, Part 2, I.A.1. In a conditional-looking sentence the **if**-clause can refer to a situation as "given" more than as a prerequisite for the main clause. Such present-tense **if**-clauses are normally followed by a main clause with a present tense or an imperative, but future is possible if that is "what you mean." The main clause in such instances gives a reaction that either does not necessarily follow from the **if** clause or follows up a hunch:

1. If *Pres.* + *Imper.*: a. If you **want** to go, **go**!

   b. If it'**s raining** out, **take** an umbrella

2. If *Pres.* + *Pres.*: a. If you **want** to do that, I **can**'t **stop** you.

   b. If you **strike out** on your own, good fortune **awaits** you.

3. If *Pres.* + *Fut.* If you **want** to go to the ball, Cinderella, you'**ll be needing** some nice shoes. (= "given that we know you want to. . .)

It is normal, then, for the verbs in such **if**-clauses to be the kind that express a state rather than an action, such as **want, like, feel**. We can call it the **Already-Existing-Circumstance Condition**, because the

if part is not really in question. Check out the daily-life drama below. The **if**-clauses all have present forms, but whether they imply future depends on the meaning of the main clause.

3. "Do you feel bad? Here, have some chicken soup. Then, if you **feel** better, you'**ll have** no excuse to stay home from school." (If *Pres.*, implying **Fut.**, + *Fut.*)

4. "There, do you feel better now? Well, if you **feel** better, you **have** no excuse to stay home from school." (If *Pres.* meaning **Existing Condition.**, + *Pres.* meaning **Pres.**)

In 3. the "feeling better" is obviously yet to come, and so, then, is the potential excuse. In 4. you assume that you already "feel better," so you already have no excuse. The verb forms after **if** don't resolve the question by themselves. You have to hear the main clause tenses.

D. In math, logic, and computer programming you talk about "**if-then**" statements. This terminology in language means that you literally use the word **then** to signal a main clause after an **if**-clause. In English it is usually not necessary, but in other languages it might be. You often hear, in the same type of sentence, the use of **why** or **well**, usually spoken with a little pause and a tone of surprise, indignation, or any of several other emotions. Imagine somebody saying,

1. If this is right triangle, **then** the length of the hypotenuse is obvious.

2. "If my work load doesn't go down soon, **why**, I just don't know what I'll do."

3. "If that mangy dog of yours messes up my yard one more time, **well**, I'll just call the pound!"

EXERCISE 9a.

REAL OR UNREAL?

Designate these conditional sentences by initial as **R**eal, **H**ypothetical, **C**ontrary to Fact or **E**xisting Circumstance. Be guided both by the verb tenses used and by what you feel to be the meaning of the whole sentence. Check the answer key. Talk it over with your friends.

1. ____ If you like peanuts, you'll love Skippy. (commercial)
2. ____ If it rains we'll cancel the picnic.
3. ____ If it rained we'd cancel the picnic.
4. ____ If it had rained, of course we would have changed plans.
5. ____ If I had a hammer I'd hammer in the morning... (folk song)
6. ____ If you don't behave, you'll be punished.
7. ____ If we won the lottery we'd go out and celebrate.
8. ____ We wouldn't have got into this mess if you had listened.
9. ____ If you give a little you get back a lot.
10. ____ "If you lived here you'd be home now. . ."
(P.R. gimmick of apartment complexes located at rush-hour-jammed highway entrances.)

ANSWER KEY TO 9a.

1-E, R. 2-R. 3-H. 4-C. 5-H. 6-R. 7-H. 8-C. 9-E. 10.-H.

II. MORE ON TENSES IN DIRECT VS. INDIRECT SPEECH

A. As you read in Chapter 8, Part 2, V.G. above, English has a tremendous tendency to adjust the use of tense forms of direct speech when that quotation becomes **indirect speech** or **reported speech**. The examples in that section make it clear that when the "verb of reporting" (say, tell, etc.) is in the **past**, the quotation makes a "backward shift" to accommodate it. Traditional grammar calls this **sequence of tenses in indirect speech** because it is automatically conditioned by the tense of the main-clause verb. In terms of a formula for, say, "She said that...."

1. A **present** quotation becomes **past** with a past verb of reporting:

   a. She said, "My car really **guzzles** gas." →
   She said (that) her car really **guzzled** gas.

   b. Since the present tense form can also imply future, it is perfectly possible for the back-shifted past to refer to the same future:

   He said, "We'**re having** a party tomorrow. I **want** to know if you **wanna** come." →
   He said he **was having** a party tomorrow and **wanted** to know if we **wanted** to come.

2. A **past** quotation that indicates a single action becomes **past perfect.** A past quotation that means a general action or on-going state usually becomes a **used to do** form. A **present perfect**, not surprisingly, then, also becomes **past perfect.** Do you feel the parallelism? Expect variations in real life. Of course, many people do not use past perfect in their speech at all. They just replace it with plain past, so that smudges the otherwise neat picture. Both the following quotes have the identical reported form:

   a. (1). She said, "My car **guzzled** two tankfuls this week!" →

   (2). She said, "My car **has guzzled** two tankfuls this week!" →

   b. She said (that) her car **(had) guzzled** two tankfuls by Thursday. (You hear both **guzzled** and **had guzzled**.)

3. A **future** becomes a **would+plain**. (This makes a third meaning of the **would+plain** verb phrase, in addition to the Frequentative of Chapter 8, Part 2, V.B.2 and the Conditional of V.E.2. More on this just below.)

   She said, "They'**ll be** here after the game." →

   She said they'**d be** here after the game.

   (Recall that **would**, from a certain perspective, is the past form of **will**, cf. Chapter 8, Section VI.C.4. That makes Rule 3 above essentially the same as Rule 1.)

B. Besides **say**, there are dozens of verbs or expressions that mean "reporting or conveying a quotation, thought, belief, or piece of information": **confirm, confess, hint, whisper, assert, whine, inject, know, believe, decide, suppose, deny, guess, swear, emphasize, declare, be sure (that).**

1. **know**: It 's raining. **Did**n't you **know** it was raining?

2. **think**: So, you 're coming, eh? I **didn't think** you were coming.

3. **hint**: He is a full-fledged member of the club. Why **did** you **hint** (that) he wasn't one?

4. You could supply dozens more without half trying. (Give yourself a pat on the back if you recognized this group of verbs as the same ones that take a **that**-clause with optional, omittable **THAT**, as you saw in Chapter 6, IV.D. In fact, the indirect quotation becomes a noun clause functioning as direct object of the verb. Everything falls into place.

C. Sometimes you do not shift from Present to Past, depending on whether you consider the statement you are reporting to be of general validity or not. It is not bad not to back-shift, although if you listen to yourself you probably catch yourself making the shift more often than not, e.g., "Life **is** uncertain, my friend. Did you know that life **is/was** uncertain?"

EXERCISE 9b.

REPORTING SPEECH
Key: p. 350

Reconstruct the original Direct Speech from which these reportings came. Include the verb of reporting if convenient and have a live context in mind. Be creative, but watch the tense forms. Adjust pronouns as you see fit. Some quotations submit more readily to this procedure than others.

Examples: He said he **knew** the way. →
1. (He said,)"I **know** the way."
2. "I **know** the way," (he said). And don' forget:
3. "I **knew** the way."

1. He promised he'd never do that again!

2. She thought she was seeing things, but she was sure she had seen him before.

3. He knew the plan wouldn't work.

4. I confessed I had slacked off recently.

5. Did you know he was planning to arrive at 7:00?

6. He claimed he worked at McDonald's.

7. He claimed he used to work at McDonald's.

8. Little did they suspect that *IT* would be waiting for them...

III. WOULDWATCH!!

Review the many lives of the compound forms with **would+plain**. Watch out that the contraction of **would** is identical to the contraction of **had**: **'d**, cf. Chapter 8, Part 1, III.D.1. The **would** form serves to mark:

A. **Hypothetical conditions**, as in Chapter 8, Part 2, V.D.

B. **Frequentative past**: repeated actions in the past, even if repeated only occasionally or regularly but at long intervals, as in Chapter 8, Part 2,V.C.

C. **Reported future**: an action reported as coming after a past action, or **future with respect to the past**, as you just drilled in Chapter 9, II.

D. You might even add another one, namely, the **predictive**: the fulfillment of prediction or acting according to pattern, without any apparent condition. (This is probably just a special case of conditional.) In speech you give the auxiliary **wóuld** a bíg stréss and de-stress the main verb. Imagine situations like,

   "The boss really piled on the work just before closing time! He **wóuld** do that!"

   You can consider it a sort of unexpressed condition, e.g., "If you gave/were to give him/her the opportunity, that is the way s/he **would act**."

EXERCISE 9c.

WHICHWOULD?

Decide which **would** is represented in the following sentences according to the surrounding context. Designate it as **C**onditional, **F**requentative past, **R**eported Future, or **P**redictive.

_____ 1. Oh, yes, I remember how my little Fluffy would romp and play in the neighbors' finely cultivated flower beds. We would have such fun watching him...

_____ 2. Ruin your garden? Oh, no! my little Fluffy would never do anything like that!

_____ 3. The neighbors assured me they would give Fluffy a little present.... (Sounds like Raymond Burr in *Rear Window*, doesn't it?)

_____ 4. If I'd a-known you was (sic!) comin' I'd-a-baked a cake.

_____ 5. We would do our share by putting out crumbs for the birds, and they would come and partake. They don't come back this way any more, though.

_____ 6. We would do our fair share for your organization if we thought the government would meet us half-way. . .

_____ 7. You knew you'd finish on time! Congratulations!!

_____ 8. I wouldn't do that if I were you....

ANSWER KEY TO 9c. 1-P. 2-F. 3-R. 4-C. 5-F. 6-C. 7-R. 8-C

IV. TWO OBSERVATIONS ON TENSE USAGE:

A. In some parts of the English-speaking U.S., there is a tendency in unreal conditions to match the tense form in the **if**-clause with that of the main clause. You hear hypothetical conditions like 1. and contrary to fact conditions like 2:

1. If I would have a dollar I would get a cup of coffee.

2. If I would have known, I would have told you.

This kind of tense sequence is frequent in normal speech, but it is considered "incorrect" to have a **would**-form in the **if**-clause in writing. In some languages this parallelism between the main clause and conditional (subordinate) clause--both with **would**-forms or their equivalent--is the norm.

B. **Asking, Re-asking and Politeness**

In repeating questions or requesting information a second time from somebody, especially a sales person, travel agent, or similar "official" person, you usually hear a past tense form even when the action in question is obviously not past:

1. (In the bus station at 4:00)
   Passenger: "Excuse me, when **does** the next bus **leave**?"
   Agent: "5:00."
   Passenger (didn't hear or wants to confirm):
   a. "When **did** you **say** that bus **left**?"

   b. "When **did** the next bus **leave**?"

   In a. you have normal back-shifting in reported speech, and in b., the bus obviously hasn't left yet.

2. Hotel customer: I have a reservation.
   Clerk: Certainly. . . What **was** your name?

   Obviously the person's name hasn't changed. It still is what it was when the reservation was made.

3. a. Burger customer: Give me a cheeseburger and fries.
   Server: OK, here's your fries.
   Customer: But I **wanted** a burger, too!

   b. Burger customer: Give me a double-tofu broccoliburger.
   Server: **Did** you **want** fries with that?

   The sense in a. is, "I **asked** for a burger, and I still want it." In b. the server is not concerned with the customer's past desires and dreams. If s/he does not want the fries *now*, there is nothing to discuss.

You can consider these as extensions of the principle of back-shifting the tenses in reported speech, but they sound odd because you almost purposely *by-pass* the verb of reporting. Furthermore, you normally utter questions with question words--**when, what,** etc., cf. Chapter 14--without a rising pitch in your voice. However, when you utter both of these **re-asking** types your voice has a high-rising contour, as you will see in Chapter 14. Listen carefully. You'll become aware of all sorts of things you never **knew** you **did**.

5. Several "polite" forms use past tense forms alongside plain forms, such as:

   a. I want → I would like

   b. Do you mind. . .→ Would you mind. . .

   c. Can you . .. → Could you please. .

   d. I wonder → I was just wondering. . .

V. A LITTLE MORE ON INFINITIVES

A. As you saw in Chapter 8, Part 2, V., the infinitive can act as a noun, either subject or predicate noun. (See V.F., just below on infinitives as adjectives.)

1. To speak out is /our duty/. (or is it: "/To speak out/ is our duty."?)

2. The Enterprise's mission is **/to** boldly **go/** where no one has gone before.

B. The Notions of Verbal "Control" and "Subject of the Infinitive"

1. Certain verbs in English are said to "take" or "govern" an infinitive after them to complete their meaning. You might find these under the title "**infinitive complement**." Some frequent ones are:

   a. She **wants to study** medicine.

   b. He **likes to cook.**

   c. We **try to behave** ourselves.

   d. She **promised to defend** the constitution.

   e. You **have to go** now.

   f. They **ought to be** ashamed.

   g. Poppa's **going to scream** if he finds out!

   h. Max **offered to help** us with our income taxes.

   i. Mimi **swore to uphold** the law.

   That is, you cannot just say, "She wants," or "He likes," by themselves as complete sentences. They need an object, whether a noun ("She wants shrimp.") or an infinitive. But an infinitive is also a verb, so you are now dealing with two verbal actions. Since verbs have to have subjects or doers, you have to ask who is doing each of the two actions. It happens that of the verbs exemplified here, the subject and doer of one is also the subject and doer of the other. One term for this is that the same subject is the **controller** of both the main verb (**want, like, promise**) and of the verb in the infinitive complement. Simply stated, in a., "she" is doing both the **wanting** and the **studying**. In b., "he" is doing the **liking** and also the **cooking**, etc. (Admittedly, modals and auxiliaries like **ought, going to, have to** do not exactly belong with these control-type verbs, but they take infinitive complements all the same.)

2. Look what happens in these:

   a. Larry **convinced me to dive** into the half-empty pool.

   b. Sarah **persuaded Harold to give** her a lift to the station.

   c. The mayor **asked the city council to raise** the parking fines.

   d. Fanny **begged the fireman to get** her cat down from the tree.

   In all these there are two verbs--one conjugated to agree with the subject of the sentence--and one infinitive, but the crucial difference between this set and the one just above is that in these examples, each of the verbs has its own controller! In a., **Larry** did the **convincing** but **I** did--or will do--the **diving**. In b., **Sarah** did the **persuading**, but **Harold** is the one who **gives** her a lift. Get the idea? Since at some abstract level you really have two subjects in your sentence, you call the second one **subject of the infinitive**. In English you can sometimes construct these with two obvious clauses, exchanging the infinitive complement for a **that**-clause. Parsing the above ones you get:

   e. Larry convinced [me] {that I should dive into the pool}.

   f. Sarah persuaded [Harold] {that he should give her a lift}.

3. The subject of the infinitive is serving two overlapping purposes at once. It is both the direct object of the first verb (convince, persuade) and the "subject" (controller) of the second (dive, give). This is why the subject of the infinitive has the same form of pronoun as the direct object, namely, **me** and not **I,** more on which in Chapter 11. The constructions are **me to dive** with the infinitive but **(that) I should dive** when you have two obvious clauses.

4. Some English verbs do not readily accept the "two-clause" paraphrase, or if they do,they sound awkward or old-fashioned. How do you feel about these:

    a. The mayor asked the city council **that they increase** the fines.

    b. Fanny begged the fireman **that they get** her cat down.

    Letter a. probably sounds vaguely "Biblical" to you, and you probably reject b. as an English sentence. Many languages insist that your sentences have as many distinct clauses as there are controllers. Others allow two-controller infinitive complements for the **convince** type of verb but require a separate clause for the **want** kind.

5. Some verbs can be either one- or two-controller.

    a. For example, **want**. You can say both, "He wants to psychoanalyze me," in which case **he** is the controller of both, and, "He wants **her** to psychoanalyze me," in which case **he** is doing the **wanting**, but **she** is doing--or will do--the **psychoanalyzing**.

    b. Recall Chapter 5, I.B.7.c and you will agree that **tell somebody to do something** is a two-controller verb. What about this:

        (1). "Herman, why aren't you mowing the lawn? I **told you to mow** the lawn."

        (2). "Herman, why aren't you mowing the lawn? I **said to mow** the lawn."

    Do you feel what happened? Who's doing the **saying** and who, the **mowing**? **Say** is very much like **tell**, as you will see at closer range in Chapter 20. Both are two-controller types, but **say** *prevents you from expressing the second controller*! It takes an infinitive complement, all right, but an incognito subject of that infinitive. Prove it: "I said {that **you** should mow [the lawn]}." So, despite appearances, **say** is a two-controller type.

C. These infinitive complements of one-controller verbs are themselves acting "noun-like" as direct objects of their verbs. Besides that, though, since infinitives are verbs, too, they can perfectly well have their own direct objects, if they are inherently transitive or predicate nouns or adjectives, if they are inherently copular. They can also be just plain intransitive. If you parse them on paper you could go blind trying to double-bracket and slash-bracket the object-within-the-object, as in:

1. She wants [to taste [my muffins]].

2. He wants [to appear /wealthy/].

so just think about what kinds of relationships you are expressing when you utter such sentences. If you parse such sentences on two levels you might find the relationships clearer, and your eyes will thank you, too:

3. One-controller: a. She wants ↓
She taste(s) [my muffins].

b. He wants ↓
He appear(s) /wealthy/.

4. Two-controller: a. Larry convinced [me] ↓
I dive into the pool.

b. Sarah persuaded [Harold] ↓
Harold give ⟨her⟩ [a lift].

D. One interesting peculiarity of these infinitives is the way they can answer questions or make assertions about an action:

1. "Why are you laughing?" "'Cuz I like to (laugh)."

2. "Do you play piano?" "Well, I've tried to (play)."

3. "Let's go out." "I'd like to (go), but I can't (go)."

As you might suspect, the reason for making a point of this obvious fact is that your new language might not have such an "infinitive introducer", so you would never have just a "part" of an infinitive in a sentence. It is already true of "semi-infinitives" without **to** after modals (**can, may, might, should**), cf. Section VII below.

E. **Infinitives and Tense**

1. The reason for calling these things **in-*fin*-itives** is that they are not bound (con-***fin*-ed**) to any tense reference or person agreement. But what about these:

   a. It is better **to have loved** and **(to have) lost** than never **to have loved** at all.

   b. She loves to travel. By next year she wants **to have seen** Kalamazoo and Oshkosh.

   c. Ugh! I seem **to have got up** on the wrong side of the bed this morning.

2. This is the so-called **perfect infinitive** because it involves the infinitive of the auxiliary **have** plus the **-ed** form of the main verb. It expresses an action which is physically in the "past" relative to some other action or circumstance and not the "past" of the speaker. More important than time reference, this form focuses on the action's being **completed** with respect to some other circumstance. In some languages, this is a separate form from the regular infinitive.

3. The same holds true for the **progressive infinitive**, e.g., **to be hyperventilating**. There is no time reference involved other than the one in the main-clause verb. The progressive infinitive--true to its nature of expressing something in progress **simultaneously** with another action--merely means "pure simultaneity," no matter when the scene takes place.

   a. "Tah, tah, I must **be going**."

   b. "Summer's coming. We'd best **be putting in** our peas, so they'll be up come fall.

   c. "Look at her: she's so lucky **to be studying** astrophysics!"

4. In some contexts, especially newspapers, the infinitive sounds "future-oriented." Actually, this usually happens in headlines when you leave out an auxiliary that tells you the tense, as in, "GERMANY TO RE-UNITE" in the sense of, "Germany **is going to** reunite," or "U.S. TO SCRAP ALL NUCLEAR WEAPONS!" in the sense of, "The U.S. **plans to** scrap all its weapons. . ."

F. Infinitives in English can also modify nouns the way adjectives do. They could be paraphrased as whole adjective clauses with a verb in one tense or the other. Not all languages permit infinitives to modify nouns like this, so beware:

1. This will be a **night** **to remember**.
   {which we will remember}.

2. The Wright Brothers were the first **people** **to fly** a plane.
   {who flew}

3. Last **one** **to climb** the tree is a rotten egg!
   {who climbs}

4. Lolla Palooza is a **dancer** **to be reckoned with**!
   {with whom one has to reckon}!

5. Water, water everywhere, and not a **drop** **to drink**.
   {that one can drink}.

G. **Purpose**

Connected with future-like feeling of the infinitive, as discussed just above in E.4, is the use of the infinitive to suggest **purpose**. You can be explicit about this by simply adding "in order to" to your sentence or "for the purpose of ---**ing**". Some languages require you to do that. Of course, you can also stretch out such **purposive infinitives** into a whole clause with "in order that. . ." or "so that . . ." Which of the infinitives in the following sentences feel "purposive", that is, which ones could you add "in order to" to?

1. We work to support our families.
2. What do you have to do to get a cup of coffee in this joint?
3. She persuaded me to co-sign her loan.
4. I co-signed her loan to get her out of debt.
5. The first one to cross the finish line gets the prize.
6. Robin Hood stole from the rich to give to the poor.
7. Now is the time for all good people to come to the aid of their party.
8. I send my kid to college to get an education.
9. My kid goes to college to get out of mowing the lawn.

If you felt you could paraphrase #1, 2, 4, 6, 8, and 9 with "in order to", good! You could further parphrase them with whole clauses, such as (1) "so that we can support our families", (2) "in order that you might get a cup of coffee", (4) "so that I could get her out of debt", and so on. Did you notice, by the way, how often such clauses have **modals** and **subjunctive**-like forms in them (see VII. and VIII., below)? No accident. More on this later.

H. **To Split or Not To Split?!**

1. This is one of those issues that make normative grammarians red in the face. The traditional rule says you must **never** put anything between a **to** and its plain verb, so the Star Trek slogan "**to boldly go where no one has gone before. . .**" is a grammatical blunder, according to the rule.

2. But is it such a sin to split an infinitive? Such a rule is probably the result of applying Latin grammar rules to English. (Recall that the assumption since the Middle Ages has been that Latin was a proper and "logical" language, and to model English after it was somehow good, even if it makes you go against your native intuition as an English speaker. In Latin the infinitive is a single word, and you could not split it if you tried.)

3. This issue has mostly to do with the place of adverbs. They usually come before the whole verb phrase including the infinitive-taking verb or after the whole infinitive phrase, cf. Chapter 7, IV.B. Different types of adverbs come in different places:

   a. I want you **to run** to the store **quickly.** (manner of running)

   b. We'd **seriously** like you **to consider** the matter. (comment on the whole idea: we are serious about wanting you to consider.)

   c. We'd like you **to consider** the matter **seriously.** (we want you to consider in a serious manner; don't just brush it off.)

4. Sometimes, though, it makes better sense to split an infinitive than not to split (than to not split it?!), and you can get a subtle difference in meaning.

   a. I want you **to quickly run** to the store.

      If you agree that this sounds all right, you will probably also agree that it means something slightly different from 3a., above, more like "I want you to do something that won't take a lot of your time and that I need to have done right away, namely, **to run** to the store. Whether you run slow or fast depends on you."

   b. We'd like you **to seriously consider** the matter. (We want you to show your seriousness by considering it?)

   c. The management wishes **to sincerely thank** the staff for their efforts. (not "thank in a sincere manner", but rather, "show sincerity by thanking?" Where else would you put **sincerely:** to thank the staff **sincerely**? That sounds even funnier. To say, "sincerely wishes to thank the staff" is better but still not great, since it means, "is sincere about wishing to thank. . ."

   d. The average listener will probably get the message no matter where you put **sincerely**, but again, you should know that adverb placement can be a problem and that splitting an infinitive is an issue in traditional grammar. You might modify the wrong thing and make a misleading statement. Fortunately, the differences will usually be subtle and most people won't notice. But check what your target language does.

VI. THE *-ING* AND *-ED* FORMS: PARTICIPLES AND GERUNDS

A. We know **-ING** and **-ED** as the verbal forms that combine with the auxiliary **be** to make progressive tenses, **is cooking, was defrosting**, on the one hand, and, with **have** to form perfect tenses **have cooked, has defrosted.**

1. Used alone, **-ING** refers either to the action in general or to a particular instance of the action. To make a long story short:

a. If it acts as a noun English grammar calls it a **gerund** or **verbal noun**:

(1). **Smoking** is bad for you.

(2). **Jogging** is not so great as it was once thought, either.

b. If it acts as an **adjective** it is called a **participle** or **verbal adjective**.

(1). A **smoking** chimney indicates that somebody is home.

(2). A **barking** dog never bites.

c. The **-ED** form is also an adjective, called the **passive participle**:

(1). **Smoked** salmon is called "lox".

(2). **Spoken** English is harder to learn than **written** English.

2. Many languages have forms with these names but they do not always work the same way. Transferring grammar terms from one language to another is sometimes handy and sometimes terribly misleading.

B. Gerunds

These are fairly easy to identify because they are subjects or objects of verbs or objects of prepositions. Most of the time they can be paraphrased by infinitives. Try these:

1. Subj.: **Playing** hooky is kid stuff! (To play hooky)
2. Pred.: Our job is **pleasing** our customers. (job is to please)
3. Dir. Obj.: Don't you just love **dancing**/ to dance?
4. Ind. Obj: She decidedto give **fencing** another chance.
5. Obj. of Prep.:

   (1). Are you sure **about taking** a right turn on red in this state?

   (2). What do you mean **by bringing** that disreputable thing home?

   (3). Thank you **for sharing** that cheery thought.

   An infinitive, despite all its other noun-like properties, cannot serve as object of a preposition. English makes you substitute this verbal noun instead. You can also supply a "bland" object for the preposition and modify it with a whole adjective clause, something like, "Are you sure **about the fact that** you cannot take a right turn on red?"

C. **Participles**, as adjectives formed from verbs, serve to modify nouns:

1. a **talking** horse 2. a **determining** factor 3. a **crying** baby

In such cases the **-ING** form is called the **present participle**, but present in the sense that it is merely **simultaneous with** the other actions in the context or a **potential action**. A **talking** horse need not be talking at the moment you describe it as such, for example, while a **crying** baby probably is really crying. Paraphrase them as "a horse that **can** talk" or "a baby that **is** crying."

2. Some verbs can take either the infinitive or the participle (gerund?). Do you feel a difference?

a. Participle only: (1). Stop **yelling!**

(2). Keep **walking.**

(3). Quit **complaining.**

(4). Finish **eating.**

b. Infinitive only: (1). We decided **to make** a run for it.

(2). They managed **to keep** the secret.

c. Either: Start **running/to run.**

3. Verbs of **perception**--like **see** and **hear**--take either the participle or the **plain** form. The difference is that the participle gives the accompanying action as a process, and the plain form gives it as either a process or a single event:

   a. We saw you two **smooch** (one peck)
      smooching (really going at it. . .)

   b. Didn't you hear me **call ?!** (a single call)
      calling?! (over and over)

   c. (1). "Hey, Rocky, watch me **pull** a rabbit out of my hat."
      (B.W. Moose, T.V., ca, early 1960's)

      (2). "I can't watch you **pulling** rabbits out of hats when Boris and Natasha are on the loose!" (R.J. Squirrel, ditto.)

D. **Participle phrases.**

1. These **-ing** forms often give a kind of "accompanying circumstance" to the main clause. They tell of one thing that was going on at the same as another one. You can sometimes rephrase these participles as whole verbs.

   a. The king was in his counting house, **counting** out his money. (The king **was** in his counting house and **was counting**. . .)

b. We sat for hours, chatting about this and that. (**sat** and **chatted**)

2. Participles can also be like compressed whole clauses, that is, the subject of the main clause verb is usually the controller of the participle, as well. They often come at the beginning of sentences and modify the subject:

   a. **Coming** up over the hill, **they** saw the town in the distance.

   b. **Slurping** down her 6th cup of coffee, **she** realized she would not finish her paper tonight.

   They can be paraphrased by whole clauses with audible subjects:

   c. {As they came up over the hill} they saw the town in the distance.

   d. {While she was slurping down her 6th cup of coffee} she realized {(that) she would not finish her paper}.

3. **Does your participle dangle?**

   Here is another normative hobby horse: the **dangling participle!** This is what happens when you start off with one subject in mind in the participle phrase and by the time you get to the main clause you've switched things around so that the original subject isn't the subject anymore. English teachers hate these even more than split infinitives, and with some justification: the dangling participle makes the listener fill in a logical gap. How often do you catch yourself saying or writing things like:

   a. **Coming** up over the hill, **the town** loomed large in the distance.

   b. **Slurping** down her 6th cup of coffee, **the paper** seemed like it would never get done.

   Is the problem clear? It's not the **town** that came up over the hill, nor was it the **paper** that slurped down her (sic!) coffee. If such a sentence is part of longer narrative, most listeners have no difficulty filling in that gap with some subject they identify elsewhere in the context. That is, the good listener wiill hear this "dangling" participle and mentally "undangle" it, converting it to a full clause so that it is clear "to whom" the town loomed large. Just know that it is a common phenomenon, but it is not considered good style.

E. Absolute Phrases

These are another variation on the participle phrase theme, though they are not too common in English. An absolute phrase has a subject *different* from that of the main clause, and its verb is a participle. Examples:

1. We'll go for a picnic on Sunday, **weather permitting.**

2. You'll ace the exam, **God willing.**

3. **It being** morning, the fog was rather thick.

Clearly you can expand these into full adverbial clauses with fully tensed verbs: **if weather permits, if God wills it, since it was morning**. Some languages have special forms for this kind of construction.

F. The -ED Participle

There is a section on the **passive voice** coming up in Section IX below, so it is enough to say for now that the participle formed with **-ed** (also a few with **-t, -n**) is also a **verbal adjective**, but it produces an adjective that describes **results of actions**, rather than actions themselves. All that you have just read about active participle constructions applies to passive ones, too.

1. Modifying a noun: a **torn** shirt, a **wrecked** car, a **depressed** area.

2. After verbs: We've got you **licked**!
(a sort of 2-stage predicate adjective, cf. Chapter 4, I.C.3.)

3. Perception: They saw us **pulled over** by the the cops.

4. Phrases: **Startled** by the knock, **Andrew** dropped his cup.

5. Dangling **Startled** by the knock, Andrew's cup fell. (*GRR!*)

6. Absolute: **Andrew startled** by the knock, **Harriet went** to answer the door instead.

This last one is more literary than spoken. In speech you would probably expand it to a full clause, **Since Andrew was startled by the knock, Harriet went to answer the door.** Another option is to make two main clauses: **Andrew was startled by the knock, so Harriet went. . .**

G. Is it possible to distinguish a participle from a gerund? Usually, yes, but you have to keep your grammatical wits about you. Look at this classic contrast. The singular/plural agreement of the verb is normally the clue, but when that agreement is blurred--as with the modal verbs with no **-s** ending--you can interpret the sentence either way, depending on what you mean. You can paraphrase a gerund with an infinitive and a participle, with a whole adjective clause:

1. Gerund: Flying is /dangerous/. (To fly is. . .)

2. Ger. + Dir. Obj.: Flying [planes] is /dangerous/. (To fly planes is. . .)

3. Participle: Flying planes are /dangerous/. (Planes that fly are)

4. Ambiguous: Flying planes can be dangerous. →

   a. Participle: Flying planes can be /dangerous/. (Planes that fly)

   b. Gerund: Flying [planes] can be /dangerous/. (To fly planes)

VII. MODAL VERBS. (rhymes with total!)

While tense forms tend to mean actions that are narrated based on some kind of observation, there is a small list of verbs which have to do with "potential action" which you cannot see at any given moment: **can, must, may, might,** for sure, and also **will, would, should, could**, as discussed in relation to tenses above. These are the **modals**, also called **modal auxiliaries**.

A. They are called sometimes "defective" verbs for four reasons (cf. Chapter 8, Part 1, III.C.2):

1. They take no endings:

a. no **-s** ending in the present: **he can, she might, it may.**

b. no **-ing**, so no present participle.

c. no **-ed**, so no past participle.

2. They neither form nor take an infinitive: ***to can, to might** do not exist and the verb that follows them does not have "**to.**"
can go, must run, may enter, might rain, will decide.

3. They cannot follow another modal or auxiliary, so they can not form a future or a perfect (cf. also 1c.). ***I will can go** has to be paraphrased, "I will **be able to** go." Also ***He has canned**. .." has to be, "**He has been able to**. . ."

4. The connection between their present and past tense forms is not obvious: **can-could** is almost recognizable as a present-past pair, but what about **may-might, will-would, shall-should**? (**Must** was originally a past form, too, though for us it means present. Notice that it has no pair.)

B. One consequence of this is that in answering questions with a following verb, you need only answer with the modal:

1. "Can you go?" "No, I can't."; "Must you leave?" "Yes, I must!", etc. This makes them look like auxiliaries, cf. "Has he gone?" "Yes, he has." They are, in a way. The difference is that "auxiliary" is a function that the otherwise independent verbs--**have, do, be**--fulfill. Modals are only modals and do not stand independently as a main verb. They shade the meaning of the following infinitive-like construction.

2. The modals followed by plain verb without **to** all have paraphrases that do take a regular infinitive. Do you feel any difference in meaning or style between the modal type and the modal-replacement?

can go	→	be able to go
must run	→	have to run
may enter	→	likely to/have permission to enter
might rain	→	liable to rain
will decide	→	want to decide? (questionable)

3. **A note on sound vs. spelling:** In normal speech the **to** becomes part of the word it follows. You hear only one **t**-sound, not two, and an "uh" vowel. This is not "sloppy" or "slurring" speech, but a natural and regular sound process.

   a. In informal writing, as in comic strips or dialogue in novels, some normally infinitive-taking verbs and modals are allowed the luxury of representing in spelling the way these things actually sound.

want to	→	wanna
got to	→	gotta
ought to	→	oughta
going to	→	gonna

   b. These spellings are usually put into the mouths of children, tough guys, or uneducated people, as if to show how crude they are. Bad news: we *all* sound like that, but us educated city folks is snobs 'bout spellin'.

   c. Note that this only happens before infinitives and not with the preposition **to** meaning direction or destination.

   "I'm going **to the store** and I'm gonna spend lots of money."

   d. These look like "pseudo-modals." In a few generations **going to** and **gonna** might be recognized as separate things.

Note that **wanna** is probably not a good candidate for separate modal status. There is no **want to** phrase that comes with other than an infinitive. It cannot mean anything different. Not all such auxiliaries are spelled as they sound, either. You don't usually see **used to** written as **yoosta,** or **have to** as **hafta,** but they might eventually join the group, too.

4. What about **will**? Is it a modal or an auxiliary? It seems to straddle the fence. It leans more towards modal, though we made a big deal of calling it auxiliary in Chapter 8. A lot of the uses of the future tense that it forms refer more to the attitude toward or supposition about the action than to observed fact, so you could well ask if the future is, indeed, a real "tense." The forms of English grammar are telling you that the grammatical form called "future tense" has partly to do with time reference and partly to do with the "potentiality" that goes hand in hand with futuristic thought. It is one of the places in grammar where **tense, modality,** and **mood** all intersect.

C. What Do Modals Mean?

1. This is a very slippery topic, and we will mention only a few things about it. These are very tricky to learn in other languages, and if you translate them as words into your target language, you will sound silly. You need the concepts. For now it is useful to know just a few of the realms of meaning modals usually deal in. Several of the modal verbs can be ambiguous in some constructions but quite unambiguous in another construction. Look at these:

   a. The party **may** start at 7:00. (possibility or permission)

   b. The party **can** start at 7:00. (possibility or permission)

   c. The party **must** start at 7:00. (insistence or deduction)

   d. The party **should** start at 7:00. (opinion or deduction)

2. They can all be read at least two ways. It is hard to say exactly what the differences are and under what circumstances you would choose

one or the other. Here are a few suggestions, but they are only approximate. Use your own sense.

a. Permission vs. possibility.

(1). You can understand **may** as either **permission** or a **supposition**, a possibility you are not sure of or only guess at: "It may start at 7:00, or it may not. . ."

(2). You can also understand **can** as permission, but you can see it in the sense of an arbitrary possibility, as in, "The party's starting at 8:00? Well, it **can** start at 7:00 for all I care!"

(3). American English tends to use **can** for both possibility and permission and reserve **may** for possibility. Perhaps you were taught from earliest school age to say, "May I have a cookie," but you already knew perfectly well that, "Can I have a cookie" was just as good. The game Simon Says is probably the only place that everybody uses "May I?" for permission.

b. Judgment or assertion vs. deduction or assumption.

(1). In **must** you either impose an opinion or take an educated guess based on what you know about the party's planners or the fact that a special guest is scheduled to arrive at 7:30. It is similar to **ought to** and **have to**.

(2). With **should** you impose your opinion subtly, probably according to some outside criterion, so it may not be just your opinion. **Should** can also make an educated guess. (It feels a little "milder" than **must**.)

3. If you put them in the past you get only one of these readings, and permission is not one of them:

a. The party **may have started** at 7:00. → Supposition.

b. The party **can have started** at 7:00. → Conclusion.

c. The party **must have started** at 7:00. → Deduction.

d. The party **should have started** at 7:00. → Opinion.

4. This is enough to get a taste of how elusive these modals can be. Listen to people who are learning English and see how much trouble they have with these.

VIII. MOODS.

Verbal **mood** is traditionally defined as the form of the verb that gives the "speaker's attitude toward or commitment to the reality of the action of the verb." That is, instead of using a tense form to express the action as you observed it, you use a mood form to express what you would have liked to observe or whether you believe or approve of what you did observe or expect to observe. A lot of languages have special forms for these. English squeezes even more nuances out of its two basic forms, e.g., **look(s)/looked**.

A. The regular present and past tense forms, if you are discussing them in the context of moods, are called the **indícative mood**, assumedly because they "indicate" the state of the world as you see it or saw it. In grammar books for many languages you will encounter the terms like **present indicative** or **past indicative**. This is the same as good old **present** and **past tense.**

B. The **imperative**, which you worked on under the rubric of tense in Chapter 8, is actually a mood because there is no direct observation of action involved, but rather, your own input on what you would like to see. In Chapter 8 there were several types of wishing constructions related to the imperative. Many languages have separate forms for them and separate terms. They include:

   1. **Óptative**, the wishing mood: **May it be. . .**

   2. **Hórtative**, the 1st person imperative: **Let's go! Let me see. . .**

   3. **Jússive**, the 3rd-person imperative: **Let him go.**

C. Sometimes the **infinitive** is also called a mood because the action is expressed as potential or abstract and not as observed fact.

D. Subjunctive

Like the other moods, the subjunctive in English is not really a tense or a verb form. It is a special type of sentence construction that requires a perhaps odd-sounding combination of forms. (Some grammar traditions use the term **conjunctive** for the same thing.)

1. One type has to do with expressions of "desire", "volition", "conjecture", basically, your judgment of what ought to be but is not at the moment. These are all **that**-clauses with the plain form of the verb, regardless of person. You would never say **he go, you be, she put** in a main clause, but note these:

   a. It is time **that he go** home./ It is time **that he went** home.

   b. It was important **that you be** there early.

   c. It is appropriate/fitting **that we be** promoted.

   d. It was necessary **that she put** her foot down.

2. The tendency in American English is to replace this plain form with the full present tense, including the **-s** form for **he-she-it**, or with the phrase **should+plain**. Different speakers use different options.

   a. It is time **that he should go** home (?). (that he goes home?)

   b. It is fitting that **we should be** promoted.

3. In older writing, like from the end of the 19th century and even into the 20th, you often encounter such things in subordinate clauses with **if** and **although**. For most of us nowadays the process of replacing the plain form with the **-s** form is completely normal in this type of clause, even if not in the "it is time that we. . ." type construction.

   a. I shall go tomorrow even **if it rain.**

   b. He wishes to see you, **though it be** late.

4. The other type of construction termed "subjunctive" in English is what you have already learned to call **hypothetical conditions**, where

you use the form for plain past in the sense of a kind of future. (The one oddity here is that for the verb **be** you always use **were**, the form you normally think of as **plural**):

a. If **I were he/him** I'd accept that offer.

b. If **he were I/me** he'd be happier than a clam.

Of course, a lot of speakers of 20th century American English feel so uncomfortable about this apparent singular/plural clash that in normal speech and popular song you sing, "If **I was** a carpenter. . ."

(1). Whether this is right or wrong is debatable, though **were** is still expected in writing. It is clear that the distinction between "regular" and subjunctive sentences just is not part of people's language feeling. This does not mean that the English language is deteriorating, that people are "bastardizing" it, or that American civilization and democracy are on the brink of disaster, as the language purists would have us believe. In such constructions, the words "necessary, appropriate, important" already do the job of signalling attitude. That the verb form does not go out of its way to underscore that is no great tragedy!

(2). It is also an interesting question whether this variation is the influence of schooling, itself. We were all taught to say **I am** and not **I be; he was** and not **he were; he goes** and not **he go**, How ironic that teachers might have destroyed one of the very things they were trying to preserve!

IX. INTRODUCTION TO VOICE: ACTIVE VS. PASSIVE

A. As if all these tenses and moods weren't bad enough, the English verb, like most verb systems in the world, has yet another category of ways to express actions. This is called **voice**. That means you concentrate not just on the fact that there is a subject and an object, but also on the **point of view** from which you look at them in relation to the verbal action. Chapter 18, below, will deal with this more, but for now you have to recognize that verbs--specifically transitive verbs--come in two major varieties, called **active voice** and **passive voice**.

B. The term **active** is meant to conjure up a picture of the subject of the verb "doing" the action, as in **Geese fly. My brakes squeal. This ointment stings.**

C. This term **active** also applies, however, to states that it is hard to consider "active", as in, "You represent good in the community." or "Actions speak louder than words," or "My petunias grow faster than yours."

D. **Passive** means that the subject of the sentence is not the doer of the action, but rather the receiver of the action. (Sounds kinda like direct object, doesn't it? More on this in Chapter 18.). You may or may not mention the actual doer in the same sentence, but at least the subject does not "do" anything.

1. Now that you are versed in the ways of participles, cf. 9.V.B. above, you cansay that you form the passive with the auxiliary **be** and the **-ED** participle, which in addition to being the **past participle** now acquires the nickname **passive participle**.

2. Given that the auxiliary **be** can run through the tense-form gauntlet of Chapter 8.1, II, the passive gives you familiar combinations in all those tenses. You might encounter these terms, but you can create them yourself as the need arises, too.

   a. Present Passive: I am disgusted

   b. Past Passive: They were mistaken for lawyers.

   c. Perfect Passive: The law has been passed.

   d. Pres. Progr. Pss.: She is being rewarded.

   e. Past Progr. Pss.: Their car was being towed.

   f. Passive Infinitive: Who wants to be served first?

3. If you also want to express the actor, you normally do it in a **by**-phrase, but you still have regular **subject-verb** order. You describe the same reality from the point fo view of the "do-er" in the active and of the "do-ee" in the passive.

a. Jane declared [the meeting] /adjourned/ →
b. The meeting was declared adjourned **by Jane.**

While a. is a statement about **Jane**, b. is a statement about **the meeting**. It would be just as good a sentence whether you mentioned **Jane** or not.

4. Naturally you have to watch for the entire verb phrase, since **be** itself is not a passive. (It is not really "active" either, but if a grammar has to choose between the two, active is the broader term):

   a. We **have been** there several times and **have** always **been pleased**.

   b. She **was** a good leader and **was** even **considered** presidential material.

5. Compare the following pairs of sentences. The same items are involved in both, but the relationship between them is different. In some you do not need a **by**-phrase, and others sound incomplete without one:

   a. Act: Ivory Soap **has brought** you this program.
   Psv: This program **has been brought** to you by Ivory Soap.

   b. Act: The sponsor **has cancelled** this concert.
   Psv: The concert **has been cancelled** (by the sponsor).

   c. Act: The president wants Congress **to pass** this bill.
   Psv: The president wants this bill **to be passed** (by Congress).

   d. Act: The committee **is carrying out** its plan.
   Psv: The committee's plan **is being carried out.**

   e. Act: Children, **dress** so we can leave in 5 minutes.
   Psv: Children, **be dressed** in 5 minutes so we can leave.

   f. Act: If you **elect** me, I **will clean up** this town!
   Psv: If I **am elected**, this town **will be cleaned up**.

   g. Act/Psv: **Has** it **created** you or **has** it **been created** (by you)?

6. So, in principle you can take a transitive active sentence and create the corresponding passive by

   a. making what was the direct object into the subject and

   b. expressing the actor as the object of the preposition **by**.

7. Whether it is good or desirable to use passive forms is a question for your sense of style and focus. Whether the two sentences really mean the same thing is a much more crucial question. Read newspapers and listen to newscasts closely and see how often, say, a White House source is quoted.

   a. Journalists and politicians can do this deliberately to absolve themselves of blame. School grammars often tell you to avoid the passive, apparently because it is better to take responsibility (actively) instead of just having things happen (passively).

   b. I was astounded one day when I asked a class what a passive was. The first response somebody offered was, "You're not supposed to use 'em." The assumption in this book is that English did not go through the trouble of evolving such complex constructions just so that students would learn to avoid them! The passive serves a purpose, and sometimes you have to use it because you do not have enough information to claim that "somebody did something," only that "something was done." In fact, looking for an "active" replacement is sometimes more difficult and produces a more awkward text than just using a passive, despite high school rules for "good" composition.

   c. Imagine a reporter covering a 2-car accident. She has to say, "Car-A collided with Car-B (active?), and Driver-B was killed (passive)." She cannot claim, "Driver-A killed Driver-B," and still keep her job or avoid a law suit. She does not even have the right to assume, say, "Car-A killed Driver-B." All we know is that, "Driver-B ended up dead," but that sounds very odd. See why passives are useful? Watch out for how your target language uses them. The norms might be quite different from English.

E. **Ending Sentences With Prepositions: Again!**

1. In Chapter 7, III.E. we discussed the normative ban on prepositions as things you should not end sentences with. There it was largely a question of relative clauses, as in the old cigarette commercial, "Taste (that is) worth fighting for." (You could add infinitive phrases, too: "You haven't got a leg **to stand on**.")

2. When you choose passive verbs over actives, you often force prepositions--and more often, **particles**--to be stranded at the end of the sentence. In normal English there is just no other way out. Essentially, besides making the former direct object of an active verb into the subject of a passive verb, English allows you to make a **prepositional object** into a subject of a passive.

3. Genuine preposition:

   a. Nobody's slept **in this bed** all night. →
   This bed hasn't been slept **in**.

   b. They talked **about that issue** at length. →
   That issue was talked **about** (at length).

   c. The enemy shot **at us** at point blank range. →
   We were **shot at** at point blank range.

4. Particles, not prepositions:

   a. He **hung out** the wash. →
   The wash was **hung out**.

   b. The committee **went over** the plan many times. →
   The plan was **gone over** many times.

   c. The coach **decided on** a new strategy. →
   A new strategy was **decided on.**

EXERCISE 9d.

ACTIVE OR PASSIVE?

Forget about tenses and moods for now. Simply underline the verb phrases in each clause of the following sentences and label them as Active or Passive. Nothing else.

1. _______ Once upon a midnight dreary, while I pondered weak and weary. . .

2. _______ Pearl Harbor was a nice place until it was bombed in 1941.

3. _______ The number you have reached has been disconnected.

4. ________ The delegation has greeted the proposal with enthusiasm.

5. ________ The delegation was greeted at the airport.

6. ________ Well, I've never been so humiliated in my entire life!

7. _______ Buy Swillwater Beer: it's swell 'cuz it's brewed with pure swill!

8. ______ The party that voted for the new tax was voted out of office.

9. ______ The meeting was scheduled for 2:00 but it will have to be changed.

10. _______ All the Perrier in the world comes from one spring, and it's bottled on the spot!

KEY TO 9c:

1. pondered-A	6. have been humiliated-P
2. was-A, was bombed-P	7. buy-A, is-A, is brewed-P
3. has been disconnected-P	8. voted-A, was voted-P
4. has greeted-A	9. was scheduled-P, to be changed-P
5. was greeted-P	10. comes-A, is bottled-P

E. GET ---ED!

1. English has another way to express passives--better to say, **semi-passives**--namely, with the verb **GET** and the passive participle. Such predicates as **get washed, get fixed, get written, get involved** feel awfully close to passives, but there is a subtle difference. In the sentence

   The funds **were distributed** to all branches of the company.

   you can imagine that the funds are already in the hands of the other branches. That is, the **be ---ed** passive refers to a **state or the result** of the process. You can imagine the process, itself, going on in the background, but it is not necessarily stated.

2. Now, in the very similar sentence

   The funds **got distributed** to all branches of the company.

   it is more likely that you envision the funds actually changing hands instead of sitting there already distributed. That is, the **"get ---ed semi-passive"** includes *both* the process *and* its result.

3. Some languages that distinguish these two types refer to the **be --ed** as the **state passive** (also **statal passive**) and to **get --ed** as the **process passive** (also **processual passive**). Since the **be**-passive suggests the process, anyway, you hardly feel any difference at all between it and the **get** type. Keep your ears open and decide for yourself. Under what circumstances would you say either of these:

   a. (1). I was fired.
      (2). I got fired.

   b. (1). She was offended.
      (2). She got offended.

   c. (1). The house was built (in 1826)
      (2). The house got built (in 2 months).

X. ASPECTS OF VERBAL ASPECT

A. This is far and away one of the stickiest topics in grammar and poses one of the greatest challenges to the language learner. As you saw in Chapter 8, verbs typically express time of the action relative to somebody's point of view. As you also guessed from the existence of progressives and perfects, the time the action occurred is not the only factor verb systems consider important, although it is the one we have all been taught to focus on since grade school and that foreign language textbooks seem to concentrate on.

B. One typical definition of verbal aspect as compared to tense is that while tense concentrates on ***when* the action took place**, aspect concentrates on ***how* that action took place or evolved in time**.

1. So, what we have been calling "progressive tense" is actually a "progressive aspect functioning within a tense." This is why you can have "plain present" and "progressive present" with no contradiction.The notion of the action "in progress in a certain situation" does not require the vantage point of a given speaker at a point in time. No matter when an action happens, anybody can imagine it "in progress." Only secondarily need you place it in time with respect to a certain observer.

2. Another kind of aspect is the type intimated in Chapter 8, Part 1, I.B. above. Some languages are very fussy about expressing **completion** or **completeness** of the action (knowing the whole course f the action from beginning to end, including all its effects) versus "plain ol' action" without stressing completeness, even if there was some tangible evidence of completion. The terms often associated with completeness vs. incompleteness are **perféctive aspect** vs. **imperféctive aspect.**

   a. This is often realized as a contrast between one-timeness or result versus repetition of the action. English has no form for this but the context of the sentence sometimes makes it clear.

   b. Take the examples in Chapter 8, Part 2, I.B.2, above. In **Columbus discovered America** you clearly have one act of discovery that yields a result. This could be called "past perfective." In **The Romans built aqueducts**, you know the building action yielded some result--you can still see them standing today!--but the thrust of such a sentence is to underscore the regularity and repetition of building. You could call this "past imperfective."

c. If you add some information, as in **The Romans built *these* aqueducts**, you have not changed the structure of the sentence, but you are pointing to specific tangible results of the building action. This is one way of expressing *perfective* aspect. (Russian is a famous example of this, and the verb in Russian has different forms for the verb **build** depending on whether you mean habit or tangible result. For a bit of consolation, you can imagine that Russian speakers, whose verb system has no progressive form, have just as tough a time learning to distinguish whether an action in English is progressive or not. We English speakers have no trouble and cannot imagine doing without it.)

3. Strictly speaking, the perfect forms, like **have arrived**, are not really one tense but two, because they deal with the factual "pastness" together with the relevant "presentness" of the action. Some people call this bridging of two physically and chronologically separate situations an aspect, too. The truth is, the term "aspect" is very broad, and in recent years lots of grammar people have come to use it whenever "tense" does not fit. It becomes a catch-all category.

C. The phenomenon we encountered in Chapter 7, III is also considered a kind of perfective aspect, and the aspect notion criss-crosses with the meaning of the verb word and the kind of action you expect it to name. When you say, "We **ate pizza**, " it is an activity. When you say, "We **ate *the* pizza**," none is left, that is, the action of **eating** has run its complete course and bears its evidence on the pizza. In addition, if you say, "We **ate up** the pizza," you are underscoring that you did a thorough job of it. So English can use articles and particles to get across what other languages express with different--perhaps, perfective or imperfective--verb forms. You need to develop a sense of what you expect a given verb to do.

a. You naturally expect some verbal actions to go on indefinitely, and you cannot actually "see" them happening: **live, think, hope, know, understand**. This is a kind of **imperfective** we called **state** in Chapter 7, or **stative verbs.**

b. Other actions that are clearly more "active" can also go on indefinitely, like **eat, drink, write, build, walk, talk**. If that's all they do--just "go on"--they are also **imperfectives**. You can call them **activities**.

c. If the same actions in b. naturally lead to something or bring about some expected change, they are **accomplishments**. If you **eat** or **drink** successfully, there will be no more pizza or Perrier. If you **write** or **build** successfully there will be marks on the paper or a 3-dimensional structure in your back yard. When you are engaged in the activity it is probably imperfective. When you "accomplish" the expected goal, you have a candidate for **perfective.**

d. Other verbs are the kind that happen all at once, in one fell swoop. The transition from one state to another is instantaneous and unstoppable, as in **burp, wink, hop** (if you mean each one once and not repeatedly), and more involved things like **reach the summit, cross the finish line, arrive in town**. This "all or nothing" action is called **achievement**.

e. So the four big categories of verb meanings are **state, activity, accomplishment** (the 'eat, build' kind), and **achievement** (the 'reach' kind). As you can imagine, other languages might be very sensitive about how they express these ideas. These four types criss-cross with the ideas of perfective and imperfective, but they are separate categories. You should not think that they are equivalents of each other.

f. English is already pretty subtle about activity vs. accomplishment. In fact you do not even see it in the verb, but only in the direct object. Compare **eat pizza** (activity) and **eat the pizza** (accomplishment.) Compare pairs of different verbs: **go to town** (activity) vs. **arrive in town** (achievement). On the notion that what **don't** say in language is just as important as what you **do** say, you can observe an interesting property of **state** verbs in English: even though you can form a **progressive** from them, you almost never have occasion to use it. You do not normally say,

***I am knowing her. *He is liking it. *Are you understanding me?**

D. Verbs like **start, begin; keep on, continue; finish** have to do by their nature with **phases** of an action, so they combine most naturally with activity verbs and also activities that lead to accomplishments, but not with states or achievements.

1. This is why you can say **start running, building** but it would never occur to you to say ***start knowing, arriving**

   Of course, you can say, "The guests have started arriving," but then you are talking about many arrivals of many guests, each of which is an individual achievement, and the plural subject masks that fact. If you did talk about a single achievement you would not say, *"I'll **start arriving** tomorrow" or, *"Oh, good: the train **is starting to arrive** at the station."

2. In similar fashion you can say **keep on reading, snarfing** (activity or accomplishment) but probably not ***keep on liking** (state).

3. And finally, we finish discussing this topic by reminding you that you can say **finish embroidering** but not ***finish living.**

CHAPTER 10

THE ADVENTURES OF NOUNS

After all that verb work, don't nouns deserve equal time?

I. NOUN COMPOUNDING

A. Nouns vs. Adjectives

Things are not always what they seem. Look back at Chapter 3 on parts of speech. Note that adjectives are supposed to precede nouns and denote some kind of quality or description.

1. But is everything that precedes a noun and describes or modifies it really an adjective? Consider these:

   a. **big** building, **old** building, **municipal** building

   b. **university** building.

2. All four of these boldfaced words do tell you about **building**. The dictionary would list the first 3 as adjectives and **university** as a noun only.

3. The truth is that practically any noun can precede another noun and create a phrase that means "a more specific kind of **building**" or "a subset of the class of **building**", so it seems to serve the same function as an adjective.

   a. "Adjective" as a class of words in English, then, is defined as much by its position (before the noun) as by its meaning.

   b. In the above examples, **big** and **old** are undeniably qualities. **Municipal**, on the other hand, is a "relation" more than a quality, because it means "related to or part of the machinery of a municipality".

c. Try to flip the adjective around into a predicate. Quality adjectives go there willingly. Relational adjectives put up a fight. You could point to a building and say, "That's big" or "That's old," but you wouldn't likely exclaim, "That's municipal!"

B. Noun-Adjective Contrasts

Look at the following sentences and the different ways you can and cannot rearrange them.

1. A **quality** adjective, e.g., **big**, gives a description. It can occur in different sentence arrangements: alone, together with its noun, or with the all-purpose word "one."

   a. This is a **big building.**

   b. This **building** is **big**

   c. This **building** is **a big one.**

2. A **relational** adjective, e.g., **municipal**, is English's way of relating two nouns, disguising one of them as an adjective. It tends to go with a noun and "one," but it does not occur alone in a predicate:

   a. This **building** is **municipal** (??)

   b. This **building** is **a municipal one** (?) (better, but still

   c. This **building** belongs **to the municipality**, in which case you see the connection between the noun and the adjective.

3. A clear-cut noun like **university** has to go with the modified noun or be replaced by a whole phrase:

   a. *This **building** is **university** (doesn't make it)

   b. **This building is a university one.** (??) (still weird!)

   c. This building belongs **to the university.** (reasonable)

4. Some grammar books might say that **university**, in such a case, is a noun "used as an adjective."

   a. That means they prefer to define part of speech based on position or function in a given sentence and not on general meaning of the word or its behavior in other types of sentences. You choose your own approach.

   b. It is, nonetheless, fair to say that noun phrases come in two basic types: those composed of **adjective + noun** (like **big building**) and those which are really **noun + noun** (like **university building**). These latter are sometimes called **noun compounds.**

   c. The upshot of all this for studying another language is that your new language might insist that nouns always remain nouns and that if you want to talk about one noun in terms of the other you have to change form or construction. So you could have, e.g., **big building** (A+N) but **building of-the-university** (N+Prep. phrase), as French does, or **university-ish building** (A+N, where the A is clearly "derived" from the original), as Russian does. English never really forces you to distinguish the two types, unless you want to paraphrase them as in 1.-3. above. If it did you would have to think about which modifier is a noun and which is an adjective.

C. Stress, Pause, Intonation

Noun compounds come in many varieties that show different kinds of relationships between their two nouns. Here are just a few. How many more can you come up with? Notice how you use your voice to pronounce these phrases. What part do you stréss? Can you pause ever-so-slightly between the first part and the second?

1. **Containers**, where the second N designates a container and the first N, the contents. This usually implies that the container is "**intended** for use" with the given substance. Listen to yourself say these:

   a. A **wáter bottle** is a bottle intended for water, whether or not water or anything else is in it at the moment. Note this is not the same as **bottle of water**, which does say there is water in it, whether or not the particular bottle is intended for water.

Likewise: **súgar bowl** vs. **bowl of sugar; wíne glass** vs. **glass of wine**, etc., though sometimes the two constructions refer to just about the same thing, as in **aír pocket** vs. **pocket of air; wínd bag** vs. **bág of wínd.** You pronounce them with stress on the **first N**, right?

2. **Materials, Composition,** even **Flavors: cotton shírt, linen jácket, iron fénce, paper nápkin, peach shérbet, veggie pízza**

   You could paraphrase these "shirt made of cotton", etc. Note that these are usually stressed on the **sécond** N.

3. **Function: hóle puncher, páper clip** (cp. with paper nápkin), **cán opener, cúrtain rod, bóok shelf, ring finger, trigger finger**

   You could paraphrase these "puncher for making holes", "clip for holding paper", "opener for cans", "finger for wearing ring," "finger for pulling trigger," etc. Note that you stress these on the **first** N. (Do you agree that the "containers" mentioned above are just a specific type of function? Could be.)

4. **Typical location,** also stressed on the first N:
   stréet musician, cóuch potato, bédbug, wáll poster, water buffalo, flagpole sitter

5. **Typical place (N_2) to find product or commodity (N_1):**
   gás station, búrger joint, T-shirt shop, cáttle ranch, dírt farm, récord store

EXERCISE 10a.

ADJECTIVE OR NOUN?

Label the following garden-variety noun phrases **A+N** or **N+N**, marking stréss on the first or second element. (Say them aloud in normal rhythm to determine which type is which. Confirm your diagnosis quickly below and with stress marks in the answer key on page 351.)

1. hungry cat __________
2. alley cat ________
3. busy street ________
4. city street ___________
5. school year______
6. exciting year _______
7. hot-fudge sundae______
8. fattening sundae___
9. efficient clerk______
10. government clerk____
11. TV program_____
12. computer program__
13. magnificent horse____
14. wonder horse____
15. beauty pageant ____
16. beautiful pageant_____
17. boring teacher____
18. history teacher ____
19. double bed___________
20. marriage bed_____
21. basement apartment _
22. luxurious apartment___
23. big spoon_______
24. soup spoon _______
25. block party__________
26. wild party_______
27. pen name_________
28. mellifluous name _____
29. famous painter____
30. house painter______
31. good president ______
32. bank president____
33. fluorescent lamp___
34. Tiffany lamp________
35. mushroom pizza___
36. spicy pizza_______

KEY TO 10a.:
A+N = 1, 3, 6, 8, 9, 13, 16, 17, 19, 22, 23, 26, 28, 29, 31, 33, 36
N+Ń = 4, 7, 10, 21, 34, 35
Ń+N = 2, 5, 11, 12, 14, 15, 18, 20, 24, 25, 27, 30, 32.

D. Notice what sometimes happens in spelling and stress:

1. **A+N** is two separate words, as in **big room, big spoon**. You pronounce each part with separate stress and possibly the tiniest pause between them: **bíg róom.**

   a. The noun may get the main stress, as in **big róom.**

   b. The adjective gets the mani stress only if you are *contrasting* it with another adjective:

      (1). Don't sleep in the líttle room. Take the bíg room.

      (2). "You take the hígh road and I'll take the lów road, and I'll be in Scotland 'afore ye. . ."

2. Compare with **N+N**: the two may be written together, and then you give one stress to the whole unit: **bédroom, téaspoon.** Often, writing the two as a single word is a visual tip-off that they are also stressed as a single word and mean something different from the two parts taken separately. This is especially true when an A+N phrase becomes, as it were, a single N.

   a. You will certainly agree that not every **blúe bírd** (A+N) is a **blúebird** (single noun).

   b. There are many **whíte hóuses** (A+N) but only one **Whíte House.** (acts like a single noun)

   c. Not every **Frénch téacher** (A+N) is a **Frénch teacher**

3. What if there is an adjective before a **N+N**. Does it modify the first **N** or the second? Take **big university building.** Does this mean:

   a. **[big university] building** = a building belonging to a big university?

   b. **big [university building]** = a big building belonging to a university?

   c. How about **big city boy**: Is **he** big or is the **city**?

d. In the Dr. Seuss classic, *Green Eggs and Ham,* is the **ham** green, too? These questions are often answered by the intonation and phrasing with which you speak such a combination, but in a written text it is not always obvious.

⇒ For as critical as stress and intonation are to speech and language, hardly any writing system for any language has a way of writing them consistently. When you read written language, you still have to "hear" it as you read.

5. Your new language may not create such predicaments. As mentioned above, it might make you literally transform a noun into an adjective by adding an ending or some other device. If that language has the phrase equivalent to, say, **housewife** you might have to restate it as **domestic woman** (which means something else in English-speaking culture), **housish person**, or something similar or an entirely different word or concept.

E. One way to keep track of which part does what is to think of these A+N and N+N phrases as having a "center" and things that surround and amplify it. You sometimes see the term **head** of the phrase and the things **dependent** on it. The head is the thing **modified** because it is modified by a **modifier**.

1. Symbolize this **modifier+modified** group as **[mr+md]** or **[dep+hd]** for **dependent+head**, if you like. This covers A+N and N+N in English, since N+N is always in the order [N_{mr}+N_{md}] or [N_{dep}+N_{hd}] Call them N_1+N_2, if you like. Then N_2 will be the head of the phrase (the modified), and N_1 will be the dependent (the modifier).

2. Languages differ in the order of these elements. English and German have [A+N] and [N_{mr}+N_{md}] compounds. Russian also has [A+N], but most often [N_{md}+N_{mr}] compounds. French and Spanish have [N+A] and [N_{md} of-N_{mr}] compounds.

F. Genitive Case

Of the so-called "case languages" mentioned in Chapter 4. VII., it is often the case that whatever case a clause requires the head-noun (N_{md}) of a phrase to be in are in, the dependent or modifier-noun (N_{mr}) is in the **genitive** case. This is especially true of the relationships discussed in C. above, where the modifier gives the material or function of the modified. The nearest English equivalent is the prepositional phrase with "of", even though English does not use that option much, as in special phrases like "a coat of armor," "a house of cards."

II. NUMBER: SINGULAR, PLURAL, DUAL

Number is a basic inflectional category of nouns. The usual terms are **singular, plural**, and **dual**.

A. **Singular** is the name of the form without the **-s**, the form you find in the dictionary. But that does not mean it refers to only one thing. It can refer to either **one or more than one** thing, while the form called **plural** refers only to **more than one**.

1. Take, for example, the generic use of the singular form in **The elephant is native to Africa**. Obviously you mean more than one elephant. You can also say, of course, **Elephants are native to Africa**.

2. In compound noun phrases (N_{dep}+N_{hd}) the dependent part is most often in the singular form, even if it refers to a plural in the real world:

   a. A **three-storey house** has three **storeys**.

   b. A 3.2-**liter** engine contains 3.2 **liters**.

   c. In a hundred-**meter** race you run a hundred **meters**.

   d. In a **record store** you buy **records**, but you go to the **records office** in a university to get you **record**! (There is some sense to this apparent chaos. Do you see it?)

3. In a few counting expressions you use the singular form even when you obviously mean plural, like after numbers. The normal plural

forms of **hundred, thousand, million** are **hundreds, thousands,** and **millions**, but only when they occur without specific numbers. The moment you literally count them, you have **two hundred, three thousand, four million**. Similarly, a cattle rancher can have **five hundred head** of cattle.

4. Some languages use only their singular form with numbers and their plural form only without numbers, the equivalent of **I like beans** alongside **I'd like 14 bean, please.** Since numbers already do the pluralizing, the form of the noun does not have to say so again.

B. Mass nouns are usually treated grammatically as singulars, even when they are collectives of single items, like **furniture**. If you use the plural form of a mass noun you probably mean different kinds of the mass: **the wines and cheeses of France.**

C. Some count nouns are only plural: **scissors, pants, clothes, jeans.**

1. You can individualize such "plural-only" nouns with a unit word like **pair**: **a pair of scissors, jeans, pants; a suit of clothes** or more likely not individualized, just **some clothes.**

2. There are several such words for individualizing or counting mass nouns. They go by the name of **classifiers**, and many nouns are very fussy about which one they get: an **ear** of corn, a **bail** of hay, a **head** of lettuce, a **clove** of garlic, a **sprig** of parsley. (Some of these classifier words ahve no other meaning or use in the whole English language.) Count nouns can have classifiers, too: a **gaggle** of geese, a **herd** of sheep, a **school** of fish. Some languages are notorious for having dozens of these specialized items.

D. **Special Plurals**

1. May languages have special forms of the plural for special meanings. The English pair **brother-brothers** is regular **singular-plural**. There is also a third form **brethren**. It refers to a group composed of individuals, but a group, the individual identities of whose members you have no intention of counting or establishing.This is called a **collective plural**. Hardly any other noun has separate plural and collective forms, but other candidates for collectives in English might

be: **shrubs, Venetian blinds, curtains**, even **bacteria, microbes.**

2. In addition to singular and plural some languages have a form called **dual**. This refers specifically to **two things**. The "classical" languages, e.g., Greek, Sanskrit, Arabic, are known for having these.

   a. This means that the "singular" form can refer to one or more than one; the "plural" form means more than one, and the "dual" form refers to "specifically more than one: the minimal amount that can be plural."

   b. English had special dual pronoun--"wit" for "we two"and "yit" for "you two"--alongside "we" (= more than two of us) and "you" (=more than two of you). Around 700 years the plural expanded to mean just "more than one." Other "dual" words in English are **both, a pair of, a couple of.**

III. NOUNS: COUNTS AND MASSES

In Chapter 3 you discovered the important difference between **count nouns,** which refer to individual items or groups of individual items, and **mass nouns,** which give a single indivisible entity. They act differently. Here is what English does:

A. **Count nouns** include things that you can imagine, whether concrete or abstract, such as

   1. individual items that you can also make plural like **table(s), chair(s), student(s), day(s), vacation(s), elephant(s)**, or

   2. a whole class of items of which each item is a member of the class, e.g., "The **table** is a useful piece of furniture," and you do not mean any one member of the set of tables in the world. This is the so-called **generic** use of count nouns.

B. **Mass nouns** are just that:

   1. indivisible wholes, often materials like **air, fire, water, oxygen, milk, wine, fur, mud**

2. abstracts like **thirst, peace, love, truth, beauty, art, resolve, unity.** Neither of these B-types is easily pluralizable. (You can say **fires, wines, loves, truths, arts**, but they mean something slightly different, more on which below.)

C. Some nouns can refer to either count or mass depending on whether you mean a single representative of a species or the idea or institution as a whole.

1. I like **radio** more than **television**. (mass)

2. I like **my radio** and **my television**. (count, the contraption, itself)

D. Simply put, count nouns represent a **set made of members**, while mass nouns are **their own set, their only member.** More on this in connection with **definiteness**, below.

IV. DEFINITE AND INDEFINITE: THE DETERMINERS

A. The **Articles**: **A, THE, Ø ("zero" article)**

The little words **A** and **THE** are called **articles** or **determiners**. According to traditional terminology, **THE** is the **definite article**, and **A** is the **indefinite article**.

1. These traditional terms are misleading because they do not always mean, "I know which one," or "I don't which one."

2. They can be an enormous problem in language description and learning, because it so hard to pin down what exactly they do mean and when exactly you use them. They are really a special-purpose adjective, but they mean something slightly different depending on whether they modify a count noun or a mass noun.

B. **THE** with a **count noun** means either of two things:

1. The noun is a **pre-identified member of a set**, that is, you and your audience know which item you mean. This is the idea of **definiteness**. This normally means that you or somebody else has already mentioned the item earlier in the conversation or in a previous conversation. So you could say that **THE** signals the **second mention** of an item in the context (and the first time you mention it, it

gets an **A**). Here is a mini-story illustrating the kind of "**A → THE**" switch you make thousands of times a day:

> "When I walked in she was reading **a book. The book** she was reading was a best seller, so I asked her if she was enjoying **the book.**"

2. The same word **THE** can also signal what seems to be the opposite meaning, namely, a count noun in a **generic** sense, and you assume that whoever you are talking with knows what one of the mentioned items is. That is, it can refer to every member of the set in equal measure. You do not have to have mentioned it before in your conversation because it is part of general knowledge:

   a. **The pen** is mightier than **the sword.**

   b. Today we will study **the ant. The ant** is a gregarious creature.

   c. **The elephant** is native to Africa and Asia.

   d. **The meek** shall inherit **the Earth**. (Are these the same use of **THE**?)

3. This notion of "general knowledge" is a very powerful factor in learning another language and culture. When you talk about particular things you have to assume that your audience knows at least what you know about their composition or other associations. If you buy **A** car, you know any car has **Ø**-wheels, **A** motor, etc., and that **A** class has **A** teacher in it.so even when you mention them the first time in the context they are still **THE**:

   a. I got a great new car. **The seats** are upholstered in polyester.

   b. "Are you taking **a** psych class this semester?" "Yeah, but **the prof.** is terrific."

C. **THE** with a **mass noun** refers not to any individuals--since there are none by definition--but rather to a **particular kind or manifestation of** the mass stuff, the way the mass appears at a given time and place. Mass nouns meant as masses usually have neither article. Since knowing when ***not*** to use **A** and **THE** is just as important in language structure as knowing when ***to*** use them, some people with a more positive outlook call this lack of article **zero-article**. We will write it "Ø-" (slashed-zero with hyphen, as in Ø-wheels in B.3 just above.

1. We had a lot of **Ø-rain** this year. vs. **The rain** did us good!

2. He exhibited great **Ø-strength.** vs. **The strength** he exhibited

3. **Ø-Water** is necessary for life. vs. Don't drink **the water** there!

D. The **indefinite article A** does not usually occur with mass nouns. With a count noun A also means two things:

1. The item is making its **first appearance** in the conversation or text, and you merely acknowledge it as a member of a set:

   a. Have you ever seen **a tiger**? This is **a tiger**. In fact, this is **the tiger** you saw in my slides. (See why *two* **a**'s?)

   b. I want **a girl** just like **the girl** that married dear old Dad.

2. Similarly to the generic idea of **the, a** with a count noun can also mean: "any member of the set individually, but you never know which one you really mean because you consider each member of the set equal to every other member of the set for the purpose at hand." Compare:

   a. **An elephant** eats Ø-grass.

   b. **An elephant** is approaching the camp.

   c. **The elephant** eats Ø-grass.

   d. **The elephant** is eating Ø-grass.

3. Do you feel the difference between the two types of A and THE? Do **a.** and **c.** feel generic and **b.** and **d.** feel like individuals? One of the ways English helps you decipher which A or THE you have to do with is by using verb tenses as indicators of generic vs. count.

   a. It is not a rule, but the **generic** tense type, namely the **plain form** of the verb (cf. Chapter 8), tends to co-occur in sentences where A and THE are used generically.

b. Similarly, the **identifiable individual** given by A and **THE** are compatible with the **progressive** forms, namely, the ones that give you a view of the action as **close-up**. Make sense?

4. It is also clear why mass nouns do not combine well with the article A. They usually use **zero article** (Ø). There are no individual members of the set. If you do use A with a mass noun you probably mean "a certain quantity of the potential whole, like a measure in terms of a container".

   a. **A beer** means **a glass** or **bottle of Ø**-beer.

   b. **A coffee** (if you use that expression) is **a cup of Ø**-coffee.

   c. **A sugar** is **a packet** or **teaspoon of Ø**-sugar.

   So when you ask for "two sugars, please," you do not mean, e.g., "cane" and "beet," but in another context, like biology class, if you talk about metabolizing "two sugars" you probably mean fructose and glucose.

5. A noun like **hamburger** can serve as both the mass and its related count, and you bring out that distinction very clearly by combining it with articles, including "zero" article:

   a. My turtle eats Ø-**hamburger**. (mass)

   b. I'd like **a hamburger**, please.
   (Individual: You assume there exists a set of burger-items, and you have not selected a particular one yet, but it does not matter which one. Any member of the set is as good as any other member of the set.)

   c. McDonnell's makes **a good hamburger** .
   (Generic: You also assume that a set exists, but you do not point out or try to select any particular member of the set.)

   d. Did you like **the hamburger**? (an established identity)

   e. Ketchup glorifies **the hamburger**. (generic: all the ones that exist are included, no matter whose)

f. Note that "Ketchup glorifies **a** hamburger" is also possible, but to make c. into *"McDonnell's makes **the** good hamburger" is pretty strange.

6. It is also worth mentioning phrases involving obvious count nouns with zero article:

   a. **in class, to class, after class, in bed, at work, around town.** (In British English you also have **in hospital, at table.**) These are sort of generic because they refer to the nouns as institutions, rather than as concrete entities.

   b. Compare these:

      (1). **Gotta go to class** with **Gotta go to a class**. Do you feel a difference? A clearer contrast might be:

      (2). There's a critter **in the bed** (so get out the Raid!) vs. There's a critter **in bed** (so be quiet and don't wake it.)

   c. Several expressions referring to time also have no article but are felt to be definite: **next year, last week,** which you could paraphrase to show its definiteness as **in the next year, during the last week.** Many languages say just that.

7. **Zero article** is typical in expressions like

   a. **a lot of** because what follows is either a singular mass noun like **a lot of Øair** or a plural count noun like **books**, which wouldn't have an A anyway. If you say **a lot of the books** you mean "a lot of the members of an established set of books."

   b. **what kind of** or **some sort of**, which is often followed by a singular count noun: **What kind of Ø-car did you get?** or a mass noun: **What kind of Ø-coffee is this?**

   c. A lot of people say **what kind of A car**. Grammar books say that A here is incorrect. From the perspective of this book, it is moe useful to point out that the two kinds of meaning conflict:

      (1). A speaks of a single member of a set.

(2). The expression **some kind of** has to refer to the entire potential set and not just a single member.

They just don't mix. It is possible that some speakers prefer the rhythm of **whatkínduva X.** Hard to say, but when speakers create variations of a supposed "norm", there is usually some basis in logic or feeling of analogy.

8. One more aspect of these articles is important to note: their use with proper nouns, especially when the proper noun has an adjective modifying it:

    a. **Proper nouns** (cf. Chapter 3.) are by definition "one of a kind," the only member of their set. This gives them a lot in common with mass nouns. When you call a person "John," a dog, "Fido," or a country, "Sleepyland," you do not refer to a whole set of such items. They are their only item, and they normally do not occur with articles or allow the plural ending. But you can combine proper nouns with articles to produce some interesting effects. Look at these:

    (1). I opened the door and in stumbled **a tired John**.

    (2). This isn't **the same Paris** I once loved.

    b. Sentences like these tell you that this obviously single item is being considered not as if it were one of many similar items, but as if it were composed of several aspects or had several faces. The expression **a tired John** does not ask you to look over the whole set of **Johns** and identify a tired one, but rather, it gives you a particular manifestation of **John**, whom you know to be a single-member set. Similarly in **the same Paris**, you aren't saying there are **many Parises,** but that Paris has many faces, whether over time or some other circumstance.

    c. Try this analogy on for size: It's sort of a question of the ordering of operations. With count nouns you consider each item like a wedge of pie and build up the whole pie out of the separate wedges. You consider proper nouns and masses a whole pie to start with, and then you have the option of slicing it into wedges, but you don't have to.

9. The big principle about **A** and **THE**, then, is that

   a. **A** establishes or seeks to establish an identification.

   b. **THE** assumes an identification or existence, either in the immediate context or in the broader world situation.

E. Three other kinds of markers indicate **definiteness** and if need be can be paraphrased with **THE**:

1. **Nouns with possessive pronouns,** namely,

   a. my-your-his-her-our-their-Jack**'s** book →

   b. **the** book **of** me-of you-of him-of her-of us-of them-of Jack, and some languages do say "the my book."

   Even though you would not say the b. type phrase, that's the sense of it. Some languages have only the latter option.

2. Nouns with the demonstrative **this-these, that-those**, understood as **the one pointed out.** So, **that book → the** book that I point out. (Some languages even say literally, "the that book."

3. **Proper nouns** are also inherently definite, with or without the article. They are by definition the only member of their set.

   a. Normally if you modify a proper noun with an adjective there is still no article: **wonderful Paris, beautiful Downtown Burbank, poor John, lucky Elmer!**

   b. Of course, proper nouns that *do* consist of sets *can* have articles. They are the ones that mean "a representative of a product made by such-and-such a company" or "item produced by such-and-such an artist": **a new Chevy, my old Jeep, that ol' Smith and Wesson, the priceless Picasso**

   c. A few place names have **THE** as part of their name: the Bronx, the Netherlands, the Philippines, the Ukraine, the Big Apple, The Hague.

d. If an adjective is involved, however, the article acts like a real article and not like part of the name: **the dear old Bronx, the monsoon-ravaged Philippines**, and not ***dear old the Bronx, *monsoon-ravaged the Philippines.**

4. Finally, the other group of words that is always definite is **personal pronouns** because, by definition, they always refer to something previously referred to. They are always "pre-identified":

   a. This is a good book. Have you read **it**? (= the book)

   b. Francesca's an OK kid, even if **she** is my little sister. (=that kid)

5. The "pronouns" for masses are **some** and **any**: "I got some popcorn. Want **some/any**?" The "pronoun" for an **in**definite count noun is **one**: "I have a couple of spare Superbowl tickets. Want **one**?"

F. The lesson you learn from this is that the traditional labels "definite article" and "indefinite article" are not really adequate to capture their whole essence. The differences between **A** and **THE**, as well as the specific vs. generic meanings of both, are sometimes very slippery and hard to pinpoint. What is fairly clear is that **THE** is, in a way, less definite than **A** in the sense that it gives you less information about the noun that is about to follow it:

1. **THE** might modify either a mass noun or a count noun.

   a. With a mass it gives the whole set (**the air**) and with a count it gives either the whole set or a single member of the set (**the elephant**).

   b. It can modify a singular or plural count (**the book, the books**).

2. **A** can modify **only a singular count**, that is, as soon as you hear it in a sentence you know that a singular count noun follows. It implies that there is a set of which you can determine the members and that you may or may not wish to determine a particular member.

3. It is worth noting that the **singular-plural** contrast typical of count nouns has a kind of parallel in the articles: **THE** is the same for both singular and plural, but think about the fact that the plural of **A** is

zero. You say **the book/s** but **a book/Ø-books**. (Sometimes you use **some** as the plural of A, more on which below.) In many languages you have one **THE** for singulars and another **THE** for plurals. Old English did this until about 1100 A.D. As it developed into Middle English, it decided one THE was enough.

G. Other languages that have articles may use them in different ways. They are among the subtlest, slipperiest things to learn in a language because of all the assumptions they make about the world the speaker of that language knows. English is like French, Spanish, and German in having both an indefinite and a definite article, as well as a "zero option," but that far from guarantees they use them the same way. Hebrew. for example, has only a definite article and zero. Russian and Latin have no articles at all, but they find other means of expressing what we call **definiteness-indefiniteness**.

V. QUANTIFIERS AND INTENSIFIERS

The articles **a** and **the** are concerned with **identity** of nouns. There are several groups of modifiers of nouns that talk about **quantity**, and sometimes both concepts are lumped together. That is, **quantifiers** assume there is a set of items or a mass of stuff.

A. **Some** and **Any**. These can modify either counts or masses. They act partly like articles and partly like quantifiers, depending on which kind of noun they are modifying.

1. With mass nouns they are quantifiers. They designate "part of the total possible mass": "Do you want **some tea, any tea**?"

2. With singular count nouns they are like articles. They refer to a single member of a total set but suggest that the choice is arbitrary or inconsequential. You can underscore that by adding "or other" or "at all": Buy me **some book** (or other), **any book** (at all).

3. In terms of sets and members, you might say that in order to use **some** you have to assume that a set exists.

   a. If the set is a mass it is its only member, so to quantify it means a part of the whole.

   b. If the set is a count, then it has individual members, any one of which is suitable for the purpose at hand.

4. **Any** suggests that the existence of the set is in question. Listen to how you ask question and make statements. It is often the case that with masses use **some** in positive statements and **any** in questions or negations. (Questions indicate that the existence is not established, and negations mean that there is, indeed, no set. You can ask the question with **any** and answer with **some.**

   a. In the following mini-dialogue, either of the questions is very natural, but only one of the positive and one of the negative answers works:

   Q: Do you want **any tea?** or Do you want **some tea?**
   +A: Yes, I'd like **some tea.**
   -A: No, I don't want **any** tea.

   To answer, "Yes, I'd like **any** tea," or "No, I don't want **some** tea," would be very odd-souding.

   b. Of course you may not always be able to put your finger on what the difference is. Probably, when you say, **Do you want some tea?** you imply that you've already made it--namely, that the set of tea does, indeed, exist. When you say **Do you want any tea?** you may or may not have made it. (You probably say **some** if you've just made it and somebody drops in unexpectedly.)

   c. To have **any** in a positive answer probably makes your ears perk up to the role of **stréss**. You could give strong stress to **any**: "Yes, I'd like **ány** tea," in which case you would mean "any *kind* of tea." You probably leave the choice up to the server.

5. With plural count nouns **some** and **any** act much as they do with masses, that is, they refer to "an indeterminate number of individuals".

   (1). "Buy me **some peanuts** and Cracker Jack. . ."

   (2). I went to get **some bananas**, but they didn't have **any bananas**. (You assumed a set existed but you were wrong.)

B. **How Much is None?**

The "negative" counterparts of **some** and **any** are the quantifying adjective **no** and the quantifying pronoun **none.**

1. Some people say this means the absence of the thing, but it actually means **zero quantity**. Whether this is positive or negative in mathematical terms is an interesting question, but language seems to consider **zero** like any other number.

    a. I have **six** hot dogs and **no** buns.

    b. "I'm nobody. Who are you?" (E. Dickinson)

    c. "I got plenty o' nothin'. . ." (Porgy and Bess)

    d. You can even substitute the word "zero" in some styles of speech for both counts and masses: "Look, pal, I've got zero patience with you."

2. In English you have the choice between **no/none** and either **not any** (for masses or plural counts) or **not a, not one** (for singular counts). Logicians may argue over whether **They have no scruples** is the same as **They don't have any scruples**. Language treats them as almost entirely interchangeable. But you have to admit it would be pretty strange if you were asked, "Do you want **any** tea?" and you answered, "No, I want **no** tea," rather than, "I do**n't** want **any** tea." The same goes for, "This little piggy had roast beef, and this little piggy did**n't** have **any**. . ." There is no grammatical reason why, but someone learning English would have to be aware which one sounded normal and which sounded odd.

C. **Each, Every, the Whole/Entire, All (the).**

The first three of these apply to count nouns. **All** can go with masses and either singular or plural counts. But they overlap a lot and play sort of logical tag with each other. Here are just the barest guidelines.

1. Both **each** and **every** modify only singular count nouns. They have to do with **individual countables**, but beyond that it is not easy to characterize them. You might get the feeling that **each** is kind of "slow motion" or stopping on the individuals, while **every** may or

generalization, while **each** requires more attention to the items. Imagine saying, "I've read **every book** in this library, and **every/each one** was a greater pleasure than the last." You would be less likely to say, "I've read **each book** in this library.. ." unless there were some reason to stress their individuality. Not all languages make this kind of distinction.

2. You can usually restate **every book** as **all the books**, using a singular to represent a plural, cf. IV.A., above. This is not always possible, though. You cannot restate "I get goose bumps **every time** you say that" as ". . .**all the times** you say that. . ." As for the phrase **all books**--that is, without the definite article--it is questionable whether this is the same as **every book**. At least you can say that **all the**--*with* the definite article--can go with either masses or plural counts: **all the time** (in the world), **all the hours** (in the day).

3. Only a few singular counts can combine with plain **all**. They all (!) have to do with time measurement: **all year, all month, all week, all day**, but nothing smaller: ***all hour, all minute**. In this case you can paraphrase them with **the whole**. Here again, you play with the count/mass distinction, treating the singular countable **day** like an indivisible mass.

4. Pronouns can combine with **all**, too. While nouns can make phrases with or without **of**--**all the books, all of the books**--pronouns can go either before **all** or into an **of** phrase: **we all, you all, they all; all of us, all of you, all of them**, and only **all of me, all of it.**

D. Much. Many. More. A lot of (lots of).

1. **Much** modifies **masses**: much work, much money, much time, much beauty.

2. **Many** modifies plural **counts**: many projects, many dollars, many hours, many beauties (people)

3. You can replace both **much** and **many** with **a lot of/lots of**. Although **much** and **many** are sensitive to the count-mass distinction, **a lot of** is not:

a. a lot of time (mass) vs. a lot of hours (count); lots of food (mass) vs. lots of peanuts (count).

b. The difference is that **a lot of** or **lots of** tends to occur in informal speech, while **much, many** are typical of written language or more formal speech. That does not make one more correct than the other. Both are fine, but their implications are a little different. Some languages do not have this stylistic option.

4. The comparative degree for both **much** and **many** is **more**. That is, **more** goes with either masses or counts:

   more time vs. **more hours; more work** vs. **more projects.**

   Just as with **a lot of**, the quantifier word leaves the difference between mass and count up to the meaning of the noun itself. **More+singular noun** means "greater **amount** of X" and **more+plural** means "greater **number** of X's."

E. **Little, Few. A Little, A Few**

The choice between these two groups is also tied up with the mass-count distinction, and they have a built-in judgment call about the size or quantity of the noun.

1. **Little** and **a little** go with masses. The difference is that **a little** is just "small quantity" with no emotional overtones, but **little** sounds as if you wished the quantity were bigger, as you see from these situations:

   a. We have **a little money**. Let's go to the movies!

   b. We have **little** money. How can we go to the movies?!

2. **Few** and **a few** are the count-noun counterparts of **little** and **a little.**

   a. He has **a few friends** in Oshkosh. Let's go visit them.

   b. He has **few friends** because he is so hard to get along with.

3. There is no pair to **a lot of** for small quantities. (The only candidate might be **a bit of.**) That is, if you are dealing with a lot, you can get by without making an issue over whether it is count or mass. The noun alone will tell you. If you are dealing with "not a lot," however, you *must* mark it as count or mass with the appropriate quantifying modifier. Did you have any idea you could be so subtle?

4. The comparative of **little** and **a little** is **less**, that is, for masses. The comparative of **few** and **a few** is **fewer**, namely, for counts. This is why some brands of ice cream can promise you **25% fewer calories** and others can have **25% less fat**.

5. In spoken American English there is a tendency to throw out **fewer** and use **less** for both counts and masses. English teacher shudders at hearing this, but look at the sense behind the "mistake." You know that in the "big" direction, the comparative **more** has one form for both masses and counts. So you extend that principle in the "small" direction to make the two comparatives act alike. The mass-count distinguish is not hurt at all by this, since the following noun is by its own meaning either mass or count. In fact, the same person can switch between **less** and **fewer** and not even notice it: "This candy bar has **less calories** than that ice cream cone," and "My computer has **fewer bugs** than yours."

6. **What part of speech are these quantifiers?** They seem to act like adjectives in English because they come before nouns and modify them. (Of course, we learned our lesson about relying on that definition in I. of this chapter.) Some grammars call them **adverbs of quantity**.

   a. Whatever you call them you should be able to distinguish the *quantifier* **little** from the *adjective* **little**. Notice that the quantifier **little** goes with masses, but the adjective **little** works only with count nouns. Your target language probably has different words for these. The chart below contrasts noun phrases with and without determiners (**A, THE, Ø-**) and with adjective or noun modifiers. The point is that the sequence of words looks very similar, but you can see that the meanings are different.

QUANTIFIERS AND ADJECTIVES IN NOUN PHRASES

	little cardboard	**Quant +N**
a	little cardboard	**Quant +N**
a/the	little box	**Det. +A+N**
Ø/the	little boxes	**Ø/Det.+A+N's**
a/the	little yellow box	**Det. +A+A+N**
Ø/the	little yellow boxes	**Ø/Det.+A+A+N's**
a/the	little cardboard box	**Det. +A+N+N**
Ø/the	little cardboard boxes	**Ø/Det.+A+N+N's**

b. The comparative of the adjective **little**, by the way, is more likely **smaller** than **littler**. Ask yourself why it sounds perfectly normal to say, "Texas is smaller than Alaska," but very funny to say, "Texas is littler than Alaska." **Smaller** does not assume that the thing is "small," although it may be, while **littler** *does* assume that the thing *is* "little" to begin with.

F. **Enough** goes with either plural counts or singular masses: **enough air, enough books.**

G. Here is a chart for keeping track of which determiners and quantifier-modifiers go with which kinds of nouns. Notice how often plural counts and masses go together. As always, think of them more as "types of meaning", rather than words, because your target language will no doubt have different ways of expressing these meanings. (The nouns *air* and *lip* serve here as typical masses and counts, respectively, and were chosen only because they are short.)

MODIFIER AND MASS-COUNT REVIEW CHART

DETERMINER, QUANTIFER		MASS	PL. COUNT	SING. COUNT
the		*the air*	*the lips*	*the lip*
a				*a lip*
"Ø"		*(Ø) air*	*(Ø) lips*	
some	Quant:	*some air*	*some líps*	
	Det:		*sóme líps*	*sóme líp* (or other)
any	Quant:	*any áir*	*any líps*	
	Det:	*ány air*	*any lips*	*ány líp* (at all)
no		*no air*	*no lips*	(*no lip*)
much		*much air*		
many			*many lips*	
= a lot of		*a lot of air*	*a lot of lips*	
more		*more air*	*more lips*	
(a) little		*(a) little air*		
less		*less air*	*(less lips?)*	
(a) few			*(a) few lips*	
fewer			*fewer lips*	
enough		*enough air*	*enough lips*	

H. Intensifiers

You can modify quantifiers and adjectives of quality in terms of a range of **intensity**:

INTENSIFIED QUANTITIES	INTENSIFIED QUALITIES	
very much	**very** fat	**pretty** incredible
so little	**so** delicious	**rather** eccentric
too few	**too** sinful	**mighty** suspicious
this much	**this** tolerable	**real** good
that many	**that** magnificent	**powerful** hungry
quite (a) few	**quite** deliberate	**móst** invigorating
	right neighborly	**(a) most** restful. . .
	such (a) fine. ..	**what** (a) silly. . .
	so fine **a**. . .	**that** pristine **a** . . .

1. English grammar considers these adverbs, and most of them are not taught in school because they are too "informal," like **powerful.** The reason for making a point of them here is that they can catch the English speaking language learner off guard. Many languages have distinct words for these meanings, while English uses words that you might think of first as adjectives.

2. Some of these are reserved for quantifiers or predicate adjectives. In "**That many angels** can't dance on the head of a pin!" **that** is clearly an intensifier for the quantifier **many**. (It answers the question, "how many?")

3. In "**That merciful angel** of a judge waived my parking fine," **that** is a demonstrative for **angel**, just as **merciful** is an adjective for **angel**. You could still have a good sentence without **merciful**, but not without **that**. It answers the question, "which (merciful) angel?"

4. Furthermore, you if you wanted to intensify **merciful**, you could only do so in the predicate, and then it would answer the question, "How merciful was that judge?" "That judge waived my parking fine. She was **that merciful**," and you might even hold out your hands, spread with palms facing. (Leave aside for now the possibility of the quantifier with inserted indefinite article in "**That** merciful **an** angel would never charge you with contempt of court..."

5. The last five intensifiers in the chart--the ones with the article in parentheses--come only with a noun and cannot occur by themselves.

   a. If the noun is a mass there is no article: "**such/most** clear water." If it is a singular count, it gets the indefinite article, A: "**such an** upstanding citizen/ **a most** upstanding citizen" (not the superlative **the most** . . .) If it is a plural count it also gets the indefinite article, Ø: **such/moist** moist brownies (though "most moist" sounds like Madsion Avenue exploiting sound. (**Móst** in this use gets a big stréss.)

   b. **So** and **such a** are a pair based on whether or not the modified noun or pronoun appears in the phrase: "These brownies are **so moist/such moist ones**." You also get, "I have never baked **so** moist **a** brownie," but only in the singular.

6. It isinteresting that the quantifiers **some** and **any** cannot be intensified. You can say, "She has **very many** nice things," "She has **quite** nice things," and "She has **some** nice things," but you cannot say, "*She has **quite some** nice things." You have to switch to "**quite a few** nice things."

EXERCISE 10b.
COUNT THAT MASS!
Key: p. 351

Identify all the noun phrases in the following sentences by underlining them. Write below whether they are definite or indefinite. If it makes sense, try to add some designation of whether they are count or mass, generic or particular. (Some are borderline; others, just unclear, so don't bother.)

Example: The first flowers of spring are a wonderful sight.
def.-c indef. indef.-c

1. Go to the store and get eggs, butter, and flour.

2. Did you get the eggs, the butter, and the flour I asked for?

3. Next year we will take a much-needed vacation to sunny Spain.

4. Don't fire until you see the whites of their eyes.

5. This little piggy went to market; this little piggy ordered out for pizza.

6. Snickers will give you quick energy in school, at work, or at play.

7. The unit of currency in ancient Transylvania was the droplet.

8. A stitch in time saves nine.

EXERCISE 10c.

DEFINITENESS AND DIRECT OBJECTS

Key: p. 352

Definiteness and Direct Objects This is another sensitivity training exercise that combines two not usually combined categories: **definiteness/indefiniteness** of nouns and the function of that noun as a **direct object.** The reason for highlighting this particular combination is that several languages use a different form of a noun depending not only on whether it is serving as a direct object, but also on whether it si definite or indefinite in that function. (Hebrew and Turkish are examples. There is a similar phenomena in Russian involving the direct object of a negated verb. Spanish distinguishes a person--automatically definite--used as direct object from a non-person.) So in these sentences, underline all **indefinite direct objects once** and all **definite direct objects twice.** Nothing else.

Examples:

The weather in New England is really unstable. I can't stand unstable weather. Now, Bermuda has the nicest weather I've ever experienced.

Did you ever sell your old computer? I'm looking to buy a computer, but I don't think I can afford a new one.

1. Sally doesn't drink wimpy coffee, but she'll like Momma's sturdy brew.

2. Have you heard any good rumors lately? You must have heard the rumor about you-know-who. . .

3. Little Ms. Muffet sat on a tuffet, eating her curds and whey.

4. On the third day of Christmas my true love gave to me 3 French hens, 2 turtle doves, and a partridge in a pear tree.

5. I'll buy you anything: a car, a house, the Ritz.

6. You've made me a generous offer, perhaps the most generous offer of my life, but I can't accept such an offer.

7. You've made me very happy with your offer.

8. I'll give you one more chance. Don't blow the chance of a lifetime!

CHAPTER 11

ABOUT PRONOUNS AND SPEECH DYNAMICS

I. PERSONAL PRONOUNS

These little words are among the most fascinating in human language. There are several groups of pronouns for various functions, and they all have traditional names. Most of them come in pairs.

A. **I, we, you, he, she, it,** and **they** function as **subject of the verb.** Sometimes you see the term **subjective case.**

B. Their partners **me, us, you, him, her, it,** and **them** function as "everything that is not subject," namely, **direct** or **indirect object** of the verb, or **object of the preposition**. Sometimes you see the term **objective case**.

1. This is also the form that most American English speakers use for that stylistic see-saw called **predicate nominative** after **be**, more on which just below.

2. These non-subject pronouns are also the ones that can stand all alone as the one-word answer to questions like, "Who did that?" regardless of what the function of that pronoun would have been in a complete sentence. (Compare the answers, "Me" and "I did.")

3. Did you notice that **you** and **it** are in both the subject and non-subject sets? These two are "unpaired." The one form serves all functions.

C. There is another set of pronouns, paired with so-called **pronominal adjectives.** Earlier on in Chapter 3, II, IV. you saw these under the title of **possessive pronouns** and **possessive adjectives**. You sometimes encounter the term **possessive case**: **my/mine-your/s-our/s-their/s-her/s** and the unpaired **his, its.**

D. Most language textbooks rank these pronouns by number, more on which in II, below. Here are the subject and non-subject sets:

1st persons	→	**I-me, we-us**
2nd person	→	**you**
3rd persons	→	**he-him** **she-her** } **they-** **it** **them**

E. One more mention of the **predicate nominative** mentioned in B. above. Whether the answer to the question, "Who is at the door?" is "It is I" or "It is me" in 20th century American English is a question of stylistic appropriateness.

1. You might *write*, "It is I" in a formal essay or business letter and *say*, "It's me" (with the contraction) in normal speech, where it would even sound pretentious to say "It is I." You can also "mix" styles and say, "It is me" (without the contraction) but probably not, "It's I" (with the contraction).

2. In older literature and in poetry you get a contraction from the opposite side: "'Tis I." "'Twas the night before Christmas. . ."

3. When you learn another language it is important to notice all aspects of language, the norms for both speaking and writing. As for the pronoun functions we are distinguishing in this section, **predicate pronoun** in American speech comes under the general heading of "**non-subject**," high school teachers' admonitions notwithstanding.

F. Here is an interesting paradox about the **subject of the infinitive** (cf. Chapter 8, Part 2, V.E.4 and Chapter 9, V.B.2): the **subject** of the infinitive--in e.g., "He wants **her to run** for Congress"--is in the **objective** case. (Recall that this term represents the piggy-backing of two separate functions: the direct object of the main verb, hence the object form, and the subject--more precisely, **controller**, cf. Chapter 9, V.B.--of the verb in the **infinitive complement**.)

II. THE NOTION OF "GRAMMATICAL PERSON"

A. The 1st-2nd-3rd number scheme presented just above is really packed with information about relationships among people and the things and situations they talk about. All languages have these notions, but they apply them in very different ways. Each of these will receive more detailed attention below, but briefly put:

B. The 1st person is called **speaker**. The speaker designates her/himself by the word **I.**

C. The 2nd person is the person **spoken to**, also called the **addressee**. The speaker designates that person by the word **you.**

D. The 3rd person is the person, thing, or even general situation **spoken about** or **referred to**. But you cannot stop here. You (the 1st person) have to tell your addressee (the 2nd person) whether this 3rd "person" is a:

1. **human being**. And you have to take yet one more step, namely, whether that person is a

    a. **male person**, in which case you call it **he**, (more on which, below) or

    b. **female person**, in which case you call it **she**.

2. **thing**--which may or may not have a biological sex, but of which the sex is simply not an issue for the topic at hand--in which case, you call it **it**. This **it** also covers entire situations, as in, "My basement flooded after last night's downpour. **It** was a real bummer!" (**It** =*the fact that* my basement flooded, and you can also call the situation **that**.)

3. In biology, this **male, female, neither** trio is called **sex**. In grammar you are much better off, for many reasons, avoiding the term **sex** and using the terms **masculine, feminine,** and **neuter gender.** They are not the same. There is a lot of lively discussion these days on this topic. More below.

E. Who or What can get around gender?

1. The 1st and 2nd persons are assumed to be **human**, but the words for them do not distinguish gender.

2. The 3rd person centers on the distinction between **human** and **non-human**, sometimes called **animate/non-animate**. This allows you to include animals on the left side of the slash, instead of the right, as many languages do, and not all languages make further distinctions of gender within the animate group.

3. The pronouns **who** and **what** capture this basic **animate/non-animate** idea and leave questions of gender and number to other elements in the sentence. **Who** asks about humans. **What** asks about non-humans. This topic will return below.

F. Personal Pronouns in the Plural

When you make these pronouns plural they do not all act the same way.

1. **3rd person plural** means literally "multiple people or things spoken about or referred to." Any one or more of them can be within sight or earshot at the moment you speak of them, but they do not have to be. Schematically this is **"3rd pl. = 3rd+3rd (+3rd. . .)"** OR

they = **he+he, she+she, it+it** **he+she, he+it, she+it, he+she+it**

2. **2nd person plural** means literally "multiple persons spoken to" but there is a little difference. At least one of those persons has to be present when you speak, but the rest of the group may be present or may not be, that is, **2nd pl. = 2nd+2nd(s) or 2nd+3rd(s)** OR

you pl. = **you₁+you₂, you+he, you+she, you+it,** **you+they,** etc.

3. **1st person plural** is quite different from the others. It does *not* mean "multiple persons speaking." It means, rather, "plural group, **one of whom is the speaker**." There is still only one speaker, and the others may be present or not, so **1st pl.= 1st+2nd(s), 1st+3rd(s)**, or **1st+2nd(s)+3rd(s)** OR

we =	I+you, I+he, I+she, I+it, I+they
	I+you+he, I+you+she, I+you+it, I+you+they

III. DELVING DEEPER INTO GRAMMATICAL PERSONS AND SPEECH RELATIONS

A. Speech takes place at a certain point in time and space and involves at least two parties. It is not trivial to mention at this point--especially for you, the learner of another language and culture--that these two parties bring with them some or all of their status in society. They can confirm, magnify, belittle, or reject their own and each other's social standing. (We will deal with this under the title of "formality" below.) English does not have a grammatical way to do this, but many languages are very exacting about "who has the right to speak how to whom." This social choice affects a lot of grammatical processes, like pronouns, verb endings, and other agreements.

1. It will help if you envision people speaking and switching **speaker/spoken-to** roles. These two types of people--the 1st and 2nd persons--are called the **participants in the speech event**, since they have to be physically present in order for the addressee to receive the speaker's sound waves. Language puts a fence around these **participants** and creates an "in-group" and "out-group." Anyone outside the group who wants to understand the message has to assume the perspective of that "in-group."

2. Don't forget, human beings were speaking language for thousands of years before they came up with the idea of writing it down. (The oldest evidence of written language goes back only about 5,000 years.) So the notion of addressing an "assumed" audience, as you do in modern printing and video, is still based on a speaker-sender and an addressee-receiver.

3. You must distinguish 1st and 2nd person as a group from the 3rd persons. These are the **non-participants in the speech event**. They may be physically "there", and they may "receive" the message just as well as the addressee, but language will either include them or exclude them from membership in the group.

B. More on 1st Person

1. This is the **speaker**, the **creator** and **sender** of the speech message.

2. Literally, this is the physical being whose brain sets a pair of vocal chords in motion and causes air waves to vibrate and reach some other physical being's eardrums, where, assumedly, they get decoded and, hopefully, understood and, ideally, responded to. Seems pretty self-evident, but this littlest of words is mighty powerful.

3. The upshot of this phenomenon is that the speaker, as creator of the speech event, has the privilege of determining all sorts of relationships of time, space, and social standing as she or he sees them. Every other participant in the speech event has to assume the speaker's point of view for as long as that speaker is speaking. Of course, that point of reference--including relational words like **here** or **there, now** or **then**, and the idea of "tense," in general--literally shifts from person to person. Grammatical person is, therefore, known as a **shifter** category. Everybody else has to "follow the bouncing sound waves," as it were.

4. **Who is "we"?**

   a. The first person plural **we**, as you saw in II.F.3, above, can refer to a group that may or may not include the **addressee**. Imagine who is present and who is alluded to in these situations:

      (1). "Hey, Mikey (and Billy), are **we** goin' to the movies or messin' around on the docks?"

      → (All) addressee(s) present and included: **we** = 1st + 2nd(s).

      (2). "Honest, Mom, I was at the movies with Mikey (and Billy). **We** weren't messin' around on the docks!"

      → Addressee is excluded from the **we** group = 1st + 3rd(s).

   b. In the so-called **royal we** or **editorial we** you have a plural form referring to a single person. The speaker usually uses this form to emphasize his or her importance, actual or imagined. Sometimes you use the **we** form to absolve yourself of responsibility. You use language to appear to "hide out" in a larger group, as when you are alone in a room but answer the question, "Anybody in there?" with, "Nobody here but **us** chickens. . ." The audience knows you are included in the group, if, indeed, there is a group, but may not know whether you are in charge or just one of the crowd.

c. You can also bend and stretch the definition of "group including speaker" to refer to "group in which speaker is not an equal player but in which speaker is involved or of which speaker has important knowledge." This is actually a roundabout, ironic, sarcastic, or downright condescending way of saying **you** without pointing the finger or of sharing the responsibility with the addressee. In these cases the parties are often of different social status.

(1). Superior to Inferior: A parent can confront a child or children, "**We** were naughty in school today, weren't **we**?" Obviously the "speaker" is not part of the group, but it either softens or stiffens the accusation, depending on your tone of voice. For contrast, the baby sitter would not likely say to parents who were out an hour later than the sitter's bed time, "Hmm, **we** were out quite late tonight, weren't **we**. . .?"

(2). Inferior to Superior: The king's chamberlain asks, "And how are **we** today, Sire?"

C. **More on 2nd Person**

1. **You** is the **addressee**, the person **spoken to,** namely, the **intended receiver** of the speaker's message. This is the person who is also a **participant in the speech event**, the one the speaker selects for reception, decoding, and interpretation of those air waves that the speaker set a-quiver. The addressee may or may not want to be one, but the speaker does not consult with him or her or ask permission. This is one of the privileges of speakerhood in human language. 20th century English does not have a separate form of the singular and plural of this pronoun, though most languages you will study do. **You**, then, refers to:

a. person/s addressed within the speech event, face to face:

   (1). "Hey, Mikey, you comin' over after school?"

   (2). "Hey, Mikey and Shirl, you comin' over after school?"

b. persons addressed, not all of whom have to be present:

   "Hey, Mikey, when Shirl gets here, **you** wanna go out for a beer?"

c. Naturally, you can personify anything and make it a participant in the speech event, whether or not you expect it to respond. You can do this with the pronoun **you**, as well as with other grammatical forms, such as the **imperative** of the verb. The speaker, of course, can be his or her own addressee, as is the nature of soliloquy in literature:

   (1). "Rain, rain, go away. Come again another day. . ."

   (2). "Twinkle, twinkle , little star, how I wonder what you are."

   (3). "Out, out, damn spot!" (Mrs. Macbeth)

   (4). "C'mon, car, start! You can do it. It's only -20°. . ."

   (5). (After letting a secret slip out you scold yourself): "Great going, Charlie. Now what are you gonna do?!"

   (6). (You look in the mirror before making a big presentation): "Knock 'em dead, handsome!"

d. English **you** is unusual among languages in not having a separate plural form, given that it does have plural forms for **we** and **they**. This is a gap in the otherwise symmetrical pronoun pattern of standard English.

   (1). Historical note: up to about the 17th century, **you** used to have a singular-plural distinction for subject vs. non-subject: sg. **thou-thee**, pl. **ye-you**. This is why they sound so quaint or "Biblical" to us nowadays. (Don't forget, the King

James Bible hit the stands in 1611.) Among speakers of American English, the Quakers are still known for calling each other "thou", but otherwise it is restricted to addressing the Deity in prayers and hymns (and you write it with a capital T).

(2). In some areas of the eastern United States there are attempts in spoken language to fill in this singular-plural gap. Everyone considers **you** the singular and tries to create a plural from it.

(a). The form **y'all** (="you all"), typical of the southeast, is not just cute or folksy, but a genuine attempt to "regularize" the grammatical pattern. It is just not part of the standardized written language we are taught in school, but it is a perfectly reasonable grammatical response to physical reality.

(b). In parts of the urban northeast you hear **yooz, yooz-guys, you-guys,** and some variations on **you-ins: yunz, yinz.** Teachers probably consider these "low class", gruff, or uneducated, but here again, the speaker of that variety of English is just taking a cue from the **I-we, he-they, she-they** pattern and filling in the proportion **you-yooz**. It makes perfect sense, even all the way to using the "regular" noun pluralizer **-s** (which sounds like **-z** half the time, anyway).

D. **More on the 3rd Person**

This is the largest group of pronouns because their are millions of person/s, thing/s, or idea/s you can **speak about**, whether you acknowledge its/their physical presence or deliberately shut it/them out, regardless of whether it/they can actually hear you. They are the **non-participants in the speech event**.

1. This group is large because it makes distinctions the 1st and 2nd persons do not make, namely, **human/non-human**, as discussed in II.D-E., above, and in English and most of the languages of Europe and the Middle East, at least, **gender.**

2. The 3rd persons pronouns also have the broadest reference. You can use the forms called 3rd person even when you mean 2nd person and sometimes even 1st person. Some people "speak in the 3rd person." They mean **I**, of course, but they use language to put a buffer between their physical selves and the way they want their audience to think of them. They talk themselves from the "in-group" to the "out-group."

   a. Did you ever have a teacher or other authority figure who did this to sound sarcastic, pedantic, or guilt-tripping?

      "Now, Ms. Smith has tried to get you to do your homework, but she hasn't succeeded. . ."

   b. Parents do this in referring both to themselves and their children, usually with names instead of pronouns, but remember that all nouns--proper and common, mass and count--are by definition "3rd person", hence the verb form **is** in:

      "Daddy's going to put Jessica to bed now, OK?" (In normal adult speech you use 1st and 2nd persons: "*I*'m going to put *you* to bed. . .")

   c. Royalty seems to like to be spoken to in the 3rd person, instead of the 2nd, or with a mixture of 3rd and 2nd person forms, as in "**Has** *Your* Majesty finished his breakfast and would **he** like a bath now?"

   d. In some cultures, of course, you regularly use 3rd person forms instead of 1st persons as a sign of humility before your addressee. It is a way of allowing your addressee to feel "in control" of the "in-group," as in "Your humble servant requests an audience, Sire." The ambiguity of the 3rd person is that the speaker could be requesting for himself or, indeed, passing on a message from another "humble servant."

4. To the list of 3rd person pronouns you can add two sub-groups. They are all considered grammatically 3rd person singular, more on which in Chapter 12.

   a. **What** and **who**, as well as their adjective cousin **which**, with the suffix **-ever** introduce noun clauses:

(1). Dir. Obj.: Do [{**whatever** you want}].

(2). Subj.: {**Whoever** eats his/her spinach} gets [desert].

(3). Ind. Obj. The government will grant ⟨{**whichever** firm bids highest}⟩ [the prestigeous contract].

Grammar books sometimes call them "indefinite pronouns," but they are not so much "indefinite" as "non-committal" or "indifferent." It is not so important that, "I do not know what you want to do" in (1), but rather, "I do not *care* ."

b. The quantifiers **any-, some-, every-,** and **no-** plus the generalized person, **-one, -body,** or the generalized thing, **-thing** do not introduce subordinate clauses: "**Nothing** says 'loving' like **something** from the oven. . ." (T.V. commercial).

c. You can often paraphrase the noun-clause introducer set in terms of the quantifier set modified by a relative clause:

whoever = **anybody who** (eats spinach).
whatever = **anything (that)** you want.
whichever = **any company that** bids

d. Note, too, that the "3rd" persons can refer to "higher" persons, as well, if you consider that the answer to **who** can be **I, we, you**. (Since the answer to **what** is always a noun, it si automatically "3rd" person in the strict sense.

E. One very common use of all the plural pronouns **we, you, they** in English is to refer to a **generalized** group. In Chapter 16, below, we will discuss this as the **omnipersonal**. When you say, "**They** say it'll be a bad year for crops," or "**You** never know what twist of fate lies ahead of **you**," or "**We** are what **we** eat," do you know the specific members of the group these pronouns refer to?

F. You can now parlay the mini-chart in I.D. above into a more informative overview of the forms and their functions in normal language use:

SUBJECT/NON-SUBJECT PRONOUNS

		SING.	PL.
	1ST PRS: SPEAKER	I-me	we-us
PARTICIPANT IN SPEECH EVENT	2ND PRS: SPOKEN TO (ADDRESSEE)	you	
	(Formerly:	thou-thee	ye-you)
NON-PARTICIPANT IN SPEECH EVENT	3RD PRS: SPOKEN ABOUT		they-them
	+HUMAN		
	MSC.? FEM?	who-whom	
	MSC. (POSS. FEM):	he-him	
	FEM.:	she-her	
	-HUMAN (NEUTER):	it, what	

IV. MORE ON GENDER, HUMAN/NON-HUMAN, SOCIAL DISTANCE

A. Natural Gender and Grammatical Gender

1. English is very concerned about the gender distinction in the 3rd person singular, but it glosses right over it in the plural: **they-them** is truly gender-blind.

2. English **he-she** line up with so-called **natural gender**, that is, they correlate directly with the physical sex, male or female, of the referent. The term **neuter** for **it** is just a way of saying that sex is not a relevant issue for the item referred to, even if it has one, as when use **it** to refer to animals, "crowds" of people, etc.

3. Most of the languages of Europe and the Middle East exhibit so-called **grammatical gender**. This is really tricky. There is no good reason why English **table** is **it**, while in Russian and Hebrew **table** is referred to by the pronoun **he**, and in French **table** is **she**. Russian and French **land** is **she**, but German **land** is **it**. Sometimes there are historical and cultural reasons you can attribute this to, but your job as a language learner is to know the grammatical gender of a noun and the changes in the form of the adjectives and verbs that **agree** with it according to the consistencies of your target language.

4. Just for some perspective, if you think **he-she-it** is as natural as apple pie, in dozens of languages in the world there is only one "3rd person" with no gender specification at all: Hungarian, Finnish, Turkish, and Chinese make no gender distinctions in pronouns. What is important for their grammars is just 1st vs. 2nd vs. 3rd person, namely, the functions of **speaker-addressee-other**, but not gender within any person. But don't think their societies are any less or more aware of the sexes! They have words for "man, woman, male, female," and all kinds of sexed beings, but these are just not reflected in the grammatical forms of words. Grammar and culture are interconnected, to be sure, but not so directly as we might think.

5. The reason for stressing this is that sometimes you hear people accusing one language or another of being a "sexist language." That is absurd. People can be sexist or egalitarian regardless of the grammatical categories of their language.

   a. In French there are two gendered pronouns in the 3rd person, "masculine" **il** and "feminine" **elle**. You translate them "he" and "she", but since every noun in the language is one or the other--there is no "it"--to think of them as representing **male-female sex** is to do French a big injustice. It is no wonder that you will be aghast that **la victime** 'the victim (with the "feminine" article **la**)' looks like a "feminine" word, regardless of the sex of the actual person. This does not mean that all French think that women are vulnerable or that anyone who falls victim is somehow "weak" and, therefore, "feminine!"

   b. Similarly, in German there are three genders, as in English, but German assigns girls and children to the "neuter" class by giving them the neuter article **das** in **das Mädchen** 'the girl ' and **das Kind** 'the child'. This does not mean they think these creatures sexless. There are lots of other considerations for assigning a noun to one **gender class** or another, so if you are learning the language of such a society, you'd better grin and bear it until you get fluent enough to argue with those speakers on their own terms.

6. The whole notion of grammatical "gender" falls apart in language systems that class objects not according to sex--physical,

metaphorical, or fanciful--but such characteristics as "shape," "size," "texture," "function," and other criteria, each of which has a grammatical form, as in many East African or Native American languages.

7. If your new language has the same **he-she-it-they** pronouns as English, look a little closer at the way they are used: German and Russian also have these pronouns, but, English gender is "natural"--**he** and **she** are people, and **it** is "things"--while German and Russian gender is "grammatical": Russian **thirst** is **she; majority** is **it**, and **union** is **he**.

8. French and Spanish have only two genders, traditionally called masculine and feminine, based on the two forms of the definite article for nouns and the usual pronoun you use to refer to them. Hebrew and Arabic have the same two gender, but only in the pronouns, with only one definite article for all nouns. Dutch has one definite article for masculine-feminine together and another one for neuter nouns. (You might as well call them Democrat and Republican, except that the words for **man,woman** and related words do tend to be grammatically masculine and feminine, respectively.) However, unlike English, German, Dutch, and Russian, the plurals of French, Spanish, and Hebrew do keep that two-gender distinction in both singular and plural, so in both French and Hebrew **car** is **she**, and **book** is **he**. In the plural **cars** is **she's**, and **books** is **he's.** Arabic pulls a fast one: **he's** and **she's** are reserved for male and female **humans**, and otherwise the pronoun **she** covers both "feminine singular" and "all non-human plurals." So in Arabic, while in the singular **car** is **she** and **book** is **he**, in the plural **cars** is still **she**, and **books** is **she**, too!

7. If you think gender is a subdivision of the 3rd person only, just look at Hebrew and Arabic, where you have gender in the **2nd** person, too: **you-masc., you-fem.** in both singular and plural, that is, a different pronoun and verb form depending on whether you are talking to (1) Dan, (2) Sarah, (3) either 'Dan and Joe' or 'Dan and Sarah', and (4) Sarah and Miriam. Is this sexist above and beyond the call of duty? Why should you have to tell the person you are talking to whether you perceive her/him as masculine or feminine? At least for now, you have no choice. (Technology has made this

occasionally embarrassing, like on the phone, when you cannot see your addressee and cannot judge his/her gender by voice alone.)

B. **Gender in language vs. Sexism in society**

1. One of the biggest dilemmas for English in this age of equality of the sexes is how to get around the fact that **he** can also refer to "generic person." Equality-minded people take great offense at statements like, "Every partner in the firm logs **his** own hours." It feels as if there are no women partners in the firm, yet there is no "neutral" or "inclusive" pronoun. In writing, you can sneak by with **s/he** but that is a visual convenience that happens to work for the **subject** set of pronouns and has little to do with speech. (What about **his/him/her**?)

2. It is nonetheless true that in language after language the pronoun equivalent of **he** can refer to "human" without either making an issue of the male sex of that person or excluding female persons. The truth is, this usually happens only under special circumstances, like in proverbs: "**He** who laughs last laughs best." Do women's laughs not count? This merely indicates that **he** is the form that means "basic human," and **she** is the form that specifies female sex. To insist on specifying womanhood in every instance, even when sex is not at issue, is just as forced, as trying to equalize everybody all the time. Instead of making an issue out of saying absurd-sounding things like, "**He or she** who laughs last. . ." it would be more equal, in view of the lack of a dedicatedly non-sexed-but-human pronoun, to let **he** continue *not* to specify gender. Oh, well, we could also debate this for hours. Just be aware that it is not so black-and-white as you think. As far as language goes, **he vs. she** is more like "black-and/or-white vs. white only. . ." More in Chapter 12, II.

C. **WHO OR WHAT IS HUMAN OR NON-HUMAN?**

The pronoun **they** is one place in English grammar where you cannot express the gender distinction. Here is another.

1. When you ask questions or give information about people or things in relative clauses (cf. Chapter 6, II.) you discount gender and concentrate only on whether you are talking about a human or not. This is the essence of the pronoun **who**. It is the same form whether the answer to the question is masculine, feminine, singular, or plural.

And whatever the gender or number of the **antecedent** of **who** in a subordinate clause, it is still **who.**

a. Question: "Who's been sleeping in *my* bed?" (Daddy Bear)

b. Relative Clause: "People who live in glass houses. . ."

2. When you ask about things you use **what**, whether the answer is singular or plural. This is true at least for questions, but in relative clauses you use **that**. "**What** is making that noise?" "The things **that** go bump in the night."
3. In relative clauses in spoken English you can also blur the human/non-human distinction by using the relativizer **that** for both humans and non-humans: "the book **that** we read" and the old summer camp tune, "the boy **that** I marry will never be tall dark and handsome and 6-foot-3. . ." This is what is really going on behind the scenes in Chapter 6, II.D.4.c.

   a. In some parts of this country many speakers replace relative clause **that** with **what**. So, while the **who/what** distinction is important for questions, **what** is the general relativizer: "the car **what** we bought," "the folks **what** came to see us." It is the same rule about having two separate question words and only one relativizer, but **that** sounds "normal" and **what** sounds "folksy."

   b. Here again, Hollywood tends to put **what** in the mouths of "mountain men" or "hill folk." School books would never allow such a thing--could they prefer "valley" speech to "mountain speech?!"--but it does reflect a variety of English where speakers make **who** and **what** act alike in terms of the kinds of sentences you can make with them: the **who/what** or **animate/inanimate** distinction is valid in questions, but when you get to relative clauses, **what** takes over, and you leave the difference between animate and inanimate to the meaning of the word itself.

4. Now, if you ask a fellow human a question about him/herself, you can safely assume that the human knows s/he is a human, and you need not use th **who/what** distinction to determine that. This frees you to turn that already existing grammatical device in a slightly different direction. You can focus on intimate, close-up "personal-

related" or larger, more abstract "society-related" aspects of yourself, depending on the kind of answer you want. You can ask either:

a. "**Who** are you?", meaning identity. The answer is probably "Herman," "Eloise," "my brother's keeper," or "your new neighbor."

b. "**What** are you?", meaning membership in a group--usually ethnic, religious, political, or professional. The answer is "2nd generation Polish," "Lutheran," "Democrat," or "a dental hygienist."

D. Formality-Informality or Social Distance in the 2nd person

In many languages you have to be very careful about how you talk *to* people. Many foreign language textbooks teach this under the loose and misleading heading of **familiar** vs. **polite** or **informal** vs. **formal you**, but in many societies it is much more subtle, often a question of **the same or higher social status** vs. **the same or lower social status**. There can be a separate way of expressing, for example:

1. **you**, whom I:

   a. know, trust, or have some bond with

   b. am socially equal with or superior to

   c. do not know

   d. am socially inferior to

   e. am equal to but wish to keep my distance from

   f. defer to for these or other factors

2. For some languages, formality or distance are expressed through the form otherwise called **plural**. In French **tu-vous,** Russian **ty-vy**, or Turkish **sen-siz** the two pronouns signal singular and plural, respectively, of the a. and b. types. The same form used for plural, however, also means both singular and plural of the c., d., e., and f. types and has a plural verb form, besides.

3. In other languages, as in German, the 2nd singular-plural **du-ihr** are also of the a. and b. types. For the singular and plural of the c., d., e., and f. types they use only one pronoun: **Sie** (written with a capital

letter) which is actually a 3rd person pronoun, the same one as **sie** (small letter), which is for **she** and **they**! So, German "2nd pl." **ihr** is only partially the same as French "2nd pl." **vous**, and German expresses 2nd-person distance or deference with 3rd-person forms.

4. Polish, like German, express distance with 3rd person forms. For Polish this means the singular nouns **Pan** 'the Sir' and **Pani** 'the Ma'am', the plurals **Panowie** 'the Sirs', **Panie** 'the Ma'ams', and the special **Panstwo** for a mixed group, 'the Sirs-and-Ma'ams'. The 2nd persons **ty-vy** look exactly like the Russian, but they act like the German **du-ihr**.

5. Some languages have special pronouns used only for social distance or deference. Spanish has 2nd person singular-plural **tu-vosotros** for a. and b. and also 3rd person-looking singular-plural **Usted-Ustedes** for c., d., e., f. Dutch has 2nd person singular-plural **jij-jullie** for a., b. and just one all-purpose singular-plural **U** for c., d., e., f.

6. These are all pretty tame, as social distance marking systems go. Deciding who to consider equal or distant is one of the big issues in language learning, because you have to know the social structure of the society and the implications and possible dangers of overstepping your bounds. You can offend someone by assuming a familiarity you have no business assuming, and you can also appear stand-offish by using the formal form inappropriately. One of the touchiest issues in some languages is feeling when you can make the transition from formal to familiar forms. About the closest English speakers come to this quandry is deciding when to call their teachers, students, business associates, or parents' friends "Mr. and Mrs. Cleaver", "Uncle Ward and Aunt June", or just "Ward" and "June." Quite a big step for some people--in both directions: to call and accept being called. But they are all "you" with no other grammatical consequences like verb forms.

V. JUST BETWEEN YOU AND I. . .

A. Our elementary school teachers have done a great job of teaching us not to say, "**Me and my brother** love to tease our sister," but rather, "**My brother and I**. . ." There were two "good" reasons for this:

1. It is "wrong" to use **me** as subject. You would never use **me** by itself and say, *"**Me** loves to tease my sister," unless you were imitating baby talk or the kind of "primitive" speech that Hollywood producers used to put into the mouths of Asians, Africans, or Native Americans.

2. Grammar books consider it egotistical and bad form to put yourself first, so you should put the other person first in any event. This is why it was fine to say, "John went with **my brother and me**," since both **me** and **brother** are objects of **with**, but it is better to give **brother** first mention.

B. Now, you knew it felt perfectly natural to say **me and my brother**, that is, you somehow knew that English treats **single** subjects and objects slightly differently from **conjoined** subjects (of the form "X **and** Y").

1. The "anything but specifically subject" pronoun group--**me, us, him, her, them**--is the one that English **speech** prefers when an **and** is involved, regardless of the function.

2. **Written** English still prefers to preserve the identity of subject and object in all cases, so: John and I came down from Mt. Everest, and the reporters interviewed [John and me] and then wrote a feature **on John and me**."

3. Many American speakers have now understood this "correct" **my brother and I** as the *only* correct form, so they use it everywhere. It is like a fixed unit that moves around to any sentence function, whether subject or object. You hear more often than not, "Here, you come and sit **between my brother and I**." or "John went **with my brother and I** to the Springsteen concert." It is as if the notion of "subject" pronoun has expanded to include **single subject and either conjoined subject or conjoined object**.

   a. When you join two pronouns, rather than a noun and a pronoun, people are not sure which way to handle it, and you get variation:

      (1). Normal spoken: **Me and him** } are good friends.
      Normal written: **He and I**

(2). Normal spoken: They talk just **like he and I/him and I, me and him, him and me.**
Normal written: They talk just **like him and me.**

b. Both "John and me" and "John and I" are possible combinations in English. Each is correct in its proper place, but people have over-generalized the second one and started using it for functions it never had before. This is neither right nor wrong, just a development of 20th century American English. According to logic, since you don't say, **Me am going** and **Sit here with I**, you should also not change that just because there's an **and.**" But who said language had to be "logical?"

4. This **between you and I** type is the mirror image of the **"Me and him are going"** type. The written language tries to preserve the subject/non-subject distinction, but it feels so unnatural that people try to make **one conjoined form good for all occasions.**

   a. If they choose the "**and me**" type it makes conjoined subjects sound "bad" to teachers. If they choose the "**and I**" type, teachers will whince at your conjoined objects. They both make a certain amount of sense, and both involve some contradiction. Whichever you choose may depend on how loudly the teacher's "**he and I**" resounds in your head.

   b. Part of the problem may also be that **you**, which is so often one of the parts of the conjoined group, already blurs the subject/non-subject distinction. Just from hearing **you** you can't tell whether you are in the subject or the object. And of course, all the nouns in the language use the same form for all functions. No wonder there is confusion. Speakers have to make special accomodations for just a tiny handful of pronouns--and not even all of them! So sometimes they just throw in the towel. This does not mean English is falling apart, just cleaning out its cabinets a little.

C. Who is bigger than whom? Comparison and pronouns

1. Normal spoken English considers the comparative word **than** a preposition, so naturally you use the non-subject pronoun after it:

   a. She is smarter than **me**, but I am richer than **her**.

b. You like **her** more than **me**.

c. They talk about **him** more than (about) **her**.

2. Normal written English considers **than** a conjunction that connects two phrases **or** two clauses, and within each clause you have to distinguish subject and non-subject. If the compared-to item was subject of its clause, then you were to give the subject pronoun and supply the "understood" missing verb or preposition to yourself. This is why school teachers always insisted that you write:

   a. "She is smarter than **I**, but I am richer than **she**," meaning **than I am** and **than she is.**

   b. Noting that 1b. above is ambiguous in spoken language, you can straighten it out in written language and for the purposes of this book, illustrate it with underlining and brackets. (The "understood" parts are also subscripted:

      (1). You like [her] more than $_{\text{(you like)}}$ [me].

      (2). You like [her] more than I $_{\text{(like [her])}}$.

      (3). They talk **about him** more than $_{\text{(about)}}$ **me**.

      (4). They talk **about him** more than I $_{\text{(talk about him)}}$.

3. **Now, what about whom?**

In school book English, the pronoun **who** has a subject/non-subject pair, just like, **I-me, we-us, he-him**, etc., namely, **who-whom**. (The object form even ends in **-m** just like **him** and **them.**) There are, nonetheless, a few factors that contribute to the desire of speakers of 20th century American English to toss **whom** aside. (Do not feel bad if you do. It sounds odder to use it than not to use it.)

   a. In questions like, "Whom do you see?", you have a structure similar to the statement, "Who sees me?". It is as if your feeling that the subject should come first overtakes your knowledge that **whom** is the object of **see**. There is no other structure in a *main* clause where the direct object both comes first and has two different forms. So **whom** here is an isolated occurrence, and speakers discard what is perceived as excess grammatical baggage. "**Who** do you see?" is a perfectly normal sentence of spoken English.

b. By the same token, in a complex sentence (cf. Chapter 6, VI.A.2 above) like, "This is the guy **whom** we put in the State House?!" you also have the direct object before the subject verb of the subordinate clause. But you also have the option of replacing the relative **whom** with **that** and then dropping it, cf. Chapter 6, II.D., namely, "This is the guy we put in the State House?!" so why bother changing **who** to **whom** in the first place?

c. Unlike the difference between **he** and **him**, the difference between **who** and **whom** is felt to belong to a formal or literary style of English and not to normal speech. So, as we saw briefly above, some people just use **whom** anywhere in a mistaken attempt to sound fancy, serious, authoritative, on the hand, or to mock that attempt, on the other.

VI. PRONOUNS VS. CLAUSES

A. To use or not to use a pronoun?

English verbs give you information about past or non-past tense (look**ed** vs. look), and within the non-past tense they tell you whether the subject is 3rd singular or not (look vs. look**s**). That is all. English always requires its verbs to have a subject, whether a pronoun or a whole noun. Furthermore, you have to repeat the same subject pronoun just about every time you use a verb.

1. The same subject can operate over a series of verbs **in the same clause**, without being repeated

   a. My baby doll walks, talks, cries and wets.

   b. We bought a paper, sat down, and read it.

2. As soon as you cross over into **another clause**, you have to repeat the subject, even if each clause is very short. (This just proves that you have always known what clauses are, even if you were sure you didn't.) Observe the subordinate clauses in curly brackets. Each requires a subject:

   a. My baby doll cries {when she walks}.

   b. We sat down and read the paper {*that* we bought}.

3. About the only place English allows you to leave out a subject is where it is crystal clear from context who is who. This requires special circumstances, usually quick conversation, "telegraphic" notes, or even deliberate, slow, "laconic" narrative.

   a. you: "Hey, Harry, need a ride somewhere?" (=Do **you** need)

   b. I (slow): "Went to town today... Bought a new hat..."

   c. I (fast): "Race you to the top of the hill..." or "Gotta go!"

   d. it: "Ooo, nice day today!" for "**It** is /a nice day/."

B. A lot of languages have elaborate systems of verb conjugation. They encode all the information about person, gender, number, and sometimes other things right into the form of the verb. For some languages this makes the use of pronouns sometimes unnecessary. German and French have lots of distinct verb endings for persons, but you have to use pronouns anyway. Spanish, Russian, and Hebrew have person endings and *can* dispense with the pronoun sometimes, but not always.

1. A typical place that most languages do use pronouns is with **contrastive stress**, even if the verb form would still tell you the person:

   a. **You** may think you're going to take that last parking space, Buddy, but ***I*** know different!"

   b. **We** all have to pay taxes, but *he* thinks he can get away with murder. . .

2. Some languages do require their pronouns, but only sometimes. You may have to start off a sentence with some subject, but you may not have to repeat it, even in every different clause.

   a. Some languages make you use a 3rd person pronoun in a subordinate clause **if it is a different subject** from the 3rd person in the previous clause. In English you say,

      "Danny and Joe were discussing the movie. He said he liked it."

      It is not immediately clear, without more context, who spoke and who liked it.

   b. If your target language says something like,

      "Danny and Joe were discussing the movie. **He** said **liked** it."

      you would probably understand that **he** refers to Joe (the closest possible referent) and from the lack of subject for **like** you would assume that it is the same **he**, so **Joe** said that **Joe** liked the movie.

   c. In such a language if you say,

      "Danny and Joe were discussing the movie. He said **he** liked it."

      then you understand that **Joe** (the nearer) said that **Danny** (the farther back) liked it. Very subtle but very important. English cannot make that distinction, except by adding voice tone, and if circumstances permit, also pointing.

4. Within a context it is sometimes hard to keep track of which 3rd person you are talking about. Take, for example, **Danny and Joe were discussing the movie. He said he liked it but he didn't agree**. Normally, speech patterns will give you hints that the first **he** refers to the closer referent, namely, Joe. So the next **he** is assumed to skip over Joe and refer back to Danny, while the 3rd **he** takes its turn back to **Joe**, but you really need a scorecard.

NO EXERCISE 11

SECTION 3

THE LEAVES

SPECIAL ISSUES OF IMPORTANCE TO THE LANGUAGE LEARNER

12. AGREEMENT, DICTIONARY USE, INFLECTION, DERIVATION
13. RECOGNIZING PARALLEL CONSTRUCTIONS
14. SO, HOW DO YOU ASK QUESTIONS?
15. JUST SAY NO!!
16. DUMMIES, IMPERSONALS, OMNIPERSONALS
17. LOCATION vs. MOTION: WH-? TH-. H-.
18. "WHO DOES WHAT TO WHOM": MORE ON ENGLISH VERB TYPES
19. RELATIONS BETWEEN TIME AND ACTION: OBLIGATORY FOR, OPTIONAL (FOR), IN, WITHIN
20. FLEX UP YOUR LEXICON

CHAPTER 12

AGREEMENT, DICTIONARY USE, INFLECTION AND DERIVATION

I. AGREEMENT IN PERSON AND NUMBER

A. Once you have identified the person and number of pronouns, as you did in Chapter 11, that information will determine the form of the verb in the sentence.

1. In the English present tense, the verb adds an **-s** when the subject is **3rd person singular (he, she, it, who, what, somebody**, etc.). The verb so-called **agrees** with the subject:

    a. I, you, we, they → **look**

    b. he, she, it, who? what? (that) → **looks**

    c. The "s-less" form **look** is not really singular or plural and does not designate any person except **non-3rd-singular**. The only verb with person agreement is **be**, cf. Chapter 8, Part 1.

2. The past tense of the verb has only one all-purpose form that agrees with everything: **looked**. That is, while the present tense of the verb partially agrees with the subject in person and number, the past tense has no person and number agreement. (Again, the only verb in English that does have past-tense number agreement is **be: was-were.**)

    I-you-he-she-it-we-they-who?what? → **looked**

3. The humanness and gender of the subject do not play a role in subject-verb agreement, but in some languages they do. Verbs in English have **person-number agreement** but not **gender agreement**.

B. Other instances of agreement in English are quite scanty:

1. **Possessives**, cf. Chapter 3, II.B.2., agree in person with their possessors and, in the 3rd person singular, in gender, as well:

   I want **my** mommy!
   Mathilda wants **her** supper?
   Matthew wants **his** bottle.
   Everybody does **his-or-her** own thing. (More on this in a bit.)

2. **Demonstratives** agree in number: this/that book **is, was**
   these/those books **are, were**

3. **Adjectives** and **articles** show no grammatical agreement in English (unless you consider A to "agree" with singular nouns). Many languages change these for gender, number, and also case.

   a. Imagine if there were number agreement for all modifiers of nouns. You might say something like:

      (1). sg. 'dog': The big dog barked.

      (2). pl. 'dogs': Thes bigs dogs barkeds.

   b. One of the interesting things about English grammatical endings is that **-(e)s** on nouns signals plural, but on verbs it signals singular. Considering that there aren't too many endings in English to begin with, compared to many other languages, it is curious that English speakers over the centuries have not created some way of distinguishing the form, say, **ducks**, as a singular verb or a plural noun. Apparently, its behavior in a sentence is enough to tell: (1). The **ducks** swim in the pond. (pl. noun)
      vs. (2). The boxer **ducks** the punches (sg. verb).

C. Some kinds of number agreement can be confusing, especially when you deal with subordinate clauses. Take these:

1. a. This is the kind of **policy** {**that makes** the rich richer}.

   b. She is the kind of **person** {**who makes** us proud of our town}.

Here you have a two-stage or relay-race agreement. The singular verb **makes** in the subordinate clause agrees with the pronouns **that** and **who,** which in turn refer to the singulars **policy** and **person,** respectively.

2. a. These are the kinds of **policies that make** the rich richer.

   b. They are the kind of **people who make** us proud of our town.

   The plural verb **make** *also* agrees with **that** and **who,** which now refer to the plurals **policies** and **people**. **Who** as a question word has singular verb agreement ("Halt! Who **goes** there?"), but here as a relative clause introducer it refers to **people,** so the plural-ness takes over. (This is another place where it is important to keep in mind that the notion of **singular** really means "no specification of--but allowing for the possible reference to--more than one," cf. Chapter 10, II.)

3. Singulars and plurals can also trip over each other in other ways. (Of course, for English this is relevant only in the present tense.) Look at these:

   a. This is one of **those policies that make** the rich richer.

   b. She is one of **those people who make** us proud of our town.

   Should the verb agree with "one" or with the plural nouns? Which is really the subject? It is partly a question of restrictive and non-restrictive clauses (cf. Chapter 6, III.) and here you have restrictive clauses. What you mean, of course, is that every member of that particular class of "policy" makes the rich get richer, and every member of the class of "person" you are talking about makes us proud of our town. It is not "One who/that makes. . ." (This is a favorite "gotcha!" type question on standardized tests, by the way.)

4. Listen to what happens when the "real" subject comes *after* the verb:

   a. What we need here is some new laws!

   b. The one thing I can't stand is your bad habits.

You run into a clash of priorities. It is as if you assume that "what" and "the one thing" are singular subjects, but once you utter the whole sentence you realize that "laws" and "habits" are really the subjects, although that, too, is disputable from several points of view. By then it is too late: you already made the verb agree with the singulars. Which is right? Maybe in a. you could say, "What we need **are** some new laws," but no way could you accept, "The one thing I can't stand **are** your bad habits." The rules can lead you into some back alleys.

5. Here is a related phenomenon. Back in Chapter 10, II.A. you saw that the form called "singular" can take over the meaning of the plural in nouns. In a very few sentence types you get something similar in verbs. Listen to these "correct" sentences:

    a. (1). Where are my glasses?

        (2). Where is my coat?

    b. (1). There are nine planets in the solar system.

        (2). There is something we need to talk about.

    c. (1). Here are the files you requested, boss.

        (2). Here is my resignation.

6. Now make contractions. If you let your grammatical guard down, you'll hear yourself avoid the sound of "double r" in the contractions "where're, there're, here're". Go on: admit that you say, "Where's my glasses? There's nine planets in the solar system, "Here's the files." This is considered "wrong", but your only options are right forms but funny sound or wrong forms but better sound. Grammar is not just *correct forms*, but a whole range of considerations, including sound, especially if you feel that **here** and **there** are enough like singular nouns that you treat them as such.

7. Pronouns and relative clauses present one more instance of "awkward agreement." In 1. above we saw that the relativizers **who** and **that** took their number agreement from their **antecedent** in the preceding clause. How do you feel about these:

a. It is **I who am** responsible.

b. Is it **you who are supposed** to pick us up after work?

First of all, this kind of construction is sounds very stilted. Second of all, people are so uncomfortable with the sound of **who am**, etc., that they prefer to re-arrange the whole thing. More often you hear:

c. I am **the one who is** responsible.

d. Are you **the one who is** / **the ones who are** supposed to pick us up?

That is, they resort to a construction where there is no question that **who** refers to either the uncontestably singular **the one** or undeniably plural **the ones**.

D. Case Agreement

Implicit in the section on the Swedish movie back in Chapter 4, VII.B. is the idea that adjectives can agree with nouns not only in **gender** and **number**, but also in **case**. English happens not to do this, but you can imagine that a typical European case language will present you with things like **nominative feminine singular** or **accusative masculine plural** forms of the noun *and* adjective. So making a noun plural forces you to adjust the adjective, as well, and code its sentence function at the same time.

II. THE GENDER QUESTION, AGAIN!

A. Gender in English is a category that is expressed only in the pronouns of the 3rd person singular: **he** vs. **she** vs. **it**. The plural **they** does not express this distinction by separate forms.

B. In Chapter 11, III. we discussed briefly the notion of sexism in language. Some speakers of English and other "gender-languages" express outrage over the age-old fact that **he** is assumed to be the "normal" or "default" pronoun to refer to any person:

1. A baker has to work **his** head off to make a living.

2. Everybody does **his** thing.

3. On April 15th every tax payer thanks **his** lucky stars that the post offices stay open late.

It sounds as if there are only men in the world! The cultural bias is quite clear. But look what happens in proverbs like:

He who laughs last laughs best.

Does this refer only to men? Of course not. If a woman saw a sign, "He who enters here will be arrested," you can bet she would not assume that she is excluded (although it would make an interesting court case!). It is, nonetheless, upsetting to many people that the grammar of their language seems to include women only by implication. Even languages that have a **he-she** distinction in the singular have a plural of either **he's-she's** or a gender-neutral or gender-inclusive **they**. If they have a **he's** pronoun it almost always refers to either masculine plural *or* "mixed" masculine-feminine. Languages do not usually maintain separate pronouns for "men only" vs. "women only" vs. "specifically mixed." If they make any distinction in the plural it is "women only" vs. every other option.

C. The fact is that the pronoun **he** can be "generic human" without specific reference to either sex, but allowing for reference to either sex.

1. This does not mean that **he** is a gender-neutral pronoun. It is simply uncommitted. It means masculine in reference to male people and in direct contrast to a **she** elsewhere in the context. The pronoun **she**, on the other hand, can and must refer to feminines only.

2. People try to get around this problem by resorting to plural agreement, particularly with words like **everybody, nobody** that already have a grain of "plurality" in their meaning. The "he who" type of generalization tends to be replaced by the truly gender-non-committal **whoever**.

   a. **Everybody** does **their** thing.

   b. **Nobody** here knows what **they**'re doing.

c. **Whoever** has finished **their** supper can have ice cream.

To a by-the-book normative grammarian this sounds like chalk squeaking on a blackboard because the grammatically *singular* "everybody" is matched by the *plural* pronoun "they." That is, you say **everybody does** with a singular verb and never "everybody do," so how can you use a plural possessive to refer this singular pronoun? It seems that you draw on grammatical means--the fact that English does not have separate forms for genders in the plural in combination with the fact that "everybody" has a plural-like meaning to begin with--to get around a major cultural dilemma. It is actually a very clever solution, despite the apparent breach of logic. It just goes to show that "language logic" and "philosophical or mathematical logic" do not have to coincide. In many languages subject-verb agreement and (pro-)noun-pronoun agreement can operate on different principles.

III. INFLECTION, DERIVATION, AND THE DICTIONARY

You first met these terms in Chapter 3, IX.B. You should be familiar with them, especially since many languages that a lot of forms for one word.

A. Inflection

This is the cover term for the process of adding suffixes--or sometimes prefixes--to some kind of **stem** to get **different forms of the same word** for different purposes. When you do this with nouns you call it **declension**. When you do it to verbs you call it **conjugation**. Inflection does not produce a word with different meaning. It just gives a different grammatical nuance and is used in a different sentence function.

1. The **inflectional category** typical of nouns, for example, is **number**. In English you add **-(e)s** to the singular stem to get plural. The word **books** does not mean anything different from **book** except that there is more than one of them in the given scene you describe.

2. Another inflectional category of nouns typical of many languages is **case**. You adjust the form of the noun--and often also the adjective that agrees with it--to show a different face of the noun in a sentence.

a. In English, as you saw in Chapter 11, you have **case declension** only for pronouns: they are, so-called, **declined for case**, as you have seen hints of along the way. **Me** refers to the same person as **I**, but playing a different role in the sentence. (You can consider **John's** a case form of **John**, however.)

b. In language textbooks when you see instructions like, "**Decline** the following nouns," the intention is to list all the case forms, usually in some traditional order. Take the word **movie** as you saw it in the fictitious English of Chapter 4, VII. and 5, IV. The declension of **movie** would be:

Nominative:	movius
Accusative:	movium
Dative:	moviye
Possessive:	movie's

3. As for the dictionary--whether a mono-lingual English dictionary like Webster's or American Heritage or a bi-lingual dictionary, like an English-Swedish/Swedish-English one -- the form of a word represents the whole word in all its potential uses. This is called, simply, the **dictionary form** or **citation form**.

a. English happens not to have very many variations for any given word, and the singular is the citation form for nouns. In a case language, the citation form is usually the **nominative singular.** The dictionary will usually provide you with the plural of nouns so that you can see any spelling changes or other "irregularities."

b. The word **books** would be listed under **book**. If you needed to look up **wives, knives, leaves** you would have to know that these plurals are unexpected inflectional forms and that you would find them under the singulars **wife, knife, leaf**. Likewise for **geese** or **mice**: you would have to know that the singulars--the citation forms--are **goose** and **mouse**. If the dictionary is big enough, it cross-reference **geese** as "See under **goose**." Otherwise it will give you this extra grammatical information under the entry for the citation form.

4. When you inflect **verbs** you call it **conjugation**. The most typical inflectional categories of verbs are **tense**, along with **person** and **number**, as you saw in Chapter 8.

   a. In English you either add the ending **-(e)d** or **-(e)n** to the plain form or change the middle vowel or both. But the past forms **told, eaten, took** do not mean anything different from their plain forms **tell, eat, take**.

   b. The citation form for verbs in English is the **plain** form. If you look up an "irregular" past tense, the dictionary will either tell you to look up the plain or trust you to know it but list it under the plain.

   c. Verbs usually have the most forms of any part of speech. The dictionary traditions of many European languages--French, Spanish, German, Russian--choose the infinitive to list verbs by. In Latin you learn to identify verbs by the 1st person present tense (the **I**-form). In Hebrew and Arabic dictionaries verbs appear in the form of the past tense of the "3rd person masculine singular" form (the **he**-form). You can imagine that if you are learning a language where every different person in every tense has its own verb form, you have to already know the grammar in order to use the dictionary. English lets you get by most of the time because there are so few changes in word forms.

5. As for the inflectional categories of adjectives and adverbs, you can think of the **comparative** with **-er** or **more** and the **superlative** with **-est** or **most**, but the dictionary will list the "plain" form of the adjective and give the degrees under that entry.

6. As a general rule, then, dictionaries do not cite *inflectional* forms separately.

B. Derivation

This is also the process of adding prefixes or suffixes to stems, but the resulting meaning of the new word is different from the original. You saw some of this in Chapter 3, IX. Derivation is how you get from noun to verb, verb to noun, adjective to adverb, or other changes.

1. Verb → Noun

   a. Add **-(e)r** to a verb stem to get "the person who does the action": **drive-driver, dive-diver, work-worker, hit-hitter, [go to the movies]-[movie-goer]**, etc.

   b. Add **-(ic)(a)tion** to get "the verbal action itself or the end result of the verbal action": **unify-unification, evaporate-evaporation, civilize-civilization,** and on and on. People often reverse the direction and assume the pattern is **evaporation-evaporate**, so you hear noun-to-verb pairs like **fortification-*fortificate** or **orientation-*orientate**. School teachers will mark these wrong and smug people will chuckle at people who say such things. But hold on: they might catch on and become the norm in the next generation. (Again, this does not license you to say just anything you please. Just be aware that there are patterns, but it is not etched in stone which items go into which patterns.)

2. Adjective → Abstract Noun: add, for example, **-(i)ty** or **-ness** to an adjective, as in **electric-electricity, pure-purity, certain-certainty, friendly-friendliness, useful-usefulness**. You cannot do this to every adjective. It is not automatic but a part of learning the vocabulary of English. This is the main difference between inflection and derivation.

3. Adjective → Adverb: add **-ly**, as in **frank-ly, wise-ly, inadvertent-ly**, but this is not automatic, either. You cannot do this to adjectives like **fast, asleep, Russian**. It has to be a **quality adjective**, cf. Chapter 3, IV.A.

   a. In a few cases, the same process of adding **-ly** can get you from noun to adjective: **friend-ly, dai-ly** (= day+ly), **home-ly,** or keep you in the adjective realm: **sick-ly, live-ly.**

   b. A few of these **-ly** adverbs have only a vague or restricted meaning connection to the noun or adjective they were derived from: **short-ly** has to only with time and not height. **large-ly** means "for the most part" and not "in a large way." **name-ly** means "a specific example of the general principle just mentioned."

4. Sometimes it is so hard to see the connection in meaning between two words that you can see are related to each other. If **humble-humility** seem to be fairly closely related, **humility-humiliate** should look even closer, but the meaning connection in the first pair is much closer than in the second pair. And do not forget that **humble** is also a verb meaning "make someone humble" and the noun from **humiliate** is **humiliation**.

5. Gender can be a derivational category of nouns, too, as in typical male-female pairs like **actor-actress, prince-princess, lion-lioness,** and the nouns you add **-ette** to with the meaning of "little or cute." You get a word of the same part of speech but with a different meaning. The dictionary may list the feminine word separately or make a note of it under the masculine, which is, after all, the gender-non-specific cover term. (Both actors and actresses join the "actors' union." Both lions and lionesses live in a "lions' den." Of course, when it is a question of function or status, you cannot say that "princess" is a female prince or that "countess" is a female count.)

6. Sometime it is hard to decide whether the adjective is derived from the noun by removing an ending or the noun, from the adjective by adding an ending. It is often important to be aware of the direction of the derivation because of other changes in the word that you do or do not expect, as in the **orientation, evaporation, unification** group above. Their noun forms all look the same, but they derive from different types of verb stems, **orient, evaporate, unify**, respectively.

7. Other derivational schemes include:

    a. **prefixation**, like **re-** for "do again" or "back up and ~", but you cannot do this to any word you like. You can **rewrite, reread,** and **reapply**, but when you **repay** you do not "pay again" but "pay back." You can **refill** but you cannot **re-empty**. Some of these will get separate entries in the dictionary, and others will be "assumed." Still others you can create on the spur of the moment as needed, and they will be English words, but they will fade back into nothingness unless people start using it a lot. It will really take on new life when its meaning becomes different from its origin, as in, say, **search/research**, which you hardly feel as being connected at all. It is not always easy to tell when a derived word becomes a separate new word or the combination of the "meaning of the original word+the meaning of the prefix or suffix." How many other **derivational prefixes** and **suffixes** can you identify in English?

b. A very common derivation pattern that is just to **change stress** on the word. This can easily escape notice if you think **visually**: our writing system has no way to indicate place of stress, so it *looks* the **zero derivation** you saw in Chapter 3. But *listen*! This can take between nouns with stress on the beginning and verbs with stress not on the beginning: **rébel-rebél, récord-recórd, cónvert-convért, énvelope-envélop** (with minor spelling adjustment). This even works for particle verbs (Chapter 7, III.) that derive nouns: **run dówn** the list/give a **rún down,** have your tire **blow óut**/have a **blów out**, and hundreds more. Of course, the meaning connection can get very fuzzy: **óbject-objéct, súbject-subjéct, cóntent-contént, cómbine-combíne.** Adjective-verb dèrivátion does not so much change stress as change vowel *sound* without rèpreséntíng it in spelling. You hear the verb with both **prímary stress** on the beginning *and* a weaker, **sécondàry stress** on the end but the ádjectìve with only primary stress on the beginning: **séparàte-séparate.**

NO EXERCISE 12

CHAPTER 13

RECOGNIZING PARALLEL CONSTRUCTIONS

Recall the Distributive Property from high school math:

$$X(A+B+C) = AX+BX+CX.$$

That is, the one element X applies equally to all elements within the parentheses. Language has an analogous property whereby one representative of a grammatical construction can work equally over a string of similar elements without being repeated. (Note that square brackets here do not mean direct object.)

I. PARALLEL VERB PHRASES

A. **Infinitives**. She likes **to** [run, jump, scuba dive, and eat quiche].

We have **to** [get up, make the bed, and put on the coffee].

1. In principle, you could repeat the **to** with each of these verbs, since they are all infinitives after **like** and **have to**. In practice, however, you would need some special stylistic circumstances, like the slow, deliberate itemization you might hear a political candidate deliver:

   I promise **to cut** taxes, **to increase** benefits, and **to play** less golf.

2. The reason it is important to be aware of this is that your target language might have, for example, a single-word infinitive, and if you interpret **jump, dive** as present-tense verbs equal to **like**, you will produce nonsense. Such a sentence might mean **She likes to run; she jumps; she dives**. Difference clear?

B. The same is true of modals and the verb phrases they form. They take "plain" verb forms, so there is no **to**, but you needn't repeat the modal:

We **can** [eat, drink, and be merry].

C. Similarly, **auxiliaries** also apply over several participles or plain forms:

a. He **is** [work**ing** and rais**ing** a family] and doesn't [**have** time for or **care** about] your political campaign.

b. I **have** [skrimp**ed** and sav**ed**] for this new car.

c. You **didn't** [**write, call**, or **send** flowers] while you were away.

D. This is also the case with particle verbs, cf. Chapter 7, III.B.: **get up, get out, get around**. In a string of these, you needn't repeat the actual verb, just string the adverbs: **get** [up, out, and around]. Again, if you are translating from English, it is perfectly possible that the target language will have separate verbs for each of these expressions, so there would be no parallelism.

II. PARALLEL ADJECTIVE-NOUN GROUPS

A. Articles

The articles **A** and **THE** come at the beginning of a noun phrase and apply their meaning throughout the noun phrase. The whole phrase is definite or indefinite. You repeat the article only if each part of the phrase has a separate identity.

1. **the** [monkeys, tigers, lions, and kangaroos]

2. **The Owl** and **The Pussycat** ; **The Tortoise** and **The Hare**

B. Adjectives

These are a little trickier because an adjective does not necessarily modify all nouns in a chain. Voice intonation and breathing will solve a lot of the problem in speech, but in writing you have to "hear" it in your head.

1. In **smart boys and girls,** are the girls smart, too?

2. In **my brother and sister-in-law** is the brother also "in-law"?

3. The question came up earlier, but in *Green Eggs and Ham*, is the ham green, too?

C. Conjunctions

Compound subjects with one verb present a classic case in ambiguity. In **John and Mary went to the movies** it is clear that John went and that Mary went, but:

1. Did they go together? or

2. Is this sentence merely the sum total of two unrelated facts?

3. Compare, for example:

   a. Lithuania and Uzbekistan declared independence from the Soviet Union. (both in 1990 during the same wave of political, economic, and ethnic upheaval)

   b. The United States and India won independence from England. (separated by almost 200 years under entirely different circumstances.)

   English grammar expresses the two situations by the same construction, but you must use your knowledge of the situation to make the final decision of how loosely or tightly the **and** "conjoins" the two parties.

D. Prepositions

Nothing prevents a preposition from having a "compound object." You have to decide how many nouns are object of the same preposition.

1. "Do you take this person **in** sickness and **in** health?" but:

2. The mail gets delivered in rain, sleet, snow, and hail.

EXERCISE 13:

WORKING WITH PARALLELS

Key: p. 352

In the following sentences, decide which constructions are parallel. That is, determine how far the grammatical influence of words goes. Indicate this by literally enclosing the whole phrase in parentheses and drawing an arrow from the repeatable part to wherever you *could* repeat it. Punctuation may help you decide, but hearing the sentence in your mind's ear is the best clue.

Examples: My (sister and brother) like to (scream and fight.)

1. John knits and sews but can't garden or cook.

2. Children should be seen and not heard.

3. I'm sick and tired of your conniving, trickery, and deceit.

4. The heroes were welcomed, decorated, and honored.

5. The Dakotas and Carolinas are paired states.

6. The Hague, Paris, and London are capitals and cultural centers.

7. They like skiing and hiking and kayaking interests them, too.*

8. The doctor wants her to eat well and exercise and says she should take a daily walk.

9. The baby can sit up, recognize people and likes to grab their hair and pull.

10. We support you in your fight and struggle and declare your enemies our enemies!! (No real causes intended here.)

(Just for fun, what would be the difference between #7. and these two items:

7a. They like skiing and hiking and kayaking interest them, too.

7b. They like skiing and hiking and kayaking, too.)

CHAPTER 14

SO, HOW DO YOU ASK QUESTIONS?

I. TWO KINDS OF QUESTIONS

Back in Chapter 6, VI.B. you saw the term **interrogative** for question sentence. You can distinguish two kinds of sentence structures that ask for different answers.

A. **Confirmation questions**. The answer is "yes" or "no".

B. **Information questions**. These begin with a **question word** and require a real answer. The question words are

1. two pronouns: **who? what?**

2. one adjective: **which?**

2. adverbs: **when? where? why? how?** including **how long? how much? how many?**

II. FORMING YES/NO QUESTIONS

A. Basic procedure: Start with an assumed statement (with a subject and verb) and **invert** (flip places, not turn upside down) the subject and the verb.

B. This works fine for verb phrases with the three auxiliary verbs **be, have, do**, as well as the modals.

1. Invert auxiliaries, namely, in progressive, perfect, emphatic, future.

   a. He is working. → Is he working?
   b. I was spying. → Was I spying?
   c. They do protest! → Do they protest?
   d. You have defected. → Have you defected?
   e. I will elaborate. → Will I elaborate?

2. Invert modals:
   a. She can cooperate. → Can she cooperate?
   b. We should consolidate → Should we consolidate?

C. **All other verb forms**: plain past and present. If they do not have an auxiliary already, **give them one: DO**!! Then you can invert it. Auxiliaries play a central role in the English verb system. (So, "plain" becomes "do+plan".) In fact, any marking of present tense (like **-s**) or past tense (**-ed**) turns up on that stuck-in auxiliary and not on the plain form of the verb.

1. He works. → **Does** he work?

2. This hurts. → **Does** this hurt?

3. The guests **left**. → **Did** the guests **leave**?

D. To answer such inverted questions, all you need is **yes** or **no,** and you can also repeat the auxiliary, but you need not use the main verb.

1. **Are** you going? Yes, we **are**.

2. **Have** you seen E.T.? No, I **haven**'t.

3. **Has** E.T. phoned home? No, he **hasn't**.

4. **Do** you take this person to be your lawfully wedded spouse?

(Imagine trying to perform this ceremony in a language without auxiliaries!)

E. Now, if you think this is all painfully obvious, just wait till you hit a language that does not invert subject and verb to ask questions. Try to suppress your instinct.

F. **Voice Signals.**

1. When you speak a statement in English your voice normally ends up at a lower pitch than when you started. When you utter a **yes/no question** in English your voice rises in pitch. It is hard to describe that pitch on the printed page, but prove it to yourself. Say out loud, "We want to eat." Then ask, "Shall we eat?"

2. A yes/no question can express shock or disbelief at somebody else's statement. Here you have no inversion of subject and verb. You simply repeat the statement with a sharply rising pitch on the crucial word and then your voice remains at a high pitch till the end of the sentence. Imagine these contexts and say aloud:

   a. "Hello, I'm a candidate for office. . ."
   "***You're*** a candidate for office? G'wan! You're puttin' me on!"

   b. "Oh, valet, please park my vintage car."
   "You want me to drive ***this*** heap? Get serious!"

   c. "Here, try this new non-dairy spread."
   "***This*** isn't butter??!! That's incredible!"

III. INFORMATION QUESTIONS

A. Pick the question word that will elicit the answer you want and start the sentence with it.

1. First of all, six of the seven questions words start with **wh-**, so these are called the "WH- (Double-U Eych) questions." The answer words start mostly with **th-** and can all be rephrased in terms of just a few:

a. Question Pronouns

who?	**this/that**	= person
what?	**this/that**	= thing
which?	" "	thing

b. Question Adverbs

when?	**then**	= at that time
where?	**there**	= at that place
why?	**therefore**	=for that reason
how?	**thus**	= in that way

2. Since the question word itself is enough to signal a question you do not raise your voice pitch. That is, questions with a question word have basically the same **falling** intonation as a statement. Say out loud, "We want to eat." "OK, what do you want to eat?" or "What do you want to eat?"., but when you got to **eat** you were down low again.

B. To invert or not to invert?

1. **who, what,** (and **which**, too) are pronouns and serve the functions you expect them to:

a. **subject of the verb**: No inversion and no extra auxiliaries.

(1). Who is cooking tonight? What is happening?

(2). Which shirt looks better? Who cares?

(3). Who's been sleeping in my bed?

b. **object of verb or preposition**: Do as in IIIA. above, then invert as in II.A.,B.

(1). [Who(m)] are you meeting? [What] are they doing?

(2). [Which shirt] do you like better?

(3). **Who** were you talking **to**? (=**to whom**!)

(4). **What** have we been waiting **for**? (=**for what!**)

2. **when, where, why, how** all require some kind of **adverbial** answer. These also require auxiliaries and inversion.

   a. **When** does the show start?

   b. **Why** did she say that?

   c. Mary, Mary, quite contrary, **how** does your garden grow?

   d. **How many** roads must a man walk down? (B. Dylan)

   e. **How much** wood would a woodchuck chuck?

   f. **Where** do you live? (position)

   g. **Where** have all the flowers gone? (Destination. More on this location vs. in Chapter 17.)

3. Note also the archaic **Wherefore?** meaning **for what reason?**. We still have the answer is **therefore** (=for that reason). This is not just a fancy, old-fashioned **where**, though. When Juliette stands on her balcony and asks, "Wherefore art thou, Romeo?" she is asking, "What is it in you that makes you 'Romeo'? Why are you 'Romeo'? Is there some inherent quality of 'Romeo-ness'"?

IV. INDIRECT QUESTIONS: NON-ANSWERS, WAFFLING, PASSING THE BUCK

A. Yes/No type with "whether"

This is a non-answer, essentially just a repetition of the question. You find it most typically as a subordinate clause after verbs like **know** and **ask.** There is no subject-verb inversion, as there is in the question. (In American English there is a great tendency to substitute **if** for **whether**.) It is sometimes called an **indirect** or **embedded question**. (Recall the curly brackets for subordinate clauses.)

1. "Is he going?"
"I don't know {**whether** he is going}, but I'll ask him {**whether** he is going}."

2. "Have they ever been to the Grand Canyon?"
"I don't know {**whether/if** they have (ever) been there}. Why don't you ask them {**whether/if** they've been there}."

3. "Does she speak Italian?"
"Who knows {**whether** (or not)/**if** she speaks Italian}?"

B. If you do use **if** for **whether** in your own speech, just be careful to distinguish the "Condition **If**" from the "Waffle-on-the-Question/Pass-the-Buck **If**" in your mind. They are not 100% the same. **Whether** is the only possibility the so-called **alternative construction "whether X or Y."** How do the following snips of conversation sound to you? Does your new language permit such a substitution?

1. "I don't know **if/whether** my paper will be done today **or not.**"
"You'll turn that paper in today **whether** you're finished **or not**!"

2. "I don't know **whether or not** I'm going." (***if or not**)

3. "You meet the Grim Reaper **whether (if?)** you sip cognac in Beverly Hills **or** sweep streets in Altoona."

C. **Question-word questions restated**: There is subject-verb inversion in a genuine question but not in the indirect, restated answer. Note the single and double underlinings:

1. "What time is it?"
"I don't know {/what time/ it is}."

2. "Where are they going?"
"Who knows {where they are going}."

3. "Why did he do that?"
"Why don't you ask him {why he did that}?"

4. Listen closely to non-native speakers of English. They often invert subject and verb or inject auxiliaries in a question, whether it is direct or indirect. For example, "Do you know what time **is it**?" or "I don't know where **does she live**." (This person either is translating directly from a language that treats direct and indirect question the same or comes from a language where there is no inversion and has over-learned the inversion rule.)

V. QUESTION TAGS

A. You can make a statement into a confirmation-type question by adding a question tag. The generic question-tag word is **right?** or more lavishly, **isn't that right?**

1. Today is Tuesday, right?

2. Hey, you're that famous celebrity, right?

B. The other device relies on your ability to identify and manipulate auxiliaries and modals. Look at these:

1. You'**re coming** with us, **aren't** you?

2. He knows his way around here, **does**n't he?

3. They arrived last week, **did**n't they?

4. She'**ll walk** away with first prize, **won**'t she?

5. You **wouldn't be kidding** us, **would** you?

6. I **can go** camping and back-backing again, **can't I**, Doc?

Simply repeat the auxiliary in the same person, number, and tense as in the clause in question--creating a **do** auxiliary if there isn't one!--and reverse the charge: a positive statement gets a negative tag, and a negative statement gets a positive tag. The voice intonation of each one is variable depending on whether you really want a positive or negative answer. Foreign learners of English have quite a job mastering the auxiliary tag. Recall, too, that the imperative can have only a **will** or **would** tag, cf. Chapter 8, Part 2, V.

CHAPTER 15

JUST SAY NO?!

I. NEGATION IN GRAMMAR

There is a bit more to **negation** in language than just saying, "No." Now that you know what is involved in interrogative sentences, you will see that negation operates similarly.

A. Basically, there are two "negativizer" words in English: **no** and **not.** Each has its own kind of usage.

1. **No** can stand alone as the one-word answer to questions regardless of the structure of the rest of the sentence. It is also the signal of **zero-quantity** of nouns, cf. Chapter 10, IV.B.

2. **Not** is the word that means, "Sorry, wrong number. Make another selection." It does not necessarily mean, "There is none of what you want," but rather, "The element you suggest is not found in this sentence."

3. Some languages may have a special word for each of these functions. Others may use one all-purpose negativizer for the one-word answer, the quantifier, and the grammatical element within the sentence. Still others have more specialized negativizers. There are also languages with special verb forms for positive and negative, not to mention special forms for the subjects or objects of positive and negative verbs.

II. NEGATING VERBAL ACTION

A. RULE: Put **not** after the verb:

1. This works in formal, poetic, or ceremonial English, not to mention the English of Shakespeare's day, including the King James Bible:

a. **Ask not** what your country can do for you...

b. **Waste not, want not.**

c. **Lead** us **not** into temptation...

d. **Fear not**, fair damsel!

e. He acts as if he **hadn't** a care in the world.

f. She loves me; she **loves** me **not**.

2. When you think about it, you see this will work only for the verb **be** in our English, and marginally for **have**.

B. So, amend IA. to read: Put **not** after the **auxiliary verb**. If there isn't one already, insert **do**!

1. **Do not go** gentle into that good night...

2. **Did** the Old Woman In The Shoe **know** what to do? No, she had so many had so many children she **didn't know** what to do.

3. She enjoyed the lecture but we **didn't** (enjoy the lecture).

Note that, similarly to questions or any such repetition, you can parallel a whole verb with just the auxiliary, and it carries all the markings for tense (past **-ed**) or number (3rd. prs. sg. **-s**).

C. **Contractions** (Review Chapter 8, Part 1, III.D., above)

1. The verbal negativizer **not** has a long and short variant in normal speech. Actually, "unstressed" is more to the point than "short." Since it has no independent stress it also loses its independence on the printed page. You spell it **n't**, with an apostrophe, and you attach it to the preceding word. In most cases this is the auxiliary. (After all, the rule is to put **not** after the auxiliary. . .)

2. The other option is to contract the auxiliary, itself, and attach it to the preceding noun, as in Chapter 8. This will normally be the subject. This gives you the variants:

   a. He is not → He **isn't.**
He**'s not.**

   b. We, you, they are not → We, you they **aren't.**
We're. you're, they**'re not.**

   c. *BUT*: I am not → only **I'm not**, and not *I amn't, at least not since Chaucer's time.

3. Contracting **have-has-had** also gives two options:

   a. He has, had not → He hasn't, hadn't.
He's not (same as **is**!). He'd not.
(but only has part of a perfect verb phrase, e.g., **He's/He'd not been home all day**.).

   b. You (etc.) have, had not → I, you, we, they haven't, hadn't
I've, you've, we've, they've not
I'd, you'd, we'd, they'd not

4. **Will not** normally gives only **won't**, although in formal writing you also see **He'll not go**.

5. Other auxiliaries allow only one option:

   a. **Do-does-did** give only **don't-doesn't-didn't**.

      (Note the vowel sounds that spelling masks: **do-does**, rhymes with 'who was'; **do-don't**, rhymes with 'you won't'.)

   b. **Shall not**, to the extent that you use it all, gives only the very old-fashioned-sounding and funny-looking **sha'n't.** (One apostrophe for **-ll** and one for **-o-**.)

6. In negative questions, or course, you get only the forms with the negativizer on the verb, because the verb starts the question and not the subject: **Isn't he? Aren't you?** (and also **Aren't I?** for **Am I not?**).

7. By the way, how do you answer such **negative-interrogative** questions (cf., Chapter 6, VI. B.4): "yes" or "no"?

   a. In English, if the question is, "Didn't you do you homework?" and you, in fact, *did*, the answer is, "Yes, I did it." If you, in fact, did not, the answer is, "No, I didn't."

   b. Sounds straightforward enough until you learn a language that does it the opposite. Since the question is about *not* doing your homework, if you *did* do it, the answer could be, "No, I did it." If you didn't do it, the answer could be, "Yes, I didn't." Don't you see the logic in that approach, too?

8. In Chapter 8 we discussed the normative bias against using contractions, at least in writing. In the negative interrogatives just mentioned, you have no choice *but* to contract if you have any thoughts of sounding normal. Even if you want to be very correct you do not say, "Did you not do your homework?" It sounds like a parody of itself or an attempt to imitate "older" or upper-class British speech or Victorian literature!

9. Naturally you do not contract if you mean to stress the negative. Listen to the different ways you say, e.g.,

   "Will you please pick up the cigarette butt you just dropped?"
   "No, I **wón't** pick it up!" or "No, I will **nót** pick it up!"

D. **And that ain't all**:

   1. In some varieties of American English, the negative contraction of any form of **be** or **have** is **ain't**, as in **I ain't goin', they ain't home, Ain't you finished yet?**, **He ain't done his chores, We ain't got no culture,** etc.

   2. Your elementary school teacher probably blasted these out of the water as "uneducated," "low-class," even "vulgar." After all, as the saying used to go, "**Ain't** ain't in the dictionary." (This assumes, of course, that only the dictionary knows what is right, includes nothing wrong, and anything not therein contained is to be reviled! It is an

age-old question whether the job of a dictionary is just to *collect* the words of a language or also to *judge* them.)

3. No matter how uneducated you are--which has nothing to do with how *intelligent* you are!--there is no way you will hear **is not** or **have not** and spontaneously change them to **ain't**. This is not a question of education, but of varieties of language. The fact is that one variety of English uses **isn't** and **hasn't**, while another variety uses the all-purpose **ain't**. The first variety is the one that has become "standard", but not because it is inherently "better" than any other variety. Whether you consider it low-class is a separate matter. Remember that contractions used to be considered low-class, but they ain't no more! Standards change. Do learn the current standard in your target language, but do not judge other varieties as good or bad. They may one day become standard!

III. NEGATING NOUNS

A. **Option 1**: Put **no** before the noun wherever it occurs in the sentence.

1. "Yes, we have **no bananas**. . ."
2. We'll have **no more trouble** from you. Is that clear?!
3. Ask me **no questions** and I'll tell you **no lies**.
4. The evil teacher showed the students **no mercy.**
5. **No mercy** was shown the students.
6. We will sell **no wine** before its time.

B. **Option 2**: Negate the verb with **not** and use **any** before the noun.
In Chapter 10, V.B. we asked whether "**no X**" was the same as "**not any X**". You decide for yourself. Just be aware that English grammar often treats them as alternates of each other.

1. We do**n't** have **any** bananas.
2. Do**n't** ask **any** questions...

3. We w**on't** sell **any** wine....

4. There are**n't any** cars....

C. This is exactly the kind of ambiguity Homer played on in the famous scene between the one-eyed beast, the Cyclops, and the hero, Ulysses. The latter introduced himself to the Cyclops as Noman (that is, No Man, Nobody). When they get into a fight and Ulysses blinds the Cyclops, the poor creature calls for help. His buddies say, "Who's hurting you?" Imagine the irony and embarrassment of having to admit, "No-man is hurting me!"

D. To negate nouns and adjectives without negating the sentence you use prefixes **un-, in-, non-**.

1. **Adjectives:** unfair, inflexible, unhappy, intolerant, non-toxic.

2. **Nouns:** tell an **untruth**, suffer an **injustice,** be a **non-entity**, sign a nuclear **non-proliferation** treaty.

3. Careful: this is different from the prefix **in-** of **in**scribe, **in**undate, **in**corporate, **in**vigorate, which has a meaning like the preposition **in**, namely, "end up **in**side or together."

4. **In** in both these meanings has the variants **ir-, il-,** and **im-** before words beginning in the consonants **r-, l-,** and **m-, b-, p-:**

   a. **Negative**: ir-rational, il-logical, im-probable, im-balance, im-modest.

   b. **"Physically 'in'"**: **im**plant, **im**plode, **im**bibe, **il**luminate, **ir**radiate

   c. This is the source of the confusion behind **inflammable**, which means *both* "*not* flammable" and "capable of going up *in* flame."

5. This is not the case with **un-**, which does not change: unreliable, unlimited, unpredictable, unmitigated.

6. There a few other prefixes, suffixes, and separate words that "feel" negative:

a. **anti-** = against, for adjectives (anti-bacterial, anti-war)

b. **-less** = without, for adjectives (painless, toothless, penniless)

c. **de-** = take away, for verbs (defoliate, debug, demilitarize)

d. **hardly** and **barely,** which do not permit the verb to be negated

e. **without**, which does not take "no" for an answer.

E. That dreaded Double-Negative!!

Since earliest grade school you were probably severely punished for uttering such monstrosities as, "I **don't** have **no** money." or "**Nobody didn't** give me **nothing**." or "That kind of talk **won't** get you **nowhere**." That is, one negativizer per clause is plenty for standard English. Whether it goes on the verb or the noun is another question, but the two are not supposed to mix.

1. The fact that English speakers feel the need to construct such sentences, whether or not the establishment approves of them, is enough to tip you off that maybe speakers of some other languages feel that need, too. Some languages do, indeed, have a regular, normal, even necessary, use of double negatives or things that look like them.

2. The last thing to say about these negatives is that language is not arithmetic. Two negatives in language do not cancel each other out, as school teachers may have told you, and make a positive. If anything, they reinforce each other. So, "I don't want nothing" does *not* mean, "I want something."

NO EXERCISE 15

CHAPTER 16

DUMMIES, IMPERSONALS, OMNIPERSONALS

AND A FEW OTHER GOODIES

I. DUMMIES AND IMPERSONALS

A. English speakers feel strongly that a clause must have a subject.

B. A noun or pronoun serves as subject.

C. Pronouns, by definition, refer to or stand for nouns.

D. But what about sentences like these:

1. It's raining; it's pouring.
2. It's a lovely day.
3. It's not nice to fool Mother Nature.
4. It's a damn shame!
5. 'Twas the night before Christmas.
6. It behooves you to speak out against injustice.
7. It bothers him to hear such talk.
8. It gladdens the heart that they get along now.
9. It stinks in here!
10. It just happens to be my birthday today. . .

E. They clearly have a subject, and that subject is the pronoun **it**. But does the **it** refer to anything that came before? Certainly not in the same way that it does in a sentence like, "This book is too expensive and **it** 's boring, too."

F. In the sentences in D. you could claim that **it** refers to the whole unfolding situation as you speak it. That would force you to expand your definition of pronouns to words that can represent whole situations, which is sometimes the case (sic!), cf. Chapters 6, III.C.

1. The **it** in the above sentences is called a **non-referential it**. It just occupies "subject position" in the sentence because English sentences really want to have subjects. It gives no information. So you can now call this **it** a **dummy subject**, a mere place holder. The actual information in the above sentences comes in the predicate.

2. Such constructions are sometimes called **impersonal sentences** because the subject neither does anything nor has anything done to it.

   a. Very frequently such dummy subjects will be followed up by an infinitive construction or a noun clause to explain the **it** retroactively, as in I. D. 6-8, above. This is the kind of style some high school English teachers deem undesirable and label "verbose" because **it** is a "wasted word, devoid of semantic content." They insist you begin with that infinitive or noun clause.

   b. But are they the same? Is either **To err is human** or **Erring is human** the same as **It is human to err**? Maybe 90% of the time the three variants could be used interchangeably, but they each have their own flavor. It is a choice you have to make, a stylistic option you can exercise in English. Some languages may not allow dummy subjects, and you will not have the option.

G. **Clefting**

You can expand sentences in various ways. (Back to Chapter 1 for this use of single underlne for whole subject and double underline for whole predicate.)

1. I want to go home. → a. What I want to do is go home.

   b. Going home is what I want to do.

   You haven't added any information to the original sentence, but you have rearranged the information to create an anticipation in the mind of your listener. The **do** in the subject clause is the "all-purpose verb" and you have to wait for the predicate to get the "real" verb **go.**

2. Take another example and you can see one more permutation. All three are normal sentences.
   a. Incompetence makes me mad.

   b. What makes me mad is incompetence.

   c. It is incompetence that makes me mad.

3. All three "mean" the same thing, that is, refer to the same situation. But do you feel they are all somewhat different? In a sense, you have started with a subject and predicate, each with its own information, and reshuffled them. (In the process you have made subordinate clauses where there were none before.)

   a. The "**what I want to do is**" variety puts half of the original predicate information in the subject.

   b. The "**going home is what**" variety puts the other half of the predicate information in the subject.

   c. The "**It is**" variety puts the all subject information into the predicate and creates a dummy subject.

   d. This phenomenon of reshuffling the subject information into the predicate and the predicate information into the subject is called **clefting**.

H. English can also use a dummy subject to unmask a hidden direct object. Take this classic contrast:

1. John is eager to please.

2. John is easy to please.

They look like the same kind of structure, but try paraphrasing them. You really can't alter the first one. But you have no trouble making 2. into **It is easy to please John,** in which case you discover that **John** here is really the direct object of **please**, but it is "posing as the subject of **is.**" In 1, **eager** describes **John**. In 2, **easy** describes **to please**. Prove it: you can further rephrase 2. into a gerund phrase where **John** is still the object of the gerund: **Pleasing John is easy**.

3. The fact that 1. and 2. above are visually similar is real sleight of hand. The two sentences mean very different things. English likes to play with this kind of construction. Here is a borderline case, depending on whether the subject is alive and capable of feelings and making decisions or not:

   The chicken is ready to eat.

   Do you see the ambiguity? Because of the meaning of **ready**, the subject can have its own mind or not. In one context the chicken expresses its volition, and you read **ready** in the same sense as **eager**. On the other hand, in a context where the chicken is beyond expressing anything, you read **ready** in the same sense as **easy** and can paraphrase, "The chicken is ready **to be eaten**," or "We-you-anybody **is-are** **/ready/** {**to eat** [the chicken]}."

   a. You would never confuse the meaning of such a sentence in a natural context, but it is interesting to see what the possibilities are. One of the hallmarks of the comedy of the Marx Brothers and other comedians is that they say such a sentence in one context, then slip into the other context so that you read it the other way at the same time and catch yourself off guard.

   b. Refer back to Chapter 9, V.B. This comes down to a question of **control** of the infinitive complement. Such sentences as the **easy to**-type do not express the controller of the infinitive complement, but do express the object of the infinitive (John) as the *subject* of the copula.

II. OTHER DUMMIES

A. You use **there** in a similar place-filler role (not the locational "there" as in "over there"):

1. **There** is a book over there.

2. **There** is nothing to fear but fear itself.

B. This is called **there-insertion**. You can do it in all kinds of ways:

1. a. A birthday present seems to be hiding behind the couch →
   b. **There** seems to be a birthday present hiding behind the couch.

2. a. A great clatter arose in the garage. →
   b. **There** arose a great clatter in the garage.

3. a. Suddenly three strangers appeared →
   b. Suddenly **there** appeared three strangers.

4. a. I want no dirty dishes left in the sink →
   b. I want **there** to be no dirty dishes. . .

C. What is the subject of the b. sentences? Is it **there** or **present, clatter** or **strangers**? Why did you stick this **there** in in the first place? What about #4? Did you sort of fill out with **there** the clause that was in the back of your mind anyway? That is, isn't #4 a compressed version of the two-clause **I want {that no dirty dishes will be left}** to begin with? What does your target language do with these types of sentences?

D. This is not the same as the place-pointer adverb **there**, as the A.1. example above shows. Both can occur in the same sentence and mean entirely different things: "Have you been to Cincinnati? **There** are lots of chili parlors **there**." (cf. Chapter 12, I: "There**'s** lots of chili parlors. . .")

E. English also uses this **it** as a **dummy object**. Look at this contrast:

1. a. This is a beautiful city. I really like **it** .

   b. This is a beautiful city. I really like **it** here.

2. a. I like this car. I'll take **it**.

   b. I'm so upset! I just can't take **it** anymore!

3. a. How's the cheesecake in this deli? Have you had **it**?

   b. I've had **it** up to here with your silliness!

4. a. This pot's too hot. I can't hold it another second.

   b. Hold it right there, varmint! This here's the sherriff.

Are the **it**'s different? The a.'s refer to **city**, **car, cheesecake**, **pot**, but the b.'s refer to whole sets of circumstances. Verbs such as **like, hate, stand, tolerate, stomach, take** (in the sense of **tolerate**) usually take this kind of "dummy object" **it**. For some reason, this is very noticeable in the speech of, say, aerobics instructors: "March it out." "Step it high."

F. **Summary Tags**

These are almost the mirror image of dummies, but this is a good place to bring them up, nonetheless, because instead of using a pronoun to hold a place but not refer to anything, here you use a pronoun to refer to an entire thought. Like the question tags in Chapter 14.V., above, you also use summary tags to respond to questions without having to repeat whole segments of the question.

1. **Infinitive and Auxiliary types**: just repeat the auxiliary or the **to** without the verb itself.

   a. Do you want **to go**? No, I don't want **to**. (cf. also discussion of infinitives in Chapter 8, Part 2, V.F., Chapter 9, V.)

   b. Is it raining? Yes, it **is**.

2. **The Clause type**: **so** sums up the entire preceding proposition. Traditional grammar calls it an adverb. It is really more like a pronoun, perhaps better, a "pro-clause". . . Just watch your target language. Maybe it does something similar and maybe not.

a. Do you think {(that) it's going to rain}?
Yes, I think **so** (= *that it is going to rain*).

b. Is today the first day of the rest of your life?
Yes, I believe **so** (=*that today is the first day of. . .*)

III. OMNIPERSONALS

A. Back in Chapter 11, II.E. there was some discussion of the **generalized** use of **we, you,** and **they**. Observe these dialogues. How do the questions get answered:

1. "How do you get to Erma's house?"

   a. "You take Bus #45 and get off at Elm St."

   b. "I take the short cut through the Jones' backyard."

   This is obviously the linguistic trick that allows the same sentence to be understood on two different levels and leads to corny jokes like the old Vaudevillian line: "Excuse me, how do you get to Carnegie Hall?" "Practice, my friend, practice."

2. "Can you turn right on red?"

   a. "Sure you can. That law's been on the books for years."

   b. "I could if I wanted to, but I'd rather wait out the traffic."

3. "These are my friends from Belgium. They speak Flemish."

   a. "Oh, I thought they spoke French in Belgium."

   b. "They do, but they also speak Flemish."

4. a. "In the U.S.A. we vote for the president in November."

   b. "Maybe *you* do, pal. ***I***'m stayin' home. Hrrmphh!"

B. The pronouns **we-you-they** can be **narrowly personal**, referring to people you could point out and identify, or what you might call **broadly personal** or **omnipersonal**, meaning "blanket group: anybody at all and everybody equally, all speakers, addressees, and other referents, actual and potential."

1. When you read such sentences on paper, only knowledge of the particular situation in question will tell you which meaning is which. Of course you can also mis-interpret somebody else's question, as is probably the case in 4, above, whether deliberately or not.

2. In speech, the voice intonation with which you phrase the question audibly will clear it right up, but in general you can say that if a **you** question has an "**I/we**" answer it is narrowly personal. If it has a **you** answer instead, you can bet it is omnipersonal.

3. A way around this potential ambiguity--but one that is rarely utilized in normal speech--is the pronominal use of **one**, as in "**One must do as one is told**." This sounds really stilted in English, especially if you continue to use it over several consecutive sentences.

   a. Imagine describing daily life in some other place: "In East Overshoe **one** hangs out **one's** laundry in the morning before **one** combs **one's** hair. Then **one** gets dressed and feeds **one's** family." Almost comical, isn't it?

   b. But the equivalent construction in a whole host of languages is absolutely the norm. Some languages have a dedicated omnipersonal pronoun like French ***on*** or German ***man***. Russian, Hebrew, and Arabic, for example, use the verb form that agrees with "they" but without the pronoun "they." This makes the pronoun **they** in all these languages "narrowly personal" in ways that it need not be in English. In order to say **they** in these languages you have to know what group of non-participants you are referring to. Otherwise, if you say, "In East Overshoe **they** hang out **their** laundry," speakers of those languages will ask you,"*Who* hangs out their laundry?"

   c. This does not mean that the group **they** refers to cannot be very large. You do not literally have to know every member of the referred-to group. In the sentence, "In China they do wonderful miniature art," **they** is omnipersonal. In the similar-looking, "The Chinese are fine artisans. They do wonderful miniature art," **they** is personal, but the membership in the group is vast.

4. Recognizing when you mean something "omnipersonally" is a major psychological hurdle to get over because you could speak a perfectly correct **you-** or **they-**type sentence in your target language, but it wouldn't mean what you wanted it to. This kind of phenomenon really points out the difference between thinking in English and translating into the other language, on the one hand, and thinking in the terms and structures of the other language.

C. Most grammar books do not stress the difference between **impersonal** and **omnipersonal** sentences (especially since the term **omnipersonal** is appearing in print right here for the first time!).

1. Some languages have a lot of impersonal constructions. English used to have more than just the **it** types. You still see them in Shakespeare, e.g., **"Methinks** the lady doth protest too much." This is not just an old-fashioned "I think," but rather a kind of indirect object, "there is thinking concerning me." This is why the verb is 3rd person singular with **-s**.

2. Omnipersonals say that there is a subject involved, but either the specific identity of that subject is unimportant, or else every possible subject is equally impotant.

3. Another grammatical device for expressing nearly the same kind of omnipersonal concept is the **passive voice**, as we mentioned in Chapter 9, IX.D.2. The two constructions can communicate the same general idea: "something happens but I do not say exactly who did it, because I do not know, or do know and wish to conceal someone's identity." Compare these:

   a. In China **they** drink a lot of tea. (Omnipersonal)

   b. The Chinese enjoy life: **they** drink a lot of tea. (Vast, but personal)

   c. A lot of tea **is drunk** in China. (Passive, same information but very different feeling.)

EXERCISE 16:

WHO IS "THEY"?

Which of the following exchanges are **Personal** and which are **Omnipersonal**? Imagine a whole conversation. Are any of them ambiguous? Do you need more context to decide? Mark them **P** and **O**, respectively.

____ 1. "How do you get to Carnegie Hall?" "Practice, my boy."

____ 2. "Look where you're going, creep!"

____ 3. In England they drive on the left side of the road.

____ 4. The English are funny: they drive on the left.

____ 5. Don't drink that: it'll make you sick!

____ 6. A steady diet of Coke and potato chips will make you sick.

____ 7. What a crazy place: how do they stand it here, Morty?

____ 8. What a crazy place: how do you stand it here, Morty?

____ 9. If you don't pay your taxes you're in big trouble.

____ 10. In the sixties, you protested by growing your hair long. Nowadays, they don't care if your hair's long.

ANSWER KEY TO 16:
1-O. 2-P. 3-O. 4-P. 5-P. 6-O. 7-O. 8-P. 9-O. 10-O.

CHAPTER 17

LOCATION VS. MOTION:

WH-? TH-. H-.

I. THREE CATEGORIES. Contemporary English distinguishes the concepts of

A. **Location** = static location, **fixed position**

B. **Destination** = motion in a direction
an **eventual** or **intended location**

C. **Source** = away from, out of, former or **cancelled location**

Each category has its own characteristic expression for asking questions and giving answers, as the following chart shows:

	LOCATION	DESTINATION	SOURCE
QUESTION	*where (at)?*	*where (to)?*	*where...from?*
ANSWER adv.	*there/here*	*there/here*	
prep.	*at, on....*	*to. . .*	*from. . .*

II. LOCATION WORDS VS. MOTION WORDS

A. From the above chart you see that all three question phrases relating to motion or position begin with **wh-**, namely, **where.** The one-word adverb answer that designates "proximity" to the answerer begins in **h-**, namely, **here.** The adverb for "distance from answerer" begins with **th-**, namely, **there.**

1. However, the distinction between location and destination is not always clear. You have to rely on the meaning of the verb itself. The question **Where?** can be about

   a. static location: Where are you sitting?

   b. or about destination: Where are you going?

2. In the question about source the two parts of the prepositional phrase "frame" the question: **Where** are you **from**?

B. Like the question word **where**, the answer words **there** and **here** do not by themselves tell you whether location or destination is at issue. A fuller answer with a prepositional phrase will usually be clearer:

1. Location: **Where** are you? **At** school. **On** the tennis court.

2. Destination: **Where** are you going? **To** school.

3. Source: **Where** do you come **from**? **From** Tuscaloosa.

4. In many areas of the south and midwest the position-destination questions are made explicit. This is considered non-standard English, but it gets the point across even better. And it makes parallel "framing" structures for all such questions:

   a. **Where** are you **at**? Where did you buy that **at**?

   b. **Where** are you going **to**?

   c. **Where** are you coming **from**?

C. In normal speech, of course, it is perfectly possible to give a quick, one-word answer with no preposition at all. The only real way to know what information the question is requesting is by the verb in the question.

1. a. **Where** are you studying today? The library. (static)

   b. **Where** are you going? The office. (destination)

   c. **Where** are you coming **from**? The club. (source)

2. Not all languages permit you to be so terse. Some have separate forms of nouns--usually cases--for, say, the house that you are **in**--often called **locative case** (not included in Chapter 4, VII. because Latin did not have one of these, though Russian does)--and the house that you are going **to** or moving **into**. (The **accusative** or **dative** often covers these motion realms.) The house that you come **from** would, in Latin, at least, be in the **ablative case**. You can classify many verbs in terms of what case they take to express motion or position.

4. As for other prepositions, you realize that **at, to**, and **from** clearly relate to location, motion, and source, respectively. **In, on,** and **around**, for example, are ambiguous for motion or location:

   a. "The book **is on the table**" is a statement of location, while "I **put** the book **on the table**" is a statement of destination, namely, "I made the book change location."

   b. "There is a fence **around** the house" is locational, but "Go around the obstacle" is motion-related, namely, "You are now on one side of the obstacle. End up on the other side!" If you think this is dragging out the obvious, try studying a language that is sensitive to this and expresses it with different forms. English relies mostly on context and the meaning of the verb.

D. Note the special status of English **home**. Of course it is a noun ("A house is not a home."), but it is also used as what looks like an adverb equally for location and destination:

1. Where are you? Home (= at home.)

2. Where are you heading? Home (= to home, "homeward")

3. Where are you coming from? (From) home.

4. And note **get**: In "We get home at 5" **get** means **arrive at/get to**. This is also a kind of destination or intended location.

E. About the only other such odd words--in that they allow you to distinguish location/destination by the verb only, since there is no preposition (at/in vs. to) are **downtown, uptown, downstairs, upstairs**.

1. In principle these are, themselves, prepositional phrases ("down into town" or something similar) but modern English fuses the parts together into single words.

   a. I'll **be downtown** if you need me. (location)

   b. I'll **be going downtown** after lunch. (motion, destination)

2. Similarly, there are also some **place vs. activity** phrases with and without an indefinite article--cf., Chapter 10, III.D.6--that in normal usage can distinguish location from direction: **I'm in bed, in the bathroom**. vs. **I'm going to bed, to the bathroom**. But the corresponding phrases in baby-talk are purely directional: **Baby go beddy-bye/ go potty.** You can't **be beddy-bye** or **be potty.**

F. **Are you coming or going?**

This is another of several ways that English expresses the point of view of the **participants in the speech event**, cf. Chapter 11, II. The verb **come** usually means **motion toward the speaker** (and possibly the addressee, as well.) The verb **go** means **motion in a direction**, but it is not specified from whose point of view. This is why **come** combines best with **here**, which also means **in proximity of or direction toward the speaker**. In similar fashion, **go** combines with **there**. This often implies **motion away from the speaker**, but the actual direction does not have to be with relation to the speaker or addressee, as in, "My Ferrari **goes** real fast."

1. When you add in the relationship of that movement to all kinds of physical objects you get the phrases with **in(to)-out (of), back-on, up-down**.

2. Consequently, in order for you to say **come in** you must also be **in** whatever room or place you are talking about. When you say **go in**, it is pretty sure that you are **outside**. The opposite is true of **come out-go out**. Likewise: **come back-go back, come on** (urging somebody in a direction toward you)-**go on** (just continuing in whichever direction they were already going, though that is probably away from you). Get the idea?

3. Having said all that, you can observe that many languages are concerned just with the motion and do not distinguish **come** from **go** as English does. But English has, in addition to this speaker-oriented motion vocabulary, a separate set of verbs that focus on **motion with respect to a place**, and these completely ignore the point of view of the speaker. Of course, you can impose that speaker orientation by paraphrasing them with **come-go** combinations:

   a. **enter** → come-go **in** (You, the speaker, may be outside or inside when you say **enter**.)
   b. **exit** → come-go **out**
   c. **return** → come-go **back**
   d. **ascend** → come-go **up**
   e. **descend** → come-go **down**
   f. **circumvent** → come-go **around**

   The obvious difference between the groups on the left and right of the arrows is that the left-hand group probably sounds more "formal" than the right-hand group. That is true of English, but it may be the only option--and, therefore, neither formal nor informal--in your target language.

4. You might as well add one very versatile motion-like verb: **get**. It can combine with all the prepositions that **come** and **go** can, but it seems to emphasize the final destination, rather than the actual motion toward the destination. This is why it feels like a "sharp, sudden, or quick" motion. Another implication of **get**-type motion is that the destination is a "little place." Whether you are sitting in the car or standing outside, you do not say to your friend, "Come in" or "Go in," as you would to a house or a room, but rather, "**Get in**." If the movement is to take place in a small area, you say, as you might to your dog, "**Get** down." So the **come-go-get** group of motion verbs is really very interesting and very subtle.

5. Of course, it is not difficult to find examples in English where you mix points of view. Imagine the following dialogue in terms of speaker's point of view:

a. "Hey, Frankie, where are you **going**?"
"To the movies. Wanna **come** along"

b. "Hey, Frankie, where are you **going**?"
"To the movies."
"Say, can I **come/go** with you?"

In a. the first speaker sees Frankie in motion and inquires about his destination. When Frankie takes his turn as speaker, he naturally assumes his own point of view and asks his friend to move in his direction. In b. that first speaker, instead of assuming his own or even Frankie's point of view, **projects both of them ahead** to the movies and says **come**, as if they are already there and see themselves approaching. If he merely wants to join Frankie, he says **go**. Do you see how you can shift back and forth? Listen to how often you do that and ask yourself what you meant by it. (The same applies to the transitive counterparts of these, namely, **bring, take**, but that is a topic for another time.)

III. THE WAY IT WAS

A. Older English maintained a very neat three-way contrast of questions and answers for these concepts. Revising the chart inI.C., above you find:

	LOCATION	DESTINATION	SOURCE
QUESTION	*where?*	*whither?*	*whence?*
ANSWER	*there* *here*	*thither* *hither*	*thence* *hence*

B. All but **here-there-where** sound archaic, poetic, or Biblical to us nowadays, but **whither, thither,** and **hither** were part of regular literary language right up till the beginning of the 20th century. (There is one additional location adverb not listed here, **yon** which is **there** for "far-away".)

1. "**Whither** thou goest I will go. . ." (Book of Ruth)

2. This is the place **whence** we began our trek home(ward).?

3. We sojourned to the inn and **thence** to the mountain....skipping **hither, thither**, and **yon**...

4. The only one of these still in use is **hence** in formal writing but less in the concrete sense of physical position than the more abstract **here**, like "given this situation."

∞∞

EXERCISE 17:

WHITHER GO YE?

Determine whether the following sentences refer to **L**ocation, **D**estination, or **S**ource. Paraphrase them so that this becomes clear.

_________ 1. Don't sit on the new furniture.

_________ 2. Enter the room and place your books in the box.

_________ 3. Bring it here, Fido, bring it here...

_________ 4. Close the door when you leave the building.

_________ 5. The volcano erupted and spewed forth hot lava.

_________ 6. We all live in a Yellow Submarine.

_________ 7. I won't be home tonight. I'll be at their place.

_________ 8. She got home and made a sandwich.

_________ 9. Take me home! I don't want to go to their place!

_________ 10. They arrived at the party late.

ANSWER KEY TO 17
1-L. 2-D. 3-D. 4-S. 5-S. 6-L. 7-D. 8-D. 9-D. 10-D.

CHAPTER 18

"WHO DOES WHAT TO WHOM?"

MORE ON ENGLISH VERB TYPES AND ROLE RELATIONS

SUBJECT OR ACTOR? OBJECT OR UNDERGOER? TRANSITIVE OR CAUSATIVE? MIDDLE-REFLEXIVE-PASSIVE VOICE? AND OTHER DELIGHTS

CAUTION: YOU ARE ENTERING NON-TRADITIONAL TERRITORY!

Human language would be pretty simple if it were concerned only with the physical layout of subjects and objects in its sentences. When you read between the lines you discover a whole world of concepts that traditional grammar usually sweeps under the rug because many languages do not use separate verb forms to distinguish these very abstract notions the way they do with, say, verb tenses. These notions of **actor** and **undergoer** are concerned with real-world relations between actions and things. You may never see these extremely useful terms elsewhere in your language study, but an awareness of them will help you over some inevitable rough spots in your language learning life. Keep an open mind and really try to imagine the "guts" of the scenes you describe through your language.

I. SUBJECT VS. ACTOR; OBJECT VS. UNDERGOER

A. After all the aforegoing discussions and exercises, thinking about nouns as subjects and objects and about verbs as transitive and intransitive has become second nature to you. The traditional explanations of sentence structure focus all our attention on subjects, verbs, and objects of verbs. That is, as long as you can identify the grammatical subject, traditional grammar isn't much interested in what relation that real-world person or thing has to that real-world action. In this chapter we make the jump from textbook grammar to real-world relations.

1. Take these minimal sentences: **Children cry. Horses whinny. Dogs bark. Geese fly. Ants crawl.** It is clear that these verbs are active voice (cf. Chapter 9, IX.), and that the subjects are also the **actors**.

2. Compare these with the minimal sentences: **Ivory Soap floats. Trees fall in the forest. The sun rises. Time flies.** Here there is also some kind of activity, but you would not exactly say that these subjects are the actors. Rather they merely show the evidence of some kind of process that they do not initiate or have any control over. The subjects here are not actors. Call them, rather, **undergoers** of the verbal process.

   Given that all the verbs in 1. and 2. are intransitive, you seethat English sentence structure permits both actors and non-actors to be the subject of an intransitive verb. Not all languages are so accommodating.

B. Now what if the verb is **transitive**? Review Passive Voice in Chapter 9, IX and note these sentences:

   1. John has won the prize.

   2. The prize was won by John.

   The subject-verb relations are clearly different. The two sentences refer to the same situation and have the same layout, namely, **subject + verb.** Both **John** in 1. and **prize** in 2. are the "subjects" of our attention. The first sentence is about **John** and the second is about the **prize**, though they are both involved in both.

C. However, in B1., **John** as subject "does" something, while in B2. the **prize** as subject does not "do" anything, but merely sets a scene where it is still John who does the winning.

1. In both sentences, then, John is the **actor**, and the prize is the **undergoer**, regardless of the fact that they are both **subjects.**

2. In the first sentence **has won** is **active voice**, while **was won** in the second is **passive voice**. One more thing: **win** as a verb is by nature **transitive**, whether it is active or passive. What changes is the actor-undergoer relation.

3. So in logical terms, the subject of an active transitive verb is also the actor, and the object of an active transitive verb is the undergoer. That usually works.

    a. Consequently, the subject of a passive verb is *still* the undergoer of the verb.

    b. One logical consequence of making an active verb into a passive is that a verb in the passive cannot also have a direct object. The simple reason is that the subject of that passive is already the undergoer. (Verbs do not usually have more than one undergoer.)

4. One reason why traditional English grammar does not make you think about this is that English--which is not a **case language**--uses the same noun form for subject whether it is an actor or undergoer.

    a. That is, the "subject" pronouns, as discussed in Chapter 11 above can refer to people that **play the role of either actor or undergoer**. You say both "**He** fired the employee," as actor-subject of the transitive verb, and "**He** was fired for insubordination," as an undergoer-subject of the passive.

    b. Other languages may prefer to use one form for **actor** and a different one for **undergoer**, no matter what **place** they occupy in the sentence layout, or they may show by the form of the *verb* whether the subject is actor or undergoer. (English does this directly with the forms of active vs. passive and indirectly in a few other ways, coming up.)

D. One More Consideration

1. Since transitive verbs like **give, send, promise, buy, allot** have the additional ability to take an indirect object (cf. Chapter 5) you have to ask yourself what happens to this indirect object if you make the verb passive. What you get is an apparent contradiction to C.3.b. above, namely,

   a. Active: The teacher gave ⟨the pupil⟩ [a book].

   b. Passive: (1). The book was given (to) the pupil.

   (2). The pupil was given [a book] (by the teacher).

2. Excluding the actor phrase with **by** in 2., it appears that the passive **was given** in 2b. *does* have an undergoer direct object **book**, but the **pupil**, despite its being the subject, is still the recipient or benefactor of that undergoer. So, while the active sentence in 1. has an actor-subject, 2a. **passivizes** what "was" the direct object. It (2a.) expresses the undergoer of the situation as subject instead of as direct object. This is quite normal and the essence of passive world-wide.

3. It is interesting that in English, *unlike* most other languages, you can passivizes what was the *in*direct object as a subject, as in (2). Not all languages with an indirect object construction will allow you to passivize it. Sometimes you get the equivalent of a dummy subject (cf. Chapter 16) and the so-called **impersonal passive**. You preserve the indirect object as an indirect object, though it sounds funny in English:

   a. *It was given a book to the pupil. (really not an English sentence)

   b. (?) There was a book given to the pupil. (better but not great)

4. Look back at the "hidden indirect object" verbs in Chapter 5, like **pay** and **tell** and add **serve** to that list, as in We served [the roast] vs. We served ⟨the guests⟩. Now recall the notion of **control** (Chapter 9,

V.B.) and look at the sentence. "Who wants to be served first?" (Chapter 9, IX.D.2.f.) You see that the *subject* "who" is at the same time the controller of **want** but *not* of the passive infinitive complement. It is, rather, the **passivized indirect object** of **serve**. You see that the traditional ideas of "subject" and "object" are just not enough to capture all the wonders of real language. If your target language does not allow you to passivize indirect objects, such a sentence cannot occur.

EXERCISE 18a.:
PASSIVE RIDES AGAIN!
KEY, P. 353
Go back to Exercise 5, page 55, and recycle sentences 1-6. First passivize the direct objects and then see if you can passivize the indirect objects, as well. Do they all make sense? Does the meaning change? Which ones do not work?

II. ONCE A TRANSITIVE, ALWAYS A TRANSITIVE?

A. This somewhat misleading dictum is meant to counteract the even more misleading dictum that a transitive verb is one that "takes a direct object." It is perfectly possible for a verb to be **inherently transitive** and simply not express a direct object. It is no less transitive, because you automatically and unconsciously imagine an object. Take these common examples:

1. a. I'm **cooking supper.**

   b. Leave me alone. I'm **cooking**. (obviously, something!)

2. a. Children must **practice piano** every day.

   b. Have you **practiced** today? (piano? your lesson?)

3. a. A little nap really **refreshes me.**

   b. Coke: the pause that **refreshes**. (whoever drinks it.)

4. a. I'll **close the office** early and go home.

   b. I'll **close** early and go home. (the office, we assume.)

5. I hate to **type my own papers** because I **type** so badly.

There is always an implied object. Some languages treat verbs with explicit objects differently from verbs with implicit objects. Other common examples are proto-typically transitive verbs like **eat, drink, write, read,** where the activity has to have an undergoer, but it is simply left unstated:

6. So you wanna go out and **eat**?

7. That guy sure can **drink**.

8. You go to school to learn to **read, write**, and **cipher**.

B. The other side of the coin of the misleading statement about direct objects is that some inherently intransitive verbs are followed by something in the sentence that can be mistaken for a direct object. More than likely, it is not a direct object in the sense of an undergoer. It is usually a kind of measure or quantity, so traditional grammar calls it an adverb-like use of a very noun-looking thing. Use your intuition and try parsing these:

1. a. The child walks well.

   b. I'd walk a mile for a Camel.

   Would you parse this: I'd walk [a mile] for a Camel? Is the "mile" undergoing anything? Is it affected?"

2. a. Harry likes to travel.

   b. He's travelled the whole wide world.

3. a. Esther Williams swam magnificently.

   b. She even swam the English Channel.

4. a. A Porsche goes fast.

   b. It can go a hundred miles an hour.

   c. You might as well go the whole nine yards. . .

Do you feel that all these object-looking items--**mile, world, Channel, yard**--are merely answering the question "how much, to what extent"? They measure the action but are not direct objects. The verbs **go, swim, travel** in these examples have a transitive-looking structure but not a transitive meaning.

C. **Whodunit: Action With No Actor?**

1. Now consider the following pairs, most of which describe the same scene, that is, "mean" the same thing. What is the subject and who is the actor? Where is the undergoer?

   a. (1). Water **boils** at 100 degrees Centigrade.
   (2). You have to **boil** the water before you drink it.

   b. (1). Oh, fooey! The casserole **burned**!
   (2). Oh, fooey! I **burned** the casserole!

   c. (1). The store **opens** at 8:00.
   (2). The boss **opens** the store at 8:00.

   d. (1). The wind **blew**, and the door **opened**.
   (2). The wind **blew** and **opened** the door.

   e. (1). The window is stuck. It won't **open**.
   (2). The window is stuck. I can't **open** it.

   f. (1). The office **closes** at 5:00.
   (2). The employees **close** the office at 5:00.

   g. (1). Their plans **changed**, and they stayed home.
   (2). They **changed** their plans and stayed home.

   h. (1). The door **closed** and **locked**, and my keys are inside!
   (2). She **closed** the door and **locked** it.

i. (1). The show **began** at 9:00.
(2). The M.C. **began** the show at 9:00.

j. (1). The lecture **ended** on time.
(2). The speaker **ended** the lecture on time.

2. After all that, the consistency between the (1)'s and the (2)'s has to jump out at you. In the (2)'s, the subjects of these transitive active verbs are all actors. In the (1)'s, however, the subjects are not the actors, nor could they possibly be in any physical sense. So, *are* these verbs transitive and active?

   a. There is clearly an action in (1), but the actor is not mentioned. The action happens as if **all by itself**, and the subject merely shows the evidence of the action. What occupies the subject **position** in the sentence plays the **role** of **undergoer** in the real world.

   b. There are languages that use a different verb form for an expectedly transitive verb with a subject that is not a candidate for the actor. French, German, Russian, Hebrew and Turkish, for example, often use one kind of verb form for the (1)'s and a different form of the same verb for the (2)'s. The grammar books for most of these languages would do you a great favor by taking advantage of the notions of **actor** and **undergoer**, but they do not. Sometimes the (2) types are called **reflexive, passive**, or the catch-all term **intransitive**, but this is misleading at best.

   c. So the statement above that "a transitive is always transitive" can be amended slightly to "**a verb that can have an undergoer always has one even if it has no actor**." But this brings us to the topic of what kind of subjects you can expect to be actors of what kind of verbs. It's really an amazing mosaic!

III. BEYOND TRANSITIVE TO CAUSATIVE: UNDERGOERS THAT THINK THEY'RE ACTORS?

A. Causatives

This is a term by which you designate verbs and constructions that indicate a two-stage process:

1. The actor does something that affects an undergoer (normal transitive) and. . .

2. that undergoer is itself seen as either actor or undergoer of the action in the verb, whether or not the actor does it, as well.

3. Take the pair of sentences

   a. The children **returned** to their home town.

   b. The children **returned** the books to the library.

4. The children in 3a. are the actors. They do the returning. They "end up back" in the town. In 3b. they are also actors, and the books are clearly undergoers. The important thing is that the children's actual action is unspecified--they might have sent the books by mail or courier and not gone to the library themselves--but you do know that the books "ended up back" at the library. The children **caused the books to return**.

5. Causative, then, is a kind of transitive, except that the focus is on the end-state of the undergoer. This is different from a regular transitive, say, **The children read the books**, where the books are purely undergoers of **read** and may or may not have changed by the end of the scene.

6. A few other pairs

   a. (1). The bus **leaves** in an hour.
   (2). The bus **leaves** you (off) at the museum.

   b. (1). They **signed up** for the course.
   (2). They **signed** me **up** for the course.

c. (1). Danny **grew** three inches last year. (measure)
(2). Danny **grew** tomatoes last year. (something affected)

7. The (1)'s are all intransitive. (You might question whether "bus" and "they" are actors, but "Danny" is clearly the undergoer of his action. The (2)'s, the corresponding *transitives* are, more precisely, causatives. In 6.c.(2), for example, Danny is an actor who does something--dig, plant, water, fertilize, spray, worry--such that the tomatoes end up as the undergoers of a **grow**-action.

8. As with everything in this book, the point is not to sit down and memorize and think that you "know" grammar. The point is to take command of your in-born tools and start thinking about the incredibly complex and subtle relationships you perceive and express in speech.

B. **English expresses causatives a few more ways:**

1. **make somebody (do) something** (not the same as "force"!):

   a. I don't want to go, but Daddy's **making me go**. (Daddy, himself, may or may not go and may or may not have *forced* me.)

   b. The loud boom **made him jump** 20 feet. (no "forcing" at all.)

2.

Active variant	Passive variant
have somebody **do** something	**have** something **done**
get somebody **to do** something	**get** something **done**

   a. If you can't fix the faucet, have somebody **fix** it.
   have it **fixed**.

   b. The car won't start and nothing I do will get it **to start**.
   get it **started**.

3. Two different but clearly related words can be in an intransitive-to-causative relationship. Which is which in these:

1. Prices seem **to rise** even when nobody **raises them.**

2. The lumberjacks **felled the tree**, and it **fell** gracefully.

3. The flower pot **is sitting** right where she **set it** down.

4. The patrons **sat** where the ushers **seated them**.

5. The rug **is lying** well. We just **laid it** yesterday.

4. Two unrelated words often work in pairs to express the intransitive-causative relationship:

a. He **went** into the house and **took the book** in.
(=made it go in)

b. **Come in** and **bring your friend in**, too.
(=have her/him come in)

c. If the dog won't **go in** the house by himself, **put him in** the house. (another kind of **make go in**).

5. The important thing to keep in mind is that **causative** is really a type of transitive, though not all transitives are causatives. Many books will talk about the **grow**-type verb as being intransitive, as in A.4.a above, or transitive, as in A.4.b., above. This is true, but the transitive is of a special type, namely, causative.

D. Thus far, then, we have distinguished several groups of verbs that behave in various ways with respect to actors and undergoers.

1. **Always intransitives**: subject may be actor or undergoer:

a. Subject in role of Actor: John yawns.

b. Subject in role of Undergoer: John falls.

2. **Always transitives**: subject may be actor or undergoer, and in a passive, the subject is the undergoer.

a. Subject in role of Actor of transitive, Object in role of Undergoer:

John **mows** the lawn.

b. Subject in role of Undergoer, Actor expressed with optional **by**:

The lawn **was mowed** (by John).

c. Subject in role of Undergoer, no actor expressed (but this is *not* passive!):

The lawn **mows** easily when it's dry.
(= "One can mow [the lawn]. . .")

3. **Intransitive with undergoer subject → causative with an actor-subject** that also involves an undergoer. In this case, the actor-subject does an action, specified or unspecified, and the verb expresses the direct object as the actor.

a. Subject as (involuntary) Undergoer: John grew fast.

The tulips grew well.

b. → Subject as Actor, and object as "double Undergoer", both of John's external action and its own internal action:
John grew [tulips].

EXERCISE 18b.:
ACTORS AND UNDERGOERS

Decide whether the verbs in the given contexts are Intransitive, Transitive, or Causative and whether their subjects are Actors or Undergoers. Designate them as:

A/I = actor subject of intransitive verb:	She spit.
U/I = undergoer subject of intransitive verb:	She fell.
A/T = actor subject of transitive verb:	She eats toads.
A/C = actor subject of causative verb:	She boiled water.
U/T = undergoer subject of a transitive verb:	The water boiled.
	She received a letter.

Example: A/T John wrote a novel. (John is actor of transitive write.)

U/T The water boiled.
(Water is not actor but undergoer of a transitive boil, despite the fact that it is a subject. We do not know who or what was the actor.)

Some of these are open to discussion. Discuss them with another English speaker and see if you can figure out what relations you express.

1. ______ This is the way {the world ends}: not with a bang but a whimper. (Eliot).

2. _____ Oh! My tummy hurts!

3. _____ Yuck! Your cigar stinks!

4. _____ Your damn cigar stunk up my whole room!

5. _____ This smells funny.

6. _____ Take time to smell the flowers.

7. _____ Ms. Smith runs briskly in Central Park every morning.

8. ____ Ms. Smith runs a machine at the factory.

9. _____ The machine runs well.

10. ____ Birds fly, but people fly planes.

11. ____ This plane sure flies well.

12. ___ He drives well.

13. ___ His Audi drives nicely, too.

14. _____ "I'll huff, and I'll puff. . .. .

15. _____ . . .and I'll *b b l l o o w w* your house down!!"

ANSWER KEY TO 18b.
1-U/I. 2-U/I. 3-U/I. 4-A/C. 5-U/I. 6-A/T. 7-A/I. 8-A/C. 9-U/I. 10-A/I, A/C. 11-U/T. 12-A/I (T?). 13-U/I(T?). 14-A/I. 15-A/C.

IV. DO YOU HEAR VOICES?

Active and passive voice seem by now like normal language phenomena. But besides those two, there are a few more constructions you should recognize.

A. You occasionally see the term **Middle Voice**. In English this not a verb form but a construction that expresses that the subject of the verb performs the action "for her or his own benefit." Traditional grammars sees this as "mid-way" between active and passive, that is, the verb form looks and feels active and transitive. But when you look for a direct object there is none.

1. That is, it is really a kind of active voice, and the verb often feels transitive, but you don't see an object, and it might even be awkward or change the meaning somewhat to supply one. You understand, therefore, that the **actor is**, in principle, **her or his own undergoer**.

2. Some typical examples:

a. John **washes up, shaves, dresses, studies and exercises**. (He does these things intentionally and deliberately, and only he benefits from these actions.)

b. I can concentrate my efforts, but I can't **concentrate** on this problem.

It is, strictly, speaking, a sub-type of active voice, and you see clearly from verbs like **exercise** and **study** that the notion of **undergoer** is not at all the same as **direct object**, just in case you were still deluding yourself into thinking the former was just a fancy term for the latter.

3. It is fair to say that direct objects of transitive verbs are, in general, undergoers, but not all undergoers are direct objects. One notion is mechanical and layout-related. The other is more philosophical and real-world-related.

B. **Reflexive** is also a type of construction where the actor-subject is his or her own undergoer-object. If this sounds just like middle voice your instincts are fine.

1. The difference in English is that the undergoer-object of a reflexive is expressed with a **-self** pronoun: **I wash myself. He shaves himself. She dresses herself.** They are sometimes hard to distinguish, though grammar books use the term "reflexive" more than "middle voice."

2. If these sound a little odd to your ear the reason is that English does not use this reflexive construction much for actions that you **expect** to be reflexive. The shaving and dressing mentioned in A.2. are expressed as a middle voice because the undergoer is unlikely to be anyone *but* the actor. If you **wash the baby**, then you have an undergoer-object different from the subject. If you are a barber and **shave Joe**, then your normally transitive action carries over to an explicit undergoer-object just like any other transitive. But even if you are a barber by profession, in your personal life you **shave** in the morning and do not say, "I shave myself," unless there is a question about the real actor.

3. The normal cases where English uses this reflexive construction are those like:

   a. I **see myself** in the mirror.

   b. The child **feeds himself** now.

c. We hate to peel potatoes: we wish potatoes would **peel themselves.**

4. These are cases when you cannot necessarily anticipate the object, and it is just an accident that the object pronoun refers to the same physical entity as the subject noun or pronoun.

5. A lot of languages, especially the ones commonly taught in schools, tend to express both middle and reflexive by the same construction.

   a. Textbooks of these languages typically call the construction "reflexive," even though that makes little sense to an English-speaking learner for the reasons just discussed. But it does make some sense for a language to express these two types of meaning by the same type of verb form, if you bear in mind that middle and reflexive have in common the fact the subject can be both actor and undergoer to different extents.

   b. If you go one more step, of course, you can lump these all together with some kind of **passive**, since the subject of a passive is also the undergoer. (The difference is that the passive is more restricted because the subject can be <u>only</u> the undergoer and not also the actor.)

6. A couple of other **middle** vs. plain **transitive** contrasts.

   a. **Cooked potatoes peel more easily than raw ones** is a normally transitive verb with an undergoer-subject, as discussed in I.A above.

   b. (1). Middle: Birds **feed** on worms.
      (2). Trans.: Birds **feed their young** on worms.

   c. (1). Middle: Mammal babies **nurse** until they leave "home."
      (2). Trans.: Mammal mothers **nurse their young**.

C. **Reciprocity** refers to a situation like "John and Mary love [each other]."

1. Start with a transitive verb and a *plural* subject.

   a. Both members of the subject group are actors and both are undergoers. The second subject is the undergoer of the first's action at the same time that the first subject is the undergoer of the second's action. John loves Mary, just as Mary loves John. The object phrases "each other" or "one another" signal this **reciprocal** action.

   b. The same holds for transitive verbs like **see, know, believe, help** and for preposition-taking verbs like **agree with, confide in, talk about.**

2. Some verbs work the same way but do not usually go with "each other". In a sense, the plural subject contains its own "internal direct object":

   a. John and Mary **meet** at 5 and **fight** over the slightest thing.

   b. Parents and children can learn to **relate** well.

3. In 2a. we know that "John meets Mary and Mary also meets John." Each performs a "meeting" action and *each* affects the *other*, but it would sound quite odd to say, *"John and Mary meet each other." That is, the whole unit composed of "an otherwise transitive verb with a **plural subject but no explicit object**" can indicate that the subjects are all actors and simultaneously each other's undergoers.

4. Doesn't this sound a lot like reflexive and middle? You are right if it feels that way. **Reciprocal** is a kind of "double reflexive," if you will. A lot of languages, as we just mentioned above, express all three of these--middle, reflexive, reciprocal--with the same type of verb form or construction. (English is a prime example, with the formula "expectedly transitive verb with no audible direct object.")

EXERCISE 18c.:
WHOSE VOICE IS IT ANYHOW?!

Similar to what you did in Exercise 18a., in the following sentences, decide whether the subject is

A/T:	actor subject of a transitive:	She sells sea shells.
U/T:	undergoer subject of a transitive:	The shells collect on the shore. (the "all by itself" kind)
A-U:	actor and undergoer are the same person or thing, namely, subject of middle voice or reflexive:	She dresses well.
U/P	undergoer subject of a Passive:	The shell was carried out to sea.

Some of them are ambiguous depending on the rest of the situation you envision around them. Put down what you think and see if you agree with the answer key. If you don't, try to imagine what the answer key suggestion indicates.

_____ 1. She's really developed her writing skills.

_____ 2. She's really developed as a writer.

_____ 3. The film was developed at the drug store.

_____ 4. This new film develops in no time flat.

_____ 5. Wine improves with age.

_____ 6. All new Slop Cola: they've improved the formula.

_____ 7. All new Slop Cola: the formula's been improved!

_____ 8. Wow: Slop Cola has really improved!

_____ 9. It's too noisy in here. I can't concentrate.

_____ 10. The government concentrated its efforts on the talks.

_____ 11. The servant washed, shaved, and dressed his master.

_____ 12. The servant washed, shaved, and dressed. (Then he left for town.)

_____ 13. No candidate would increase taxes. . .

_____ 14. . . .yet the taxes keep increasing.

_____ 15. Bad news: taxes have been increased!

ANSWER KEY TO 18b.
1-A/T. 2-A=U. 3-U/P. 4-U/T. 5-U/T. 6-A/T. 7-U/P. 8-U/T. 9-A=U. 10-A/T. 11-A/T. 12-A=G. 13. A/T*. 14-U/T**. 15-U/P.
* More accurately: A/C, but that's not the point here. ** Really U/I, since **increase** means "become greater" and **increase taxes** is the causative "make taxes become greater."

EXERCISE 18d.

REVIEW OF ROLES

Key: p. 355

Just identify all the following items, no matter where they occur in the sentence, in the following ways:

Underline actors once. Underline undergoers twice.

Enclose /actors-as-their-own-undergoers/ (middle voice, reciprocal, reflexive) in diagonal slashes.

Square-bracket the [undergoer of a causative] (undergoer, as far as actor-subject is concerned, and actor or undergoer of the verb itself).

Curly-bracket the {indirect object of an active made passive}.

In sentences with more than one clause separate the subordinate clause by double hyphens and operate within it the same as a main clause, even if this entails your copying them onto another piece of paper. (Needless to say, put back missing **that** in subordinate clauses, since it serves a function in its own clause.)

Examples:

1. The citizens elected the candidate.
   → The citizens elected the candidate.

2. The candidate was backed by a solid committee.
   → The candidate was backed by a solid committee.

3. The citizens made the candidate promise to repave the streets.
   → The citizens made [the candidate] promise to repave the streets.

   (This brings in a problem of **control**: "candidate" straddles two clauses: object of **made**, subject of **promise**, but there is no convenient graphic symbol to indicate that without drawing elaborate diagrams. Just think about it.)

4. The citizens who elected the candidate were promised repaved streets →{The citizens}--who elected the candidate--were promised repaved streets.

As with 18b., some of these are open to other interpretations. You are certainly allowed other views, but be prepared to defend them.

1. He did not receive the car that was promised him.

2. The car he ordered did not arrive.

3. The car he was promised was not delivered.

4. You can try to anger them if they anger you, but they don't anger easily.

5. She stood the vase on the mantle, and there it stands to this day.

6. The picture was hung yesterday, and it's still hanging.

7. She was brought upstairs. Then she was brought some tea.

8. She photographed him, but he didn't photograph well.

9. Have you tasted the cake? The cake tastes good!

10. They want to sell the book, but that book won't sell.

CHAPTER 19

RELATIONS BETWEEN TIME AND ACTION:

OBLIGATORY "FOR", OPTIONAL (FOR), "IN", (WITH)IN

This chapter is concerned with sentences like these:

We gazed into each other's eyes	**(for) an hour.**
We went to town	**for an hour.**
We'll go to town	**in an hour.**
We can get to Toronto	**(with)in an hour.**

What's all the fuss about? Look back at Chapter 9, X.C. on four kinds of action:

STATE, ACTIVITY, ACCOMPLISHMENT, ACHIEVEMENT.

We will see how English uses **time expressions** and prepositional phrases to distinguish the fact that **state** and **activity** verbs have **duration** (mere measurement of time), while **accomplishment** and **achievement** verbs lead to some kind of **change.** The reason these notions are so troublesome for learners of other languages is that languages have a tremendous variety of means for expressing the relations among verbal actions, the time they take to run their course, and the way the world looks "before" and "after." If you speak your target language by "translating word for word" from English you will produce nonsense. You need an idea of what kinds of relations English accounts for. Your target language may have more, fewer, or entirely different notions. For the four kinds discussed here, English uses only two prepositions. (Two and a half if you include "zero", as in the optional **for**.) Other languages may use different expressions or combinations of prepositions and noun **cases** for each type.

I. WHEN ACTION AND TIME ARE SIMULTANEOUS

A. Time = Action

The time expression gives a simple measurement of the time the action goes on and assumes that the world was the same "after" as it was "before." English indicates this for **states** and **activities** with an **optional "for "+ time expression**. That is, you may say **for** or you may leave **for** out, and it will not hurt the meaning of the sentence. (Whether you have a personal preference for it is another matter.) Say the following examples out loud both with and without **for** and see if you feel any difference or preference. Try to paraphrase the sentence so that you feel the difference between plain "action that lasts a certain amount of time" and "actions that signal a change of circumstances":

1. State verbs:

   a. She **lived** in Seattle **(for) two years.**

   b. They **have been lying** there motionless **(for) five hours.** (Should we call the cops?)

2. Activity verbs:

   a. She read **(for) an hour** and went to bed. (action, then change)

   b. He worked there **(for) six months** and quit. (action, then change)

   c. We have been waiting for you **(for) over an hour**! (just action)

You could say all these with or without **for** with no effect on the utterance, couldn't you? The important point is that in, say, 2a., the "reading" action yields no change, while "went to bed" does. In 2b. the "working" proceeded regularly, but "quit" suggests a clear "before" and "after" situation: before, he was working, then he wasn't. In 2c. there is just a "waiting" action that lasts.

B. Time = Duration of action leading to a natural conclusion

Measure the **total time** that goes by with the action in progress and expect that when the action has run its course there is some kind of result or shift to a new action, that is, you **accomplish** one action, and that allows you to proceed to the next scene.

1. This is expressed by **in + time expression**:

   a. She ran from home to school **in 6 minutes** flat.

   b. The train goes from Seattle to Portland **in 3 hours.**

   c. You have **2 hours in which** to complete the assignment.

   d. If you're lucky, you'll read that novel **in a week.**

2. The difference between this type and the **optional-for** type is that at the end of these, something is necessarily different, but with the **for**-type things are pretty much the same.

3. You can also substitute **within** for **in** in all these. The difference between them with these time expressions is that **within** gives a maximum "possible" time, but it allows you to get the desired result in less time. **In** usually indicates that the action will take the entire stated time.

4. You can usually paraphrase both **in** and **within** with some kind of sentence like, "It takes X-amount of time for the action to run its natural course, no matter when you start timing." You do not need any particular person's point of view.

II. WHEN TIME AND ACTION ARE SEQUENTIAL

A. Time passes, then action starts.

When a certain time elapses before the action begins, English also uses **in**. The implication is, "Start timing now, as we speak. After X-amount of time, the action will begin or the state will come into being." Often this, like I.B. above, also implies an accomplishment or achievement. The difference is, unlike I.B., above, that **you do need someone's point of view to start timing from**. You need specific information about the speaker, addressees, and the circumstances of the conversation, just like the **shifter** categories of Chapter 11, II.

1. We'll leave the house **in 20 minutes** (that is, from "now").

2. The polls will close **in an hour**. (so it must be 8 P.M.)

3. We're a little lost, but we'll get to your place **in a while**.

Note the overlap with the **in**-type in I.B. If that **in** refers to "total time of action no matter when you start timing," then this **in** means, "You have to know **when** to start timing." English uses the same grammatical means to express apparently different things.

4. In the course of a narrative you can rephrase this as "X-time later": "The loving couple set about their daily routine. He made breakfast and got the kids ready for school. 20 minutes later, she left for the office." That is, "start timing from some point internal to the narrative."

B. **The reverse of II.A.: Accomplish or achieve the result of one action, then start timing second one.**

This situation usually suggests an intended or planned period. English marks this one with an **obligatory for**. If you leave this **for** out the sentence doesn't make sense.

1. We're going to Europe **for a year**
   (= start counting only once we **arrive** there and let a year elapse)

2. They went to the country **for a week.**
   (= intending to spend a week **once they had arrived**).

3. Lend me your book **for a while.**
   (Don't start counting until it has achieved the switch from your hand to mine.)

4. He dropped in **for a minute** but stayed **(for) an hour!**

So, **obligatory for** is "projection or intention of time" and **optional (for)** is "pure measurement of time." You must decide whether you are measuring the duration of an action or the time span that depends on the successful completion of a previous action. Usually, the "before" action is an accomplishment or an achievement, and the result is a state.

⇒ You can picture these four types of relationships like this:

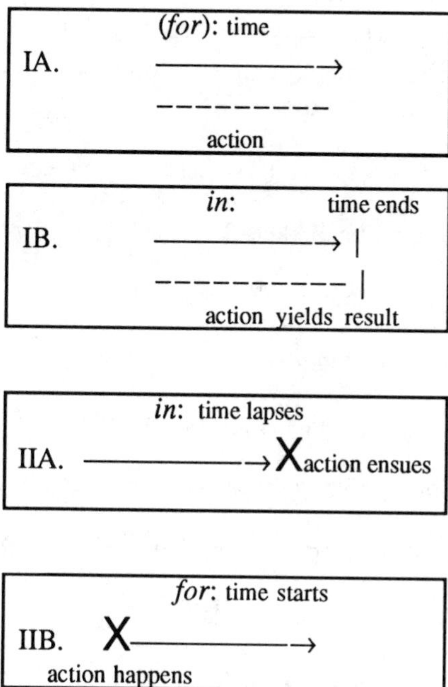

EXERCISE 19: TIME AND ACTION

Determine which of the four possible situations the following sentences illustrate:

T = A	Time = Action, cf. IA, with "optional **for**"
T = D+C	End of Timing of the Duration of the action coincides with its Conclusion and the accomplishment of a result, cf. IB with **in**
T → A	Time passes, then Action happens cf. IIA. with **in**
A → T	action is accomplished, then timing of resulting state begins., cf. IIB. with **obligatory for.**

_______ 1. Don't go away: we'll be there in 5 minutes.

_______ 2. Give him a toy and he'll amuse himself for hours.

_______ 3. They've been living here for a few years.

_______ 4. They're moving to Tacoma in a few weeks.

_______ 5. Minute Rice cooks in just one minute!

_______ 6. I'll finish cooking this in a minute and join you.

_______ 7. You will know peace for the rest of your life.

_______ 8. She'll be gone for a week.

_______ 9. She'll be gone in a week.

_______ 10. Amazing: you read War and Peace in a day!?

ANSWER KEY TO 19:
1-T→A. 2-T=D. 3. T=D. 4-T→A. 5-T=D+C. 6-T→A. 7-T=D. 8-A→T. 9-T→A. 10-T=D+C.

CHAPTER 20

FLEX UP YOUR LEXICON

The **lexicon** is, basically, the stock of words a language has, its vocabulary. It is the stuff contained in the dictionary. Part of the meaning of a word is that it can be used in certain kinds of sentences or together with certain other words but not just any word. You cannot string words together willy-nilly. The published dictionary of any given language defines or translates words, but it is usually not very explicit about how to *use* a word. This chapter is intended to illustrate the wide range of meaning of some commonly used words in English that have many--and for English speakers, often confusing--equivalents in other languages. From the suggested synonyms or paraphrases you begin to get the idea that you can really define a word only in a given context. Just as two points define a line in geometry, so two words begin to define a **semantic field** in language. Especially in language learning, for example, you cannot ask, "How do you say **leave** in this language?" You have to see the single word **leave** as a pie and realize how many wedges it has. Your target language may divide up its pie differently. That is, the word has several different "meanings," and some of these meanings insist on occurring only in certain sentence structures. So the better question is, "How do you say **leave** *in the sense of* **depart** or *in the sense of* **leave something behind?**" (In grammatical terms, is *transitive or causative* **leave** the same as *intransitive* **leave** in this language?)

A good mono-lingual (English-English) dictionary, like Webster's or the Amercian Heritage, should exemplify all of the meanings of a word, and you know how large such volumes can be. So when you use a pocket-size bi-lingual dictionary, like an *English-Spanish/Spanish-English* type, you see that it cannot possibly give you all the meanings of the English word *and* all the possible Spanish equivalents. It may give a string of words that, indeed, "mean" **leave** but not always with enough other information to guide you to pick the appropriate one for your specific context. The hardest thing to realize is that these other-language words have their own life in that language, each with its own emotional connotations, special uses, stylistic nuances and associations. You have to know, too, what kinds of sentence structures they can enter into, what government they have (cf. Chapter 7, III.), and whether they can be, for example, either transitive or intransitive, and if transitive, do you have to express an object or not (cf. the **eat, write, read** type in Chapter 18, where you do not have to state the object and the **like, conjure, destroy** type, where you do), and if you do, then what kind of object the verb can operate on (i.e. **change a tire** in Hebrew, for example, requires a different verb from **change a dollar**). That is, together with the **meaning** of the word you also have to learn the **grammar** of the word. You, as a language learner, may not yet have the experience to choose the one that fits your situation stylistically or emotionally, so use the dictionary only as a tool to **remind you of what you already know** and not as a reliable way to learn new words. If you want to *learn* from the dictionary, you need to do some flipping back and forth. Before you pick a Spanish word from the English-Spanish half of the dictionary, look it up in the Spanish -English half and see if it gives you any further examples that will illustrate whether this word means what you want to express.

To understand how important the right word choice is and how little an average dictionary can really help you choose it, you need only recall former president Jimmy Carter's trip to Poland in 1977. His American translator rendered Carter's "**desire** to help the Polish people" with a Polish word for **desire** that, first of all, Poles considered old-fashioned, and second of all, meant **desire** *in the carnal sense*! Another famous example: a German nun who wrote a note to an American sister signed it, "May the Lord pickle you." She had obviously looked up the equivalent of **preserve, keep, watch over** in a German-English dictionary that did not provide enough context along with its entries. ("Pickling," after all, is a way of "preserving", but *vegetables* and not people. It makes perfect sense in principle, but the details can be pretty hilarious.) The German nun obviously knew English "grammar", because she wrote a perfectly correct sentence **pattern**. Unfortunately, the word she put in the verb slot did not go with the other words in the pattern.

There are lots of anecdotes about this sort of mishap. The point is, the more flexible you are at re-stating words and phrases, the more likely you are to find the places where your own language and your new language converge and diverge. You have to be quite precise about the meanings you want to express--much more precise than most language textbooks insist on. This does not mean that English is a vague or imprecise language or that another language is clearer or more "logical." It merely means that another language divides up one realm of reality differently from the way English does. Russian might have separate verbs for each of the sub-definitions of the single English verb **leave**, below, but while Russian says "clock" for any of several kinds of "time pieces," English divides that realm into "the small one on your wrist" and "the big one on the wall." Neither language is better or worse for it.

The verbs, nouns, and other items below have been chosen because they typically trip up English-speaking language learners who are in the habit of translating "word for word," though you now see that that concept cannot exist! Most of the languages of Europe, at least, treat these items more or less similarly, and all are different from English. Read the suggested sub-definitions and decide which of the sentences illustrate which meaning. The answer keys are provided right below each exercise.

I. VERBS

A. LEAVE

1. depart, go away from, abandon (person or place)
2. exit, go out of (place)
3. make something or someone stay behind
4. part from, say goodbye to (usually a person)

_______a. Sorry, I left the lasagna in the oven too long.

_______b. Close the door when you leave.

_______c. It's no (*sob*!) good, Mortimer, I'm leaving you!

_______d. It's all right, Billy, we're leaving you with the baby sitter.

_______e. What a great barbecue, but now we have to leave.

_______f. So late already? Gotta leave for work pronto!

_______g. Did you leave your wallet home again?

_______h. She left the house and went to the bus stop.

_______i. She left home, assumed a new name, and started over.

KEY to IA: a-3. b-2. c-1,4. d-3. e-1. f-1. g-3. h-2. i-1.

B. **CHANGE**

1. undergoer-subject becomes different (so-called intransitive)
2. actor-subject becomes different (reflexive)
3. actor-subject acts in self-interest (middle voice)
4. actor-subject makes undergoer-object different (transitive)
5. nothing changes in nature, but subject replaces object with something else (transitive), whether another of the same kind of thing or a different one altogether

_______a. We've made plans and can't change them.

_______b. We've made plans and they can't change.

_______c. Why, Dr. Jekyll, how you've changed!

_______d. That shirt's awful. Go change your shirt.

_______e. The leopard cannot change his spots.

_______f. Your date's coming. You'd better change and get going.

_______g. Your attitude stinks. You'd better change and get booking!

KEY to IB: a-4. b-1. c-2. d-5. e-4,5. f-2. g-3.

C. KNOW

1. have command of information or ability
2. be acquainted or familiar with (person, place)
3. recognize (either in the sense of physical identification or the more abstract political use of acknowledge)

_______a. Do you know what time it is?

_______b. Do you know the woman in red?

_______c. Do you know who the woman in red is?

_______d. "Johnny, I hardly knew ya'. . ." (old Irish anti-war song)

_______e. He knew the song.

_______f. He knew the song would be a hit.

_______g. He knew how to sing.

KEY to IC: a-1. b-2. c-1. d-3. e-1,3. f-1. g-1.

D. MEET

1. become/get acquainted or familiar with (transition into "know")
2. encounter, run into, whether by accident or design
3. rendezvous with ("meet with", usually by arrangement, especially with a plural subject and no object expressed)

______ a. How do you do? Pleased to meet you.

______ b. Ah, yes, the count and I met years ago . ..

______ c. You'll never guess who I met downtown today.

______ d. That gang often meets at the local watering hole.

______ e. She knows about you and wants to meet you.

______ f. She's got a problem and wants to meet with you about it.

KEY to ID: a-1. b-1. c-2. d-3. e-1. f-3.

E. GET

The American Heritage dictionary lists 89 separate definitions for **get**. It is one of the most useful and versatile words in English with dozens of combinations with prepositions and other specific words. Here are some of its usual meanings, though they often overlap and you can't always pin it down to one. In some meanings the subject of **get** is an actor; in others, an undergoer (cf. Chapter 18). (Telling which is which may also help you find appropriate equivalents in your target language.) As you go through this set, be aware that there is some overlap and either of two definitions might work, depending on the larger context. Try to imagine as many contexts as you can where these sentences would make sense.

1. become, make transition into new state or position:
   get sick, tired
   also **get on/off/in** (the bus).

2. This includes all the **processual passives** (semi-passives), cf. Chapter 9, IX.E.: **get paid** on Friday

   get ripped off (store)

3. obtain, win, secure, procure (actor-subj): **get a promotion**

4. acquire, "come up with"(undergoer-subj.) : **get a bruise**

5. buy (actor, like 3a.): **get an ice cream cone**

6. receive (undergoer, like 3b.): **get a letter**

7. annoy, anger: You really **get** me!

8. seek revenge on: I'll **get** you for this!

9. have, possess (actually, only **got**) "I **got** plenty o' nothin'" (Gershwin)

10. with a host of prepositions and particles

   a. arrive in/at, reach (scheduled or not, often "appear suddenly") **get** + (to town)

   b. arrive, reach (scheduled, expected) The train **gets in** at 6.

   c. manage, survive: I **get by on** my salary.

   d. manage, maneuver: **get around** on foot

   e. advance: **get on** in years

_____ 1. When did you get here?

_____ 2. "Jeepers Creepers, where'd ya' get those peepers?"

_____ 3. This is my puppy. I got her at the Animal Shelter.

_____ 4. That new teacher really gets me!

_____ 5. Careful not to get sick.

_____ 6. Boy, Harry really got screwed on that exam!

_____ 7. All right, big shots, I got a royal flush. Pay up!

_____ 8. Go to the tradin' post and get some vittles.

_____ 9. You little brat! I'll get you for this!

_____ 10. By the time I get to Phoenix, she'll be risin'. ..

_____ 11. We got an eviction notice today.

_____ 12. We got evicted from our apartment.

_____ 13. It's not so easy to get by on wages alone these days.

_____ 14. Hey, how'd you get World Series tickets behind home plate?!

_____ 15. Why don't you just get smart and get lost!

KEY to IE:				
1-10a/b.	4-7.	7-9.	10-10a.	13-10c.
2-4.	5-1.	8-4/5.	11-6.	14-3.
3-4/5.	6-2.	9-8.	12-2.	15-1, 1/2.

F. **TELL**

1. say to (somebody), make a statement (usually+clause or single noun.)
2. relate, narrate a story about
3. decide, determine

____ a. Did you tell them when to get here?

____ b. Tell us about your summer vacation.

_____ c. If I've told you once I've told you a million times. ..

_____ d. Grandma, tell the one about Goldilocks!

_____ e. Who's that on the phone? I can't tell you by the voice.

_____ f. Can you tell when the baby is due? Can they tell you yet?

_____ g. I'll tell you a thing or two, you young whippersnapper.

KEY to IF: a-1. b-2. c-1. d-2. e-3. f-3,1. g-1.

G. ASK

1. pose a question, seek information
2. **ask for**: request something., request that somebody do something.

_____ a. He asked me what time it was.

_____ b. He asked me for a quarter.

_____ c. He asked me when they would arrive.

_____ d. He asked me to give him a quarter.

_____ e. Ask me no question, I'll tell you no lies.

KEY to IG: a-1. b-2. c-1. d-2. e-1.

H. CALL

1. give a name to
2. catch someone's attention in a loud voice, summon
3. contact someone by phone (an 20th century extension of 2?)

____ a. " . . .The rain is 'Tess'; the fire's 'Joe', and they call the wind 'Mariah'..." (Broadway play ca. 1940's)

_____ b. I can't talk to you now, but I'll call you later.

_____ c. Go call the kids in for supper.

_____ d. Henry get in here. Don't you hear me calling you?!

_____ e. What a cute little creature. What do you call it?

_____ f. If you don't call by midnight I'll be worried sick.

_____ g. Next witness: call Hiram J. Bildgebottom to the stand.

_____ h. Hey, kid, what did you call my mother?

KEY to IH: a-1. b-3. c-2. d-2. e-1. f-3. g-2. h-1.

II. NOUNS

A. TIME

1. hour, measurement by the clock
2. era, period (especially in the plural)
3. occasion, instance
4. opportunity

_____ a. What time is it?

_____ b. What a time we live in.

_____ c. This is the fourth time you've been late this week.

_____ d. Drop in any time you feel like.

_____ e. Drop in whenever you have time.

_____ f. It was the best of times; it was the worst of times.

_____ g. How many times have you seen the Rocky Horror Picture Show?

_____ h. This is the last time we order pizza from that place, OK?

KEY to IIA: a-1. b-2. c-3. d-4. e-1. f-2. g-3. h-3.

B. CLASS

1. scheduled learning activity, lecture, lesson
2. the people who form the group that learns
3. a positive quality of behavior, taste, know-how
4. plural **Classes**: the school year or period when individual classes (#1) meet regularly

_____ a. I really like my biology class. It's real interesting.

_____ b. I really like my biology class. They're real interesting.

_____ c. Boy, you really have a lot of classes this semester!

_____ d. Boy, you really have a lot of class!

_____ e. Her English and physics classes start at 9:00 and 12:00.

_____ f. Classes start early this semester, on September 1!

_____ g. Can't talk to now: gotta run to class.

_____ h. We should have a class party to loosen things up!

_____ i. It's already quarter past 9: class is in session.

_____ j. It's already April, but classes are in session till mid-May.

KEY to IIB: a-1. b-2. c-1. d-3. e-1. f-4. g-1. h-2. i-1. j-4.

C. **MOVIE(S)**

1. a reel of celluloid with pictures (plural: **movies**)

2. plural: **the movies**

   a. the industry that produces movies, the "cinema"

   b. the place where you go to see movies, movie theater

_____ (1). There's a great movie playing tonight. Wanna go?

_____ (2). There are some great movies this week. Which ones do you wanna see?

_____ (3). I really like these movies.

_____ (4). I really like the movies.

_____ (5). Did you see Robert Redford at the movies?

_____ (6). Did you see Robert Redford in the movies?

KEY to IIC: (1)-1. (2)-1. (3)-1. (4)-2a. (5)-2b. (6)-2a.

III. OTHER PARTS OF SPEECH (a very tiny sampling)

A. ON (preposition)

1. contact with a horizontal surface
2. contact with a vertical surface
3. about, concerning, devoted to the subject of
4. (while) using, by means of an instrument or conveyance

_____ a. Humpty Dumpty sat on a wall.

_____ b. Here is a great book on Humpty Dumpty.

_____ c. See that book on Humpty Dumpty? Get it off him!

_____ d. They saw it on television and heard it on the radio.

_____ e. They saw it on the television and put it on the radio.

_____ f. Guess who I ran into on the bus today.

_____ g. Don't sit on the television while talking on the phone.

_____ h. That picture looks better on this wall than on that one.

KEY to IIIA: a-1. b-3. c-1. d-4. e-1. f-4. g-1. h-2.

B. **WHEN**

1. adverb: at what time?, whether in a direct or indirect question
2. conjunction: at the time that, at the same time as, concurrent with, while

____ a. When are you going?

____ b. I'm going when the others go.

____ c. I don't know when I'm going.

____ d. When crossing the street, be sure to look both ways.

KEY to IIIB: a-1. b-2. c-1. d-2.

C. **SO**

1. interjection: sentence introducer, ice breaker in conversation (usually spoken with a pause after it)
2. conjunction:
   a. as a result, therefore, for that reason
   b. in order that, for the purpose of
3. adverb:
   a. intensifier of adjective or adverb
   b. in this manner

_____ a. So, uh, what's new?

_____ b. Don't be so stubborn!

_____ c. "As ye sow, so shall ye reap."

_____ d. Mom hid the cookies so we'd eat tofu!

_____ e. Mom hid the cookies, so we'll eat tofu!

KEY to IIIC: a-1. b-3a. c-3b. d-2b. e-2a.

So you see that the possibilities are endless. You can do this with hundreds of the commonest words you use all the time. Even when you do not think an English word has more than one meaning, your target language just might sub-divide the same semantic field and you have to learn to make that distinction. It's part of the fascinating business of learning a new language.

APPENDIX

1. ANSWER KEYS TO EXERCISES
2. FOR FURTHER READING
3. INDEX OF TERMS, CONCEPTS AND LANGUAGE ISSUES
4. INDEX OF WORDS, PARTS OF WORDS, AND OTHER LANGUAGES

ANSWER KEYS TO EXERCISES

1, 2a-b, 3, 4a-b, 5, 6a-c, 7a./c, 8a-b, 9b, 10a-c, 13, 18a./d.

EXERCISE 1, p. 5

1. April showers bring May flowers.
2. My bonnie lies over the ocean.
3. I pledge allegiance to the flag.
4. Peter Piper picked a peck of pickled peppers.
5. She sells sea shells by the sea shore.
6. Mary had a little lamb; its fleece was white as snow.
7. Coke adds life!
8. Over the river and through the woods to Grandmother's house we go.
9. My name is McNamara. I 'm the leader of the band.
10. The square of the hypotenuse is equal to to the sum of the squares of the other two sides.
11. George Washington threw a silver dollar across the Potomac.
12. The amazing Veg-O-Matic slices, dices, and peels!
13. The rockets' red glare, the bombs' bursting in air gave proof through the night that our flag was still there.

14. Four score and seven years ago our foreparents brought forth a great nation. . .

15. By the shores of Gitche Gumee by the shining Big-Sea-Waters stood the wigwam of Nokomis. . .

EXERCISE 2a., p. 8

1. I write the songs {that make the whole world sing}.
2. People {who live in glass houses} shouldn't throw stones.
3. He {who is without sin} may cast the first stone.
4. This is a day {that will long live in infamy}.
5. He {who laughs last} laughs best.
6. The evil {that men do} lives after them.
7. God bless America, land {that I love}. . .
8. Beware the Jabberwock, my son, the jaws {that bite}, the claws {that catch}
   (Right: no subject. Ignore "my son".)
9. This, Mr. Corlione, is a deal {that you cannot refuse}.
10. Ten Days {That Shook the World} is a book by John Reed about the 1917 Russian revolution.
    (Whole title including subordinate clause is subject.)

EXERCISE 2b., p. 10

1. {When it rains} it pours.
2. Do you know {where she lives}?
3. I won't go {unless you do}.
4. Children should do {as they 're told}!
5. I wouldn't do that {if I were you}.
6. You can't always get {what you want}.
7. I 'll understand this grammar stuff {when hell freezes over}!
8. (Take me out to the ball game . . . .) I don't care {if I ever come back}. . .
9. (Rockabye baby. . . {When the wind blows} the cradle will rock.
10. {If I had a hammer} I 'd hammer in the morning. . .

EXERCISE 3, p. 24

1. The Cat [in the Hat] came back.
2. The rain [in Spain] falls mainly [on the plain].
3. Put that [in your pipe] and smoke it!
4. Somewhere [over the rainbow] bluebirds fly.

5. The square [of the hypotenuse] is equal [to the sum] [of the squares] [of the other two sides].

6. Peter Piper picked a peck [of pickled peppers].

7. Go [to the polls] [in November] and vote [for the candidate] [of your choice].

8. Some enchanted evening you may meet a stranger [across a crowded room].

9. I pledge allegiance [to the flag] [of the United States] [of America].

10. [In a cabin] [in the woods] a little old man [by the window] stood.

EXERCISE 4a., p. 46

1. Real men eat [quiche].

2. Beef gives [strength].

3. {If you touch [me]} I 'll call [the police]!

4. Grammar will not baffle [you] any more.

5. [What] are you writing, [your memoirs]? (=suggested answer to question "what", but "what" is still the d.o.)

6. Drink [Coca Cola].

7. Support [your local union].

8. May I take [your order], please?

9. I'd like [a Big Mac and fries], please.

10. The phone company cancelled [my service] {because I didn't pay [my bill]}.

EXERCISE 4b., p. 47

1. Try [it]: you'll like [it]!

2. These are /the times/ {that try men's [souls]}.

3. You have [ring] around the collar!

4. Maybelline makes [beautiful eyes].

5. Ms. Smith defeated [the incumbent mayor] and became /the new mayor/.

6. You can take [Salem] out of the country but you can't take [the country] out of Salem.

7. [How much wood] would a woodchuck chuck {if a woodchuck could chuck [wood]}?

8. {If Peter Piper picked [a peck] of pickled peppers, [how many pecks] of pickled peppers did Peter Piper pick?

9. All the world 's /a stage/!

10. Do you take [this person] to be /your lawfully wedded spouse/. . .and will you be /a faithful spouse and parent/?

(Don't worry about the status of "to be a. . ." You will have ample opportunity to deal with it in Chapters 8 and 9.)

EXERCISE 5, p. 55 (See also 18a., p. 295)

1. I gave ⟨my love⟩ [a cherry] without no stone.

2. Promise ⟨her⟩ [anything], but give ⟨her⟩ [Arpège].

3. Will you buy ⟨me⟩ [something] nice?

4. Sing ⟨us⟩ [a song]. Tell ⟨us⟩ [a tale].

5. (a) The parents sent ⟨their daughter⟩ [a nice surprise].

   (b) The parents sent [their daughter] on an important errand. (no I.O.)

6. (a) People {who buy [their poodles] wholesale} are /cheap/.

   (b) People {who buy ⟨their poodles⟩ [presents]} must be /rich/.

7. (a) Friends, Romans, Countrymen, lend ⟨me⟩ [your ears]!

   (b) In some cultures, men lend ⟨their wives⟩ [money], and in some other cultures they lend [their wives] to their friends. (optional: ⟨to their friends⟩)

8. Ask ⟨me⟩ [no questions] and I'll tell ⟨you⟩ [no lies].

9. I'll leave ⟨you⟩ [my fortune] {if you leave [me] /alone/}!

   (Grammatical pun: I'll leave ⟨you⟩ [a loan] {if you leave [me] /alone/}.)

10. (a) I cut [myself] shaving.

(b) I cut ⟨myself⟩ a [piece] of cake.

11. (a) You've had [your supper]. Now you have to pay [the bill].

(b) You've done [your dance]. Now you have to pay ⟨the piper⟩.

EXERCISE 6a., p. 63

1. Hurry [to] K-Mart [for] the sale [of] a lifetime!!
Adv. ph = where to? *Adv. ph. =why?* *Adj. ph. =which sale?*

2. We were sailin' along [on] Moonlight Bay....
Adv. ph.= where sail?

3. "What light [through] yonder window breaks?"
Adv.ph. = where break?

4. "It seems she hangs [upon] the cheeks [of] night [like] a rich jewel
Adv.ph = where *Adj. ph.= which* *Adv. ph = how?*

[in] an Ethiop's ear."
Adj. ph. = "located in" or what kind of jewel

5. The stockings were hung [by] the chimney [with] care [in] hopes
Adv.ph=where *Adv.ph=how* *Adv. ph.=why*

that St. Nicholas soon would be there...

EXERCISE 6b., p. 79

A. 1. a. Come [up] and see me sometime.

b. Come [up the stairs].

2. a. Don't put that [down]!

b. Don't put that [down the laundry chute]!

3. a. Let's go to the schoolyard and hang[around].

b. They live [around the corner].

B. 1. a. I don't want to do it now. I'll do it [after].

b. I'll do it [after the movie].

c. I'll do it {after the movie ends}.

2. a. He'd never seen anything like it [before].

b. Don't eat that [before supper]!

c. Don't eat that {before you go running}!

3. a. We haven't done that [since childhood].

b. We haven't done that {since we were kids}.

c. We haven't done anything like that [before] or [since]!

EXERCISE 6c., p. 81

1. {What you think [of them]} is no business [of mine].
   NC *AvP* *AjP*

2. I wouldn't go [in that old house] {if I were you}....
   AvP *AvC*

3. {Whoever thought this stuff up} is [off his/her rocker]!
   NC *AjP (AvP?= where? what kind?)*

4. {If you miss the train}{(*that*) I'm on} you will know {that I am gone}. . .
   AvC *AjC* *NC*

   (What to do with on? It is, of course, a transposition of *the train on which I am*, but leave it alone for now.)

5. I 'm leavin' [on a jet plane]; I don't know {when I'll be back again}.
   AvP *AvC*

6. Everything {we've achieved [until now]} will go for naught {unless you accept the task} {(that) I'm putting [before you]}....
   NC *AvP* *AvC* *AjC* *AvP*

7. We were doing fine [without help] {until they showed up}!
   AvP *AvC*

8. They met [before class] and had made arrangements {before the teacher walked [into the classroom]}.
   AvP *AvC* *AvP*

9. Anyone {who finds the answer [to the magic riddle]} can have anything {(*that*) he desires}!!
   AjC *AjP* *AjC*

10. Do you know that guy {who 's campaigning [for governor]?
AjC AvP

11. Do you know {(*that*) that guy 's campaigning [for governor]?
NC AvP

12. Whose woods these are I think I know, his house is in the village though.→

I think {(that) I know} {[of whom] these are /the woods/}
NC AjP NC

{though his house is [in the village]}.
AvC AjP

BONUS:

What did you bring the book I don't like to be read to out of up for? →

We really don't have the tools to handle this one easily yet, so we'll fudge a little and do it in 2 stages:

Stage 1: Why did you bring up the book out of which I do not like to be read to?

But this does not submit itself very readily to the kind of parsing we are doing, so the most convenient thing to do is make the question into a statement, even if it sounds a little funny.) →

Stage 2: You did bring up the book {[out of which] I do not like to be read (to) why = [for what]}.
AjP AjC AvP

There are two other problems: one with the verb phrase bring up the book, *as you will see in Chapter 7, III., and the other is with the indirect object of* read. *Verb phrases like* to be read **to** *involve the notion of passive voice, more on which in Chapter 9.*

EXERCISE 7a., p. 86, Parsed

1. /Who/ are you?

2. [Who] are you visiting?

3. [What] are you driving nowadays, Mario?

4. **What** are you driving **at**, anyway?

5. What makes [you] /so sure/?

6. **What** is the moon made **of**?

7. /Who/ was that lady {*that* I saw [you] **with**?

8. /Who/ are those new kids on the block?

9. [Who[are those new kids on the block bothering?

10. **Who** are those new kids on the block talking **to**?

EXERCISE 7c., p. 97

1. He finished his cigarette and flipped the butt [out the window].

2. He looked [at his mail] and [flipped out] the minute he saw her handwriting.

3. [Help me out] here. I need some advice.

4. Help me [out of this monkey suit], will you please?

5. She's been [looking for] you all day.

6. She's been [looking for] a present [for Clara's birthday] all day.

7. The shuttle [blasted off] [from Cape Canaveral] just [after dawn].

8. Take your blasted fishing gear [off my white shag carpet], if you don't mind!

9. When we raise the funds [for this program] it just will [take off].

10. That new nuclear plant [gives off] more radiation [in an hour] than you can scrub [off the whole white-coated staff] [in a day]!

EXERCISE 8a., p. 112

1. You have a lot of guts to do that!
   present

2. You have earned everybody's admiration!
   present perfect

3. A 4-leaf clover! I do believe I 'll have good luck today.
   emph. pres. *future*

4. While my wife is busy in corporate dealings I do the dishes and the laundry.
   present *present*

5. "Who did that?" "What? I didn't do anything!"
   past *emph. past*

6. It was such a nostalgic trip. We hadn't been back there in years!
   past *past perfect*

7. Mr. Gorbachev has taken bold steps toward *glastnost.*
   present perfect

8. Mr. Gorbachev has less support in the government now than he used to.
   present

9. Who are you and who do you think you're kidding?
present *present (question)* *present progressive*

10. We were so happy when we were carrying a mortgage and car payments. . .
past past progressive

EXERCISE 8b., p. 137

1. If I had known you were coming I would have baked a cake.
pst.pf.= contr. *past prg=ind. prs.* *cond.pf.= contr.*

2. If I had my way, I would tear this building down.
pst=hyp. cond. *cond.*

3. Why are you asking so many questions?
prs.prg.

4. Why are you so mad?
prs.

5. Do you want anything?
prs.(emph.)

6. Do me a favor.
imp.

7. We've been looking for you all day long!
prs.pf.prg.

8. I looked over Jordan; what did I see: a band of angels was coming after me . . .
pst. *pst.emph.* *pst.prg.*

9. Friends, Romans, and countrymen lend me their ears often.
prs.

10. Michael rows the boat ashore.
prs.

11. Michael, row the boat ashore. (Did you notice the comma? It speaks volumes!)
imp.

12. Deep in my heart I do believe that we shall overcome someday.
prs. emph. *fut. (emph?)*

EXERCISE 9b., p. 350

1. You promised you'd never do that again →
"I'll never do that again!" he promised.

2. She thought she was seeing things, but she was sure she had seen him before.
→ "Am I seeing things? I'm sure I've seen him before," she thought.

3. He knew the plan wouldn't work. →
"The plan won't work! I know it!"

4. I confessed I had slacked off recently. →
"I confess: I've slacked off recently."

5. Did you know he was planning to arrive at 7:00? →
"He's planning to arrive at 7:00. Did you know that?"

6. He claimed he worked at McDonald's. →
"I work at McDonald's," he claimed.

7. He claimed he used to work at McDonald's. →
"I worked/used to work at McDonald's," he claimed.

8. He claimed he had been working at McDonald's for a year when the embezzlement was discovered. → (You need a little fancy footwork here:)
"I've been working here only a year. I can't have embezzled anything in that short time."

9. Little did they suspect that *It* would be waiting for them...
→ *It* will be waiting for them. ..

EXERCISE 10a., p. 189, with stress marks

A + N hungry cát, busy stréet, exciting yéar, fattening súndae, efficient clérk , magnificent hórse, beautiful págeant, boring téacher, 19. double béd, luxurious apártment, big spóon, wild párty, mellifluous náme, famous páinter, good président, fluorescent lámp, spicy pízza

N + Ń city stréet, hot-fudge súndae, government clérk, basement apártment Tíffany lamp, mushroom pízza

Ń + N álley cat , schóol year, Tee-Vée program, compúter program, wónder horse, béauty pageant, hístory teacher, márriage bed, sóup spoon blóck party, pén name, hóuse painter, bánk president

EXERCISE 10b., p. 212

1. Go to the store and get eggs, butter, and flour.
   def-c ind-c m m

2. Did you get the eggs, the butter, and the flour I asked for?
   def-c def-m def-m

3. Next year we will take a much-needed vacation to sunny Spain.
   ind-c prop.

4. Don't fire until you see the whites of their eyes.
   def-c def-poss-c

5. This little piggy went to market; this little piggy ordered out for pizza.
   def-c gen-c def-c gen-m

6. Snickers will give you quick energy in school, at work, or at play.
   prop m gen gen gen

7. The unit of currency in ancient Transylvania was the droplet.
   gen-c m prop gen

8. A stitch in time saves nine.
   ind-c m

EXERCISE 10c., p. 213

1. Sally doesn't drink coffee, but she'll like Momma's sturdy brew.

2. Have you heard any good rumors lately? You must have heard the rumor about you-know-who. . .

3. Little Ms. Muffet sat on a tuffet, eating her curds and whey.

4. On the third day of Christmas my true love gave to me 3 French hens, 2 turtle doves, and a partridge in a pear tree.

5. I'll buy you anything: a car, a house, the Ritz.

6. You've made me a generous offer, perhaps the most generous offer of my life, but I can't accept such an offer.

7. You've made me very happy with your offer.

8. I'll give you one more chance. Don't blow the chance of a lifetime!

EXERCISE 13, p. 254

1. John (knits and sews) but can't (garden or cook).

2. Children should be (seen and not heard).

3. I'm (sick and tired) of your (conniving, trickery, and deceit).

4. The heroes were (welcomed, decorated, and honored).

5. The (Dakotas and Carolinas) are paired states.

6. The Hague, Paris, and London are capitals and cultural centers. (right, none!)

7. They like (skiing and hiking), and kayaking interests them, too.

8. The doctor wants her to (eat well and exercise) and says she should take a daily walk.

9. The baby can (sit up, recognize people) and likes to (grab their hair and pull)

10. We support you in your (fight and struggle) and declare your enemies our enemies!!

EXERCISE 18a., p. 295
= EXERCISE 5, p. 55 REVISITED

The a.'s show direct objects as subject.
The b.'s show *in*direct objects as subject.
(?) and (??) indicate that the result is barely English.

1. I gave my love a cherry without no stone. →

   a. A cherry without no stone was given (to) my love (by me).

   b. My love was given a cherry without no stone (by me).

2. Promise her anything, but give her Arpège.
(You cannot passivize imperatives, but try using some modals. The meaning is a little different, and the sentences are rather awkward, if not awful.) →

   a. (?) Anything can be promised (to) her but Arpege can be given (to) her.

   b. (??) She can be promised anything, but she can only be given Arpege.

3. Will you buy me something nice? →

   a. (?) Will something nice be bought for me?

   b. (?) Will I be bought something nice?

4. Sing us a song. Tell us a tale. (Again, an imperative.) →

   a. A song should be sung (to) us. A tale should be told (to) us.

   b. We should be sung a song (to). We should have a tale told (to) us.

5. The parents sent their daughter a nice surprise. →

   a. A nice surprise was sent (to) their daughter (by her parents).

   b. Their daughter was sent a nice surprise (by them).

   The parents sent [their daughter] on an important errand. →

   Their daughter was sent on an important errand. (That's all!)

6. People who buy their poodles wholesale are cheap. →

   (?) People whose poodles are bought wholesale are cheap.

   People who buy their poodles presents must be rich. →

a. (??) People by whom presents are bought for their poodles. . .?

b. (??) People whose poodles are bought presents (for). . .?

[*So you see this is not just a mechanical process. The more complex the sentence, the harder it gets to passivize. You get either a sentence that means not quite the same as the active one or non-English, period. Keep your grammatical wits about you and do not produce nonsense because you think the book wants you to. You must always end up with "normal" language.*]

EXERCISE 18d., p. 310

1. He did not receive the car -- that was promised {him}.

2. The car -- (that) he ordered -- did not arrive.

3. The car -- (that) {he} was promised was not delivered.

4. You can try to anger them if they anger you, but /they/ don't anger easily.

5. She stood the vase on the mantle, and there it stands to this day.

6. The picture was hung yesterday, and it's still hanging.

7. She was brought upstairs. Then {she} was brought some tea.

8. She photographed him, but he didn't photograph well. (also /he/)

9. Have you tasted the cake? The cake tastes good!

10. They want to sell the book, but that book won't sell.

• •

FOR FURTHER READING AND ENJOYING

Some of these are good general references for details of English grammar and "good" language. Others are more serious "studies." Others are rather meager. They all have something to offer. See what suits your needs and interests.

Braun, Frank X. *English Grammar For Language Students*. Ulrich. 1947.

Fuller, Graham. *How To Learn a Foreign Language*. (Washington, D.C.: Storm King Press) 1987.
(Very general ideas of what you can expect from other languages and cultures.)

Gordon, Karen. *The Well-Tempered Sentence: A Punctuation Handbook for the Innocent, the Eager, and the Doomed.* Times Books. 1983.

____________. *The Transitive Vampire: A Handbook of Grammar for the Innocent, the Eager, and the Doomed.* Times Books. 1984.
(Both volumes are self-consciously "cute", very literary, and English-only.)

Greenbaum, Sidney. *The English Language Today*. New York: Pergamon Press. 1985.

________________*Good English and the Grammarian*. London: Longman. 1988.

Herman, Ethel and Everett, Karen. *Grammar For Teens*. LinguiSystems. 1989.

Herman, William. *The Portable English Handbook*. 1983.

Lederer, Richard. *Crazy English: The Ultimate Joy Ride Through Our Language*. 1989. (Amusing and informative, but totally without structure or a difference in principle between speech and spelling, or derivation and inflection, on which, see Chapter 3, IX and 12, III., above.)

Liles, Bruce. *A Basic Grammar of Modern English* . Prentiss Hall. 1987.
(Sober presentation in small format of most normal grammatical phenomena.)

Morton, Jacqueline. Editor of a series of six little volumes called *English Grammar For Students of "X"*. Olivia and Hall. The separate authors are:

French.	1979.	Morton, Jacqueline.
German:	1980.	Zorach, Cecile.
Italian:	1982.	Primorac, Karen and Sergio Adorni.
Latin:	1983.	Goldman, Norma and Ladislas Szymanski.
Russian	1987.	Edwina Cruise.
Spanish.	1980.	Emily Spineli.

Newman, Edwin. *A Civil Tongue.* (1977). *Strictly Speaking* (1982). *I must say: On English, the News, and Other Matters.* (1988). Warner Books. (3 well-known books on how "bad" our English has become, by a real language "purist.")

Quirk, Randolph. *A Grammar of Contemporary English.* New York: Seminar Press. 1972.

______________. *A Comprehensive Grammar of the English Language.* London: Longman. 1985. (A real encyclopedia of almost 1800 pages!)

Reed, Alonzo and Brainerd Kellogg. *A Work On English grammar and Composition, in which the science of the language is made tributary to the art of expression.* New York. Clark and Maynard. 1886.

(This is where the diagramming technique of the Post-Script to Chapter 1-5 comes from. It used to be very popular in elementary and junior high schools.)

Wouk, Herman. *The City Boy.* New York. Doubleday. 1952. (especially Chapter 9, pp. 102-105, "Promotion Day," where the popular tough guy tries his hand at grammar and poetry.)

There are others with titles like *English Grammar Made Simple, Painless English,* and dozens more on persuasive vocabulary, writing styles, and other topics. Nothing wrong with that, but make sure you don't think that this is "grammar"! Of course, there are also more complex books on introductory linguistics. Great field to get into, but not to everbody's taste.

INDEX OF TERMS, CONCEPTS, AND LANGUAGE ISSUES

D

E

F

H

I

O

P

Q

Z

INDEX OF WORDS, PARTS OF WORDS, AND OTHER LANGUAGES

LANGUAGES

ABOUT THE AUTHOR

Robert A. Fradkin was born in Fall River, Massachusetts in 1951. From earliest childhood he had a passion for language and languages. His first taste of French in elementary school and Hebrew in religious school lead him to try Russian in high school. That exciting venture moved him to declare a Russian major at Boston University in 1969. In 1974 he entered the graduate programs in Slavic, Semitic, and Turkic languages and general linguistics at Indiana University in Bloomington. His experience as a graduate assistant there, teaching both Russian and Hebrew made it clear to him that he would make a career teaching language, coupling practical skills with bringing students to an awareness of linguistic structure beyond and between the lines of textbook grammar rules. In 1982 he left for Seattle to direct the Hebrew language program at the University of Washington. Upon completing his Ph.D. in Slavic and Semitic linguistics at Indiana University in 1985, he accepted an assistant professorship in the Judaic Studies Program at Brown University and undertook to build a new program in modern Hebrew. Now returning to the Slavic field, he has just begun directing the program in Russian in the Department of Foreign Languages and Literatures at Old Dominion University in Norfolk, Virginia.

Franklin Pierce College Library
00060659

PRAISE FOR *INVEST YOURSELF*

"Millions of Catholics think they have to live a divided life, with their careers quarantined from their faith. John Abbate writes from his own hard-won experience as a businessman who not only wanted to enrich his Catholic life, but also integrate it into his business vocation. With a deft handling of business, economics, and theology, he explains clearly how you can do the same in your own work and life."

—JAY W. RICHARDS, PhD
New York Times bestselling author and host of
A Force for Good on EWTN

"This book was a journey of discovery. John Abbate brings the beauty and majesty of the Catholic faith into sharp focus, and while many of us tend to admire that beauty, this book is a call to action: to live our faith daily in our family, business, and social lives."

— STEVEN MICHAEL RAMIREZ
Former McDonald's owner-operator

"Whether you're the CEO of a Fortune 500 company or your domain is a suburban minivan, prepare to embrace all that God has in store for your life by studying and sharing the precepts in *Invest Yourself*. John Abbate, a successful executive with a vibrant spiritual life, candidly invites each of us to ask the big questions that sometimes stand in the way of the true prosperity God desires for us. God desires our best and wants to give us the best! Dare to commit yourself to true encounter, lasting change, and the abundance that comes from mission-oriented vision."

— LISA M. HENDEY
Author of *The Grace of Yes*

INVEST YOURSELF

INVEST YOURSELF

DARING TO BE CATHOLIC IN TODAY'S BUSINESS WORLD

JOHN M. ABBATE

BEACON PUBLISHING
North Palm Beach, Florida

This book was written by John M. Abbate in his personal capacity. The opinions or ideas expressed in this book are the author's own and do not in any way consistently reflect the views, policy, or opinion of McDonald's Corporation, its employees, or any such affiliation associated with McDonald's or the Brand.

Published by Beacon Publishing

Design by Madeline Harris

ISBN: 978-1-63582-023-2 (softcover)
ISBN: 978-1-942611-87-5 (ebook)

Names: Abbate, John M., author.
Title: Invest yourself : daring to be Catholic in today's business world / John M. Abbate.
Description: North Palm Beach, Florida : Beacon Publishing, 2018.
Identifiers: LCCN 2017057174 | ISBN 9781635820232 (softcover : alk. paper) | ISBN 9781942611875 (e-book)
Subjects: LCSH: Work—Religious aspects—Catholic Church. | Vocation—Catholic Church. | Wealth—Religious aspects—Catholic Church. | Success—Religious aspects—Catholic Church.
Classification: LCC BX1795.W67 A23 2018 | DDC 248.8/8—dc23

For more information on this title or other books and CDs available through the Dynamic Catholic Book Program, please visit www.DynamicCatholic.com.

The Dynamic Catholic Institute
5081 Olympic Blvd • Erlanger • Kentucky • 41018
Phone: 1-859-980-7900
Email: info@DynamicCatholic.com

First printing, January 2018

Printed in the United States of America

ACKNOWLEDGMENTS

To my wife, I am so blessed and appreciative of your influence on my faith and vocational journey these past thirty years. You are the perfect antidote to my personality, and you have impacted my life beyond measure. Thank you for the support and courage that allowed me to tell a bit of our story. Your love, empathy, and self-giving are truly unmatched.

To my mom, a huge thanks and gratitude for your faith, encouragement, and dedication to our entire extended family. I am indebted to your love and commitment to raising a Catholic family.

To my dad, you are the epitome of reverent leadership. What an incredible role model you have been for me and others.

To Our Lady Queen of Peace for her unrelenting call that first led me on a pilgrimage to Medjugorje, and the never-ceasing challenge to live a life uncommon.

To my children, Matthew, Kathryn, and Andrew, what a gift from God you three are to your mom and me. I strive each and every day to be the kind of father to you that my dad is to me . . . though your Poppy is a tough act to follow. Let us strive to keep the legacy alive.

To Monsignor Joseph Pacheco for his early encouragement and unwavering belief in my talents and abilities.

To my brothers and sister, we have always challenged each other to keep our faith at the center of our lives. You are the source of much of my joy and inspiration.

To my brother Jim and friends Brian, Steve, Jamie, and Doug, your guidance, perspective, and example have been invaluable to me as a husband, father, and friend.

To Katherine Adams for your early help in challenging me to focus my message and guidance in the editing of the raw manuscript.

To the leadership at Dynamic Catholic for their vision, courage, and belief in the power of the laity to lift the Catholic Church in American to a new level of passion and purpose.

Lastly, to the team at Beacon Publishing for their fresh insight and advice on creating a manuscript that ultimately reflects my intended idea and mission.

CONTENTS

ONE

Choosing Prosperity

We make a living by what we get.
We make a life by what we give.
—Winston Churchill

The most extraordinary power we have been given as human beings is our freedom to choose. St. Thomas Aquinas eloquently called it "the dignity of causality."[1] Simply stated, this means that through the power of our free will and intellect given to us by God, we have the capacity to decide the direction of our own life and our own prosperity. We can choose whether to make a lasting difference that sees beyond a temporal world bound by scarcity and fear or simply toil through life seeking perpetual self-gratification, never reaching true fulfillment.

I believe most of us would agree that we all want three basic things out of our brief time here on earth. We all need hope; we all yearn for happiness; and we all crave the satisfaction of knowing that our life has counted for something. These three elements constitute a life well lived—an abundant life.

But living such an abundant life requires tapping into our essential purpose as human beings—a purpose that is far greater than realizing the fulfillment of our own desires or passions.

Because we are created in the image and likeness of God (see Genesis 1:27), we can start by looking at him. And there we discover that the essence of our authentic humanity is in self-giving. This is our Christian inheritance, powerfully expressed by Christ and his teachings. Self-giving is the key that will free us from the burdens of a world dominated by the "scarcity mentality" we have inherited.

We all have the potential to live a life of Christian abundance now, regardless of the reality of our past choices. Yet this is possible only when we deliberately and courageously decide to think differently about our life's vocation and are willing to exercise choices to live this higher calling. In this book, using my own journey as the backdrop, I will explore the concept of vocation as the medium to live out our God-given purpose, live a life that matters, and experience the true abundance we desire.

I am a very practical and logical thinker, and most of my life has been dominated by the norms of the business world. Deep down, I am a finance and economics guy. I love creating a good spreadsheet and analyzing the next opportunity. I truly enjoy the everyday challenge and unpredictability of maintaining financial, personal, and professional success.

Along the meandering path of my life, I have discovered a few things about how to balance my financial portfolio, and more crucially, my personal and faith lives as well. Of course, I still fail at times, yet the risk of catastrophic failure is mitigated when I am living my true vocation.

My Catholic faith is not an exercise in irrationality or credulity. It is a faith built first and foremost on God and the revelation of his son, Jesus, but also centered on the wisdom and intellect of thousands of men and women who have come before me. Most of these men and women have spent their entire lives dedicated to the rigorous scholarship of this discipline called theology. Catholicism is steeped in the rationality, wisdom, and practicality of being scrutinized, studied, and applied in our culture for two thousand years. Isn't it time we stopped believing that our Catholic faith is built on foolish and nonsensical imagination or arcane mysticism? As you read this book, I will introduce you to a few of the brilliant thinkers who have dedicated themselves to Christ and worked selflessly to make these truths accessible to the rest of us.

I hope that as I share my own journey and discoveries, you will gain a deeper understanding of the fact that business success and a thriving Catholic faith aren't mutually exclusive, but instead together can form the basis of a life of abundance—a life that is rich in what matters to God.

I've learned how investing in both the practical and spiritual matters of life have revolutionized the way I live, and I hope to share these ideas with you in a way that is engaging, entertaining, educational, and practical. I believe that the hope, happiness, and meaning we all seek can only be found in Jesus Christ and a life of self-giving rather than self-serving. This is the foundational message of this book, and it sums up our vocational call as Christians.

Standing on the Shoulders of Giants

I have had a lifelong passion for biographies. I love the unique and inspiring stories I've encountered through reading about the lives and accomplishments of others. When we hear or read about the ways another person overcomes adversity or lives with excellence, it allows us to think and relate differently to our own lives and our not-so-unique struggles. As Sir Isaac Newton put it, "If I have seen further, it is by standing on the shoulders of giants."

Immersing myself in stories about Jack Welch, Ronald Reagan, Immaculée Ilibagiza, Thomas Merton, John Adams, Albert Einstein, St. John Paul II, Steve Jobs, St. Francis of Assisi, St. Catherine of Siena, and Jesus Christ has allowed me to find common ground with their lives, their struggles, and their successes and failures. Their candid self-revelation and vulnerability have led me to reexamine my own reality and allow a deeper examination of my core ideology.

I cannot overstate the power these stories and others have had on my life and my evolution as a businessman, father, husband, and struggling Catholic. Much of my reading in my late teens and early adulthood was focused on business and politics. Over the past twenty years, I've developed an insatiable appetite for reading the profiles of successful businesspeople in books and in magazines such as *Businessweek* and *Forbes*. I have been driven by a desire to unlock the mystery of other people's success and gain insight into their motivation.

I thought that understanding the success drivers of these men and women would propel me to maximize my own potential. However, once I saw beyond the secular world's view of success, I became disenchanted with much of the material provided by many of these books and magazines.

Through years of personal and professional growth and failure, I have defined my own principles, vision of success, and process for attainment. I no longer need to spend my time reading others' stories of business success or failure. One more story of a person working seventy hours a week and making a financial windfall has become stale and uninspiring.

My experiences with Catholic conferences, pilgrimages, and professional business organizations such as Legatus have opened my eyes to the abundance of talented and faithful men and women who are willing and able to carry on the mission of the Church. These heroic people are the future of this great faith. Their enthusiasm, sacrifice, and talent are infectious.

Unfortunately, the vast majority of Catholics never see much of the charismatic and inspirational side of our Church. Many don't seek out opportunities to hear great Catholic speakers, experience Mass in new and inspiring locations, spend a week on pilgrimage with other Spirit-filled Catholics, or read a great book about these dynamic members of our faith.

Instead, they are bombarded with stories told through the lens of the secular and slanted media of fallen priests and fringe groups whose idea of pro-life work is bombing women's clinics.

The stories of individual Catholics that the media reports are equally unfortunate. They are not the stories of ordinary Catholics doing extraordinary work in their communities. Media reports focus on marginal Catholic celebrities or politicians who do not embody the faith and the teaching of the Church. They use their celebrity status to promulgate their distorted and individualistic versions of the truth.

Disappointingly, statistics say that less than 1 percent of Catholics will read a single Catholic book in the course of a year. The true beauty of the Catholic faith can be fully realized only when we utilize our intellect to acquire knowledge to grow in our faith. We aren't meant to have a blind and uninformed spiritual journey. Our faith takes real effort and scholarship.

In the encyclical *Fides et Ratio* (*Faith and Reason*), St. John Paul II reiterates the natural inclination we have to seek truth using our innate creative intelligence: "We ultimately seek the truth because 'in the far reaches of the human heart there is a seed of desire and nostalgia for God.' God has created man with an internal homing device so that we may long to seek his truth and peace" (24).

We simply cannot divorce faith from reason if we are to truly understand our relationship with God and his purpose for our life. It is reason that sheds the light that allows our faith to prosper. Without a proper philosophical understanding of God, faith becomes merely a blind and childish trust that can be easily manipulated by other people. However, without faith, pure rationalism and scientific positivism will also lead man down a path of carnage. A simple look at the history of the past century proves what happens when man relies predominantly on his rational nature for guidance. In hindsight, we can all agree that there was nothing remotely rational about the leadership and subsequent genocide inflicted by people such as Hitler, Mao, and Stalin. Yet all three of these men had one thing in common: a belief in the power of the secular over the divine.

Jesus' death on the cross is a stark revelation that God's saving plan is not congruent with human logic. "God chose what is foolish in the world to shame the wise . . . God chose what is low and despised in the world, things that are not, to reduce to nothing things that are" (1 Corinthians 1:27–28).

Therefore, the wisdom of God cannot be fully understood or contained by human reasoning. Only through revelation and faith can we come to fully know and understand God's salvific plan for us.

In *Fides et Ratio*, John Paul II writes that through the paschal mystery—Jesus' life, death, and resurrection—we are given the opportunity via faith to get a glimpse of our Father's plan for us. Therefore, Christ is the link between philosophy and faith that allows us to overcome our human limitations.[2]

Millions of Catholic Books

Books can change lives. Books allow us to see beyond the limited walls of our daily existence and share our insight and wisdom with each other. As C. S. Lewis said, "We read to know we are not alone."[3]

I've discovered that most Catholics want to understand their faith on a deeper level, but not necessarily via traditional Catholic channels provided through their parish. They want to be inspired in their faith through heartwarming or interesting stories that can translate to their own life. Most Catholics are not interested in reading about the theology of consubstantiation, transubstantiation, or in-depth Christology. People want to spend their valuable and limited time on topics that directly relate to their lives today. They'd like to know how this book can help them on their unique path to becoming better, happier, more hopeful people. And readers are looking for material that not only teaches and entertains but also inspires them to action.

The mystery for us fragile and broken humans is to understand what motivates people of talent to push themselves in a direction that is so countercultural. This gap in understanding has the potential to compel and captivate us to seek not only answers for their life's path, but ultimately the answers for our life's path.

Based on my own experience, it is a joy to appreciate firsthand the power and mystery of our faith, and share it with other dedicated and inspired Catholics. Our Church is rich in tradition and talent; however, we must be willing to explore and seek the opportunities that are available to us. This cannot happen when we confine our faith journey to a single parish or attending Mass once per week.

However, books can only point the way to a new faith in Christ. As Pope Francis wrote in an encyclical letter to the bishops, "Faith is born of an encounter with the living God."[4] We encounter him in the sacraments, through reading and meditating on Scripture, and in experiencing a vital, ongoing relationship with Jesus Christ in prayer. Encountering the living God in these ways empowers us to live fully and deeply, enjoying the abundance we long for and that God has planned for us since the beginning.

The Challenge of Sharing Our Faith in Today's Culture

To speak or write publicly about my Catholic faith journey and the ways in which I strive to integrate it in my life, work, family, and culture is always a challenge for me. It is much easier to talk about topics such as finance, marketing, and entrepreneurship, which relate to my business. These are the things I know so well; they are much less personal, and allow for much less vulnerability. When it comes to sharing my faith, I am forced to face the reality of my fragile humanity. And so are you.

We are all acutely aware of our unique shortcomings, and no one wants to feel like a hypocrite. That's why many times we remain silent. We dismiss our role in the mission of sharing our faith and hope with others rather than accept our past shortcomings. It reminds me of the following story in the Gospel of Mark.

Jesus is in a synagogue in the town of Capernaum. It is very early in his ministry. Already he is an enigma; certainly he's not well known or understood by the people around him. In this synagogue, Jesus meets a man with an unclean spirit that immediately confronts him.

The demonic spirit that has possessed this man is the only one who truly recognizes Jesus for who he is: the Son of God. The spirit basically says to Jesus in a harsh, angry voice: "I know who you are, Jesus of Nazareth! What do you want with me?"

"I know who you are!" Those are the troubling words that run through our minds as we think about our life's purpose, the mission God has for us. Those words play on our insecurities, our history, our fears. This is what confronts us when we have an opportunity to share our faith with someone; it's a false voice that claims to know who we are and what we have done in betrayal of our faith. This voice wants to shut us down, keep us from being true to our mission, and shame us with the actions of our past, creating just enough doubt and discomfort to silence us.

But while we must embrace the reality of our failings and imperfections, it is still true that God uses us to reach each other for the kingdom. Thomas Merton said, "It is Christ who draws us to himself through the action of our fellow men."[5] So, to speak about one's faith journey is the way Christ reaches others, even though it demands a certain amount of acceptance, vulnerability, and most of all, humility.

St. Paul said this in Romans 7:21–25:

> So I find it to be a law that when I want to do right, evil lies close at hand. For I delight in the law of God, in my inmost self, but I see in my members another law at war with the law of my mind and making me captive to the law of sin which dwells in my members. Wretched man that I am! Who will de-

> liver me from this body of death? Thanks be to God through Jesus Christ our Lord!

I find this to be an incredibly poignant passage from St. Paul. I can certainly relate to his struggles and frustrations when I reflect on my own life experiences. I am constantly fighting attitudes and behaviors that I know are contrary to God's desire for me as well as to my true desires. I fall victim again and again to the fragile humanity of a will affected by sin. However, I am consoled by St Paul's message of liberation through the resurrection of Jesus Christ and his living Church.

I have come to understand that it is the future that tells us what our past is about. It is our life experience that allows us to become that unique self-gift that we are called to be for others. The most compelling form of evangelization comes when people are willing to share their personal encounter with Christ. As humans, we connect with stories. They move us, draw us in, and captivate our attention. I believe we must push ourselves outside our comfort zone and into our past in order to draw on the experiences that allow us to pave the way for others.

We keep our heritage alive by telling our unique stories, keeping our traditions, cooking our cultural foods, and finding time to be together as a family. It is our history and our connection to our past. The power of our Catholic culture is built upon our faith tradition. We partake of the sacraments, celebrate feast days, and learn from the teachings of the Church. We must dare to share our story with those around us and invite others to tell their stories as well.

We have all received an abundant inheritance from our forefathers. We stand on the shoulders of so many resilient and courageous figures of our past. Today *we* must choose to be the link that keeps our Catholic history alive in our families, our communities, and our culture. When we choose to learn about and share our own family history and embrace the richness of the tradition of our Catholic faith, we become the instrument that continues the mission of Matthew 28. We spread the Good News to all corners of the world.

Passing on the Legacy

When I was a teenager, my brothers and I would spend time in the late evenings with my father just hanging out in our spa. We would talk about his early childhood, college life, his work, and the Catholic faith. He would tell us stories of his upbringing during the Great Depression, and the struggles and joys of a childhood during this period of America's history. He would also talk about his family's daily commitment to its Catholic faith and why he had held so steadfastly to it throughout his life. Whether it was the fear and guilt of missing Mass on a Sunday, an obligation to eat fish on Fridays all year long, or always seeking a Catholic Church to say a prayer in when he first moved to a new town, these were the stories of his faith, and through this sharing they become the stories of our faith as well.

My mother and father have always been committed Catholics. As children, missing Mass on Sundays was never an option for us. My parents have never been overly pious, but simply matter-of-fact as to how and why the Catholic faith is the best and most practical way to live your life. They have passed on the traditions of their faith to their grandchildren as well. They both place great importance on the sacraments of baptism and first Communion, and their vital importance as lifetime gifts of grace to heal and elevate the human spirit in times of triumph and tragedy. As Pope Francis says, "Do you open your hearts to the memories that your grandparents pass on? Grandparents are like the wisdom of the family; they are the wisdom of a people."[6]

I am Catholic because of these two people. They are my original connection to the beauty and majesty of this two-thousand-year-old culture. What an incredible gift it has been!

As you read this book, I hope you take the opportunity to consider your own unique life experiences, both the good and bad, in shaping your mind and heart toward a life in Christ.

TWO

In the Beginning . . . There Was Economics

The economy of salvation refers to God's activity in creating and governing the world, particularly to his plan for the salvation of the world in the person of Jesus Christ, a plan which is being accomplished through His Body the Church, in its life and sacraments.

—CCC, Glossary

As we begin our pursuit of true prosperity, it makes sense to explore the impact and implications of economics on our faith journey. I think we can agree that humans are all driven by the temporal nature of the earth and the impact of a world defined in many ways by its limited resources. The reality is that many of our daily behaviors are directed by our innate fear of this scarcity, as well as the subsequent application of the laws of supply and demand we use to manage the problem. This phenomenon is commonly referred to as our biological anthropology, and it creates the foundation for a society that is governed by the science of economics.

As Christians, we grasp that we are eternally connected with our original parents, through the consequences of original sin. Because of them, we struggle to manage the limitations imposed on our lives. And that's where God's economics enter the picture—his activity as he governs the world and plans for its salvation through Christ. The Church now carries on this grand economy of salvation.

The role of economic management has always had a deep history within the context of our evolution and our Catholic faith as well. Whether in St. Paul's letters or in parables within the Gospels, we find many direct references to the word *economics,* along with the overarching theme of managing our lives within financial parameters.

The etymology of the word *economics* is from the original Greek word *oikos,* which means "house." The *oikonomos* would describe the "steward" or "manager" of the house. The *oikonomia,* or "economy," is the plan for the management of the house. The evolution of this concept, starting with the household, has led to our current understanding of modern economics and the process of managing not only our household but also state, national, and international economies.

St. Paul was pastoral in his approach to evangelization. He was always very concerned with the implementation of our faith, with the "how" of living our faith in culture. That's why he spoke and wrote often on the topic of economics. St. Paul's intent was to help the early Christians understand how to manage their house or family (*oikos*) and larger community/economy (*oikonomia*) in light of the new and very radical philosophy of Jesus Christ.

Existing and managing ourselves within economic boundaries is a focal concern in Christianity. The challenge of daring to live the radical message of Christ in the marketplace is the preeminent struggle for all of us. We all face the reality of the necessity of work to support our biological needs and those of our families.

But what happens once we have met the basic needs for our family and ourselves? Is it acceptable to want more? How do we reconcile the fact that we are all given different gifts, but some are compensated at a much higher level than others? What is our responsibility to acknowledge this disparity, and are we called to then redistribute?

Our faith must be lived in the cultural and economic reality of a world that has provided many of us with a material abundance far beyond our basic needs. How do we deal with the complicated by-product of capitalism and stay in right relationship with God's family? How do we administer the nonessential wealth that our labor has produced?

These are just a few of the questions that I have reflected upon over the past twenty-five years. In the next several chapters, I'll share some of my struggles, and I hope it will shed some light on your path and give you a better understanding of these age-old, often troubling questions.

Basis of Economics: Scarcity

The first lesson of economics is scarcity: There is never enough of anything to fully satisfy all those who want it. The first lesson of politics is to disregard the first lesson of economics.
—Thomas Sowell

I was first introduced to the theory of economics in 1983. I was a senior in high school, taking the first of many economics classes. Mr. Paske, one of the few teachers I still remember from those days, was witty, with a sarcastic sense of humor. He was the perfect antidote for a bunch of smug and self-absorbed high school seniors.

Learning about macroeconomics was a profound intellectual experience for me. It all made so much sense. Mr. Paske taught me the logical principles behind how and why the world seemed to work on a financial and economic level. This introduction to the science of economics would eventually lead me to seek an undergraduate degree in economics in college. Thus, I began my journey toward seeing the world through the eyes of an economist.

Just for clarification, I am not an economist. Having an undergraduate degree in economics is the equivalent of having an undergraduate degree in psychology. I am just qualified enough to be an annoyance at Thanksgiving dinner. However, being familiar with the basic principles of economics has helped me more fully understand the actions of humanity in a world defined by limited resources.

Throughout most of human history, the overarching problem was simply surviving. The bulk of everyday life was spent seeking a share of a limited supply of food, water, shelter, warmth, and safety. As a species, humans existed on the brink of starvation and with the threat of physical harm for thousands of years. Even up to a hundred years ago, most of humanity continued to struggle with problems of scarcity.

Until the latter part of the twentieth century, most of people's waking hours were spent on work or household chores. During the mid-1800s the average man worked sixty-five to seventy hours per week with virtually no leisure time. One hundred years ago, less than 10 percent of the workforce actually took vacations.

Interestingly enough, in 1848 a famous economist named John Stuart Mill described a scenario in his book *Principles of*

Political Economy. He wrote of a future in which there would be enough economic growth for mankind. He truly felt that at some point, economic output and productivity would render a certain material contentment in society. When that time arrived, people would be able to work less or not at all, while enjoying material goods, along with the time to pursue the higher goals of life. Mill wrote:

> There would be as much scope as ever for all kinds of mental culture, and moral and social progress; as much room for improving the Art of Living, and much more likelihood of its being improved, when minds ceased to be engrossed by the art of getting on. Even the industrial arts might be as earnestly and as successfully cultivated, with this sole difference, that instead of serving no purpose but the increase of wealth, industrial improvements would produce their legitimate effect: that of abridging labour.

I find this to be an extraordinarily interesting thought to ponder from today's perspective. John Stuart Mill assumed that man had the capacity to eventually overcome the psychological and physical encumbrance of scarcity and desire. He could have never imagined the amount of goods and services provided by today's economy. But what would have baffled him even more is the insatiable appetite man still has for acquiring more stuff, and the fear of losing out on the incremental nature of having more. He certainly could never have envisioned humanity waiting in line outside overnight for the opportunity to buy the latest iPhone.

The simple reality is that there is still never enough of anything to satisfy our deeply embedded materialistic and scarcity mentality. You need look no further than our national debt statistics. Today our consumer debt is at a record high of $12.84 trillion. Our credit card debt makes up more than $784 billion of the total, with the average monthly unpaid credit card balance at $16,883 per household.[7] What happened to the so-called "new normal" postrecession mentality that was so highly discussed in the years following the 2008–2009 recession?

The late philosopher George Santayana wrote, "Those who cannot remember the past are condemned to repeat it." Based on the current evidence, it seems a decade is just about enough time to forget the post-austerity mentality of the most recent recession.

Certainly the philosophies of individualism and materialism can be directly linked with our deeply embedded biological anthropology: greed, envy, and fear of scarcity. Obviously, Mill underestimated the instinctive nature of their power and grip on humanity as a whole.

As we have started to overcome the physical struggles of the true scarcity faced by our ancestors, we are still psychologically burdened with their legacy. We are innately fearful of not having enough for our family and ourselves. Yet the most fundamental embodiment of scarcity that impacts our lives is time. The late economist Gary Becker pointed out that even in a utopian world where price and quantity reach an equilibrium that mitigates the fear of material deficiency, we must deal with the issue of scarcity of time. Regardless of one's accumulation of wealth, the reality of the physical flow of time still provides us only a finite period to consume and purchase.

The Greek word for *time* is *chrónos*, which refers to the unending chronology of the physical nature of the earth moving around the sun; this is the passage of physical time. It is this unending cycle of movement that creates an ever-widening gap from our past, as well as the perpetual aging of our bodies. *Chrónos* embodies the scarcity of time that causes the anxiety of facing (literally and metaphorically) the reality of aging and lamenting life's missed opportunities.

However, the Greeks had another word for time, *kairos*, which can be found in the New Testament. This implication of time suggests a transcendence of the constraints of a physical time subject to scarcity. Whereas *chrónos* is quantitative (seconds and minutes), *kairos* is qualitative, measuring moments, not seconds. It refers to the meaningful moment, the perfect moment, the next significant moment.

In Ephesians 5, St. Paul instructs us to redeem the *kairos*, meaning to pay attention and take advantage of the opportune times and seasons of our lives. It is a perspective that sees life not as seconds, minutes, or hours slipping through our fingers like sand, but as unique moments of opportunity to live our faith in culture. If we are physically and psychologically bound by the constraints of our temporal world, the element of time will always be a limited resource for us, and a major cause of anxiety.

Fear of Scarcity

You can never have enough of what you don't really need.
—Matthew Kelly

As humans we all must come face-to-face with the economic reality of limited resources and the impact of supply and demand in our life. Scarcity and competition have led humans down a very slippery slope, a path where we begin to act and react out of the fear that they kindle within our psyche. It is a fear that grips us and leads us to irrational thought and actions. It leads to feelings of panic and anxiety, which results in poor choices: corruption, deceit, violence, or some other form of sin that distances us from God and each other. Make no mistake—sin is often foundationally rooted in fear. Perhaps that's why St. John Paul II started his entire papacy with a simple but profound statement: "Be not afraid."

The reality is that we all must deal with our natural fear of scarcity; it grips us all. This is a by-product of our history; it's our innate desire to survive. It's our biological anthropology. We need look no further than any history book, including the Bible, for confirmation of our capacity to allow scarcity and fear to dictate irrational behavior that has led to much murder, deceit, and sin. The twentieth century turned out to be the bloodiest period in history. Unfortunately, the twenty-first century is continuing along this same path of annihilation. As Thomas Merton wrote, "The world is the unquiet city of those who live for themselves and are therefore divided against one another in a struggle that cannot end, for it will go on eternally in hell."[8]

All of us have acted irrationally due to our natural inclination toward these fears. Take a moment and examine your own life. How have you acted when faced with the fear of missing out on some material good? Can you remember a time when fear and greed led you down a path toward excessive risk against your better judgment? How did you react to the housing bubble of the early 2000s, and the subsequent crash? How did the stock market drops of 2000 and 2008 affect you?

Take some time to examine other areas of your life that have been influenced by feelings of scarcity and fear. Maybe those areas were financially related, or maybe they were influenced by your self-esteem. Here are some examples:

- The desire for that critical job promotion
- The "perfect" girlfriend or boyfriend who led you down a path of sin
- The perfect house that you just had to have, so you overextended yourself
- The scarcity and panic of missing out on the bull market. Everyone was getting rich but you, so you bought at the top and eventually sold at the bottom, like 85 percent of investors.
- The need to get your "brilliant" child into that elite college
- The simple daily battles in life, such as fighting for your seat at the airport, fighting traffic on the way to work, or fighting to get your money's worth at Disneyland

There is no denying that we all must find a way to deal with the reality of our innate fear of losing and that overwhelming desire to be the first in a world of limited supply.

The *Catechism of the Catholic Church* and theologians in general have spent a considerable amount of time reflecting on the issues we face. In fact, one of Catholicism's pivotal concepts in dealing with scarcity is the belief in the transcendental nature of faith and its impact on the constraint of time, or *chrónos*. The Church believes that we are nothing more than sojourners on this earth, pilgrims on the path to heaven.

Through Christ's life, death, and resurrection, he has not only conquered death—he has conquered time. No longer do we need to be bound by a limited life that ends in death. We can truly see our time on earth as a bridge to greater possibilities. We can learn to see time in a fresh, new context.

How would you spend your life differently if you truly embraced the idea of a lifetime of abundance rather than scarcity? Would you take more opportunity to savor the beauty of God's natural creation, choose to delve into a more satisfying vocation, or simply invest in deeper relationships? The emotional and physical toll of living with time as a limited resource certainly shapes our worldview and, sadly, our actions.

With that understanding, let's delve into the "theology" of American capitalism.

American Capitalism and Our Catholic Faith

American capitalism has been the philosophical and practical antidote to counterbalance the challenges related to the earth's limited resources. I am certainly a part of this culture and have been rewarded for my ability to maximize the opportunities afforded by the system of commerce. I do believe capitalism is the most efficient way we have to allocate the earth's limited resources and to redistribute wealth.

America was the very first country built on an economic foundation based on individual responsibility and the freedom of initiative. The United States has been the safe haven for the world's entrepreneurs, small business owners, and the poor seeking the opportunity to maximize their talents and expand their dreams. This was the foundation our forefathers envisioned and the inspiration for the industrial revolution of Europe.

Today we live in the wealthiest country in the history of the world. The per capita material abundance of the United States is truly astonishing by any measure. However, that does not mean we don't have issues with uneven distribution of wealth or pockets of abject poverty in America. Yet the reality is that even the "poor" in this country would be considered very well off in much of the world. As of 2015, according to the United States Department of Health and Human Services, a family of four in the United States is considered poor if their household income falls below $24,250.

According to Gallup research, the median household income in the United States is $43,585. As a comparison, again based on research done by Gallup, the worldwide median household income is just under $10,000 per year, with most of Africa, Asia, Mexico, South America, and Eastern Europe averaging far below this number.[9] According to that data, capitalism has tremendous power to elevate the wealth of a society, but it is only a tool of the people, and thus dependent on their execution and intentions.

Today, the philosophical tradition of entrepreneurship and capitalism is on trial. There is much dissension and debate over disparity of income, class distinction, and the role and responsibility of government in our lives. As of 2016, the United States has some of the highest tax rates in the world on individuals and corporations. The debates continue to rage as to the "right" form of governmental intervention in the economic system of our society.

I believe it is important that we understand what the wisdom of our faith has to tell us on these contentious issues pertaining to capitalism and wealth distribution. If you're not familiar with it, you might be surprised at the Church's position in this debate. St. John Paul II addressed Catholic social teaching with regard to capitalism:

> If by "capitalism" it is meant an economic system which recognizes the fundamental and positive role of business, the market,

> private property and the resulting responsibility of the means of production, as well as free human creativity in the economic sector, then the answer is certainly affirmative, even though it would perhaps be more appropriate to speak of a "business economy," "market economy," or simply a "free economy."[10]

However, he goes on to remind us that capitalism must be "circumscribed within a strong juridicial framework which places it at the service of human freedom in its totality."[11]

The words of Pope John Paul II certainly support the notion of capitalism, but with several caveats to consider. The key elements that define a better understanding of capitalism on behalf of the common good are as follows:

- a free and democratic state where people are allowed to exercise their own will and intellect
- a sophisticated governmental judicial system to handle civil disagreement
- a culture that embodies natural moral law

The esteemed Catholic author Michael Novak built upon the foundational benefits and justification of capitalism in *The Spirit of Democratic Capitalism*. At one time, Novak believed in socialism because he felt its economic system seemed ethically superior. However, he realized through observation of human affairs and personal reflection that he was mistaken. He grew to understand that capitalism is superior to socialism, both in practice and in theory. Most important, Christian virtues can not only survive, but can flourish under democratic capitalism. In this seminal work Novak states:

> Few theologians or religious leaders understand economics, industry, manufacturing, trade and finance. Many seem trapped in pre-capitalist modes of thought . . . Many swiftly reduce all morality to the morality of distribution. They demand jobs without comprehending how jobs are created. They demand the distribution of the world's goods without insight into how the store of the world's goods may be expanded . . . They claim to be leaders without having mastered the techniques of human progress.[12]

Democratic capitalism taps an individual's God-given creativity and initiative and relies on self-interest to direct its actions. It offers an outlet for greed and reinforces habits of prudence, fortitude, and tolerance if one is to be successful in his or her endeavors. These virtues are consistent with Christianity and are reflective of the Protestant work ethic that has so profoundly influenced commerce in the early days of our country.

Modern economic thought tends to have a zero-sum concept of man, nature, and wealth. This view implies that no gain can be realized without a subsequent cost. No one can obtain material wealth without it being taken from someone else. It follows that without strong control by government, there would be perpetual conflict and each person would seek to maximize his or her own gain. Thus, control is needed to prevent excessive individualism and avarice. Under the socialist view, capitalists become wealthy by exploiting workers, and nations become wealthy by exploiting Third World nations. Of course, the ultimate solution to end such abuse is the elimination of private property.

Much of Catholic social teaching was formed in the precapitalist world of medieval society, which appreciated stability rather than dynamic economic growth. The Church teachings were thus more concerned with the fair distribution of available goods than with an economic system that created incremental long-term societal wealth based on exponential growth.

Certainly the New Testament supports the poor. The spirit of socialism thus initially appears to be closer to the Gospel than the competitive nature of capitalism. However, by fostering a form of capitalism that values freedom, individualism, and innovation, society as a whole is lifted to greater economic prosperity.

Today, the Catholic Church stands firm in its position on the role of democratic capitalism to enhance the mission of the Church:

> The illusion that a policy of mere redistribution of existing wealth can definitively resolve the problem must be set aside. In a modern economy, the value of assets is utterly dependent on the capacity to generate revenue in the present and the future. Wealth creation therefore becomes an inescapable duty, which must be kept in mind if the fight against material poverty is to be effective in the long term.[13]

Democratic capitalism is certainly worthy of support when it is based predominantly on markets and incentives driven by scarcity, a democratic state, and a moral and cultural system that is diverse and open-minded. The free-market system fosters economic growth, social mobility, and self-reliance. Political liberty introduces diversity, democracy, and the idea of a constitutional government. The moral-cultural system is supported by the structures of family, Church, and other civic-minded associations. The key component of democratic capitalism is freedom.

No other system has produced an equivalent yield of benefits that have also achieved the loosening of the bonds of the feudal class culture. Yet, as Novak points out, the reality of sin must always be considered as part of the ongoing evolution of man, as we structure ourselves and measure our intentions. Let us also keep in mind that diversity is an integral element in the process of healthy capitalism. As much as we can become frustrated with the polarizing and overtly influential reporting of our free press system, it is a vital element of the democratic capitalism project. Diversity of culture, skill sets, and opinions helps fragment a society and check its power, preventing it from forming homogenous groups that may desire to overwhelm and dominate the marketplace, leaving the minority with less opportunity or worse.

An amazing by-product of democratic capitalism is that it produces not only wealth but also virtuous people whose worldly enterprises can and do complement the work of God. As history demonstrates, capitalism is able to convert an individual's talent and ambitions into the creation and distribution of wealth, and subsequent benevolence toward those less fortunate. In fact, according to the Philanthropy Roundtable, charitable giving in the United States has increased 3.5 times over the past sixty years, adjusted for inflation and population growth.[14] This is an extraordinary and grace-driven by-product of income surplus, driven by our market economy and the productivity and ingenuity it has cultivated.

From a macro perspective, the American democratic economic experiment has worked masterfully. We are an extremely wealthy nation that historically has been supported by a strong middle-class workforce. Our society was founded on the principles of religion and natural moral law. We have had all the critical elements defining capitalism for the common good (see page TK) in place to allow for large-scale success.

However, as we look into the twenty-first century, do we continue to meet the basic criteria for a successful economy that benefits the vast majority of its citizens? As society has become increasingly secular and its emphasis on civic organizations and extended family connections has diminished, can we sustain the American experience?

Our society is predisposed toward individualism and the fear of scarcity. What happens to mankind without the guiding principles of religion, natural moral law, family tradition, and civic pride? This is where you and I have both the opportunity and the obligation to introduce the transforming truths of our faith to the disordered world around us.

THREE

From "Me First" to "Daring to Be the First"

Lord, you have made us for yourself, thus our hearts are restless until they rest in you.

—St. Augustine

For most of my life, my mantra was "Me first." It was the perfect vision for a young and aggressive kid. I have always wanted to win; I'm competitive and have been this way for as long as I can remember. In fact, I hate losing more than I like winning.

Even today, I struggle with an overly competitive nature. In full disclosure, I have been known to "toss" a club after a poor golf shot, or release a rather inappropriate comment in frustration after losing a close pickup basketball game. I have certainly improved in this area of my life, but I still have to be conscious of my temperament in the heat of battle. Much of my proclivity toward an aggressive mentality in sports also transfers to business.

In the heat of battle over an idea or direction at a business meeting, that same competitive fire can emerge. Many years ago, I became so frustrated with the position of a business colleague that I called him a "complete idiot" in front of about twenty other colleagues. It certainly was not one of my finer moments.

Money, Prestige, Power Means I Win, You Lose

I have always admired the businessmen of the world, the ones I've read about in books and magazines, watched on TV, and seen in the movies over the past twenty-five years. I was in college when the movie *Wall Street*, starring Michael Douglas, hit theaters. Though Gordon Gekko was a callous, greedy scoundrel, there was an attractive charm to his presence. His character was certainly an enigma to me.

In the movie, Gekko gives his infamous speech that sums it all up:

> *The point is, ladies and gentleman, that greed—for lack of a better word—is good.*
>
> *Greed is right.*
>
> *Greed works.*
>
> *Greed clarifies, cuts through, and captures the essence of the evolutionary spirit.*
>
> *Greed, in all of its forms—greed for life, for money, for love, knowledge—has marked the upward surge of mankind.*
>
> *And greed—you mark my words—will not only save Teldar Paper, but that other malfunctioning corporation called the USA.*[15]

I remember thinking, *But isn't the point of all the education, work experience, discipline, and grit to separate ourselves from the rest for greater success?* My definition of greater success was increasing my ability to acquire more of the earth's limited resources.

For me, it meant a large stock portfolio, a nice house, and other material comforts. At work, it meant a better bottom line, greater ROI and return on assets, and greater power and influence. Looking back, much of my motivation was not just for the money, but for the challenge, the competition, and the ego boost. It was my view of life's scorecard.

I've been reading the *Wall Street Journal* since I was fourteen years old. I was raised in the business world. After receiving my MBA, I returned to the business world to make my mark. I wanted to separate myself from the crowd and prove that I was the smartest, most hardworking, most focused person around.

But as I've mentioned, despite my competitive nature, the Catholic Church has always been an important part of my life and my identity. I have rarely missed a Sunday Mass in my entire life. I never went through a stage in life when I questioned my faith. Much of my identity has always been Catholic. It is who I am and much of what I do. In my family, we celebrate rich Catholic holiday traditions and attend Sunday Mass, even holy days. I attended Catholic grade school, college, and graduate school. I really enjoyed being part of the larger Catholic family.

However, as an adult, I could never quite come to terms with the relationship between my faith and my work. Many times, I would question some of my motives or ambitions. I had a sense that something was not quite right, but I was never able or willing to figure out the puzzle. Most often, my competitive spirit could not find a way to acquiesce to the Holy Spirit. My inner conversation went something like this: *How can I be the hard-driving business leader that I've been reading about in all the books and magazines, and yet also blend in my Catholic faith? How can I make the tough decisions if I'm burdened with God's call of benevolence, compassion, and empathy? I have to make tough decisions. I have to terminate people, demote people, and negotiate hard. I'm competitive. I want to win, and if by my winning someone else loses, that's just part of business and life. It's a zero-sum game. It's easy talk about how business and faith can live in harmony, but the practicality of the day-to-day grind is a whole different story. Then again, maybe I just don't understand the "how."*

If I reflect honestly, there might have been something else at work. There are many *-isms* in Catholicism. Minimalism is one of them. It's that voice that asks:

- What is the least I can do and still convince myself that I'm being a good Catholic?
- If I'm attending Mass each Sunday, isn't that enough to qualify?
- Do I really need to commit my entire life to Christ? Is that what he is asking? Because I am certainly not interested in being one of "those people"—the ones who seem to have no life outside of church.

Catholic minimalism has reached epic proportions in the world today. There are close to seventy million Catholics in America today. Yet most are lapsed or at best lethargic. I was in that lethargic category—I still attended Mass, but without any real desire to spend time or effort in the daily implementation of the core ideas of the Gospel message I heard there.

One day I came across these words of Jesus: "He who does not take his cross and follow me is not worthy of me. He who finds his life will lose it, and he who loses his life for my sake will find it" (Matthew 10:38–39).

I've spent twenty years on this reflective treadmill. At times I've been a little confused and troubled, but certainly not enough to change tactics. I was compelled by my work, and I lived for the daily challenge and personal fulfillment of doing the job well. I was also very aware of the difficulty of making a business work in such a competitive, litigious, and cutthroat environment as exists in today's culture. Maybe I was a bit afraid to move from a "me first" position to daring to be the first to really follow Jesus. Take up my cross and lose my life for Christ's sake? Let down my guard, change direction? I just wasn't ready to go down that road. Yet there was another nagging message, from Luke 12:48, that would never quite leave my consciousness: "Everyone to whom much is given, of him will much be required; and of him to whom men commit much they will demand the more."

I knew how privileged I was, and I often felt a bit of guilt about it. I came from a strong, close-knit Catholic family. I received a solid education and great job opportunities, I married my beautiful college sweetheart, and we have three healthy kids. I have been blessed beyond what one could or should expect. "To whom much is given . . ."

By nature, I am a very introspective person. I'm constantly reading, thinking, and searching for better ideas, greater meaning, and self-improvement. Yet I began to realize that most of this energy was being focused in a linear direction. Business success is where I had the most control and certainly the greatest clarity.

My wife has been my most vocal and challenging critic. Over the years she questioned my motives, decisions, attitudes, and priorities—even accusing me of being hypocritical at times. I felt she was just naive and unaware of what it takes to prosper in business today, that she knew nothing about the reality of economics and the need to be first. I thought that maybe she wanted all the benefits without accepting the sacrifice. I would tell her, "It's easy to be a Christian when you have no skin in the game and people aren't trying to steal from or sue you every day."

The concept of Catholic social justice that I understood back then was not my vision of successful American democracy, much of which is based on self-discipline and personal responsibility.

But was that just another justification for a minimalist attitude?

I own a commercial office building that had been vacant for many months without much prospect for finding a new tenant. One day, the broker called me and said he had a tenant who wanted to lease the space. But then he added that he wasn't sure I'd be willing to accept the tenant because of my Catholicism. It turned out the prospective tenant was Planned Parenthood.

I thought for a minute and then said with clarity that I had no issue with that. After all, this was business. They had to rent space somewhere. I said to myself, "It's not as if they're going out of business if I don't rent to them."

I've always been pro-life and considered myself to be unwavering on this issue. However, I had convinced myself there must be some degree of separation between work and faith, thus allowing me to justify accepting Planned Parenthood as a tenant on our property.

Thankfully, my family talked some sense into me, and a few days later I called the broker back and declined to rent the space to those tenants. It was a poignant moment for me. It was almost as if I could hear that cock crow, that same one the apostle Peter heard after denying that he knew Jesus.

The Catholic Church has not backed down from this controversial issue. The universal call to holiness that we all share as priestly people of God holds every one of us to a higher standard of living than simply following the State's civil obligation for good conduct. Pope John Paul II was very active in voicing the position of the Church on this topic throughout his papacy:

> Christians, like all people of good will, are called upon under grave obligation of conscience not to cooperate formally in practices which, even if permitted by civil legislation, are contrary to God's law. Such cooperation occurs when an action, either by its very nature or by the form it takes in a concrete situation, can be defined as a direct participation in an act against innocent human life or a sharing in the immortal intention of the person committing it.[16]

Socrates said, "An unexamined life is not worth living." As I reflected upon my actions, I was disappointed with myself and wondered how I could have considered such a decision. How had my moral compass become so skewed? Certainly there was an element of greed involved. However, there was also something more—perhaps indifference or even apathy. I had begun to numb myself to truly listening to my conscience.

It is much easier to make choices in business or life without thinking about their deeper implications. Operating this way has become a cancer within our culture.

To honestly evaluate the decisions we make, developing a deeper and more complex moral rubric takes time, deeper reflection, risk, and vulnerability. Looking at the decisions of life within the shallow guidelines of civil obedience is a much simpler path. It is certainly the path of least resistance for many, myself included.

There were other watershed moments that began to create a crack in my work-faith foundation. Specifically, there was a distinct rift developing between my wife and me. She was finding it very difficult to live with my work attitude, focus, and priorities.

I was always attached to my BlackBerry or computer, and I continually thought about work. I said that my family was my priority, but deep down, I knew it was a lie. It just wasn't reflected in my actions. I would tell myself that if I didn't keep my focus, I would jeopardize my goals, and I would certainly not be the type of leader I wanted to be. My role models were guys who worked eighty-hour weeks and traveled twice as much as I did. I would say to myself, *If she only knew the real world.*

By the summer of 2005, my wife and I were treading on thin ice. Our one-year-old son, Andrew, was a sickly child. He constantly suffered from a multitude of allergies, and the air quality of the central San Joaquin Valley caused him severe breathing problems, which led to deep congestion and an inability to sleep. We spent many nights next to him, giving him breathing treatments every few hours or just comforting him as he struggled to breathe.

Then my wife's best friend, Andrew's godmother, was diagnosed with cancer. She spent the better part of one summer in the hospital undergoing a myriad of experimental chemo procedures that left her body and mind a wreck. When she died, her loss was devastating for us; she was just thirty-eight years old.

This was a very strange period of time for my family and me. We had just spent the past decade building our family through many tribulations resulting from infertility issues. We should have been rejoicing and basking in the gift of our three children, ages six, three, and one. Instead we were emotionally exhausted and drifting away from each other and our faith.

No Coincidences

In the fall of 2005, my wife, Kaaren, and I decided to attend a Catholic conference together. We were struggling under the weight of stress and sadness in our lives, and we needed a few days of reflection, spiritual nourishment, and renewal. At this conference there was an emissary from the little village of Medjugorje, in Bosnia and Herzegovina, where it is believed by many Catholics throughout the world that Marian apparitions have been taking place for the past thirty-five years.

As the conference continued throughout the day, a rather odd feeling came over me, a feeling as unexplainable today as it was more than a decade ago. I felt an internal tug to go on a pilgrimage to this remote village in Bosnia and Herzegovina.

Over the course of the afternoon, the feeling just kept getting stronger and more pronounced. I believed it was a ridiculous thought, and I struggled to ignore it. With my work schedule and my family obligations, I could not fathom pursuing this crazy idea. I had hardly been out of the country, and certainly was not ready to go to some obscure village in Europe for a week of prayer. After the conference, I dismissed the idea for two months, again believing it to be a sophomoric and in-the-moment thought and not worthy of further pursuit.

However, the feeling of being called persisted. In early 2006, I convinced myself to call the only company I knew that offered pilgrimages to Medjugorje. They had sponsored the Marian conference that Kaaren and I had attended. As it turned out, there was a message on the answering machine stating that they were no longer doing pilgrimages because of the retirement of the pilgrimage coordinator. In a strange way, I felt relieved. This information released me from making a decision or leaving work for some crazy pilgrimage. I had done my part and at least explored the opportunity.

Two weeks later I was still restless and unable to stop thinking about going to Medjugorje. I was sitting at my desk one afternoon and spontaneously decided to redial the pilgrimage group number. This time the pilgrimage coordinator answered the phone. I proceeded to stumble and stammer, stating that I was calling even though I knew they were no longer doing pilgrimages.

She asked me why I'd called back if I thought there weren't any more pilgrimages, and I told her I didn't know. She said that a few days ago, she was able to get someone to take over for her and that the group would offer another pilgrimage in early March, during Lent. She then said something like, "I think I know why you called." I was speechless. I replied, "I'm glad you do, but I certainly don't."

As Paulo Coelho said, "It has been said that there is no such thing as coincidence in this world."[17] Maybe I really was being called.

FOUR

Pilgrimage: Who Do You Say That I Am?

To go on pilgrimage means to step out of ourselves in order to encounter God where he has revealed himself.

—Pope Benedict XVI

In early March 2006, I left for Bosnia and Herzegovina. I was still unsure of my intention for going on this pilgrimage. I was a bit uneasy about being completely disconnected from my work and away from my family. And the truth was, I felt very skeptical of what might await me there.

My interpretation of Catholicism has always directed me more toward the pragmatic and rational, rather than the mystical. I just wasn't sure how much of the charismatic or supernatural I could take. I did not want to be in an environment where people were frantically searching for miracles or "signs." That just isn't my style or comfort zone. And I also wondered how I could possibly handle ten days without a gym or e-mails and conference calls to keep me occupied.

From the moment we arrived in a still-war-torn Sarajevo, the trip was different from anything I had previously experienced. After twenty-eight hours of travel, we loaded onto a bus for the final two-hour ride to Medjugorje. It was late at night, and we were all exhausted. I was looking forward to sleeping on the bus. I was thinking like a tourist.

Our Croatian tour guide, Miki, had other plans for me. The first thing we did upon boarding the bus was say a prayer of gratitude for the opportunity of the experience that awaited us, followed by praying the Rosary together. It would certainly be a pilgrimage, not a vacation.

For the first time in my life, I spent several hours of my day dedicated solely to reflection and prayer. One of the extraordinary highlights of Medjugorje was the Mass itself at St. James Church. There were hundreds of priests and thousands of pilgrims in Medjugorje who all had one thing in common: a desire to experience Christ in the sacraments.

There were at least ten priests and deacons on the altar at every Mass. Throughout the week, each priest would alternate being the lead celebrant at the Mass. The homilies, liturgy, and the music were filled with an awe-inspiring energy and enthusiasm. It was unlike anything I had witnessed in my local parish Mass.

Right outside St. James Church, there were about twenty confessionals, with priests listening to confessions in a dozen languages. How amazing to see people in a rush for an open seat at the ten a.m. American Mass, or waiting in line ten deep for their first confession in twenty years.

The days were spent with Mass, walks up Cross Mountain and Apparition Hill while reciting the Stations of the Cross or the Rosary, conversing with some of the visionaries, and much fellowship with other pilgrims from all over the world. The local wine was very good too! It was an opportunity for prayer, reflection, and a humble appreciation for being a part of this unified spiritual journey we call Catholicism.

I was sincerely overwhelmed by the experience, the peace, the love, the worship, and the community of Catholics—truly one faith body. The weather that week was cold and rainy, and the little room I stayed in was cramped and chilly as well, but it made no difference. I quickly embraced the fact that I was a pilgrim, not a tourist. The minor hardships just seemed to add to the spiritual experience.

In our Catholic faith, the tradition and theology of pilgrimage has a deep and meaningful history. For thousands of years, Catholics have embarked on difficult physical journeys as a means to go deeper into the spiritual core of their lives in Christ. Going on a pilgrimage indicates a desire to journey toward some greater spiritual growth through hardship, periods of solitude, self-examination, and prayer.

In the early period of the Church, people would travel for months to make a pilgrimage to the holy sites of Jerusalem in veneration of Jesus Christ. After the conquest of the Holy Land by the Muslims in the seventh century, many people shifted their pilgrimages toward Europe's holy sites such as Santiago de Compostela in Spain, and other Marian apparition sites such as Fatima, Lourdes, Knock, and La Salette.

As part of my spiritual journey, I have come to appreciate the wisdom of our tradition with regard to this ancient practice. I too have integrated pilgrimages as part of the faith plan for my life. Since my initial trip, I have been back to Medjugorje twice, while also taking similar journeys to the Holy Land, Fatima, Assisi, Orvieto, and Rome. Each trip has provided a unique opportunity to push myself outside my spiritual and physical comfort zones, and recharge my faith. I look forward to the opportunity one day to join in the tradition of thousands before me and walk the Camino de Santiago.

My life has been forever changed by those days in that remote village in Bosnia and Herzegovina. I remember my personal theme for the week was simply "Be not afraid." Be not afraid to live your faith. Be not afraid of branching out into the unknown. Be not afraid of the world's view of failure. And be not afraid to alter your life's mission.

It was there that I finally had the courage to ask myself the most fundamental question in human history: "Who do you say that I am?"

It was the question that Jesus posed to his disciples at Caesarea Philippi. It is the same question that he asks of you and me. This question is so profoundly important to mankind that it can be found in all three synoptic Gospels (Matthew 16:13, Luke 9:20, Mark 8:29). I have realized that if we get this question wrong, it is impossible to understand our essential purpose and ever be in right relationship with our Creator. It is certainly the central question of our lives.

Reflecting back on the arbitrary events that led me to Medjugorje and beyond, I am awed by the determination of the Holy Spirit in my life. I simply can no longer believe in coincidence. There have been so many opportunities to take a different path in my life over the past decade. Yet, somehow, I am continually pulled back to the power of my experience in Medjugorje and the fundamental question of our lives: "Who do you say that I am?"

FIVE

Realizing Our Christian Identity

We can believe what we choose. We are answerable for what we choose to believe.

—Cardinal John Henry Newman

"Who do you say that I am?"

After Jesus poses this provocative question to his disciples, St. Peter responds, "You are the Christ, Son of the living God." Peter has realized that Jesus is the anointed one, the long-awaited Messiah of Israel. Jesus responds to him, "Blessed are you, Simon Bar-Jona! For flesh and blood has not revealed this to you but my Father who is in heaven" (Matthew 16:15–17).

Jesus can never be accused of being oblique, and he does not mince words. Here he makes a definitive claim to be the Messiah, the anointed one, and by doing so he is forcing us to make a choice in how we see him: He is either who he claims to be, or he is a lunatic or a liar.

British novelist C. S. Lewis captures the radical nature of Jesus' assertion in the following excerpt from *Mere Christianity*:

> I am trying here to prevent anyone saying the really foolish thing that people often say about Him: I'm ready to accept Jesus as a

> great moral teacher, but I don't accept his claim to be God. That is the one thing we must not say. A man who was merely a man and said the sort of things Jesus said would not be a great moral teacher. He would either be a lunatic—on the level with the man who says he is a poached egg—or else he would be the Devil of Hell. You must make your choice. Either this man was, and is, the Son of God, or else a madman or something worse. You can shut him up for a fool, you can spit at him and kill him as a demon, or you can fall at his feet and call him Lord and God, but let us not come with any patronizing nonsense about his being a great human teacher. He has not left that open to us. He did not intend to.[18]

"Who do you say that I am?" → ***"Who do I say that I am?"***

When you and I accept the reality of Jesus' identity as the Son of God, logic then impels us to ask the same life-altering identity question of ourselves. "Who do I say that I am?" This is the entryway and opportunity to discover our true nature, our Christian anthropology. For if we believe in the nature of Jesus Christ and God the Father, we must accept his claim upon us as well.

> God created man in his own image, in the image of God he created him; male and female he created them. (Genesis 1:27)

> See what love the Father has given us, that we should be called children of God; and so we are. (1 John 3:1)

> For we are his workmanship, created in Christ Jesus for good works which God prepared beforehand, that we should walk in them. (Ephesians 2:10)

> And if [we are] children, then heirs, heirs of God and fellow heirs with Christ. (Romans 8:17)

> But you are a chosen race, a royal priesthood, a holy nation, God's own people, that you may declare the wonderful deeds of him who called you out of darkness into his marvelous light. (1 Peter 2:9)

The defining characteristic of humanity is that we are made in the image and likeness of God. We have been created out of his freely given love for us. God has provided us with an intellect and a will. We are distinctly human because we possess this dual capacity of intellect and freedom of ownership over our will.

Man is unique in his ability to harness both intellect and will, allowing him to make rational decisions in right relationship with his nature.

> Being in the image of God the human individual possesses the dignity of a person, who is not just something, but someone. He is capable of self-knowledge, of self-possession and of freely giving himself and entering into communion with other persons. And he is called by grace to a covenant with his Creator, to offer him a response of faith and love that no other creature can give in his stead. (*CCC*, 357)

However, when we separate the intellect and the will, it leads to a lessening of our humanity and impacts our ability to make the decisions that place us in right relationship with God.

Currently, the most obvious example of the dichotomy between the intellect and the will is the pro-choice movement. Humanity has chosen to separate the intellect from the will in order to justify the termination of an unborn human life.

The sophistication of today's science has proven repeatedly that even at conception, the zygote is a completely unique living organism. Even at this point of its evolution, the zygote is in full possession of its own set of DNA that is separate from that of its parents. Within the first trimester of pregnancy a routine ultrasound confirms visually the fact of a living and active human person. Furthermore, the developing embryo has a heartbeat and its own circulatory system just twenty-two days after conception; at twenty weeks, the baby in the womb is capable of hearing and recognizing a voice, and can respond to other external stimuli. This is all scientific fact, not opinion. It is man's use of his rational nature. As G. K. Chesterton said, "Fallacies do not cease to be fallacies because they become fashions."

Yet many will ignore the intellect in favor of the will in order justify their decision to terminate a pregnancy. Thomas Aquinas argued that the will and the intellect are partners, and freedom must be consistent with the truth. Man must utilize his rational intellect to find and understand the truth, rather than simply asserting the will in order to justify his actions.

When humanity says, "I have a right to choose," it is simply applying a philosophy of voluntarism to justify a desire to abort a living baby because of circumstance. It is the systematic favoring of the will over the intellect. In essence, if I desire it to be true, I can make it true. This is also the modern philosophy of moral relativism, which supports and promotes a society to live without any concrete universal or knowable moral truth. It is a perspective that believes the individual's version of truth that suits or justifies his or her desire is all that matters.

This is critical because man cannot possibly understand his true potential until he understands foundationally who he is as a human. Ultimately, intellect leads to knowledge, and will leads to the capacity to freely love. This combination of knowledge and love is what allows a person to be truly free.

However, our Christian reality calls us to a much deeper understanding of intellect and will than simply freedom for ourselves. The real questions are: Freedom from what? Freedom for what purpose?

The Law of the Gift

St. John Paul II said, "For we are at our best, we are most fully alive and human, when we give away freely and sacrificially our very selves in love for another." This is what it means to be a fully functioning person.

Personhood

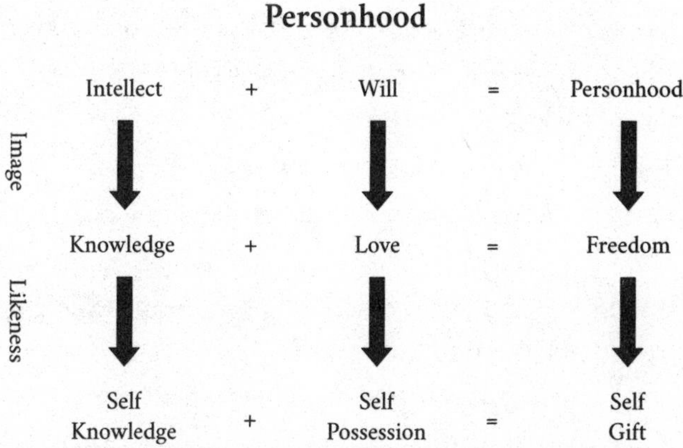

Source: The Augustine Institute, Theology 504: Moral and Spiritual Theology, Dr. Michel Therrien, PowerPoint slide.

Our intellect leads us to reason, knowledge, and ultimately self-awareness. Our will allows us the capacity for choice and enables us to love and be loved, and to choose our unique life's path toward self-possession. We possess freedom because we have the capacity to harness our intellect and free will.

Our Christian reality is about not just our personal freedom, but a freedom that dares to attain something much greater beyond ourselves. We can find many examples of our intended reality as human beings made in the image and likeness of God throughout Catholic doctrine. In *Gaudium et Spes* (*Pastoral Constitution on the Church in the Modern World*) we are told, "Man cannot fully find himself except through the gift of self."[19] There are many more instances in the Bible, such as these:

> Whoever seeks to gain his life will lose it, but whoever loses his life will preserve it. (Luke 17:33)

> A new commandment I give to you, that you love one another; even as I have loved you, that you also love one another. (John 13:34)

> You shall love your neighbor as yourself. (Matthew 22:39)

Bishop Robert Barron describes a significant issue plaguing our world today:

> One of the most fundamental problems in the spiritual order is that we sense within ourselves the hunger for God, but we attempt to satisfy it with some created good that is less than God. When we try to satisfy the hunger for God with something less than

> God, we will naturally be frustrated, and then in our frustration, we will convince ourselves that we need more of that finite good, so we will struggle to achieve it, only to find ourselves again, necessarily, dissatisfied. At this point, a sort of spiritual panic sets in, and we can find ourselves turning obsessively around this creaturely good that can never in principle make us happy.[20]

Take a moment and reflect upon the reality of Bishop Barron's words. How do they relate to your understanding of Christian reality and your essential purpose? How often do you get caught up in trying to satisfy the hunger for God through worldly means?

At this stage in my life, I should know what would satisfy my desire for happiness. But I still fall into the trap of seeking substitutes for this happiness. Thomas Aquinas said that the four typical substitutes for God are wealth, pleasure, power, and honor. I am . . . guilty, guilty, guilty, and guilty!

Almost every day I have an internal battle with myself over the substitutes for God's happiness. It doesn't mean I shouldn't pursue certain goals or desires for my life. But I'm learning that I must always be vigilant about putting these pursuits in their proper context of my life's fundamental goal.

There are times when the things you enjoy pursuing (and are good at) may lead to wealth, pleasure, power, and honor. But with a deeper understanding of yourself and the ability to reflect on your actions, you can differentiate the material rewards from the reality of your essential purpose and use your gifts in a meaningful way.

The Parable of the Bags of Gold

In one of Jesus' parables, he describes what various servants do with the gifts they've been given by their master:

> For it will be as when a man going on a journey called his servants and entrusted to them his property; to one he gave five talents, to another two, to another one, to each according to his ability. Then he went away. He who had received the five talents went at once and traded with them; and he made five talents more. So also, he who had the two talents made two talents more. But he who had received the one talent went and dug in the ground and hid his master's money. (Matthew 25:14–18)

The parable continues with the master eventually returning home to evaluate the stewardship of his servants. When he discovers that the servant who received one bag of gold simply chose to bury it rather than at least attempt to invest, the master calls him a "wicked, lazy servant!" He proceeds to command his men to "throw that worthless servant outside, into the darkness, where there will be weeping and gnashing of teeth."

The point of this passage is a rather stark example of what Jesus wants from us and our talents. Simply put, he wants a return on his investment. He has given all of us unique and powerful gifts for the benefit of ourselves and mankind. So often we choose not to invest our time, talent, and treasure because of complacency, greed, insecurity, or fear. This parable is a warning: God is calling us to live our lives boldly! Dynamic Catholic's tagline is "Be Bold. Be Catholic." It is so fitting for our faith. I know that if and when I allow myself time for self-reflection and self-awareness, it will lead me away from seeking the temporary happiness of a life determined by moral relativism, and instead toward boldly daring to use my gifts for the common good of mankind.

SIX

A Novel Perspective: Work as Vocation

For whoever would save his life will lose it, and whoever loses his life for my sake will find it.
—Matthew 16:25

Shortly after returning from my pilgrimage, I read a profile in a business magazine about the CEO of one of the largest corporations in the world. The article told of him working eighty hours a week for twenty years to reach the coveted position of chief executive officer. I remember doing the math in my head: That's 11.5 hours a day, seven days a week. In the article he also mentions taking his eighteen-year-old daughter off to college, with the irony of it all completely escaping him.

For the first time, I saw the story of a successful businessman totally dedicated and absorbed by the job in a new light. I finally had the clarity to see that this life was not for me. It all finally clicked. Saying no to this kind of life would require a deeper yes, a clearer understanding of what is truly important.

Unless you're St. Paul on the road to Damascus, life typically doesn't change radically in an instant, a week, a month, or year. My life and my attitudes weren't just magically altered either. Yet I had acquired a greater vision of what God was calling me to be. I heard a universal call to holiness designed specifically for me.

To have the courage to leap into the disruption of a life in Jesus Christ, we must truly understand our essential purpose. We must know our Christian anthropology. This anthropology is never about scarcity and fear, but always about investing ourselves in a life of spiritual abundance in partnership with a God who does not compete with humanity.

However, in order to experience our rightful abundance, we must be able to see ourselves as children of God and so choose to accept this relationship. His abundance is defined by love, not by our notions of scarcity, or whether we possess the material items that are subject to supply and demand.

The survival mechanism that sees the world through the prism of limited resources can have a profound effect on how our attitude is shaped, turning it away from the optimism and hope of happiness through God and toward pessimism and cynicism of competition for limited resources.

If we see the world through the prism of scarcity, then as soon as we feel threatened by something we perceive will limit our ability to survive, we turn away from the benevolent and optimistic nature of hope. We become burdened by the fear of potential future events that carry the possibility to alter our earthly abundance. We become obsessed with the notion of scarcity and what that might mean for our limited view of happiness.

A Shift in Perspective

You must realize now, more clearly than ever, that God is calling you to serve Him in and from the ordinary, secular and civil activities

of human life. He waits for us every day, in the laboratory, in the operating theatre, in the army barracks, in the university chair, in the factory, in the workshop, in the fields, in the home and in all the immense panorama of work.
—St. Josemaría Escrivá

In 2006, author Matthew Kelly emailed me an early draft of his new book, *The Dream Manager*. He had just spent a month in solitude walking the Camino on pilgrimage, and had been inspired to write a book about this idea of work as a deeper vocation. The book is a parable of sorts, written about a fictional company with a high percentage of unskilled or first-time employees in a very labor-intensive and service-oriented business. The company is plagued with low morale and high turnover, thus costing the company a tremendous amount of money in lost productivity, hiring costs, and training hours.

Knowing my background and experience as the owner of multiple McDonald's restaurants as a franchisee, he was looking for some feedback regarding the book's premise and ultimate conclusions.

If I had received the book five years earlier, I would have dismissed its premise as unrealistic and a bit naive. However, I had recently started to rethink my life's mission and my ultimate purpose as an employer, father, and husband.

I had just read the book *Ordinary Work, Extraordinary Grace*, by Scott Hahn. This book encouraged me to understand that my work must be integrated into my spiritual life, as one more opportunity to serve God and his kingdom. With that mind-set, I was profoundly impacted by Matthew's book. While reading it, I could feel butterflies in my stomach as the fable evolved.

Matthew's story centers upon a company dealing with serious problems of high turnover and low morale. This was certainly something I could relate to as a franchisee in the quick-service industry. The managers begin to investigate what really drives the employees' satisfaction. What they discover is that their employees' main motivation is not necessarily the promise of a bigger paycheck or title, but rather the actualization of their dreams.

More often than not, the employees have neither the vision nor the opportunity to dream. Most of them are stuck in a world focused on day-to-day subsistence. Whether it is struggling to find daycare, transportation issues, dealing with relationship strife, or simply a lack of discipline, the employers recognize that these are their employees' barriers to dreams. That is why issues with productivity or turnover can never be solved until employers can assist the employees in addressing the immediate problems of their daily lives.

Until we find the ability to overcome the hurdles of our basic needs, dreaming of a more robust life is impossible. *The Dream Manager* chronicles how the management team assembles a program using company resources to individually and collectively address the immediate needs of their employees, while also teaching them to dream.

The book's vision certainly hit home. I live in a community that faces a multitude of social and economic issues that manifest themselves in the workplace. I could fundamentally relate to the story line, people, and problems this company faces.

Instead of seeing these issues in the light of negativity and dysfunction, I began to see them as a business and personal opportunity for me. I believe we have always been a very fair employer and certainly strive to create a functional, safe, and fair work environment. It's my intent as a McDonald's franchise owner to be very mindful of our civic responsibility, and I certainly have taken on the hardships of employees.

However, this story's message goes far beyond the basic notion of "good employer." The book challenges the reader to "be not afraid" to confront the employee-employer business model relationship that permeates our economy. It is a model that simply evaluates and recognizes the employee within the context of how he or she performs in the work environment. However, the model does not pay much attention to the issues of daily life for people of a certain socioeconomic level.

Yet, if employees face issues with transportation, housing, or childcare, these problems will eventually cause problems in the work environment. Of course, the easy solution would be to terminate their employment or accept their choice to quit, and not really pay attention to the hidden cost of this turnover.

The problem is that I paid attention to these hidden costs. I knew what we were paying to maintain this model. But having the courage to change is something else. Becoming physically and emotionally involved with the daily struggles of your employees can bring on its own challenges and disappointment. Over the course of the past decade, I have certainly experienced an abundance of both. Committing time and resources does not always guarantee success or gratitude.

After I read the book, as a company we committed to supporting the Dream Manager program within our McDonald's franchisee organization. Since that time, we have consistently dared to incorporate the concepts into our daily managerial process and mission objectives.

While this hasn't always been easy, we have been a part of some incredible success stories. Getting to know our employees at a deeper level and using our resources to help their lives have been the most rewarding parts of my job over the past decade.

Today more than ever, I see McDonald's as a unique and wonderful bridge for our employees—a bridge to a long-term career with McDonald's or to college, a short-term help for family, or simply another job opportunity. When we are thinking about the needs of the employee first, we find the by-product to be greater dedication, productivity, and loyalty to the McDonald's brand and our customers.

I know much of my paradigm shift on the integration of my faith into my business would never have been possible without my initial pilgrimage experience in Medjugorje. That experience was the catalyst that allowed me to "be not afraid" and dare to truly think differently about my role and responsibility as a Catholic leader in our culture today. It is responsibility that demands magnanimity—a virtue I had not applied to my life until then.

Magnanimity is a desire to push toward greater achievement morally, spiritually, physically, and mentally. More important, it is truly desiring that same success for others as well.

The perpetual challenge for any business leader is the communication of a vision. Today, I spend a large portion of my time applying my philosophical approach to business through my actions and words. In order to be truly successful on our mission, I need all key stakeholders to buy in and help us execute the vision, every day and in each of my restaurants. We simply cannot be successful in this endeavor unless all our supervisors, general managers, and department managers buy into the philosophy of being magnanimous leaders.

The most powerful question of my life has continued to be "Who do you say that I am?" My journey to find the answer has profoundly redirected my life. Using the platform of my work as a vocational opportunity to live my faith has created a synergy to allow me to see the work-life equation through a fundamentally different lens. Now, using the insights I've gained, I believe the possibilities are endless.

Whether it is thinking differently to help our employees obtain access to college through scholarships and application assistance, providing access to computers for their children, helping them learn financial skills for their future, helping them address transportation barriers, or simply accommodating their schedule needs, it has all become part of our collective job responsibilities.

Living a Culture of Catholicism

My pilgrimage opportunities have opened my eyes to the significant loss of Catholic culture we are experiencing in the Western world. When you are enclosed within the current Catholic environment of many of our parishes or Catholic schools, it is easy to assume that this is just the way it is; it's not supposed to be inspirational, charismatic, or motivating—it's just church.

Yet, so often, what I have heard and experienced on pilgrimages and attending conferences is the exact opposite perspective. Both the priests and the laity constantly comment on the overwhelming sense of community and shared ideology that is experienced in environments such as Medjugorje, Fatima, the Holy Land, and local eucharistic or Marian conferences. It is an understanding of who we truly are as a people made in the image of God. It is a shared ideology that bonds us and unifies us toward a common vision and philosophy of life.

As the United States continues its ambivalence toward God and natural moral law, we see a society moving toward greater fragmentation, and an unraveling of the unity that once was the fabric of the American democratic success story.

As John Adams, the second president of the United States and one of the architects of the United States and its constitution, stated in 1789, "Our constitution was made only for a moral and religious people. It is wholly inadequate to the government of any other."

In the original American democratic experiment, there was a shared sense of moral values, patriotism, and work ethic. Today we cannot find a common ground that allows for collective identity, unity, and collaboration. Our inability to rally around a shared vision of America may ultimately lead us toward the historical path of the once-great Roman Empire.

The great doctor of the Church St. Augustine wrote of this in his philosophical work *City of God,* in the mid-400s. It was a challenging time for Catholics living in the Roman Empire during this period. The decay and decline of this formerly magnificent state was becoming obvious to the citizens of Rome and their enemies as well. The critical questions of the time were "What caused the decline?" and "What or who was to blame?"

Those who adhered to the pagan faith were quick to blame the Christians, claiming that the gods had abandoned Rome because of the acceptance of Christianity in the empire in AD 325. These Romans claimed that Christians were loyal not to the state, but to this "kingdom of heaven."

St. Augustine used *City of God* to refute the pagans' charges that Christians brought about the fall of Rome. He suggested instead that the Roman Empire became weak because they gave themselves up to the moral and spiritual corruption that was accepted by the pagan culture of the day. His premise was that humankind must pursue the city of heaven to maintain a proper sense of order and civility within the context of the earthly state, which in turn leads to true peace.

In effect, *City of God* is the eternal challenge to human society. To which city does your primary allegiance lead you? St. Augustine's philosophical accounting of Rome could as well have been written for us today.

Catholic philosopher Alasdair MacIntyre has written extensively on the issues surrounding the significance of shared identity and belief in a common culture to sustain a unified and flourishing society.

In his book *After Virtue*, MacIntyre concludes that individualism and its insidious by-product, moral relativism, as a guide to truth have led to an inevitable and irretrievable loss of a common culture: "Modern society is indeed often, at least in surface appearance, nothing but a collection of strangers, each pursuing his or her own interests under minimal constraints."[21] However, more damaging is the loss of a common ethical reference point to allow for productive and healthy debate.

This reality has moral, religious, social, and economic effects that are only just beginning to permeate and fracture our American culture. The most obvious examples of this lack of a common reference point from which to begin consequential debate are the pro-choice/pro-life and euthanasia issues. Without a shared reference point surrounding the intrinsic value of a human life, all debate becomes an exercise in futility.

In the midst of a secular and temporal vision of life that hardly goes beyond our generation, how can we see the vast canvas that

God has been creating for humanity? The answer lies in seeing ourselves in the proper context of who we are as members of the body of Christ. It is a citizenship that transcends today's world of pleasure and pain, in which we see ourselves in the proper context of our Christian faith.

SEVEN

Finding Our Strength in Humility

So the last will be first, and the first last.
—Matthew 20:16

One of the great challenges of my life has been embracing the concept of Christian humility. Far too often, the confidence and assertiveness that made me successful and proficient in the tasks of my daily life eventually led me down a path toward arrogance, egoism, and insensitivity toward others.

Part of this mentality is a function of my competitive spirit and desire to win. I have always addressed life's obstacles with an aggressive and assertive self-confidence in order to be successful. Yet, as many in my life can attest, I have been less than understanding when others either fail to model this same behavior or don't find value in its ideology. It's caused strife in my personal life and in my working relationships.

However, I have come to understand that our role and responsibility as Christians must always be fundamentally rooted in the humility that I realized I lacked (and far too often still do). It is not the humility that is so often perceived as weak or feeble, but a humility of strength, confidence, and fortitude. I have realized that it is only through the prism of humility that we will ultimately have the power and grace to live our lives enthroned in this principle of self-gift.

When Jesus speaks of the last to be first in Matthew 20:16, he is simply reiterating the new role of humility in the life of a true Christian. In the fifth chapter of Matthew's Gospel, Jesus speaks at length about this new and radical way of thinking about life. In fact, in this moment Jesus purposely speaks from the Mount of Beatitudes in Galilee as the "new" Moses, a bit of symbolism that was not lost on his perceptive Jewish audience. Certainly, Moses and the Decalogue was a prefiguring or typology of these eventual teachings of Jesus in the Beatitudes.

His Sermon on the Mount was a radical extension of the original Ten Commandments for the Hebrew people. In Jesus, we finally come to a moment in the economy of salvation where God has determined that man has the capacity to grasp a deeper understanding of our essential purpose. Jesus preaches that there is a new standard required of man.

The Beatitudes, found in Matthew 5:3–11, are at the heart of Jesus' preaching. They take up the promises made to the chosen people since Abraham, fulfilling those promises by ordering them no longer merely to the possession of a territory, but to the kingdom of heaven.

The Beatitudes praise and honor the meek, the humble, and the peacemakers. It is no longer good enough to live a life of an eye for an eye and a tooth for a tooth, because that is a life fundamentally rooted in the scarcity and limitations of our biological nature. We are now being called to greatness as described by Christ in the following passage delivered just after the Beatitudes:

> You are the light of the world. A city set on a hill cannot be hid. Nor do men light a lamp and put it under a bushel, but on a stand, and it gives light to all in the house. Let your light shine before men, that they may see your good works and give glory to your Father who is in heaven. (Matthew 5:14–16)

This now must become our goal. This is man's mantra for choosing to "be the first" in humble servitude and obedience to one another.

However, today there seems to be an ever-increasing propensity to choose to be "less than" or some second-rate version of ourselves. Why?

We have become a society that purposely chooses to be either too wary or too self-absorbed to be the first. Perhaps we are simply not willing to muster up the courage to vigorously pursue our God-given talent—out of either fear or mere complacency.

I am as guilty of this behavior as the next person when it comes to self-absorption or lack of humility. If I'm not vigilant about my essential purpose, I will find myself drifting into a mentality that is focused on money, pettiness, or minimalism.

Sadly, some days I can go into one of my establishments knowing full well the impact my presence and personality has upon the team, yet I fail to act. I fail to come outside myself and my own personal agenda and meet the needs of the employees in their moment.

I have found that some days, all it takes is me giving a genuine smile and hello to my employees as they are working, acknowledging my gratitude for their commitment to their effort. Some days it means sitting down and listening to an issue that seems to be holding them back from becoming more successful or content in their jobs or lives. Mainly it is as simple as being present, putting the cell phone or computer away, and having the commitment to be with them in that moment. My task-driven personality can be my Achilles' heel when it comes to recognizing immense value in these moments. Today I keep a little note on my desk and computer that reminds me to check myself. The note simply states, "Be here now."

St. Francis said, "For it is in giving that we receive." It's a paradox of life that if you want to receive, you have to be willing to give. This directly contradicts the message we get from our culture, which teaches us that we are the center of everything. *Give me. Let me have it. I want to possess your life!* How many relationships are dysfunctional because of this desire to possess rather than give in selflessness?

The one thing that is impossible to do with the divine life is to possess it. Why? Because the divine life is a life of love, and true love means self-giving. Real love is about giving it away. To have the divine life is to have love in you, and to desire to give away what you have received. By giving you will have it. You will have divine life in the measure you give it away. And this will lead to the death of being "less than," of self-absorption, apathy, and pettiness. In its place, becoming a self-gift (giving yourself away) will bring the abundance and prosperity we all seek.

EIGHT

The Power of Christian Hope

Where there is hope, there is faith.
Where there is faith, miracles happen.
—Author Unknown

At Sunday Mass one weekend an obscure reading from the prophet Habakkuk affected me intensely. I listened to the reading and then read it to fully absorb its message. Take a moment and read this passage before continuing in this chapter.

How long, O Lord, must I cry for help
    and you do not listen?
Or cry out to you, "Violence!"
    and you do not intervene?
Why do you let me see iniquity?
    Why do you simply gaze at evil?
Destruction and violence are before me;
    there is strife and discord. . . .

Then the Lord answered me and said:
    Write down the vision;
Make it plain upon tablets,

so that the one who reads it may run.
For the vision is a witness for the appointed time,
a testimony to the end; it will not disappoint.
If it delays, wait for it,
it will surely come, it will not be late.
See, the rash have no integrity;
but the just one who is righteous because of faith shall live.
(Habakkuk 1:2–3; 2:2–4, NAB)

In the midst of our incredibly turbulent and dark times, the distress and frustration conveyed in the words of Habakkuk seem so relevant to our twenty-first-century existence. "How long, oh LORD, must I cry for help and you do not listen?" Why is it that God doesn't seem to listen to those in Syria or Lebanon or anywhere ISIS persecutes? "Why do you let me see iniquity? Why do you simply gaze at evil?" Why must we hear and read about corrupt priests and politicians and never-ending gang violence?

How often do we fall into this way of thinking in our lives? How often do we cast away hope only to have it replaced by discouragement, apathy, and despair at the loss of our God in today's culture?

But then, God's beautiful response to Habakkuk reminds us of his grander vision and time frame. "See, the rash have no integrity; but the just one who is righteous because of faith shall live." This is God's eternal message for mankind throughout salvation history! He implores us to grasp patience and hope built on trust in him and his time.

The Book of Habakkuk was written just prior to the imminent Babylonian invasion of modern-day Israel in 605 BC. Habakkuk's prophecy was directed to a world that was again faced with looming disaster. Another powerful foreign army was invading Judah, and the people, like Habakkuk, were wondering what God was doing to protect his chosen people and the land he had rightfully given them. So much evil and death surrounded them, but it seemed God remained strangely silent. Habakkuk was asking the age-old question: Where is God? How long will he allow this pain to continue? Where is the justice?

The Book of Habakkuk reminds us that while God may seem silent and uninvolved in our world, he always has a plan to deal with evil, pain, and loss as well as goodness. Eventually, justice is always served. The example of the prophet Habakkuk encourages believers to wait for the Lord, expecting that he will indeed work out all things for our good in time. It is the everlasting message of hope.

The Book of Habakkuk teaches us that no place is too dark for God's grace to penetrate when we have faith that reaches above and beyond mere human reason. Faith must be an attitude of trust in the presence of God. Faith gives us the power that unlocks the doors to hope and optimism for an uncertain future. When we have faith and hope, we acknowledge that we are not in control, but we can still move forward in fidelity to his will. A world without God is a world without hope (see Ephesians 2:12).

Thomas Aquinas defines hope as "a future good, difficult but possible to attain . . . by means of the Divine assistance . . . on Whose help it leans."[22]

God is the source and object of our faith, hope, and love (what we call the theological virtues). The "highest" good we hope for ourselves, of course, is everlasting happiness in God's presence. We must see hope in the proper context as it relates to the kingdom of heaven. We can be hopeful even in the midst of chaos because our faith allows for us to see through the current secular battle that is raging around us to understand that the war has already been won via the promises of the paschal mystery. I'll share my own story of hope.

A Decade of Hope

My wife, Kaaren, and I were married in the summer of 1992. When we were just beginning to think about starting our family, Kaaren was diagnosed with severe endometriosis, a disorder that thrives on estrogen; the more it is exposed to the hormone, the more it grows and causes internal scarring. We learned that achieving pregnancy with endometriosis is extremely difficult.

After several appointments with doctors at UCSF Medical Center, the consensus was that Kaaren needed surgeries to help clean up the endometriosis, and then we needed to pursue pregnancy immediately. The doctors feared that if we waited, Kaaren's odds of conceiving a child would be extremely low.

Thus began a laborious journey that would be filled with many surgeries, infertility treatments, pain, and much sorrow. It turned into an odyssey that would last for the next thirteen years. From 1992 to 1997, Kaaren underwent several surgeries and a myriad of infertility procedures. We went from a young and enthusiastic married couple to a pair of harried, frantic, and bickering young adults trying to come to terms with physical and emotional pain, surgeries, and the distinct possibility of a life without the children we had envisioned having.

Unfortunately, neither of us was equipped to deal with the consequences of our situation. We were in an emotional and physical dogfight that required our full commitment and partnership. At that point, I had neither the emotional bandwidth nor the maturity to provide the support Kaaren needed. She was in a new and challenging job, living in an unfamiliar town with few friends, and with a husband who wanted to focus on his own career opportunities, learning the game of golf, and playing basketball.

By the winter of 1995, our marriage was in shambles and our lives were an emotional mess. Shortly before Valentine's Day 1995, Kaaren and I separated. We had seemed to be the idyllic young couple with the brightest future imaginable just a few short years before. It was a surreal time for both of us. Kaaren and I were separated for six long months. However, through much work, we developed a stronger commitment to each other and our marriage vows. We would certainly need that sacramental commitment in the years to come.

God Writes Straight with Crooked Lines

After repeated failed infertility treatments, Kaaren and I finally decided to pursue adoption in mid-1997. It was not what we had originally hoped for when dreaming about our future family, but over time we embraced the idea as another adventure and God's will for our lives and those of others.

As thousands of couples can attest, adoption is a very difficult process. We were involved in several domestic adoptions over the course of two years that eventually ended in frustration and disappointment. We seemed unable to make the right domestic adoption connection that would lead us to becoming parents.

During this time, we had several vigilant prayer warriors fighting on our behalf. My parents traveled to the Holy Land in 1996. While in Israel they visited the holy and ancient monastery on Mar Saba overlooking the Kidron Valley. The monastery dates back to AD 483 and has continuously had monks living there for more than fifteen hundred years. It was the home of St. John of Damascus, and it also contains the relics of St. Sabbas. In keeping with thousands of years of tradition, only men are allowed inside the monastery. Therefore, only my father and other men in their pilgrimage group were able to enter the monastery and interact with the monks.

While we were inside this ancient monastery, a monk asked my father if there was anything he would like the monks to pray for on his behalf. My father told him about Kaaren's health issues and infertility. The monk casually mentioned that when a person drinks tea made from a palm leaf at the monastery and is anointed with special chrism oil, through the intercession of St. Sabbas, a miracle is possible; many have been recorded throughout history.

My father is a very devout but practical Catholic. He has never searched for miracles. However, he was struck by the honesty and simplicity of this monk living a faithful life in a manner that has hardly changed for more than a thousand years. Before departing, my father went back and accepted this small gift of hope from the old monk. After reuniting with my mother outside the monastery, my father conveyed the story to her; she was equally moved by the event.

Back in the States, my mother kept the palm leaf and chrism oil in her purse, waiting for the right time to offer this representation of hope and faith to Kaaren and me. Both my mom and dad were a bit unsure of how we might react. It felt so meaningful and significant to them, but would we be dismissive and look upon them with a sardonic credulity? Or would we be open to the unbound mysteries of our Catholic faith?

It's that same feeling we all encounter from time to time when we have an opportunity to share our faith, isn't it? It's the hesitancy driven by a feeling of not wanting to be looked upon as a lunatic or an "over-the-top" Catholic. It reminds me of St. Paul's words to the Corinthians: "For if we are beside ourselves, it is for God; if we are in our right mind, it is for you" (2 Corinthians 5:13).

Shortly after returning home from their trip, my mother and father found the right opportunity to tell Kaaren and me about their encounter at the ancient monastery. We were moved not only by the story but also by their love and concern for us and our cross. We readily drank the palm tea and then were anointed with the oil of Mar Saba. It was a special moment for all four of us, and Kaaren and I were grateful for this small gift of faith and hope on our behalf.

One day in September 1998 I received a page from Kaaren during the middle of the morning. She was a special education teacher and rarely paged me during the day. I thought it was strange, so I called her back immediately. She asked if I would come home for lunch that day.

My initial thought was to say no. I always worked during the lunch hour and was not keen on driving twenty minutes back to the house for lunch. However, I agreed, figuring something was up. I arrived home to Kaaren, a bottle of champagne, a card, and two bows—one blue and one pink. I was immediately very concerned, thinking Kaaren was getting herself too emotionally connected to the next "perfect" adoption opportunity to come our way. I couldn't have been more wrong.

The hope and prayers of so many were finally answered. After almost seven long years of struggles, my wife had become pregnant. It was an overwhelming sensation of the utter goodness of God. Our hope and fidelity were being rewarded in greater abundance than we had ever expected. Matthew, our gift from God was born in May 1999.

Eventually Kaaren and I began to realize that if our hopes of more children were to come to fruition, once again we would have to look to adoption. It was certainly with trepidation that we reconvened the journey. The process turned out to be as difficult as our prior experiences, before the miracle of Matthew. We encountered several potential birth mothers who ended up being more interested in our money and a free trip to California, the beach, and Disneyland than finding a safe and loving home for a child.

In the spring of 2002, we were in the middle of yet another arduous adoption process. The birth mother wanted us to pay for her and her boyfriend to live by the beach in California until her due date. The boyfriend was in jail at that time, but was due out within a few weeks. The birth mother had already shown herself to be very unpredictable and was obviously looking for a way out of rural Texas. It felt like another looming adoption disaster story. However, the emotional nature of adoption grabs hold of you when you're so desperate for a child to call your own. My wife was very vulnerable and hanging on for dear life, beyond all rationality.

In the spring of 2002, we received an unexpected call from the little agency we had contacted back in 1997, inquiring about whether we were still interested in adoption. They informed us of an infant available for adoption in the Marshall Islands. We weren't even sure where the Marshall Islands were. I vaguely remembered them from reading about WWII history, but I did not know a thing about their location or people.

When we received the call, it seemed like someone was throwing us a life vest just before we were swallowed into the abyss. Our immediate response was yes! As usual with our God, little did we know what that yes was to mean for our lives.

The Marshall Islands are a group of hundreds of atolls in the western Pacific in a region of the world called Micronesia. It is classified as a part of the developing world, with very high birth rates, infant mortality, and medical standards far beneath those of North America.

We found out that we were to adopt a little boy. Within a month we received a call that a little girl was also available. The agency wanted to know if we would be interested in adopting both children. We felt such gratitude already and believed God was truly acting and leading in our lives, so we immediately agreed.

During the long waiting process, we received a picture of both but little else. It is very difficult to obtain any medical history from the Marshall Islands or anything concrete about a baby's family. This may seem like a minor detail to some, but for anxious and high-strung adoptive parents it was certainly a concern, and a major leap of faith and hope.

A few months later we received a call from our adoption facilitator with some bad news. The little boy we were to adopt had been taken by his grandparents to the out islands and was no longer available to us. We were very disappointed. It is amazing how quickly one can become attached to a picture and a dream for the future. However, we were so thankful for the opportunity to say yes to the other baby—who turned out to be our Kathryn! Yet the next few months were filled with anxiety as we prayed that our baby girl would remain available. Finally, the time had come. There was a five-hour flight twice a week from Honolulu to the Marshall Islands and then on to the Cook Islands. We flew to Hawaii and then caught the flight to Majuro, Marshall Islands. The atoll is very narrow, comprising sixty-four islets on a reef that is approximately twenty-five miles long. It is a land mass of less than four square miles and contains thirty thousand people.

We visited Kathryn for the first time on the Tuesday we arrived. She was living with fourteen people in a small one-bedroom house divided by a curtain. The was no actual door on the entrance to the house, and the floor was hard packed dirt. The water came from a large catch basin on the roof of the house. Kathryn was sitting on a dirty blanket when we arrived. There were several other little children of various ages playing and drinking coconut milk.

The night of adopting Kathryn was her first night being away from her young mother and her breast milk. Poor Kathryn was in a state of shock and anxiety. To make matters worse, she was covered with scabies, a condition caused by parasitic mites that burrow into the skin and lay eggs, causing extreme itching and rash. We had been forewarned, so we had brought topical medication to begin treatment and at least relieve some of the itching. Needless to say, it was a very long and sad night for her and painful for us as well.

After a few days on the island we were ready to take Kathryn back to California. We had our official adoption paperwork and her Marshall Islands passport. Legally, that is all we needed to return. Due to a special compact agreement between the United States and the Marshall Islands, the Marshallese passport is still one of only a few in the world that allow for free travel between the two countries.

During this period, a handful of dishonest adoption agencies were illegally taking children from the Marshall Islands into the United States without proper adoption paperwork. They were then selling the children on the black market to desperate parents. That's why the Immigration and Naturalization Service (INS) was considering putting a moratorium on allowing children into the United States without going through the US Embassy in the Philippines for visa approval. Our adoption agency had assured us that this would not be a problem for us. We would have proper adoption paperwork done through a US judge in Majuro and the INS had not officially decided on a visa solution.

When we arrived at the little airstrip on Friday to fly out of the country, we were immediately denied permission to bring Kathryn back with us. Somehow the INS had been notified, and they instructed the airport personnel not to allow Kathryn on the airplane back to Honolulu. We were notified that she was not allowed to board the plane to Hawaii.

We were faced with a major dilemma. Kathryn was now officially our child and our responsibility. We could leave her to stay in the Marshalls for the next couple of months while we ventured to the Philippines to attempt to reconcile her visa paperwork. However, due to high-level terrorist alerts after 2001, the State Department was discouraging any travel to the Philippines in general. We also had Matthew at home. He was not yet three years old and couldn't be away from his mom for the next eight weeks, but Kaaren was not willing to leave Kathryn under any circumstances.

We began pleading with the official at the airport to allow us on the plane. We showed him our official adoption paperwork. We tried to talk logically to him about our situation and the fact that we'd been assured of getting out of the country with Kathryn. He said, "My hands are tied. The INS in Hawaii told me to not let her on the plane."

By this time, Kaaren was starting to become frantic and eventually started weeping with Kathryn in her arms. I continued to plead and argue with the man, begging to be allowed on the plane. I told him that once we arrived in Hawaii I would deal with the INS. I continued to fight, but eventually realized it was not working. I was almost out of hope.

It was then, in total exasperation, that I began to pray the Rosary. I walked in a circle around the lobby area, my mind screaming for a solution. Kaaren was also praying, while holding Kathryn. As we prayed, the moment of departure was quickly arriving. I pleaded and begged again, but to no avail. We continued to pray while the plane was boarding. I could tell the airline official was stressed over the situation and had spoken a couple more times with the INS, but they reaffirmed their stance.

With minutes left before the departure, I frantically spoke to the official one last time in complete and utter despair. He looked at me and said, "Just get your family and get on the plane. You can deal with them in Hawaii. I don't want to be a part of this!" I was stunned! I thanked him profusely. We ran onto the plane right before the door was closed, while all the passengers stared at us in disbelief.

We arrived in Hawaii late Friday night and approached the customs line, expecting to wait our turn. But an angry INS agent was waiting for us, and immediately escorted us out of line and to a back room for interrogation. We spent an hour in the room being interviewed by the agent and berated for our conduct.

But we knew there was little they could do now that we were on US soil with our child, who had been officially adopted in the Marshalls and approved by a US judge. The INS knew this also, which is why they were so adamant that we not get on the plane.

After the interrogation, they informed us that we would be required to show up in immigration court in San Francisco sometime in the near future to deal with the illegal entry of Kathryn in the United States. By then, we simply didn't care. We had our daughter in the United States and knew we could handle anything else that came our way.

Several months later we had not yet heard from the INS court. I was worried that if we did not resolve the issue, Kathryn's eventual citizenship would be compromised. I called the court to inquire about the original notice to appear. The clerk searched and searched the computer for the file, but ultimately could not find anything. She told me that no file existed on this issue.

I was dumbfounded. What could possibly have happened to the file? Did it disappear or just get thrown out? Eventually, with the help of our immigration attorney, Kathryn became an official citizen of the United States and of the Marshall Islands too!

A year and a half later, Kaaren and I arrived in Honolulu for the birth of our third child, Andrew. His birth mother had come to Hawaii on her Marshallese passport to have the baby in the United States. We arrived the day after he was born. What an incredible experience to be with his birth mother and grandmother during this time. We now had legal guardianship of Andrew, and he was already a US citizen!

Over the next year we worked on the adoption process for Andrew. It was a long process because we had to attempt to contact the birth father in the Marshall Islands for his approval. After the search period and administrative work, which took a year and a half, we were finally able to adopt Andrew. In the summer of 2005, the entire family flew back to Hawaii for the official adoption.

After thirteen long years of fighting Kaaren's health issues, multiple surgeries, marital strife, infertility, adoption trouble, and the INS, our family was complete! It was all we could have ever originally hoped and prayed for in our married lives. Through all the triumph and tragedy, we remained faithful and trusted in the power of God's grace. I still marvel at his goodness and the power of hope through faith. "The LORD takes pleasure in those who fear him, in those who hope in his steadfast love" (Psalm 147:11).

Living a Life of Hope

How would your life be different if you chose to "be the first" in living a life of hopefulness rather than despair or pessimism? How would your attitude and relationships be different if you truly embraced the hope that is the foundation of our Catholic faith?

Research shows that when we adopt a positive perspective and attitude about the future, it reduces our anxiety and improves our physical and mental health as well. In turn, we are motivated to actively seek improvement in our lives and become a self-gift to others. We are innately programed to transform our thoughts into the reality of our lives. Optimistic thoughts lead to positive action and a hopeful attitude.

Catholic leadership starts with a hopeful, magnanimous spirit. I have found that when I stay positive and optimistic about the people and events that surround me, others begin to absorb this optimism and embrace this spirit.

Parallel studies show that pessimism promotes apathy and depression, which are often accompanied by a sense of helplessness that feeds the depression and hinders achievement. This has become a very serious problem.

Diagnoses of clinical depression have increased tenfold in the past fifty years. Though this is due in part to more accurate diagnoses and more open-minded attitudes concerning mental illness, it is also largely a result of environmental factors that surround our secular culture and are continually reinforced by the media.

I believe we must begin to police ourselves in terms of the negativity of our culture. If Fox News is making you pessimistic, turn it off. If MSNBC makes you feel less than hopeful, choose to fast from its content. It is important to remember that the media outlets make their living on driving viewership through content. It is rarely important what type of content they provide, as long as people are willing to tune in. If we look back on the best viewership ratings over the past thirty years, we find that it is a function of negative events that then become "news" over many days. This is the business of the media and the holy grail of their success. We can choose not to be manipulated by their business plan.

The first thing we must acknowledge, although we may not want to, is that we all face times when we are very disappointed with God. We feel no different than Habakkuk. I have felt that way many times in my life, whether it was during deep and seemingly insurmountable marital strife, the disappointment of another failed pregnancy, or a failure in a business venture.

Yet, through the sacramental nature of my faith I have eventually been given some small ray of hope. Sometimes it is just enough to sustain me for a few days. In Luke 17:6, the Lord says, "If you had faith as a grain of mustard seed, you could say to this sycamine tree, 'Be uprooted, and be planted in the sea,' and it would obey you."

Sometimes my faith is as small as that mustard seed! We see this reference to mustard-seed faith twice in the Scriptures. The mustard seed is one of the tiniest seeds found in the Middle East, but the mustard plant can spread very quickly and grow to be unusually large. The point Jesus makes is that the amount of faith needed to sustain and do great things is very small. In the midst of our struggles, even if we just keep a little faith, it will eventually lead us to hope and success we could never have imagined in the depths of our turmoil.

Conveying a Vision of Hope

So often our young people don't feel hopeful about their future opportunities in America. They see the socioeconomic environment as rigged against them. Certainly the shallow messaging from our politicians only exacerbates these feelings as they wrangle for votes. Many of my employees are of Hispanic origin and believe that our form of democratic capitalism is beneficial for everyone but them. Or worse, many never take the time to thoughtfully consider their goals and aspirations for their future. So many come from homes where English is their second language and their parents have had little opportunity to advance in a career beyond manual labor.

Today, this country has so much to offer our young people. However, without the proper guidance, messaging, and direction of a parent or mentor, many of our young Hispanic men and women become stuck in a vicious economic cycle of mere subsistence or worse.

I truly believe that service and hospitality businesses such as McDonald's can provide an incredible ray of hope for so many Americans who face these realities. Whenever I have the opportunity, I preach McDonald's as an incredible bridge of hope to the future young people envision for themselves. If continuing education is the goal, we provide scholarships, flexible scheduling, and even tutoring. If someone's dream is to learn some basic work and hospitality skills, McDonald's provides a great first step toward any future career in hospitality or people management. If a career in the restaurant or hospitality industry is the hope, McDonald's has very sophisticated training programs that allow for a high level of learning and execution at every stage of advancement and complexity of the business. The beauty of McDonald's is that a person can become a very successful general manager, supervisor, or more without a college degree.

The only requirement is a burning desire to learn, work diligently, advance, and get outside one's comfort zone. The cultural opinion of McDonald's as a dead-end job is so sadly off base. The reality is that the company is truly a channel of hope for millions of Americans who need a place to jump-start their dreams.

As a Catholic business leader, I feel it is part of my responsibility to bring the virtue of hope into my business and into the lives of my employees. I am very fortunate to have the opportunity to touch thousands of employees' lives every year. It is an awesome opportunity and a responsibility that I take very seriously.

NINE

A Journey toward Happiness

What we are looking for is happiness. Not a momentary happiness, but one that is deep and lasting and both human and supernatural.
—St. Josemaría Escrivá [23]

It is only appropriate to talk of happiness after exploring the concept of hope. Hope is the entryway and foundation of happiness. Once we are able to grasp Christian hope, we can begin our path toward a life of happiness.

There are so many great books that describe the foundation of living a life of happiness, and they all say fundamentally the same thing: Our happiness is simply a matter of perspective. It is a function of how we see the world and of the choices we make rather than the "stuff" we have. If we choose to see the world through the eyes of consumerism or hedonism, then our path to happiness will always be tied to feelings of pleasure and instant gratification. The problem is, there is always more stuff to buy or people to compare ourselves to who have more stuff than we do.

However, if the choices we make are based on the virtues (prudence, justice, fortitude, and temperance) and a willingness to embrace delayed gratification, then we can find lasting happiness. In Catholic theology an example of delaying gratification is engaging in the practice of fasting. By denying yourself some impulsive desire, you allow your mind to begin to control your body. That's when you allow your Christian identity to dominate your biological identity.

In the experiences of my own life and working with thousands of young people over the past twenty-five years, I believe some measure of happiness can be achieved by concentrating on a few key areas. However, a caveat must be mentioned here. The pure happiness we all innately seek but never fully achieve is actually not possible on this earth. So managing our expectations must play a part in the journey toward happiness. Ultimately we are just sojourners, knowing that the everyday ups and downs we all face are leading us to something great—and this is why we can dare to be happy even in the midst of our daily struggles.

Finding Purpose and Self-Worth

Purpose and self-worth begins with first accepting the fact that we all possess the right talents and abilities that are needed to carry out the duty God has chosen us to fulfill.

> It is Jesus who stirs in you the desire to do something great with your lives, the will to follow an ideal, the refusal to allow yourselves to be grounded down by mediocrity, the courage to commit yourselves humbly and patiently to improving yourselves and society, making the world more human and more fraternal. (St. John Paul II)[24]

> It is difficult to make a man miserable while he feels worthy of himself and claims kindred to the great God who made him. (Abraham Lincoln)[25]

We should never waste time fretting about the talent we do not possess. Wouldn't it be ridiculous for a hall of fame wide receiver such as Jerry Rice to lament the fact that he does not have the skill set to throw a football like Tom Brady? Or a masterful computer programmer who mourns his inability to sell the software to the end user? If we don't have it, then we simply do not need it.

This goes for our loved ones as well. How often do we (not so) secretly grieve the fact that our child is not better or more interested in a certain type of sport or subject in school? How much time do we spend worrying about what our children's current skill set will mean for his or her future vocation? How many of us clandestinely try to manipulate our children's paths toward a certain type of college or career that will make them happy, but deep down it's really about our own egos? Sadly, we can spend so much time thinking about and coveting other people's talents, when in fact those talents would not lead us or our children to happiness. Why? Because that is not God's unique plan. When we pursue a path of happiness based on other people's talents or desires, we will eventually be left feeling dissatisfied and unfulfilled. So often we hear of people who are completely dissatisfied with their career choice, but they now feel trapped by the investment of education and time. Many have spent the vast majority of their lives in pursuit of what others wanted for them, only to find it was never really suited to their talents or interests.

In order to be happy, we must feel like our life means something to us and others, and we must dare to believe that we are making a difference with our time and talent. Investing ourselves in this pursuit will leave us with a feeling of self-worth.

Playing "Moneyball"

Every year in my companies we develop and implement a new business theme for the year. A few years back we branded the year "Moneyball." It was a riff on the book of the same name, written by Michael Lewis. The basic concept was to embrace the philosophy of the Oakland Athletics baseball team and its development process. The general manager of the Athletics, Billy Beane, realized that it does not take a bunch of highly paid, five-star players to make a winning team in baseball. What is needed is a bunch of two-, three-, and four-star players who work together to become a five-star team.

At my McDonald's, we don't have men and women with MBAs or degrees from top colleges. We have a bunch of hard-working and dedicated men and women from a myriad of social, cultural, economic, and academic backgrounds. In order for us to succeed at the highest level, we need to complement each other's strengths and mitigate our weaknesses.

There is great hope and happiness for all of us when we come together as a team of complementary talents. We must honor and cherish each member of the team's strengths (and understand each other's weaknesses) to combine them in a way that makes the whole so much greater than the sum of the individual parts.

I tell my employees that if they have limited English skills, we'll leverage their strength in the kitchen. If they don't like administration or accounting but are incredible hospitality ambassadors, we'll place them up front with the customers, where they can focus on service and hospitality. If they are going to school and can only work evenings, fantastic. Their availability in the evenings will be a strength for our dinner and late-evening business.

The concept of Moneyball reinforces the fact that we all have something to add to make the business succeed. It is about conveying a sense of purpose and self-worth to each employee that he or she is worthwhile and possesses a skill set that is integral to our team and our success.

Many of our employees have résumés that the normal business culture deems less than adequate. Maybe it's because of a lack of language proficiency or certain academic shortfalls. However, the talents so many possess are highly beneficial given the right amount of nurturing and partnership. Maybe we are a bunch of average players individually, but together we have the ability to win the World Series!

Family First!

For me, the opposite of scarcity is not abundance. It's enough. I'm enough. My kids are enough.

—Brené Brown

I've discovered that the reality of my long-term contentment is not predicated on things I can afford to buy or my accolades at work. For me a measure of joy and contentment is possible only when I grasp the "enough" that begins with my wife, children, friends, family, and faith. It is a contentment that is based on relationships and experiences of time spent together. Yet at times I still struggle with the application of this reality in my life. God has blessed me with gifts to create material abundance in my life.

There are few monetary restrictions on my ability to acquire stuff. That's why I am in a constant battle with myself to come to terms with the concept of enough. I am continually practicing restraint for no other reason than to assert control over my innate tendency toward materialism and instant gratification, rather than find the joy I seek in people and experiences.

The material goods of our world come and go, and they eventually lose their luster for all of us. But the happiness built on the love within a beautiful relationship is timeless. So often successful men and women wrap their self-esteem around the power and success they feel in their work rather than their family life. At work people have to listen to us, and we tend to feel a certain measure of control that does not always happen in the messiness of our home lives and relationships. Having an enjoyable and fulfilling career is important in our journey, but not at the expense of our relationships. The reality is that success and happiness at work is a very temporal existence. Eventually, we all become less and less relevant in our jobs and are all ultimately replaceable. If I die tomorrow, the restaurants will still open at 5:00 a.m.

As leaders and those who aspire to make a difference in the lives of others, we must dare to be first in setting the standard for what it means to put family first with our actions. We cast a long and powerful shadow over our environment. What we do and say impacts how others think and act. It is a difficult task to balance the demands of a family and being successful at work. It is so easy to talk or write about but incredibly difficult to execute. But the fact that something is difficult does not give us the excuse to not put forth the effort to accomplish this balance.

One of the ways I have found to foster a family-first mentality is to encourage flexibility in the workplace. In my experience, mature and dedicated employees value a work environment that allows flexibility and trust more than any other employment benefit, including financial compensation. When you choose family first for yourself and promote this attitude with your employees, you will find an abundance of new and creative ways to remain as productive as or more productive than before.

In my company, I give my general managers and supervisors broad flexibility with their schedules and vacation time. Over the course of my career, we have had multiple key employees take anywhere from a month to six months off for a multitude of reasons—major illnesses, weddings, the birth of a child, or just a great trip in pursuit of their dreams. Invariably other people are more than happy to step up to help cover the productivity gap associated with their absence. They all do this willingly and with a good attitude because they believe in the system and its value for all members of the team. I, as well as many in our company, love our McJob, but it is only a means to a greater end. The ends we seek are functional relationships built on a dedication to our families and the legacy we hope to leave.

Embracing Restraint

It is Jesus you seek when you dream of happiness; he is waiting for you when nothing else you find satisfies you; he is the beauty to which you are so attracted; it is he who provokes you with that thirst for fullness that will not let you settle for compromise.
—St. John Paul II

Unless we are completely clear about what constitutes true happiness, we will allow the secular world to dictate a happiness that is relative to circumstances and defined by popular culture.

This culture of instant gratification, based on *pleasure* versus long-term happiness, has been magnified by the insidious influence of moral relativism in all aspects of our society.

Although this philosophy has always been around in some form or another, today we are at a unique and dangerous crossroads. Pharmaceuticals and advancements in information technology such as the Internet allow humanity to pursue destructive pleasures without the short-term dangers that were deterrents for our forefathers. The "morning after" pill, creams for STDs, instant access to pornography, and one-click purchasing have opened up a Pandora's box of complex problems.

As we say in business, there are no barriers to entry. We have always had an inclination toward concupiscence. However, prior to the baby-boomer generation, short-term pleasure seeking associated with sexuality, drug use, and consumerism was much more difficult. There was an expectation of a standard moral code of behavior, fewer goods and services available to procure, and a painful, stigmatizing outcome associated with sexually transmitted diseases, unwed and unwanted pregnancy, and indebtedness.

In today's culture there is very little stigma attached to promiscuity, drug use, STDs, poor credit, and increasing debt. Worse, there is the issue of immediate access to extremely negative influences. For example, prior to the Internet revolution, accessing pornography was impossible without leaving the house. And today, mind-altering drugs are legal in many states and available for home delivery. Contraception is now more accessible than ever before.

The message we hear through all forms of media is: Moral relativism equals real freedom and happiness.

Still, there is a universal and inescapable objective moral truth. We innately understand that certain conduct is morally wrong. Throughout culture and history, there has always been a consistent moral norm that kept the fabric of society intact.

History has shown that society must have a standard for "right" behavior. Without some form of moral equilibrium, chaos ensues. And a culture's popular opinion at a moment in time cannot justify a moral standard. Consider the events in Germany in 1938 or the United States' immoral stance regarding slavery in the 1820s. In both examples, the majority of the citizens were overwhelmingly supportive of the policies.

Where does that moral truth come from? It starts with natural moral law. It is the light of understanding God places in us, and it results from our acceptance of his wisdom and goodness. Man has been formed in the image of the Creator and therefore instinctively knows the difference between right behavior and destructive behavior.

On a macro level, humans know that murder is unacceptable, and that lying or stealing is not constructive conduct for a healthy society. We understand this intuitively without necessarily having to be taught the concept.

Additionally, we have the revealed laws of the Old Testament, including the Ten Commandments, and the laws of the New Testament, especially the Beatitudes. Lastly, we have our cultural tradition, education within our family, and our Church's teaching to provide and form our conscience.

The Judgment of Conscience

The Catholic Church defines conscience as the application of natural moral law to a particular circumstance. The conscience allows the judgment of reason to guide our behaviors so that we may seek good and avoid evil. It must be formed by a strong moral education and aided by the gifts of the Holy Spirit.

In today's state-run educational system, the process of formation of conscience has taken a backseat to teaching a sophomoric ideology of tolerance and relativism at the expense of moral standards. Worse, our schools are primarily focused on the praxis of specific skills rather than teaching a curriculum rooted in the virtuous life.

Christianity has proven that true freedom is possible only with God and the application of the virtues—prudence, justice, fortitude, and temperance. Our understanding of freedom must be directed toward the truth of who we are as children of God. Human freedom can exist only in reasoned and ordered communion with others through the application of moral law. Thomas Merton explains it this way:

> Now at last I came around to the sane conception of virtue—without which there can be no happiness, because virtues are precisely the powers by which we can come to acquire happiness: without them, there can be no joy, because they are the habits which coordinate and canalize our natural energies and direct them to the harmony and perfection and balance, the unity of our nature with itself and with God, which must, in the end, constitute our everlasting peace.[26]

There is no denying that we live in a very confusing and dynamic world, where the lines between right and wrong can be nebulous for anyone. That is why we need the grace of the Holy

Spirit and the guidance of the Church to assist our conscience in making the right choices that will lead us to long-term happiness.

Practicing Self-Compassion

I have often wondered why so many unhappy people don't make the connection between a divine relationship with Jesus Christ and their ultimate happiness. They spend beyond their means, take pills, drink too much alcohol, work day and night, or lose themselves in a sexual relationship to overcome their feelings of unhappiness. Maybe this is because developing their faith seems too simple, too boring, or just not a quick enough solution to their immediate problems.

I have a friend who has struggled on and off with alcohol, overeating, and dejection for some thirty years. He is acutely aware of his issues and the hollow nature of his tactics to solve the dilemma that holds him back from being who God desires him to be. A few times in his life, he has even had glimpses of the beauty and peace of a spiritual life in Christ. Yet, he still struggles to see the virtues and mercy of a practiced life in Christ as part of his solution. When given the opportunity to participate in the sacramental nature of his faith, he chooses another path. Why? Maybe it's because of the shame he feels about himself, or that he has no clear understanding of how merciful our God can be. Maybe it is simply the power of inertia or an underdeveloped conscience that does not provide him the fortitude to commit to a life in Christ.

Whatever the cause, he has not been able to find the catalyst to change. However, with God there is always hope. I know that when we are ready to change, our God will be ready for us. He will always be patiently waiting, just as that loving father waited and watched for his son in the parable of the Prodigal Son. Certainly, the first step comes in finding the power of God's merciful heart that leads to self-compassion.

Over the centuries the apparitions of the Blessed Mother continue to challenge us to partake in the sacrament of reconciliation. God wants us to be cleansed and begin anew. It is through this process that we can let go of all our previous transgressions and leave the yoke of our past sins behind. In places such as Fatima, Lourdes, and Medjugorje, it is not unusual to see hundreds of people waiting in line at any one time to partake in the sacrament of reconciliation for the first time in five, ten, twenty, or even thirty years. The courage it takes to overcome the fear and shame of years of sin is a special part of the resulting joy that so many millions have experienced through these special places. However, we don't need to travel to an apparition site in Europe to experience this extraordinary gift. This opportunity is available in every Catholic church across the United States and the world. What is holding us back from partaking in this sacramental experience? Maybe it's time you mustered up the courage to choose to be first and lead your family to a deeper sense of peace and liberation via the sacrament of reconciliation.

Harnessing the Power of Reciprocity

Reciprocity is our inherent willingness and desire to exchange our unique gifts with each other for mutual benefit. As human beings, we all feel a natural pull toward reciprocation. We are programmed to give and share; it is an innate human trait that is common throughout all cultures.

According to Pope Benedict XVI, "By considering reciprocity as the heart of what it is to be a human being, subsidiarity is the most effective antidote against any form of all-encompassing welfare state."[27] Our sense of empathy and compassion for others flourishes when we rely on each other through the exchange of talents and resources. It is part of our nature, and why humanity thrives in community versus isolation.

This is a gift of our Christian inheritance; we want to share happiness. Reciprocity is truly the foundation of the Church's teaching on subsidiarity. It is a theology that highly encourages the rights and responsibilities of the individual, but it also acknowledges and supports the symbiotic benefit of community. It is the community's responsibility to provide care and assistance to each other in sustenance of the common good and the dignity of the human person. However, this must not be done at the expense of the individual's right and responsibility to do her part to take care of herself. Unfortunately, too often either our collective misplaced generosity or our ambivalence clouds the importance of a capable individual's responsibility to himself in engaging in reciprocity. When this is not permitted or encouraged to transpire, it gives subsidiarity and social justice a black eye.

When the power of reciprocity is working in conjunction with our Christian nature as self-gift, we labor together as human beings for the greater good of society or business, along with the moral, spiritual, and physical growth of each of its members.

Early in my business career, when I was overly focused on daily productivity and immediate results on the job, I was never truly happy in my work. I was always dissatisfied with either the sales growth, profit margin, or operational execution in the restaurants. This was certainly at the expense of people and relationships.

The problem was that I just didn't understand the difference between never being happy and never being satisfied. I was never satisfied with the results, and that mind-set made me chronically unhappy in my work. Maybe it was because of my somewhat introverted nature, but it took some time and coaching for me to grasp the subtle but important difference between these two ideas.

It's certainly all right to strive for more in business or life. Magnanimous leadership is perpetually seeking incremental improvement not only personally, but for others as well. I believe in pushing myself and others to stretch outside our comfort zones to reach new heights in professional development and execution. However, that is much different from projecting a perpetually dissatisfied attitude.

Whether you are the CEO of a company, a parent raising children, or a leader in your parish, I have come to realize that a great leader must be a happy leader. People do not respond well to someone who is negative, unhappy, or unpredictable in his or her disposition. I am embarrassed to admit it, but there were years when my employees cringed when I came through the door.

Whether it is in marital or work relationships, dysfunction ensues when people feel like they are walking on eggshells in your presence. It is a horrible and stressful way to live and be productive. Over the long term it leads employees or family members to indifference, disloyalty, and deception.

I have overcome my emotional immaturity in this area by valuing people first and results second. By first focusing on people instead of my own feelings of dissatisfaction with work or with my employees, I have been able to understand how important, rewarding, and critical good relationships are to a successful enterprise.

I have spent the better part of the past fifteen years investing in reciprocity as a business strategy. I have found that a higher level of loyalty and execution is the result, and my happiness has been its by-product.

Small Gift, Big Reward

I believe the greatest gift you can give your family and the world is a healthy you.
—Joyce Meyer

I have always believed that when you feel good about your physique and implement an exercise routine in your life, you tend to be a happier and more energetic person. That's why I have always incorporated a consistent fitness routine in my life. I enjoy nothing more than going on a beautiful hike, riding my bike through the countryside, or jogging on a beach. No matter what state of mind I am in before I begin the activity, I am always more content and happier during or after. Furthermore, many of my best ideas have come during a long run, when I am lost in the almost transcendental experience. There are very few activities in my life that have that same effect on me.

With this philosophy in mind, a few years ago I gave out about sixty Fitbit step-tracking devices to my senior management team. I thought it would be a fun way to start the year and help theme it around the importance of activity, consistency in daily routines, and the power of camaraderie for success. We began to wear the devices, and in friendly competition, we tracked each other's progress through a social media phone app.

Part of the beauty of working at McDonald's is that we are always on our feet and moving. So the more you hustle and provide quick service, the more steps you rack up. It started as a fun way to get everyone a little more focused on moving those customers and tracking our daily exercise. But more broadly and longer term, it was about getting people to see how important a healthy lifestyle and a sense of shared identity can be to our happiness.

After several years, I am proud to say that many of my employees have taken the idea far beyond anything I had originally imagined. Many of the original participants have now brought in others, including their spouses and friends. On any given weekend you can find several of our employees running a half marathon or 5K together, sharing in the power of their reciprocity.

A Final Point: Happiness Is a Choice!

Action may not always bring happiness; but there is no happiness without action.
—Benjamin Disraeli

The very best marriage advice I ever received was that love is a choice, not a feeling, and it's a choice that proves itself with action.

I believe the same thing can be said of happiness. We must actively seek happiness through a life dedicated to self-discipline, virtue, and the grace and wisdom of the Church. Starting today, choose happiness. Here are some of the tactics that have worked well for me as I've continued on my journey.

Be the first to radiate optimism at work and home.

Be the first to share your unique gifts with others.

Be the first to smile and say hello to a colleague or stranger.

We must have the courage to choose happiness. We must have the courage to make choices that delay instant gratification, utilize a well-formed conscience, and share our gifts. This is the hallmark of our Christian inheritance.

TEN

Discovering Joy in Sacrifice

We are never so defenseless against suffering
as when we love.
—Sigmund Freud

The path of love and self-gift leads man toward a life of joy and happiness. However, the happiness that I am referring to is a much deeper, supernatural happiness, something far beyond simply having fun. It is certainly not the modern notion of happiness, which centers on fleeting feelings predicated upon all things external—a cycle of continuous pleasure and the utter avoidance of pain and suffering. As Matthew Archbold says in his book, *Faith under Fire*:

> The simple truth is that every act of self-giving love turns the world upside down. It seems like that's the one thing the world is never prepared for. Anytime we choose to love, we invite heartbreak. Some refuse to love wholeheartedly because of this; they shy away and shun love, unwilling to risk getting hurt.[28]

Make no mistake: Happiness and lasting joy derived from self-gift does not imply a life without sorrow. At some level, the path of love and self-gift will always include suffering. The honesty of Jesus in the Gospels is a refreshing antidote to modernity's false promises that happiness is possible through an avoidance of pain and suffering.

Jesus makes his point clear in all the Gospels:

> If any man would come after me, let him deny himself and take up his cross daily and follow me. (Luke 9:23)
>
> He who does not take his cross and follow me is not worthy of me. (Matthew 10:38)
>
> If any man would come after me, let him deny himself and take up his cross and follow me. (Mark 8:34)
>
> I have said this to you, that in me you may have peace. In the world you have tribulation; but be of good cheer, I have overcome the world. (John 16:33)

As St. John Paul II makes clear, the path of humanity in Christ is in accepting sorrow even though we are not always capable of understanding its meaning.

> To suffer means to become particularly susceptible, particularly open to the working of the salvific powers of God, offered to humanity in Christ. In him God has confirmed his desire to act especially through suffering, which is man's weakness and emptying of self, and he wishes to make his power known precisely in this weakness and emptying of self.[29]

It is essential to understand that a single justification of the suffering we endure is not always possible, but man must be willing to look at his hardship through the eyes of Christ the Redeemer. Seeing the difficulties in our lives or those of our loved ones through the diverse lenses of charity, humility, transformation, discipline, and redemption frees us to see beyond a specific event itself. It then becomes possible to see events through Christ's example of sacrifice and redemption.

It is only through the path of love by way of self-gift that we can find the joy that leads to sustainable happiness.

A few years back, I had a young female employee, Erica. She had started at McDonald's at the age of fifteen and had worked there for the next nine years. During this time, she proved herself to be an incredible asset to the restaurant. She was an amazingly efficient and friendly employee and was well liked by customers and her fellow crew members.

Along the way, Erica used McDonald's as her bridge through high school and college. She enjoyed the job, working as she pursued her dream of being a bilingual schoolteacher. After many years, she finally achieved her goal and was hired to teach in the local school district. She had also married a wonderful young man and was pregnant with their first child. The day she put in her two-week notice, she called me to thank me for the opportunity to work at McDonald's. I remember thanking her for all the time and dedication she had put in on behalf of McDonald's, the employees, and the customers. The last thing I said to her was simply, "If you ever need anything at all, please call me. You are a special person and I know that life has great things in store for you."

It wasn't more than a couple of weeks later that I received a call from her in a state of panic and shock. The night before, her husband, Ernie, had been in a terrible accident. He had been working with a friend, helping him build his house. After a hard day's labor, they'd had a few beers to relax. That night was extremely stormy, and on the way home he lost control of his vehicle and hit another car. Ernie ended up without a scratch, but the gentleman in the other car, who was well-respected in the community and the chaplain at a local federal prison, lost his life.

The news was completely devastating. There was such tragedy and loss on both sides. Erica had a wonderful new job, she was carrying their first baby, and she had big dreams for her family's future. Ernie was a faithful and affable young man who was devoted to his wife, his faith, and his job. Yet, he had acted irresponsibly and cost his family their future and a man his life.

Erica reached out to me for support and direction. Over the next four years, my wife and I supported them as best as we could during Ernie's incarceration in San Quentin State Prison. We had the opportunity to visit him on many occasions and experience his sorrow, anguish, and shame. Ultimately, Ernie served two years in prison and several more years on probation. After his release, I had the good fortune of having him work for me for a couple of years until he was in a position to resume his prior career.

It was a harrowing few years for him, his family, and the victim's family. The victim's wife was incredibly angry and bitter, as would be expected. All this weighed very heavily on Ernie, and I'm sure he carries that burden still. Yet this kindhearted man has never lost his faith in God's love for him.

Kaaren and I were honored to be chosen to walk with them on their via dolorosa, and to offer what little we could to support them and their family. I know that the experience has added long-term value to our lives and those of our children. We felt the impact that the poor choices of others had on society, we felt empathy for Ernie and Erica, we came face-to-face with the fear and financial burden of incarceration, and we felt the power of God supporting the families. The experience of their pain, anguish, and despair was of monumental benefit to many others in their life.

I know that Ernie and Erica have struggled mightily with their cross, but today they continue to persevere together and have another beautiful child to love and care for. Though we no longer keep as connected with them as we did during their time of suffering, their story and influence continues to resonate with us in myriad ways. We still marvel at their courage and commitment to one another and their utter faith in Jesus as their Savior and Redeemer.

The mystery of all our unique suffering certainly can never be fully understood by any of us. The questions that loom on this subject are much too complex for mere humans to comprehend. However, choosing a life of faith and hope has allowed humanity the ability to overcome the sorrow, anger, and despair that only leads to greater misery. How can we seek redemption and understanding in the suffering? Again we look to the wisdom of St. John Paul II:

> Christ does not answer directly and he does not answer in the abstract this human questioning about the meaning of suffering. Man hears Christ's saving answer as he himself gradually

> becomes a sharer in the sufferings of Christ. For it is above all a call. It is a vocation.[30]

In many ways my father epitomizes the American dream. He was born and raised according to the poor Italian immigrant experience of the 1930s. My grandfather was an unskilled laborer from Sicily, struggling to provide for his growing family in rural Ohio in the heart of the depression. Whether it was my grandfather waiting in cheese and bread lines for a little extra food or my father and his siblings going door-to-door selling vegetables from the garden, they unified around faith, family, and survival. The family lived in a two-bedroom farmhouse with no indoor plumbing until my father was sixteen years old. He was one of the very few from his socioeconomic circle to attend college and go on to achieve a measure of wealth. He has been married to my mother for more than fifty-four years. From a macro perspective—what a life! In fact, he and my mother would be the first to acknowledge, with an almost uncomfortable sentiment, the richness and abundant blessings God has provided their life together.

However, my father and mother have both endured much pain and suffering in their lives, and in that of their extended family as well. I write of this only to make an important point: My parents have never viewed their lives through the prism of their difficult times. They would never consider defining their lives by their suffering, but there is no doubt this suffering has helped define their lives in some way. I believe this to be the profound wisdom and meaning that St. John Paul II's words reveal to us: "Man hears Christ's saving answer as he himself gradually becomes a sharer in the sufferings of Christ." We must confront and embrace his cross as a part of living an authentic Christian life. It is only through the cross that we can ever hope to fully encounter him and the true happiness and abundance we seek.

I have read St. John Paul II's theology of suffering many times, but I am still a little perplexed and uncomfortable with wholeheartedly embracing the redemptive nature of suffering. This is based partly on my own fear of what that suffering might actually mean in my life. However, in reading his words in relationship to my mother's and father's lives, I have arrived at a greater sense of clarity in his meaning that, for me, comes in seeing one's life through a wide-angle lens that captures the entire journey of a life lived in Christ.

I do know that success and victory are always much sweeter when they have come after failure or defeat. It is the benefit of perspective and life's contrast that defines our ability to discern our happiness from and in the midst of our suffering.

ELEVEN

Living a Legacy Today

As each has received a gift, employ it for one another, as good stewards of God's varied grace.

—1 Peter 4:10

For we are [God's] workmanship, created in Christ Jesus for good works, which God prepared beforehand, that we should walk in them.

—Ephesians 2:10

The reality is, we all want to feel that our lives matter to someone in this world. Deep down, we want to feel that we have accomplished something beyond self-gratification. The desire to leave a legacy is in everyone's DNA. It is part of the innate longing we have to reach the fullness of our Christian nature we call self-gift. It is the epitome of true prosperity and true abundance.

St. Thomas Aquinas noted almost nine hundred years ago that God provides us with the gift of intellect and will, as well as the efficacy of prayer. With these unique gifts, given only to mankind, you and I can make a difference! We have the power to change the world.

Ultimately, to create the legacy that we all desire for our lives, we must see our time on earth through the prism of *contribution*. This means our lives must be used as a vessel to provide our unique gifts to others. Our Christian faith teaches us that the act of self-giving will lead us on our path to joy and happiness. The use of our intellect and will to contribute our best gifts to others is the true and holy evolution of what makes us human beings. As Bishop Robert Barron says, "Your being increases in the measure you give it away."[31]

Unlike the model of success or failure based on an economy of scarcity and competition, a life of simple contribution does not need to be scored or measured. Contribution as self-gift can be truly measured only in the transcendent world of God. It is he, not the institutions or social norms of the world, who ultimately determines the gauge of our impact.

Thus, we are no longer burdened with some cultural litmus test imposed on us by modernity. We are defined no longer by wins or losses, but by simple contribution to others. This was Christ's message two thousand years ago in Galilee, and this is his message today. When we embrace humility and contribution, we can free ourselves to act proactively toward others in a "be the first" mentality.

Jesus told a story that illustrates this principle of contribution and true abundance:

> And Jesus sat down opposite the treasury, and watched the multitude putting money into the treasury. Many rich people put in large sums. And a poor widow came, and put in two copper coins, which make a penny. And he called his disciples to him,

> and said to them, "Truly, I say to you, this poor widow has put in more than all those who are contributing to the treasury. For they all contributed out of their abundance; but she out of her poverty has put in everything she had, her whole living." (Mark 12:41–44)

This little story from the Gospel of Mark reiterates that the measure of our contributions will not be determined by the standards of our culture, but only by our heart.

Living Contribution in Business: Ronald McDonald House Charities

Ray Kroc, founder of McDonald's, famously said, "None of us are as good as all of us." That philosophy has been carried through his legacy, Ronald McDonald House Charities. The following is a great illustration of how the business world can tap into the power of contribution.

In 1972, the Philadelphia Eagles were fund-raising in support of team member Fred and his wife Fran Hill's daughter, Kim, who was battling childhood leukemia. After raising enough funds for Kim's hospital bills, the Eagles' ownership decided to continue to raise funds to benefit local area hospitals.

Dr. Audrey Evans, a pediatric oncologist at the Children's Hospital of Philadelphia, saw a need for families to stay in a supportive place while their children were in treatment for extended periods of time, essentially a home away from home, rather than stay at a random motel or commute each day. The general manager of the Eagles, Jimmy Murray, contacted a local advertising agency to explore how best to support this idea and to promote a way to raise enough money to make the idea a reality.

The agency came up with a simple but profoundly impactful idea that continues to this day: What if McDonald's would donate twenty-five cents from every Shamrock Shake sold in the region toward the purchase of a house?

Ed Rensi, the McDonald's regional president, agreed as long as McDonald's could take the name of the house. On October 15, 1974, the world's first Ronald McDonald House was born.

Today, Ronald McDonald House is supported by millions of people giving a few cents to support sick children and their families, and now there are 356 houses all over the world. Most of the support for the millions of people served each year comes from the smallest of donations from our customers, local communities, and the McDonald's owner-operators in the area of each house. Just one example of the many programs McDonald's and its independent owner-operators are involved in is this program; since 2010 McDonald's owner-operators have been donating one penny from every Happy Meal sold to Ronald McDonald House Charities. The total giving through 2016, for just this one of several initiatives, is more than $35 million.

This is a wonderful example of capitalism for the common good. In today's economy, there are many examples of great companies who have figured out how to leverage their employees' and customers' desire to be a part of the contribution game to help change lives.

Many companies today have realized that this dual mission of capitalism as a force for good resonates very favorably with consumers and impacts their purchasing habits. Another perfect example of this philosophy in action is Toms shoes. For every pair of shoes that is purchased, Toms will donate a pair to a needy individual somewhere in the world.

The Papacy and Legacy of Francis

Let us all remember this: One cannot proclaim the Gospel of Jesus without the tangible witness of one's life.
—Pope Francis

There is no denying that the early stages of Pope Francis' papacy have made many people uncomfortable. He is a Jesuit priest, but has taken the name and philosophy of an iconic monk: St. Francis of Assisi.

I believe he was chosen by the movement of the Holy Spirit in this moment in history for a unique purpose. His choice of the name Francis is significant and revealing. It demonstrates that he has come not to be a brilliant theologian the likes of Pope Benedict XVI or Pope John Paul II, but to be a uniquely pastoral leader. He desires to show the world love in action and what it means to live as a humble member of the Catholic Church. He is perpetually challenging us to live a legacy through our daily actions and our merciful hearts.

Francis is our first pope from South America, and he sees the world through the eyes of a people who have faced social and economic injustice since colonial times. He has seen the effects of unregulated capitalism and totalitarianism on his country and his people. Francis has witnessed the ravages of abject poverty and the indifference of many to the plight of those who live in it. He has become God's messenger to remind us of our obligation to each other and to systems of governance that provide opportunity for all people: "To all of you, especially those who can do more and give more, I ask: Please, do more! Please, give more! When you give of your time, your talents and your resources to the many people who struggle and who live on the margins, you make a difference."[32]

When we are bound by the fear of scarcity, we don't have the capacity to live outside a comfort zone that protects our wealth and social status. At best, living this way allows us to consider leaving a legacy with our material goods after we no longer need them. There is nothing wrong with the idea of leaving some of our wealth for others when we pass, but there is no risk whatsoever in this philosophy. It is a mentality that says, "I am going to live my life as I wish, providing for all my material desires, but if there is anything left after my passing, I would be willing to give a bit of it away to those in need." That is acting in the comfort zone of contribution.

Our ability to live a legacy is always contingent on our ability to embrace mercy and reject fear. When we dare to invest ourselves and embrace the philosophy of self-gift, we have the freedom to live a legacy today.

Providence and Dominion

A significant point about leadership in the twenty-first century is a commitment to the resources of the earth. Through the mighty works of God, we have been given providence with the earth's bounty. The provisions of the earth are a divine gift from our Creator, and they need to be harnessed and cherished through our prudent toil and stewardship. "Yet he did not leave himself without witness, for he did good and gave you from heaven rains and fruitful seasons, satisfying your hearts with food and gladness." (Acts 14:17).

Through our intellect and will, God has given man dominion over his creation, as well. "Then God said, 'Let us make man in our image, after our likeness; and let them have dominion over the fish of the sea, and over the birds of the air, and over the cattle, and over all the earth, and over every creeping thing that creeps upon the earth" (Genesis 1:26).

This providence and dominion requires stewardship on behalf of the less fortunate and our future generations.

Pope Francis' encyclical *On Care for Our Common Home, Laudato Si,* is directed toward business and political leaders of the world. He states:

> The ecological crisis is also a summons to profound interior conversion. It must be said that some committed and prayerful Christians, with the excuse of realism and pragmatism, tend to ridicule expressions of concern for the environment. Others are passive; they choose not to change their habits and thus become inconsistent. So what they all need is an "ecological conversion," whereby the effects of their encounter with Jesus Christ become evident in their relationship with the world around them. Living our vocation to be protectors of God's handiwork is essential to a life of virtue; it is not an optional or a secondary aspect of our Christian experience.[33]

When we are determined to find God in our chosen vocations, I believe it is possible to see everything in a new light—the light of Christ. Whether it is people or resources, the same principles of ethical behavior and virtue apply. As powerful a tool as democratic capitalism can be in wealth creation, productivity and technology advancements, and wealth redistribution, it still has its shortcomings in relation to the reality of man's fallen nature and the power of greed, gluttony, and materialism.

> Once more, we need to reject a magical conception of the market, which would suggest that problems can be solved simply by an increase in the profits of companies or individuals. Is it realistic to hope that those who are obsessed with maximizing profits will stop to reflect on the environmental damage, which they will leave behind for future generations? Where profits alone count, there can be no thinking about the rhythms of nature, its phases of decay and regeneration, or the complexity of ecosystems which may be gravely upset by human intervention.[34]

I was recently in the Marshall Islands for the first time in many years. Modern amenities such as the internet, cell phones, prepackaged goods, and processed foods have reached the Marshallese people and their culture.

Today this remote island community is partaking in the technological advancements of modernity, but without the social and educational understanding to deal with its by-products. It is a society with one foot in today's world and the other planted in the mentality of an ancient island culture that does not know how to effectively deal with the advancement and aid it receives.

The teen pregnancy rate in the Marshalls is one of the highest in the world, with almost 40 percent of the population under fifteen years old.[35] Most are living without proper plumbing, sanitation, or nutrition. Furthermore, you see street after street and beach after beach filled with overwhelming amounts of garbage—plastic bottles, aluminum soda cans, and polyethylene bags seemingly everywhere. The atoll is plagued with the by-products of imported modern conveniences such as packaged goods, processed foods, taxis, and monetary aid. These by-products include diabetes diagnoses and obesity rates that are among the world's highest.

From the magical aqua lagoon to the dilapidated concrete buildings and garbage, I am reminded of the work of the great theologian Romano Guardini and his book *Letters from Lake Como*: "Technology has created an alternative universe, self-sufficient and almost independent of given nature. Technology has become our destiny that subjugates its human creators as much as their creation. Man withering behind the destructive hands of modernity."

What happens to a culture and its people when technology permeates at a faster rate than the people's ability to acclimate to its effects on society? What is the carnage of this imbalance? Today we see it not only in the Marshalls, but all throughout the developing world. Our history teaches us that progress cannot be stopped. Thus, as Guardini states, "First we must say yes to our age. We cannot solve the problem by retreating."[36]

Therefore, humanity must adjust and assimilate without losing dignity, our ultimate purpose, and responsibility to each other and our earth. Guardini also says:

> Further, it must be possible to tackle the task of mastering nature in a way that is appropriate . . . a new order of living, standards of what is excellent and what is despicable, of what is permissible and what is impermissible, of responsibility, of limits, etc., by which we can hold in check the danger of destruction presented by arbitrary natural forces.[37]

This perspective is true not only in the Marshall Islands, but in our families and work as well. Whether it is Snapchat, Facebook, e-mail, or processed foods, we must find a way to allow our ever-advancing technology to be integrated into our life in such a way that it is controlled and harnessed for the betterment of our essential purpose, rather than transforming us into something short of God's vision for us. Something as basic as fasting from technology for a period of time, finding time to exercise, and having healthy family dinners together at home can be a first step in harnessing the power of modern technology toward the common good and our essential purpose.

I know there is much controversy surrounding the positions of the United States Conference of Catholic Bishops and the Vatican on climate change and other environmental issues. We are free to disagree with specific opinion regarding the science behind global warming or some other major global issue, but we cannot deny the awesome responsibility of our obligation to our world and its future inhabitants. We do not own this land, but are only its current tenants. No sane person can deny the destructive reality of unabated technological advancement on our culture and its people. Therefore, we cannot allow one issue to be used as a scapegoat for shunning our moral obligation to harness technology in a way that honors and advances the dignity of the human spirit. This is our legacy. What are you doing within your family or community to fulfill this duty?

Living a Legacy

Legacies that matter are connected with people. A hundred years from now all that will matter is the people that you connected with in such a way that you added value and meaning to their lives.
—John Maxwell

Recently I gave a talk to a group of business owners about our roles and responsibilities as Christian leaders for our culture. I was asked about my desire for my own legacy. I appreciated the question because it is one that we must be continually asking ourselves throughout our entire careers. As our lives evolve and our roles and responsibilities change, so must our expectations of living and leaving a legacy. I believe one's outlook on legacy must be viewed in proportion to his or her unique and ever-changing talents and resources.

Those of us who have been given so much are morally obligated to reciprocate, as Jesus tells us when he says that much will be asked of those who have been entrusted with much (see Luke 12:48). We have all been entrusted with so much—are we going to bury it in a hole or accept with courage the responsibility of these gifts?

Ultimately I place my role as husband and father at the top of my list of responsibilities. Thus, my legacy will first be contemplated and measured based on my relationship with my wife and children. I want to live a legacy of love, respect, and accountability toward my family. If I can get this right, I will have been successful in leaving my legacy.

In the business world, if you want to live and leave a legacy, you must invest your time, talent, and treasure in people. The legacy we live in business is always about developing magnanimous leaders in our organizations who are capable of imparting our mission to others.

This doesn't mean that everyone has the potential to be the next Jack Welch or Jeff Bezos. But we want to develop people who project and provide a generous spirit, inspire others to be a little better every day, are altruistic, and are forgiving. It is only through people that we have the power to change the world, and it most often happens shoulder-to-shoulder and one life at a time.

If I am vigilant about modeling this behavior while taking every opportunity to communicate in word and deed, I am confident that my legacy will impose a culture infused with magnanimous leadership.

This same understanding of success through people must also be embraced within our community activities and parishes. People are inspired by people! We must spend energy developing partnerships with others who desire a greater sense of purpose and are willing to share in our passion and commitment. This is the only way to create a sustainable and lasting legacy.

Here are four steps you can take today:

1. Declare and *believe in yourself* as a gift and worthy of contribution.
2. Dare to make a difference by investing your time, talent, and treasure.
3. Get out of the scarcity mode of success or failure and into the mentality of simple contribution.
4. Accept that we are meant not for comfort but for greatness. Has there ever been a saint who did not accept discomfort and persecution?

From the very beginning, the Church's central message has been about legacy. It is why we are always a missionary Church. The whole point of the New Evangelization is to reassert the original mission given to St. Peter and the rest of the apostles: "Go, therefore, and make disciples of all nations, baptizing them in the name of the Father, and of the Son, and of the Holy Spirit" (Matthew 28:19).

The pivotal question we all must consider: What will our legacy be? Are we willing to step out and begin to define it today?

Let's choose to be the first to offer our time, talents, and treasure for our children and our Church.

TWELVE

Leadership at the Service of Life

Place your talents, enthusiasm, and fortitude
at the service of life.
—St. John Paul II

It has been more than a decade now since I began my journey to discover the deeper responsibilities of what God is asking of me in my vocation as a Catholic business leader. This journey has led me on a meandering path toward much greater reflection on my actions and a deeper sense of accountability for my life during my short time on this earth.

Many of the modifications I have made in my life commenced with my initial pilgrimage in early 2006. One of the crucial lessons from that experience was the importance of surrendering to a greater purpose.

"Only with total interior renunciation will you recognize God's love and the signs of the time in which you live."[38] Our Blessed Mother has been proselytizing with this message across the world through her apparitions for hundreds of years. Why does she repeat the same ideas again and again? Because she knows we need to be reminded of these messages, much like we remind our children of the same messages over and over. We need renunciation—fasting, prayer, sacrifice, denial, and obedience. When we deny ourselves, we can finally begin to gain control over the body and allow our lives to be dictated by our minds and our souls.

With each opportunity that we take to engage in interior renunciation, we gain a measure of freedom that is possible only through denial and prayer. When we are so focused on our own needs, wants, and temporal desires, we simply do not have the capacity to be the self-gift that is our essential purpose.

There is no easy way to accomplish many of the ideas that have been discussed in this book. The reality is that failure is inevitable and it's something we must all face. Continuing to move in a positive direction does not mean we will not face significant setbacks along the way. To overcome these setbacks and continue to move forward along our path toward holiness, we must be willing to embrace self-compassion as well. We are our own worst critics and worst enemies. We are all far too hard on ourselves. The self-loathing that follows our mistakes is extremely detrimental to our self-confidence, hope, and ultimate path to joy and happiness. We must embrace self-compassion.

Living an authentic life in Christ is an everyday choice and must be viewed in that way. Like the alcoholic who gets up every day and says, "I will not have a drink today," we must have a one-day-at-a-time mentality.

There Is No Finish Line

Sooner or later the serious runner goes through a special, very personal experience that is unknown to most people.

Some call it euphoria. Others say it's a new kind of mystical experience that propels you into an elevated state of consciousness.

A flash of joy. A sense of floating as you run.

The experience is unique to each of us, but when it happens you break through a barrier that separates you from casual runners. Forever.

And from that point on, there is no finish line. You run for your life. You begin to be addicted to what running gives you.

We at Nike understand that feeling. There is no finish line for us either. We will never stop trying to excel, to produce running shoes that are better and better every year.

Beating the competition is relatively easy.

But beating yourself is a never-ending commitment.

—Nike [39]

When I was in high school, Nike came out with the tagline "There is no finish line" for a major ad campaign to support its line of running shoes. At the time, I was wrestling and had taken up competitive long-distance running. I was captivated by the message and the subsequent imagery of a lone runner journeying down a long and winding road. The words that described the scenario further captured my imagination and seemed to embody my personality and the spirit of work and dedication that leads to a life of success. I purchased the Nike poster and hung it on my wall as a symbol of life as a long and winding journey of consistency and daily commitment to my dream.

I kept that poster on my wall all through high school and college. "There is no finish line" became my personal tagline. It was a constant reminder that success comes to those who are willing to put in the daily work and effort to reach their goals. And even better, I learned that when you embrace the journey rather than the end result, the process can become richer and more impactful, enjoyable, and rewarding than the goal itself.

This certainly became part of my life's vision. Long after I stopped running competitively and wrestling, I have continued to exercise most days of my life. It is part of who I am and it is my daily victory over myself. It is an opportunity for me to exercise my will over my body every day.

This mentality has spilled into many other areas of my life as well. Whether the daily commitment is to my faith, family, or the world, I see it all in a very similar way. There is no finish line. Each day is a new opportunity to be successful, self-disciplined, and accountable to something greater than my own selfish needs.

I have also discovered that humans need to set themselves up for success. We need a plan that allows us to be successful even in the dynamic and ever-changing nature of life. I have come to realize that most people struggle in their faith life, not because of a lack of faith, but because of a lack of discipline and sense of long perspective.

When I look back in honesty on the ebb and flow of my own faith journey, I see the failures were much more a function of the process than anything else. I allowed the "rest of my life" to interfere with my commitment to my faith life.

Whether it was the strains of work or young children, I did not have a solid process that would allow for me to be successful on a daily basis. Ultimately, I needed to figure out a better way, a better plan that would keep me consistent. I discovered that the same process I used in business could be successful in my spiritual life as well. As I conclude this book, I think the basic notion of Jesuit leadership is as good a way as any to sum up the essential realities of leadership that we must come to terms with in order to continue making a difference in the world each day.

These principles are equally effective for your family life, your civic commitments, your church involvement—basically for every area of your life.

> We're all leaders, and we're leading all the time. Whether we are doing it well or poorly, chances are we are affecting someone else.
>
> Leadership springs from within. It is about who I am as much as what I do. Therefore, we must know who we are at our core. Even when we stray off our path, we have the foundation of knowledge to eventually come back to our core.
>
> Catholic leadership is not an act. It is my life, my way of living in a manner that honors our essential purpose.
>
> I never complete the task of becoming a leader. It's an ongoing process of self-reflection and self-evaluation.

The Jesuits' insight on leadership drives at the core of what we must accept if we are to become God's vision for us. We cannot simply stop being our best because it is inconvenient, or excuse ourselves, saying we don't have a "leadership personality." God has given all of us the task of leading people in our lives. He has also given us the tools to enhance these skills. Yet authentic leadership is not possible without the elements of virtue. It is the molecular structure of the character that is demanded of leaders.

A Vocation of Hope, Happiness, and Legacy

Work is a good thing for man—a good thing for his humanity—because through work man not only transforms nature, adapting it to his own needs, but he also achieves fulfillment as a human being and indeed, in a sense, becomes "more a human being."

—St. John Paul II (Laborem Exercens, Through Work)

Now more than ever, we need leaders who dare to live their faith in every aspect of their lives, including their work. It is easy to be a hard-nosed, apathetic, or self-absorbed leader who only values profits or his or her own short-term success. It is also very easy to be a leader who cares only about relationships and making peers and subordinates comfortable and accountable to merely average results.

The real challenge for us is to create an environment that can inspire others to live with compassion, empathy, and inspiration. It is characterized by investing ourselves and being willing to be the first. In essence, it is through virtue and charisma that we are worthy of being respected and followed. Therefore, we don't have to fall back on a given title or some coercive form of formal power to get people to listen, follow, and deliver results. Reverent power in leadership will always trump leadership based on a short-term formal power base.

Preparation and Restraint

The secret to being a bore is to tell everything.

—Voltaire

One of the essential characteristics of leadership is having the discipline to thoroughly prepare yourself for whatever challenge or job awaits. Great leaders don't just "wing it." Whether it is being a perpetual student of the vocation you have chosen, doing the prep work required for the big meeting, or practicing diligently to deliver a speech, confidence and success come from preparation.

However, another critical aspect of leadership is knowing the power of restraint. This means having the humility to curtail a desire to grandstand with your knowledge in order to impress your audience beyond the intended objective.

In my experience, I have found the latter to be one of the most challenging and uncommon characteristics of leaders. It takes a good deal of confidence and humility to restrain oneself from being verbose. As a parent and business leader, I have to admit that I have failed to do this more often than I care to remember. But the fact is that over-lecturing simply does not work in parenting, business, or faith! We are all masters at tuning each other out very quickly.

In the Catholic Church, I find brevity to be a rare commodity. Preparation is a hallmark of the priesthood and of many Catholic authors and speakers. Most are highly educated and have spent much of their adult lives learning their craft, but then they want to "prove" it, or they struggle to convey that hard-earned knowledge in a way that is relevant, entertaining, and digestible.

However, there are several individuals who I believe will stand out as champions of the New Evangelization of the twenty-first century precisely because of their ability to harness preparation and restraint. Bishop Robert Barron and Cardinal Timothy Dolan are two such individuals. Interestingly enough, both of these men have very strong ties to the Midwest. They are modern-day versions of the great American evangelist of the twentieth century, Fulton Sheen (who was also a midwesterner).

Part of the magnetism and effectiveness of these men is their ability to convey the beauty and genius of Catholicism in a way that truly resonates with the everyday life of a wide and varying population of Christians in the United States today. They are incredibly knowledgeable about the philosophy and theology of our faith, but they communicate with a plainspoken, humble, and honest charm that is accessible to the everyday Christian.

They converse with honesty and humility that never seeks to talk above or below their intended audience. They use humor, modern cultural references, personal anecdotes, familiar language, pragmatic examples, and modern modes of communication to reach their audience in unique ways. They also challenge the reader or listener to go deeper with his or her spiritual and intellectual growth, reaffirming the difficult but worthy journey of what it means to practice Catholicism. Bishop Barron has written some very dense and intellectually challenging material as well, but he does so purposely, knowing he is writing to a very linear and particular audience and not for mass consumption.

"Beige Catholicism"

Bishop Robert Barron uses the term "beige Catholicism" to describe a Catholic culture that is overly accommodating to the prevailing secular culture, bland and unsure of its position, and apologetic of Catholic moral teaching and the tradition of our faith. It is a premise in which the world sets the agenda for the Church, rather than the Church being a beacon for the world, based on the truth of our faith.

Maybe beige Catholicism is a function of the misinterpreted spirit of post–Vatican II, or the clerical abuse crisis of the past twenty years. Regardless of the reason, both Barron and Dolan preach and lead in a way that is always respectfully inclusive, but never beige. They have shown that we can be strong, confident, and bold, while also being universal and generous in our approach to the greater culture.

As I've shared in this book, for much of my business career beige Catholicism was the standard by which I measured myself. Perhaps now you will have discovered that this term summarizes your vocation as a parent or business leader. Certainly, it is a much easier path to travel for all of us, because it takes less thought, creativity, time, and risk.

As humans, we make mistakes, but the message of the Gospels transcends the fragile humanity of its caretakers. Therefore, we must not allow the mistakes of our lives or those of our Church leaders to discourage us from boldly living our faith. Jesus was never bland or beige, nor were any of the great saints. We must remember that we have been chosen, and the reality of the truth forces us to make a choice that will not always lead to comfort or cultural acceptance. However, the measure of courage will be our willingness to resist the path of beige Catholicism or "cafeteria Catholicism" (referring to those who pick and choose what teachings they want to believe).

We Change the World One Life at a Time

Love is willing the good of the other . . . and then doing something concrete about it. It's not an emotion; it's not an attitude. It's a movement of the will.

—Bishop Robert Barron [40]

I have covered a considerable amount of ground in this book. I hope there were some ideas, personal anecdotes, quotes, or excerpts from Catholic social doctrine that resonated with you or challenged you. My desire in writing this book was for you to take away at least one idea or inspiration that will propel you forward in your life's path toward deeper love and sanctity. If this has happened, then I have achieved my goal and am honored to have played a small part in the movement of the New Evangelization.

I hope you will join me on this journey of incorporating your vocation as a platform for proactively living out your faith in culture. Together, we have the power to change the world.

AFTERWORD

Majuro, Marshall Islands, July 11, 2017

Your name shall no more be called Jacob, but Israel,
because you have striven with God and
with men and have prevailed.
—Genesis 32:28

It has been almost fifteen years since Kaaren and I first traveled to this remote coral-based island in Micronesia. We have returned once again, this time not to adopt, but simply to celebrate. Today was our twenty-fifth wedding anniversary and fifteen years since the adoption of our daughter, Kathryn, from this unique atoll.

In gratitude for these events and so many other blessings throughout our lives, we attended Mass at the Cathedral of the Assumption in Majuro today. We celebrated the Eucharist together as a family and then received a blessing from the local parish priest, Father Raymond. It was a special day for our family, indeed!

In meditating upon our twenty-fifth anniversary and the significance of being here this week, I was again reminded of the wisdom and insight of God's revealed Word. The reading for today was from the book of Genesis, chapter 32, verses 24–31. It is the story of Isaac's second son, Jacob, and his peculiar but profound confrontation with an unknown assailant. As the story goes, Jacob encounters a man he doesn't know and proceeds to wrestle with him through the night. By daybreak, Jacob tires of the seemingly endless struggle, eventually reaching a truce. However, he requests a blessing from the man as a condition of this respite. The unknown man then asks Jacob his name. After hearing it, he pronounces Jacob's name to be changed to Israel, which means "he who wrestles with God." He then provides the requested blessing. The passage ends as follows: "Jacob called the name of the place Peniel, saying, 'For I have seen God face to face, and yet my life is preserved.'"

Jacob's new name would become the name of the future nation formed by the tribes of his twelve sons. As we know, the nation and its descendants would do their own wrestling with God over the course of the history of salvation.

What a prophetic message for me to ponder on this momentous occasion in my life. For I have wrestled with doing the will of God for much of my life as well. I have grappled with him through pride, avarice, twenty-five years of marriage, in sickness, health, infertility, adoption, fatherhood, and the true call of vocation. But today as we received our silver jubilee marriage blessing from Father Raymond, I could only feel the overwhelming gratitude and humility of the goodness of God and his plan for my life.

Today there was no wrestling with God, but only blessings from him. For this life Kaaren and I have hoped, for these children we have been on our knees to pray, for this marriage we have fought, wept, labored, and loved. So the struggle of Israel is a metaphor for my struggle and probably your struggle as well. Yet with the ever-abundant grace provided by the sacramental nature of our faith, Christian hope is always possible. And with hope there can be happiness as well.

Through these adversities and triumphs, we have methodically sown the seeds of a life we could have never dreamed of twenty-five years ago. As it turns out, the cross is the salvific antidote that brings about our happiness. Today I feel the abundant joy of God's love for my family and all his people.

ABOUT THE AUTHOR

John Abbate is an independent franchisee/owner-operator of McDonald's restaurants throughout the Central Valley of California, as well as a strategic adviser to the Dynamic Catholic Institute. He is also co-founder and president of Possibility Productions (www.possibilityproductions.org), a nonprofit apostolate in support of the mission of the New Evangelization.

John holds a BBA in Economics from the University of San Diego, an MBA from the University of Notre Dame's Mendoza School of Business and an MA in Catholic Theology from the Augustine Institute. This is his first book.

John can be reached by email at
john.abbate@dynamiccatholic.com

NOTES

1. Thomas Aquinas, *Summa Theologica,* trans. Fathers of the English Dominican Province (New York: Benziger Bros., 1947–48), Part 1, Question 22, Article 3.

2. St. John Paul II, *Fides et Ratio* (Libreria Editrice Vaticana, 1998), 23.

3. A quote from the movie about C. S. Lewis' life, *Shadowlands,* adapted by William Nicholson from his play and directed by Richard Attenborough.

4. Pope Francis, *Lumen Fidei* (Libreria Editrice Vaticana), 4.

5. Thomas Merton, *The Seven Storey Mountain: An Autobiography of Faith* (New York: Houghton Mifflin Harcourt, 1999), p. 186.

6. Pope Francis, "Address of Pope Francis to the Participants in the Pilgrimage of Families During the Year of Faith" (Libreria Editrice Vaticana, 2013).

7. Erin El Issa, "2016 American Household Credit Card Debt Study," Nerdwallet, https://www.nerdwallet.com/blog/average-credit-card-debt-household/.

8. Thomas Merton, *New Seeds of Contemplation* (New York: New Directions, 1962), p. 78.

9. Gallup, http://news.gallup.com/poll/166211/worldwide-median-household-income-000.aspx.

10. St. John Paul II, *Centesimus Annus* (Libreria Editrice Vaticana, 1991), 42.

11. Ibid.

12. Michael Novak, *The Spirit of Democratic Capitalism* (Lanham, MD: Madison Books, 1982).

13. Pope Benedict XVI, "Fighting Poverty to Build Peace: Message for Celebration of the World Day of Peace" (Libreria Editrice Vaticana, 2009).

14. The Philanthropy Roundtable, http://www.philanthropyroundtable.org/almanac/statistics/.

15. Michael Douglas, *Wall Street,* directed by Oliver Stone (Los Angeles: Twentieth Century Fox, 1987).

16. Pope John Paul II, *Evangelium Vitae* (Libreria Editrice Vaticana, 1995), 74.

17. Paulo Coelho, *The Pilgrimage* (New York: HarperSanFrancisco, 1995).

18. C. S. Lewis, *Mere Christianity* (New York: Macmillan, 1960), pp. 55–56.

19. John Paul II, *Gaudium et Spes*, 24.

20. Robert Barron, *Catholicism: A Journey to the Heart of the Faith* (New York: Image Books, 2011), p. 43.

21. Alasdair MacIntyre, *After Virtue* (London: Bloomsbury Publishing, 2013), p. 290.

22. Aquinas, *Summa Theologica*, Part II, Question 17, Article 1.

23. Josemaría Escrivá, *Friends of God* (New York: Scepter, 2002), 292 .

24. John Paul II, 15th World Youth Day Address, *Tor Vergata*, (2000).

25. *Life and Works of Abraham Lincoln*, Centenary Edition, ed. Marion Mills Miller, Litt. D. (Princeton), Vol. V, p. 166.

26. Thomas Merton, *The Seven Storey Mountain: An Autobiography of Faith* (New York: Houghton Mifflin Harcourt, 1999), p. 223.

27. Benedict XVI, *Caritas in Veritate* (Libreria Editrice Vaticana, 2009), 57.

28. Matthew Archbold, *Faith under Fire: Dramatic Stories of Christian Courage* (Cincinnati: Servant, 2016).

29. Pope John Paul II, *Salvifici Doloris* (Libreria Editrice Vaticana, 1984), 23.

30. Ibid., 26.

31. Bishop Robert Barron, "Parable of the Talents," November 19, 2017; https://www.wordonfire.org/resources/homily/parable-of-the-talents/818/.

32. Pope Francis, "Meeting with Young People," impromptu speech given at Santo Tomas University, Manila, Philippines, January 18, 2015.

33. Pope Francis, *Laudato Si* (Libreria Editrice Vaticana, 2015), 217.

34. Ibid., 190.

35. Pacific Institute of Public Policy, "Pacific's High Teen Pregnancy Rates," Gif Johnson, April 22, 2014; http://pacificpolicy.org/2014/04/pacifics-high-teen-pregnancy-rates/.

36. Romano Guardini, *Letters from Lake Como: Explorations on Technology and the Human Race* (Grand Rapids, Mich.: William B. Eerdman's, 1994).

37. Ibid.

38. Annual apparition to Mirjana quoted in June Klins, *I Have Come to Tell the World That God Exists: The Best of "The Spirit of Medjugorje,"* Volume 3 (self-published, 2011), p. 274.

39. Created by John Brown & Partners in 1977 for Nike advertising campaign.

40. "Bishop Barron on Faith, Hope, and Love," YouTube video, 7:59, posted by WordonFire.org, January 31, 2013, https://www.youtube.com/watch?v=PuyKsaj6GbM&feature=em-subs_digest.

NOTES

NOTES

NOTES

NOTES

NOTES

NOTES